THE LOEB CLASSICAL LIBRARY

FOUNDED BY JAMES LOEB

EDITED BY

G. P. GOOLD

PREVIOUS EDITORS

T. E. PAGE   E. CAPPS

W. H. D. ROUSE   L. A. POST

E. H. WARMINGTON

EURIPIDES

IV

LCL 10

EURIPIDES

TROJAN WOMEN
IPHIGENIA AMONG THE TAURIANS
ION

EDITED AND TRANSLATED BY

DAVID KOVACS

HARVARD UNIVERSITY PRESS
CAMBRIDGE, MASSACHUSETTS
LONDON, ENGLAND
1999

Library of Congress Cataloging-in-Publication Data

Euripides
Trojan women; Iphigenia among the Taurians;
Ion / Euripides: edited and translated by David Kovacs.
p.   cm. — (Loeb classical library ; LCL 10)
Greek text and English translation.
Includes bibliographical references.
ISBN 0-674-99574-0
1. Euripides—Translations into English.
2. Greek drama (Tragedy)—Translations into English.
3. Hecuba (Legendary character)—Drama.
4. Iphigenia (Greek mythology)—Drama.
5. Ion (Greek mythology)—Drama.
I. Kovacs, David.   II. Title.
PA3975.A2   1999
882′.01—dc21   99-17693

CONTENTS

TROJAN WOMEN   1
    Introduction   3
    Text and Translation   14

IPHIGENIA AMONG THE TAURIANS   145
    Introduction   146
    Text and Translation   152

ION   313
    Introduction   315
    Text and Translation   322

PREFACE

The Greek text, as in earlier volumes, is my own. I explain my editorial principles and the simplified system for reporting manuscript readings in the general introduction in Volume One. I have discussed in my *Euripidea Altera* (Leiden, 1996) some of the readings adopted here. I hope to discuss others in a forthcoming volume. Readers should note that text enclosed between square brackets is deemed to be spurious. Angle brackets mark words or lines thought to have been accidentally omitted by copyists. As in previous volumes, where I have marked a lacuna of a line or more I have usually filled in, purely by way of illustration, what the sense seems to require. Unattributed supplements are my own.

As in Volume Three I have marked passages written in lyric meters and sung in the original performance by translating them line-for-line to match the Greek. For spoken verse I use the ordinary typography of prose.

It is a pleasure to acknowledge help received. A grant from the Division of Research of the National Endowment for the Humanities enabled me to devote the academic year 1996-7 to this volume and its successor. My heartfelt thanks to the Endowment for its support. I was also elected, for that year, to a Visiting Fellowship at Balliol College, Oxford. My thanks to the Master and Fellows for their splendid hospitality and to Jasper Griffin for his stimulating friendship.

I have had highly profitable discussions on textual matters with Martin West, James Diggle, Charles Willink, and Chris Collard. Martin Cropp very kindly allowed me to see a draft of his forthcoming Aris and Phillips edition of the *Iphigenia among the Taurians*. George and Philippa Goold criticized both my text and my translation.

To Judith Kovacs, who consented thirty years ago this year to throw in her lot with mine, I owe much more than I can hint at in an academic preface. To her this volume is gratefully and lovingly dedicated.

University of Virginia   David Kovacs

ABBREVIATIONS

A&A	*Antike und Abendland*
BICS	*Bulletin of the Institute of Classical Studies*
CP	*Classical Philology*
CQ	*Classical Quarterly*
HSCP	*Harvard Studies in Classical Philology*
RhM	*Rheinisches Museum*
TAPA	*Transactions of the American Philological Association*
YCS	*Yale Classical Studies*

TROJAN WOMEN

INTRODUCTION

For quite some time scholars connected *Trojan Women*, put on in early spring of 415 B.C., with the Athenians' attack on the island of Melos, which ended—in the waning months of 416—with the massacre of the adult men and enslavement of the women and children. (See Thucydides 5.84-116.) The prevailing view was that the play was a sort of *pièce à clef*: in the play's Greeks, who have taken Troy and proceed to kill Astyanax, the son of Hector, we are meant to see the Athenians, while the Trojans stand for the Melians. On this reading, the play expresses Euripides' revulsion from his city's treatment of Melos and his abhorrence of wars of aggression.

But there is evidence of various sorts against this view. First, there was not enough time between the fall of Melos and the City Dionysia for Euripides to have planned, written, and rehearsed a play on this theme: see van Erp Taalman Kip 1987. Second, the play is the only surviving part of a loosely connected trilogy whose first two plays were *Alexandros* and *Palamedes*. The fragments of the *Alexandros* make it plain that the fall of Troy is to be seen against a divine background, and that it was the gods in the last analysis who destroyed Troy, with the Greeks as their instrument, a theme also prominent in *Trojan Women*. This view of the fall of Troy would be ill suited, to say the least,

3

to a play meant to criticize Athens for destroying Melos. Third, however successfully it has been put on in modern times as a play of protest against war, it contains several scenes and choral odes, notably the scene where Helen is on trial and the ode on the gods' abandonment of Troy, that add nothing to or work against this supposed purpose. Lastly, the chorus of Trojan captives, in a choral ode speculating on where they will be sent as slaves (197-229), go out of their way to pray that they may be sent to blessed Athens and not to hateful Sparta, something hard to explain if Euripides is trying to tell his countrymen how criminal Athens has been in its prosecution of the war against Sparta. We should look at the play without the assumption of allegory.

The play's first audience watched two other plays by Euripides that same day, plays on events related to the Trojan War. Here is what can be known or reasonably guessed about these plays. (See Murray 1946, Kovacs 1984, and Hose 1995.) *Alexandros* tells the story of Paris, also known as Alexandros. His mother Hecuba when pregnant with him dreamt that she gave birth to a firebrand, and the dream was interpreted to mean that her son would destroy Troy. The order was accordingly given that the child should be exposed, but the herdsman who was to have done so saved him instead and raised him as his own. When he has grown to manhood (the play begins at this point) the other herdsmen bring him bound before Priam to punish him for behavior that is too proud for his station. (Nature, as so often in Greek myth, triumphs over nurture.) He confutes his accusers and is then allowed to compete in athletic contests (ironically, contests Hecuba had instituted in memory of her exposed son). He defeats his brothers. One of them, Deiphobus, angry at being defeated by a supposed slave, persuades his mother Hecuba to kill him. How this was to be managed our sources do not say, but the truth about his parentage emerges in time to prevent his death. Though Cassandra in a moment of prophetic vision recognizes her brother and prophesies the doom of Troy unless he is killed, no one believes her, and Paris, the long-lost and deeply mourned son, is received joyfully into the royal house. The audience, however, know that he is Troy's destined destroyer.

There are tantalizing hints in the fragments of *Alexandros* concerning the role of the gods in that play and hence in *Trojan Women*. These hints suggest that in Euripides' play, as in other sources from the fifth century and earlier, the curse child, who is fated to be the ruin of his parents, is no mere fluke about which the gods happen to know in advance, but is a deliberate instrument of the gods, used to bring about that ruin. In Aeschylus, the coming of Paris to Troy with his bride Helen is described as the arrival of an Erinys, one of the ministers of Zeus's justice. A fragment of the *Alexandros* by the Roman dramatist Ennius, which was probably a fairly close translation of Euripides, describes Helen as "one of the Furiae," i.e. an Erinys. This came presumably from the prophecy of Cassandra, and if we take her words literally, they imply that Zeus wills the destruction of Troy and that his agents are Helen and her abductor Paris. That Paris survived is due, as Andromache says at *Trojan Women* 597, to the malice of the gods. But it is not only the Trojans who are doomed. In our play Cassandra speaks of herself as an Erinys, this time in connection with the death of Agamemnon and the ruin of his house (457; see also 356-60). It seems likely then that the plan of Zeus encompasses ruin for both sides, as it does in the *Oresteia* and in Homer. In fact, another fragment, assigned with some likelihood to the prologue of *Alexandros* (fr. 45 Snell), makes this explicit: "Zeus the father has contrived these events to cause grief and pain for Greeks and Trojans." This divine perspective reappears in many passages in *Trojan Women*, as we shall see presently.

About *Palamedes*, the next play, we know considerably less. The main outline of the story, however, is clear from later accounts that seem to be summarizing Euripides or the myth already current before he wrote. The setting was the Greek camp before Troy. Palamedes was the cleverest and most inventive of the Greeks. Among his many accomplishments for the benefit of the Greeks was the art of writing. But Palamedes' cleverness was the cause of his downfall. It was a ruse of his that forced Odysseus to join the Trojan expedition, unmasking Odysseus' feigned madness as pretence. Because he was angry at being detected and also jealous of Palamedes' cleverness, Odysseus decided to kill him. By an elaborate trick he managed to bury gold beneath Palamedes' tent and then arranged for the interception of a forged letter from Priam to Palamedes offering him as the price of betraying the Greek camp the exact sum of gold Odysseus had buried. Palamedes spoke in his own defense but was convicted and put to death. His brother Oeax wrote about his fate on the blades of oars, set them adrift on the Aegean, and thus managed to get his message to their father Nauplius. Legend told how Nauplius set false beacons on the coast of Euboea and wrecked the Greek ships on their homeward journey in order to avenge the death of his son.

The general tragic theme of the unknowability of the

future, that seeming blessings turn out to be curses and vice versa, was surely developed in this play as in *Alexandros* and *Trojan Women*. In particular, Palamedes, like many another tragic hero, is destroyed because of his very excellences. (Compare Paris' words in *Alexandros* fr. 44 Snell: "Alas, I am to die because of the excellence of my mind, which is the salvation of other men." The paradox is repeated once more at *Trojan Women* 742-3 if these are genuine, and more distantly echoed at 744.) It was Palamedes' invention of writing that allowed Odysseus to concoct such convincing evidence against him. In partial compensation, it is the same art that allows him to win posthumous revenge against his enemies and vindication in the eyes of future generations.

The first two plays raise expectations that are fulfilled in the third. *Alexandros* leads us to expect that Troy will fall, and *Palamedes* that the Greek fleet will be wrecked. The first is fulfilled before *Trojan Women* opens, and the second is adumbrated in its prologue. The rest of the play shows the aftermath of Troy's destruction. Zeus's plan to ruin both Greeks and Trojans has been brought, in the case of the second, to completion and, in the case of the first, to the brink of completion.

Trojan Women is the most oddly constructed of Euripides' extant plays. There is no *peripeteia* (swift change of fortune) at all: the Trojan women are miserable at the play's beginning and scarcely more so at the end: only the death of Astyanax makes any real change in their situation. The play consists of four scenes revolving around Cassandra, Andromache, Helen, and the dead Astyanax, preceded by a prologue involving Poseidon and Athena. Diverse as they are in other respects, all five of these scenes can be regarded as meditations on the archaic Greek themes of the deceptiveness of appearances, the unreliability of human knowledge, and the power of the gods.

After Poseidon has sketched the opening situation and he and Athena have plotted to wreck the Greek fleet in punishment for Greek sacrilege (Ajax had abducted Cassandra from the shrine of Athena, and his guilt was shared by the Greeks when they failed to punish him), the two divinities depart. In the first episode the Greek herald Talthybius arrives to tell the Trojan women of their fates. Agamemnon wants Cassandra as his slave mistress. About the sacrifice of Polyxena to the ghost of Achilles he speaks with misleading vagueness and tells Hecuba merely that her daughter will attend Achilles' tomb. Hector's widow, Andromache, is to be the slave of Neoptolemus, the son of the man who killed her husband. Hecuba herself has been allotted to the wily and treacherous Odysseus, a monstrous indignity. Talthybius gives orders for Cassandra to be brought out of the tent.

The next scene begins with a *coup de théâtre*: Cassandra enters brandishing torches, ostensibly in joy at her coming "marriage" to Agamemnon. Her connection with Agamemnon can be no rational source of joy, especially since she is Apollo's priestess and sworn to lifelong virginity. But Apollo has revealed to her that her union with Agamemnon will bring about the death of the Greek king and the ruin of his house. Troy will thus be avenged. After affirming once more that she is an Erinys sent to ruin Greece, she goes off.

After a stasimon in which the Chorus sing of the deceptive joy of Troy's last night, Andromache enters with her son Astyanax bound for the ship of Neoptolemus. In an antiphonal lyric they lament the fall of Troy, the death of Hector, and the cruelty of the gods, who allowed Paris to escape death and go on to destroy his country. Hecuba learns from Andromache of the sacrifice of her daughter Polyxena. In a long speech Andromache, reflecting on Polyxena's lot and her own, argues that Polyxena is better off. Since she is dead, she does not feel the loss of her former happiness as Andromache must. Andromache's situation is hopeless. She will be required to live in the same house with the son of her husband's killer. There she must either love Neoptolemus at the cost of disloyalty to Hector or remain true to her husband and incur the hatred of her new master.

Hecuba sees hope for the future. If Andromache wins over her new master, Astyanax may grow to manhood, and he and his descendants may once more settle Troy. No sooner has she said this than Talthybius enters with the news that the Greeks have decided to kill Astyanax: the son of their most dangerous foe must not be allowed to live. He is to be hurled from the battlements. Andromache's response is surprisingly lucid: the nobility of the boy's father, she says, has proved his undoing. She blames the gods for the fall of Troy and for the death of her son. Mother and child are led away.

After a stasimon in which the Chorus sing about Trojan history and lament that the gods no longer favor Troy comes the Helen episode. Menelaus enters in search of his wife, intending, he says, to kill her as soon as they get back to Argos. A sort of trial takes place. Helen speaks in her own defense, arguing that her running off with Paris had divine causes for which she cannot be held responsible.

Aphrodite won the beauty contest by offering marriage with Helen as a bribe. Had Hera or Athena triumphed, Greece itself would have been enslaved to the barbarian, for that was the bribe the other two goddesses offered. So Helen deserves partial credit for helping to prevent the enslavement of Hellas. Hecuba speaks for the prosecution and with merciless logic disputes the idea that the goddesses Hera, Athena, and Aphrodite could have entered a beauty contest and that any of them could have offered the bribes mentioned. Menelaus pronounces Helen guilty and says she will die in Argos, but the audience, who know the story from elsewhere and are given strong hints at lines 1049-52, realize that this is not the way things are destined to end.

There follows a stasimon in which the gods are once more reproached for betraying Troy. Then the body of Astyanax is brought on in the makeshift coffin furnished by his father's shield. After Hecuba has lamented him, the city is set on fire and the Trojan women are ordered to leave for the ships of their masters.

This not a nihilistic play or an angry one. The Greeks here are only slightly less pitiable than the Trojans. All alike are involved in a complex web of destruction. The Erinys that visited Troy in the shape of Helen will visit Argos in the shape of Cassandra. Troy has fallen, but the Greeks will not be unscathed either. The only consolation available is not hope, which is so often a delusion, but the assurance that the sufferers will not be forgotten by posterity. Hecuba's sentiments in 1240-5 are precisely those of Helen in *Iliad* 6.357-8: "Zeus has set an evil destiny upon us so that hereafter we may be a theme in song for men yet to be."

SELECT BIBLIOGRAPHY

Editions

W. Biehl (Leipzig, 1970).

K. H. Lee (Basingstoke and London, 1976).

S. A. Barlow (Warminster, 1986).

Literary Criticism

A. P. Burnett, "*Trojan Women* and the Ganymede Ode," *YCS* 25 (1977), 291-316.

R. A. Coles, *A New Oxyrhynchus Papyrus: the Hypothesis of Euripides' Alexandros, BICS* Supp. 21.1 (London, 1971).

M. Hose, *Drama und Gesellschaft* (Stuttgart, 1995), pp. 33-57.

A. M. van Erp Taalman Kip, "Euripides and Melos," *Mnemosyne* 40 (1987), 414-9.

D. Kovacs, "Euripides, *Troades* 95-7: Is Sacking Cities Really Foolish?" *CQ* 33 (1983), 334-8.

———— "On the *Alexandros* of Euripides," *HSCP* 88 (1984), 47-70.

———— "ΜΩΡΟΣ ΔΕ ΘΝΗΤΩΝ ΟΣΤΙΣ ΕΚΠΟΡΘΕΙ ΠΟΛΕΙΣ: Nochmal zu Euripides, Troerinnen 95-7," *RhM* 139 (1996), 97-101.

———— "Gods and Men in Euripides' Trojan Trilogy," *Colby Quarterly* 33 (1997), pp. 162-76.

M. Lloyd, "The Helen Scene in Euripides' *Trojan Women*," *CQ* 34 (1984), 303-13.

G. Murray, "Euripides' Tragedies of 415 B.C.: the Deceitfulness of Life," in *Greek Studies* (Oxford, 1946), pp. 127-48.

R. Scodel, *The Trojan Trilogy of Euripides,* Hypomnemata 60 (Göttingen, 1980).

B. Snell, *Euripides Alexandros*, Hermes Einzelschriften 5 (Berlin, 1937).

Dramatis Personae

ΠΟΣΕΙΔΩΝ	POSEIDON
ΑΘΗΝΑ	ATHENA
ΕΚΑΒΗ	HECUBA, Queen of Troy
ΧΟΡΟΣ	CHORUS of captive Trojan women
ΤΑΛΘΥΒΙΟΣ	TALTHYBIUS, a Greek herald
ΚΑΣΣΑΝΔΡΑ	CASSANDRA, Hecuba's daughter, a prophetess
ΑΝΔΡΟΜΑΧΗ	ANDROMACHE, widow of Hector, Hecuba's son
ΜΕΝΕΛΑΟΣ	MENELAUS, leader of the Greek forces
ΕΛΕΝΗ	HELEN, wife of Menelaus
Nonspeaking role:	Astyanax, son of Andromache and Hector

A Note on Staging

The *skene* represents the tent in which the Trojan captives are housed. In the background is to be imagined the city of Troy, now a smoking ruin. Eisodos A leads to the Greek ships, Eisodos B to the city of Troy.

ΤΡΩΙΑΔΕΣ

ΠΟΣΕΙΔΩΝ

Ἥκω λιπὼν Αἰγαῖον ἁλμυρὸν βάθος
πόντου Ποσειδῶν, ἔνθα Νηρήδων χοροὶ
κάλλιστον ἴχνος ἐξελίσσουσιν ποδός.
ἐξ οὗ γὰρ ἀμφὶ τήνδε Τρωικὴν χθόνα
5 Φοῖβός τε κἀγὼ λαΐνους πύργους πέριξ
ὀρθοῖσιν ἔθεμεν κανόσιν, οὔποτ᾽ ἐκ φρενῶν
εὔνοι᾽ ἀπέστη τῶν ἐμῶν Φρυγῶν πόλει
ἣ νῦν καπνοῦται καὶ πρὸς Ἀργείου δορὸς
ὄλωλε πορθηθεῖσ᾽· ὁ γὰρ Παρνάσιος
10 Φωκεὺς Ἐπειὸς μηχαναῖσι Παλλάδος
ἐγκύμον᾽ ἵππον τευχέων συναρμόσας
πύργων ἔπεμψεν ἐντὸς ὀλέθριον βρέτας.
[ὅθεν πρὸς ἀνδρῶν ὑστέρων κεκλήσεται
δούρειος ἵππος, κρυπτὸν ἀμπισχὼν δόρυ.]
15 ἔρημα δ᾽ ἄλση καὶ θεῶν ἀνάκτορα

13–14 del. Burges

¶ 1 The Trojans are called Phrygians in Greek poetry and the Greeks Argives, Achaeans, and Danaans. Troy is also called Ilium and Pergamum.

14

TROJAN WOMEN

At the beginning of the play HECUBA *lies prostrate on the ground before the* skene *on a pallet. Enter* POSEIDON *above the* skene, *on the* theologeion.

POSEIDON

I am Poseidon, and I have come here from the briny depths of the Aegean, where choruses of Nereids turn their footsteps in graceful rounds. Ever since Phoebus and I put stone fortifications about this land of Troy with straight mason's rule, good will toward the city of the Phrygians[1] has never left my heart.[2] Now the city smolders, sacked and destroyed by the Argive spear. Epeius, the Phocian from Parnassus, built a horse pregnant with weapons by the devising of Pallas Athena and sent inside the walls this image meant for ruin. [And therefore men of later times shall call it the Wooden Horse because it hid spears within its belly.][3]

The sacred groves are deserted, and the temples of the

2 Poseidon is here represented as a pro-Trojan deity. In the *Iliad* he is pro-Greek.

3 These two bracketed lines make a poor pun on δούρειος ἵππος, which usually means "wooden horse" but is treated as if it meant "horse of spears."

φόνῳ καταρρεῖ· πρὸς δὲ κρηπίδων βάθροις
πέπτωκε Πρίαμος Ζηνὸς ἑρκείου θανών.
πολὺς δὲ χρυσὸς Φρύγιά τε σκυλεύματα
πρὸς ναῦς Ἀχαιῶν πέμπεται· μένουσι δὲ
20 πρύμνηθεν οὖρον, ὡς δεκασπόρῳ χρόνῳ
ἀλόχους τε καὶ τέκν᾽ εἰσίδωσιν ἄσμενοι,
οἳ τήνδ᾽ ἐπεστράτευσαν Ἕλληνες πόλιν.
ἐγὼ δέ (νικῶμαι γὰρ Ἀργείας θεοῦ
Ἥρας Ἀθάνας θ᾽, αἳ συνεξεῖλον Φρύγας)
25 λείπω τὸ κλεινὸν Ἴλιον βωμούς τ᾽ ἐμούς·
ἐρημία γὰρ πόλιν ὅταν λάβῃ κακή,
νοσεῖ τὰ τῶν θεῶν οὐδὲ τιμᾶσθαι θέλει.
    πολλοῖς δὲ κωκυτοῖσιν αἰχμαλωτίδων
βοᾷ Σκάμανδρος δεσπότας κληρουμένων.
30 καὶ τὰς μὲν Ἀρκάς, τὰς δὲ Θεσσαλὸς λεὼς
εἴληχ᾽ Ἀθηναίων τε Θησεῖδαι πρόμοι.
ὅσαι δ᾽ ἄκληροι Τρωάδων, ὑπὸ στέγαις
ταῖσδ᾽ εἰσί, τοῖς πρώτοισιν ἐξῃρημέναι
στρατοῦ, σὺν αὐταῖς δ᾽ ἡ Λάκαινα Τυνδαρὶς
35 Ἑλένη, νομισθεῖσ᾽ αἰχμάλωτος ἐνδίκως.
    τὴν δ᾽ ἀθλίαν τήνδ᾽ εἴ τις εἰσορᾶν θέλει,
πάρεστιν Ἑκάβη κειμένη πυλῶν πάρος,
δάκρυα χέουσα πολλὰ καὶ πολλῶν ὕπερ·
ᾗ παῖς μὲν ἀμφὶ μνῆμ᾽ Ἀχιλλείου τάφου
40 λάθρᾳ τέθνηκε τλημόνως Πολυξένη·
φροῦδος δὲ Πρίαμος καὶ τέκν᾽· ἣν δὲ παρθένον
μεθῆκ᾽ Ἀπόλλων δρομάδα Κασσάνδραν ἄναξ,
τὸ τοῦ θεοῦ τε παραλιπὼν τό τ᾽ εὐσεβὲς

gods run with blood. Near the steps of the altar base of Zeus, Protector of the House, Priam lies slain. The plentiful gold and spoils of Phrygia are being conveyed down to the Achaean ships. The Greeks who have made the expedition against this city are awaiting a favoring breeze so that in this tenth year's seed time they may rejoice to see their wives and children. But since I am beaten by the Argive goddess, Hera, and Athena—together they destroyed Troy—I am now leaving behind glorious Ilium and my altars. When cruel desolation comes over a city, worship suffers, and the gods no longer receive their honors.

The Scamander River rings with many shouts of captive women who are being assigned by lot to their masters. Some are taken by the Arcadian army, some by the Thessalian, and some by the sons of Theseus, leaders of the Athenians. Those Trojan women who have not yet been assigned are in this tent, reserved for the army's chief men, and with them is Tyndareus' daughter, the Spartan Helen, who is rightly being treated as a captive.

Poor Hecuba, if anyone wants to see her, is here, lying in front of the door, weeping many tears for many reasons. Unbeknownst to her, her daughter Polyxena has been piteously killed at the tomb of Achilles; Priam and her sons are dead; and her daughter Cassandra, whom Lord Apollo left an untamed virgin, Agamemnon, contrary to the god's

γαμεῖ βιαίως σκότιον Ἀγαμέμνων λέχος.

45 ἀλλ', ὦ ποτ' εὐτυχοῦσα, χαῖρέ μοι, πόλις
ξεστόν τε πύργωμ'· εἴ σε μὴ διώλεσεν
Παλλὰς Διὸς παῖς, ἦσθ' ἂν ἐν βάθροις ἔτι.

ΑΘΗΝΑ

ἔξεστι τὸν γένει μὲν ἄγχιστον πατρὸς
μέγαν δὲ δαίμον' ἐν θεοῖς τε τίμιον,
50 λύσασαν ἔχθραν τὴν πάρος, προσεννέπειν;

ΠΟΣΕΙΔΩΝ

ἔξεστιν· αἱ γὰρ συγγενεῖς ὁμιλίαι,
ἄνασσ' Ἀθάνα, φίλτρον οὐ σμικρὸν φρενῶν.

ΑΘΗΝΑ

ἐπῄνεσ' ὀργὰς ἠπίους· φέρω δὲ σοὶ
κοινοὺς ἐμαυτῇ τ' ἐς μέσον λόγους, ἄναξ.

ΠΟΣΕΙΔΩΝ

55 μῶν ἐκ θεῶν του καινὸν ἀγγέλλεις ἔπος,
ἢ Ζηνὸς ἢ καὶ δαιμόνων τινὸς πάρα;

ΑΘΗΝΑ

οὔκ, ἀλλὰ Τροίας οὕνεκ', ἔνθα βαίνομεν,
πρὸς σὴν ἀφῖγμαι δύναμιν, ὡς κοινὴν λάβω.

ΠΟΣΕΙΔΩΝ

οὔ πού νιν, ἔχθραν τὴν πρὶν ἐκβαλοῦσα, νῦν
60 ἐς οἶκτον ἦλθες πυρὶ κατῃθαλωμένην;

49 δὲ Elmsley: τε C
59 οὔ Wecklein: ἢ C
60 κατῃθαλωμένην Elmsley: -ης C

18

will and piety, will force to become his mistress.

So, towers of dressed stone, city once prosperous, farewell! If Zeus's daughter Pallas had not destroyed you, you would still be standing firm on your foundations.

Enter ATHENA *by* mechane *to join Poseidon on the* theologeion.

ATHENA

May I put aside my earlier enmity and address one closely related to my father and a great divinity, honored among the gods?

POSEIDON

You may: the words of close kin, lady Athena, have no small power to charm the heart.

ATHENA

For these kind sentiments, my thanks. I bring, my lord, a theme for you and me to discuss.

POSEIDON

Is it perhaps a pronouncement you bring from one of the gods, Zeus or one of the powers divine?

ATHENA

No: it is for the sake of Troy, on which we stand, that I approach your power, trying to win it as my ally.

POSEIDON

Surely you have not cast your old hatred aside and started to feel pity for her now that she has been burnt to ashes?

ΑΘΗΝΑ

ἐκεῖσε πρῶτ' ἄνελθε· κοινώσῃ λόγους
καὶ συνθελήσεις ἃν ἐγὼ πρᾶξαι θέλω;

ΠΟΣΕΙΔΩΝ

μάλιστ'· ἀτὰρ δὴ καὶ τὸ σὸν θέλω μαθεῖν
πότερον Ἀχαιῶν ἦλθες οὕνεκ' ἢ Φρυγῶν;

ΑΘΗΝΑ

65 τοὺς μὲν πρὶν ἐχθροὺς Τρῶας εὐφρᾶναι θέλω,
στρατῷ δ' Ἀχαιῶν νόστον ἐμβαλεῖν πικρόν.

ΠΟΣΕΙΔΩΝ

τί δ' ὧδε πηδᾷς ἄλλοτ' εἰς ἄλλους τρόπους
μισεῖς τε λίαν καὶ φιλεῖς ὃν ἂν τύχῃς;

ΑΘΗΝΑ

οὐκ οἶσθ' ὑβρισθεῖσάν με καὶ ναοὺς ἐμούς;

ΠΟΣΕΙΔΩΝ

70 οἶδ'· ἡνίκ' Αἴας εἷλκε Κασσάνδραν βίᾳ.

ΑΘΗΝΑ

κοὐδέν γ' Ἀχαιῶν ἔπαθεν οὐδ' ἤκουσ' ὕπο.

ΠΟΣΕΙΔΩΝ

καὶ μὴν ἔπερσάν γ' Ἴλιον τῷ σῷ σθένει.

ΑΘΗΝΑ

τοιγάρ σφε σὺν σοὶ βούλομαι δρᾶσαι κακῶς.

ΠΟΣΕΙΔΩΝ

ἕτοιμ' ἃ βούλῃ τἀπ' ἐμοῦ. δράσεις δὲ τί;

ATHENA

Return first to my earlier point: will you share counsels with me and cooperate in whatever I wish to do?

POSEIDON

Certainly. But I want to know what your purpose is. Is it for the Greeks' sake or the Trojans' that you have come?

ATHENA

I want to bring joy to my former enemies, the Trojans, and to give the Achaean army a journey home they will not like.

POSEIDON

But why do you leap about so, now with one character, now with another? Why hate and love whomever you chance to so excessively?

ATHENA

Are you not aware that I and my temples have been treated with contempt?

POSEIDON

Yes: it was when Ajax dragged Cassandra off by force.

ATHENA

And he was in no way punished or censured by the Achaeans.

POSEIDON

And yet it was with your might that they sacked Troy.

ATHENA

That is why, with your assistance, I mean to hurt them.

POSEIDON

For my part I am ready to do as you wish. But what will you do?

21

ΑΘΗΝΑ

75 δύσνοστον αὐτοῖς νόστον ἐμβαλεῖν θέλω.

ΠΟΣΕΙΔΩΝ

ἐν γῇ μενόντων ἢ καθ᾽ ἁλμυρὰν ἅλα;

ΑΘΗΝΑ

ὅταν πρὸς οἴκους ναυστολῶσ᾽ ἀπ᾽ Ἰλίου.
καὶ Ζεὺς μὲν ὄμβρον καὶ χάλαζαν ἄσπετον
πέμψει δνοφώδη τ᾽ αἰθέρος φυσήματα·
80 ἐμοὶ δὲ δώσειν φησὶ πῦρ κεραύνιον,
βάλλειν Ἀχαιοὺς ναῦς τε πιμπράναι πυρί.
σὺ δ᾽ αὖ, τὸ σόν, παράσχες Αἰγαῖον πόρον
τρικυμίαις βρέμοντα καὶ δίναις ἁλός,
πλῆσον δὲ νεκρῶν κοῖλον Εὐβοίας μυχόν,
85 ὡς ἂν τὸ λοιπὸν τἄμ᾽ ἀνάκτορ᾽ εὐσεβεῖν
εἰδῶσ᾽ Ἀχαιοὶ θεούς τε τοὺς ἄλλους σέβειν.

ΠΟΣΕΙΔΩΝ

ἔσται τάδ᾽· ἡ χάρις γὰρ οὐ μακρῶν λόγων
δεῖται· ταράξω πέλαγος Αἰγαίας ἁλός.
ἀκταὶ δὲ Μυκόνου Δήλιοί τε χοιράδες
90 Σκῦρός τε Λῆμνός θ᾽ αἱ Καφήρειοί τ᾽ ἄκραι
πολλῶν θανόντων σώμαθ᾽ ἕξουσιν νεκρῶν.
ἀλλ᾽ ἕρπ᾽ Ὄλυμπον καὶ κεραυνίους βολὰς
λαβοῦσα πατρὸς ἐκ χερῶν καραδόκει,
ὅταν στράτευμ᾽ Ἀργεῖον ἐξιῇ κάλως.
95 μῶρος δὲ θνητῶν ὅστις ἐκπορθεῖ πόλεις,

86 σέβειν] τίειν Herwerden

22

ATHENA

I want to give them a grim voyage home.

POSEIDON

While they are still on land or when they are on the briny
sea?

ATHENA

When they are sailing home from Ilium. Zeus for his part
will send plentiful rain and hail and dark storm winds.
He promises to give me the lightning bolt to strike the
Achaeans and set their ships on fire. As for you, make the
Aegean swell with high waves and eddies and fill the deep
indentation of Euboea's coast with corpses so that hence-
forth the Greeks may learn to reverence my temples and
show honor to the other gods as well.

POSEIDON

It shall be so: the favor you ask requires no long discussion.
I shall throw the Aegean main into confusion. The beaches
of Mykonos and the reefs of Delos and Scyros and Lemnos
and the promontories of Caphereus[4] shall be filled
with the bodies of many dead. So go to Olympus, take the
lightning bolts from your father's hand, and wait until the
Argive fleet is making full sail.

Foolish is the mortal who sacks cities and yet, after

---

[4] Caphereus, in Euboea, was the home of Palamedes, the hero
of the play that preceded *Trojan Women* in the trilogy. The name
here, like the reference to Euboea in 84, may be an allusion to the
Nauplius' revenge for Palamedes' unjust execution. See introduc-
tion.

ναοὺς δὲ τύμβους θ᾽, ἱερὰ τῶν κεκμηκότων,
ἐρημίᾳ δοὺς αὐτὸς ὤλεθ᾽ ὕστερον.

ΕΚΑΒΗ

ἄνα, δύσδαιμον· πεδόθεν κεφαλὴν
ἐπάειρε δέρην ⟨τ᾽⟩· οὐκέτι Τροία
100 τάδε καὶ βασιλῆς ἐσμεν Τροίας.
μεταβαλλομένου δαίμονος ἄνσχου.
πλεῖ κατὰ πορθμόν, πλεῖ κατὰ δαίμονα,
μηδὲ προσίστη πρῷραν βιότου
πρὸς κῦμα πλέουσα τύχαισιν.
105 αἰαῖ αἰαῖ.
τί γὰρ οὐ πάρα μοι μελέᾳ στενάχειν,
ᾗ πατρὶς ἔρρει καὶ τέκνα καὶ πόσις;
ὦ πολὺς ὄγκος συστελλόμενος
προγόνων, ὡς οὐδὲν ἄρ᾽ ἦσθα.
110 τί με χρὴ σιγᾶν, τί δὲ μὴ σιγᾶν;
[τί δὲ θρηνῆσαι;]
δύστηνος ἐγὼ τῆς βαρυδαίμονος
ἄρθρων κλίσεως, ὡς διάκειμαι,
νῶτ᾽ ἐν στερροῖς λέκτροισι ταθεῖσ᾽.
115 οἴμοι κεφαλῆς, οἴμοι κροτάφων
πλευρῶν θ᾽, ὥς μοι πόθος εἱλίξαι
καὶ διαδοῦναι νῶτον ἄκανθάν τ᾽
εἰς ἀμφοτέρους τοίχους μελέων,
ἐπιοῦσ᾽ αἰεὶ δακρύων ἐλέγους.

96 ναοὺς δὲ Blomfield: ναούς τε C   99 ⟨τ᾽⟩ Musgrave
101 ἄνσχου Nauck: ἀνέχου C   111 del. Tyrrell
119 ἐπιοῦσ᾽ Musgrave: ἐπὶ τοὺς C

giving over to desolation temples and tombs, holy places
of the dead, perishes later himself.[5]

Exit POSEIDON and ATHENA. Hecuba rises to her feet.

HECUBA

Up, unhappy woman! Raise your head and neck from the
ground! This is no longer Troy you see, and we are no
longer Troy's rulers. As your fortune changes, endure the
change! Sail with the current in the strait, sail with your
fortune, and do not turn the prow of your life to face disas-
ters, sailing toward their oncoming wave! Ah me, ah me!
What lament is there that I cannot utter, unlucky woman
that I am? My country is gone, my children, my husband!
Great pride of my ancestors, now cut short, how slight a
thing you were after all! What should I wrap in silence,
what should I not wrap in silence? [What should I lament?]
How luckless I am, how miserably does my body recline,
my back stretched out on its hard bed! Alas for the temples
of my head and for my sides! How I long to roll my back
and spine about, listing now to this side of my body, now to
that as I utter continually my tearful song of woe! This too

[5] This generalization must be read in its context. The Greeks
are foolish not for sacking cities (they had Athena's help in this)
but for alienating their divine ally and thereby causing their own
destruction, a destruction here ironically contrasted with their
success in killing others. See Kovacs 1983 and 1996.

EURIPIDES

120 μοῦσα δὲ χαύτη τοῖς δυστήνοις
ἄτας κελαδεῖν ἀχορεύτους.

πρῷραι ναῶν, ὠκείαις
Ἴλιον ἱερὰν αἳ κώπαις
δι' ἅλ' ⟨Αἰγαίαν⟩ πορφυροειδῆ
125 λιμένας θ' Ἑλλάδος εὐόρμους
αὐλῶν ⟨σὺν⟩ παιᾶνι στυγνῷ
συρίγγων τ' εὐφθόγγων φωνᾷ
βαίνουσαι πλεκτάς, Αἰγύπτου
παίδευμ', ἐξηρτήσασθ', ⟨αἰαῖ⟩
130 αἰαῖ, Τροίας ἐν κόλποις,
τὰν Μενελάου μετανισόμεναι
στυγνὰν ἄλοχον, Κάστορι λώβαν
τῷ τ' Εὐρώτᾳ δύσκλειαν·
ἃ σφάζει μὲν
135 τὸν πεντήκοντ' ἀροτῆρα τέκνων
Πρίαμον, ἐμέ τε ⟨τὰν⟩ μελέαν Ἑκάβαν
ἐς τάνδ' ἐξώκειλ' ἄταν.
ὤμοι, θάκους οἵους θάσσω
σκηναῖς ἐφέδρους Ἀγαμεμνονίαις.
140 δούλα δ' ἄγομαι γραῦς ἐξ οἴκων
πενθήρη κρᾶτ' ἐκπορθηθεῖσ'
οἰκτρῶς. ἀλλ' ὦ

---

122 ὠκείαις Tyrrell: ὠκεῖαι C   124 ⟨Αἰγαίαν⟩ Willink
125 λιμένας θ' Seidler, Hermann: καὶ λιμένας C
126 ⟨σὺν⟩ Page   128 πλεκτάς Musgrave: -τὰν C

26

is music for those in misfortune, to utter aloud their joyless troubles.[6]

Prows of ships, with swift oar
you came to holy Ilium
over the dark blue ⟨Aegean⟩ sea
and the fair harbors of Greece
with the hateful song of pipes
blent with the voice of tuneful flutes,
and you hung down from your sterns, ⟨alas,⟩
alas, in the bay of Troy,
ropes, which Egypt taught you to make,
coming in quest of Menelaus'
hateful wife, who disgraces Castor
and brings ill fame upon the Eurotas.[7]
She is the slayer
of Priam, father of fifty sons,
and has run me, unlucky Hecuba,
aground in utter destruction.
Alas, what sort of place do I now sit in,
hard by the tents of Agamemnon!
I am taken away as an aged slave from my house,
my head ravaged in grief
pitiably! But, O

6 The rest of Hecuba's words here, and her exchange with the Chorus, are sung.

7 Castor and Polydeuces were Helen's twin brothers, later deified. The Eurotas is the principal river of Sparta.

129 παίδευμ' Tyrrell: παιδείαν C   ⟨αἰαῖ⟩ Page
136 ⟨τὰν⟩ Burges
141 πενθήρη Murray: κουρᾷ ξυρήκει π- C

27

τῶν χαλκεγχέων Τρώων ἄλοχοι
μέλεαι, κοῦραι δύσνυμφοι,
145 τύφεται Ἴλιον, αἰάζωμεν.
μάτηρ δ' ὡσεί τις πτανοῖς,
κλαγγὰν ἐξάρξω 'γὼ μολπάν,
οὐ τὰν αὐτὰν οἵαν ποτὲ δὴ
150 σκήπτρῳ Πριάμου διερειδομένου
ποδὸς ἀρχεχόρου πλαγαῖς Φρυγίους
εὐκόμποις ἐξῆρχον θεούς.

στρ. α

HMIXOPION A

Ἑκάβα, τί θροεῖς; τί δὲ θωΰσσεις;
ποῖ λόγος ἥκει; διὰ γὰρ μελάθρων
155 ἄιον οἴκτους οὓς οἰκτίζῃ.
διὰ δὲ στέρνων φόβος ἀίσσει
Τρῳάσιν, αἳ τῶνδ' οἴκων εἴσω
δουλείαν αἰάζουσιν.

EKABH

ὦ τέκν', Ἀχαιῶν πρὸς ναῦς ἤδη
160 κινεῖται κωπήρης χείρ.

HMIXOPION A

οἲ ἐγώ, τί θέλουσ', ἦ πού μ' ἤδη
ναυσθλώσουσιν πατρίας ἐκ γᾶς;

144 κοῦραι Willink: καὶ κ- C   147 κλαγγὰν post Dindorf
(del. ὅπως) Willink: κλαγγὰν ὄρνισιν ὅπως C
150 διερειδομένου Herwerden: -μένα C   Φρυγίους Wila-
mowitz: -αις C

unhappy wives of the Trojans with swords of bronze,
women unblest in your husbands,
Ilium is burning: let us wail aloud!
Like a mother bird to her winged brood,
I lead off the song of lamentation,
not at all the same song
that I led off, as Priam leaned upon his scepter,
with the confident beat of chorus leader's foot
in praise of Troy's gods.

Enter from the skene *one half of the* CHORUS *of captive
Trojan women.*

CHORUS A

Hecuba, what do you utter, what do you cry aloud?
What is the meaning of your speech? Through the walls of
   the tent
I heard the cries of woe you are uttering.
A pang of fear is darting through
the women of Troy, who within these walls
bewail their slavery.

HECUBA

My children, already toward the ships of the Achaeans
the oarsmen are moving!

CHORUS A

Ah me, for what purpose? Will they now
take me from my ancestral land?

---

156 φόβος] τάρβος Seidler
159 Ἀχαιῶν Schroeder: Ἀργείων C

EKABH

οὐκ οἶδ᾽, εἰκάζω δ᾽ ἄταν.

HMIXOPION A

ἰὼ ἰώ.
165 μέλεαι, μόχθων ἐπακουσόμεναι,
Τρῳάδες, ἐξορμίζεσθ᾽ οἴκων·
στέλλουσ᾽ Ἀργεῖοι νόστον.

EKABH

ἒ ἔ.
μή νύν μοι τὰν
ἐκβακχεύουσαν Κασσάνδραν,
171 αἰσχύναν Ἀργείοισιν,
170 πέμψητ᾽ ἔξω,
μαινάδ᾽, ἐπ᾽ ἄλγεσι δ᾽ ἀλγυνθῶ.
[ἰὼ ἰώ.]
Τροία Τροία δύσταν᾽, ἔρρεις,
δύστανοι δ᾽ οἵ σ᾽ ἐκλείποντες
175 καὶ ζῶντες καὶ δμαθέντες.
ἀντ. α

HMIXOPION B

οἴμοι. τρομερὰ σκηνὰς ἔλιπον
τάσδ᾽ Ἀγαμέμνονος ἐπακουσομένα,
βασίλεια, σέθεν· μή με κτείνειν
δόξ᾽ Ἀργείων κεῖται μελέαν;
180 ἢ κατὰ πρύμνας ἤδη ναῦται
στέλλονται κινεῖν κώπας;

HECUBA

I do not know, but I conjecture that it is ruin.

CHORUS A

Ah, ah!
Luckless Trojan women,
unmoor yourselves from the tent to hear of your misery:
the Argives are preparing their journey home!

HECUBA

Ah, ah!
I beg you then,
do not bring forth
the maddened Cassandra
to be disgraced by the Greeks,
the maenad girl, and let me not have grief upon grief!
[Ah me, ah me,]
Troy, unhappy Troy, you are gone,
and unhappy are we who leave you,
both the living and the dead!

Enter from the skene *the other half of the* CHORUS.

CHORUS B

Ah me! All atremble I have left the tent
of Agamemnon to hear you,
my queen. Surely the Greeks
have not resolved to end my poor life?
Or are the sailors now preparing
to move their oars down from their sterns?

---

166 ἐξορμίζεσθ᾽ Headlam: ἔξω κομίζεσθ᾽ C
171 et 170 inter se trai. Murray   171 fort. αἰσχύναν ⟨ἔν γ᾽⟩
Ἀργείοις   173 ἰὼ ἰώ secl. Seidler

ΕΚΑΒΗ

ὦ τέκνον, ὀρθρεύουσαν ψυχὰν
ἐκπληχθεῖσ᾽ ἦλθον φρίκᾳ.

ΗΜΙΧΟΡΙΟΝ Β

ἤδη τις ἔβα Δαναῶν κῆρυξ;
185 τῷ πρόσκειμαι δούλα τλάμων;

ΕΚΑΒΗ

ἐγγύς που κεῖσαι κλήρου.

ΗΜΙΧΟΡΙΟΝ Β

ἰὼ ἰώ.
τίς μ᾽ Ἀργείων ἢ Φθιωτᾶν
ἢ νησαίας ἄξει χώρας
δύστανον πόρσω Τροίας;

ΕΚΑΒΗ

190 φεῦ φεῦ.
τῷ δ᾽ ἁ τλάμων
ποῦ πᾷ γαίας δουλεύσω γραῦς,
ὡς κηφήν, ἁ δειλαία,
νεκροῦ μορφά,
νεκύων ἀμενηνὸν ἄγαλμα,
τὰν παρὰ προθύροις φυλακὰν κατέχουσ᾽
195 ἢ παίδων θρέπτειρ᾽, ἁ Τροίας
ἀρχαγοὺς εἶχον τιμάς;

188 νησαίας . . . χώρας Wecklein: -αν . . . -αν C
193 ἄγαλμα Lachmann: ἄγαλμ᾽ ἢ C

HECUBA

My daughter, I came in fear,
panic-stricken in my soul, awake since dawn.

CHORUS B

Has some Greek herald already arrived?
To whom am I, poor woman, assigned as a slave?

HECUBA

You are near, I think, to the drawing of lots.

CHORUS B

Ah, ah!
What Argive or Phthiote
or dweller in an island country
will take me in my wretchedness far from Troy?

HECUBA

Ah me!
For whom, unhappy
old woman that I am, will I toil, and where in the world will
    I serve?
Like a drone,[8] poor wretch,
the picture of a corpse
and the strengthless image of the dead,
shall I keep watch by the door
or tend their children, I
who once was honored as queen of Troy?

---

[8] She likens herself to a drone because being old she is of little
use.

EURIPIDES

ΧΟΡΟΣ

στρ. β

αἰαῖ αἰαῖ, ποίοις δ᾽ οἴκτοις
τάνδ᾽ ἂν λύμαν ἐξαιάζοις;
οὐκ Ἰδαίοις ἱστοῖς κερκίδα
200 δινεύουσ᾽ ἐξαλλάξω.
νέατον τοκέων δώματα λεύσσω,
νέατον· μόχθους ⟨δ᾽⟩ ἔξω κρείσσους,
ἢ λέκτροις πλαθεῖσ᾽ Ἑλλάνων
(ἔρροι νὺξ αὕτα καὶ δαίμων)
205 ἢ Πειρήνας ὑδρευομένα
πρόσπολος οἰκτρὰ σεμνῶν ὑδάτων.
τὰν κλεινὰν εἴθ᾽ ἔλθοιμεν
Θησέως εὐδαίμονα χώραν.
210 μὴ γὰρ δὴ δίναν γ᾽ Εὐρώτα
τάν ⟨τ᾽⟩ ἐχθίσταν θεράπναν Ἑλένας,
ἔνθ᾽ ἀντάσω Μενέλᾳ δούλα,
τῷ τᾶς Τροίας πορθητᾷ.

ἀντ. β

τὰν Πηνειοῦ σεμνὰν χώραν,
215 κρηπῖδ᾽ Οὐλύμπου καλλίσταν,
ὄλβῳ βρίθειν φάμαν ἤκουσ᾽
εὐθαλεῖ τ᾽ εὐκαρπείᾳ·

198 τάνδ᾽ ἂν ... ἐξαιάζοις Wilamowitz: τὰν σὰν ... ἐξαιάζεις fere C   201–2 νέατον ... νέατον Seidler: -οι ... -οι C   201 τοκέων δώματα Parmentier: τεκέων σώματα C   202 ⟨δ᾽⟩ Seidler

CHORUS

Ah me! With what pitiable cries
could you bewail this outrage?
No more shall I whirl my shuttle
and move it back and forth on a Trojan loom!
I look my last on the house of my parents,
my last ! Greater troubles than these shall I have,
either brought to the bed of a Greek
(a curse on that night and its fate!)
or going as a pitiable slave to draw water
from the sacred spring of Peirene.[9]
O that I might come to the famous
and blessed land of Theseus!
Never to the whirl of the Eurotas
and the hated abode of Helen,[10]
where as a slave I will encounter Menelaus,
the sacker of Troy!

The holy territory of the Peneus River,
the lovely plinth on which Olympus is built,
is laden with wealth, I have heard tell,
and plentiful fruitfulness.

[9] The principal spring of Corinth.
[10] Sparta.

---

205 ὑδρευομένα Heiland: -σομένα C
211 ⟨τ᾽⟩ Musgrave

τάδε δεύτερά μοι μετὰ τὰν ἱερὰν
Θησέως ζαθέαν ἐλθεῖν χώραν.
220 καὶ τὰν Αἰτναίαν Ἡφαίστου
Φοινίκας ἀντήρη χώραν,
Σικελῶν ὀρέων ματέρ', ἀκούω
καρύσσεσθαι στεφάνοις ἀρετᾶς,
τάν τ' ἀγχιστεύουσαν γᾶν
225 †Ἰονίῳ ναύτᾳ πόντῳ†,
ἂν ὑγραίνει καλλιστεύων
ὁ ξανθὰν χαίταν πυρσαίνων
Κρᾶθις ζαθέαις παγαῖσι τρέφων
εὔανδρόν τ' ὀλβίζων γᾶν.

230 —καὶ μὴν Δαναῶν ὅδ' ἀπὸ στρατιᾶς
κῆρυξ, νεοχμῶν μύθων ταμίας,
στείχει ταχύπουν ἴχνος ἐξανύτων.
τί φέρει; τί λέγει; δοῦλαι γὰρ δὴ
Δωρίδος ἐσμὲν χθονὸς ἤδη.

ΤΑΛΘΥΒΙΟΣ
235 Ἑκάβη, πυκνὰς γὰρ οἶσθά μ' ἐς Τροίαν ὁδοὺς
ἐλθόντα κήρυκ' ἐξ Ἀχαικοῦ στρατοῦ,
ἐγνωσμένος δὴ καὶ πάροιθέ σοι, γύναι,
Ταλθύβιος ἥκω καινὸν ἀγγελῶν λόγον.

225 Ἰονίῳ ναυτᾶν πορθμῷ Willink
237 δὴ Mistchenko: δὲ C

This would be my second choice after the holy
and sacred country of Theseus.
And I hear that the land of Aetna and Hephaestus,
opposite Carthage,[11]
mother of Sicily's mountains,
is proclaimed by heralds for its crowns of excellence,
as also is the land that neighbors
the Ionian sea,[12]
watered by Crathis the lovely,
who turns your hair the color of gold,[13]
who cherishes the land with his holy streams
and makes it blessed in its brave men.

Enter TALTHYBIUS *by Eisodos A.*

CHORUS LEADER

But look, here comes the herald from the Greek army,
dispenser of bad news, with haste in his step. What does he
bring, what does he say? For we are now slaves of a Dorian
land.

TALTHYBIUS

Hecuba, you know that I have made frequent journeys to
Troy from the Achaean army as a herald: as one previously
known to you, I, Talthybius, have come to report news.

---

11 This refers to Sicily and to its success in the panhellenic
games at Olympia and elsewhere (anachronistically, since neither
these places nor the games existed in the Bronze Age).

12 Probably an allusion to Thurii, a colony on the instep of Italy
founded under the leadership of the Athenians in 444/3 B.C.

13 Because of the minerals it carried, the Crathis colored yel-
low anything dipped into it: see Ovid, *Metamorphoses* 15.315-6.

ΕΚΑΒΗ

τόδε, φίλαι γυναῖκες, τόδε, Τρωιάδες,
ὃ φόβος ἦν πάλαι.

ΤΑΛΘΥΒΙΟΣ

240 ἤδη κεκλήρωσθ᾽, εἰ τόδ᾽ ἦν ὑμῖν φόβος.

ΕΚΑΒΗ

αἰαῖ, τίνα πόλιν Φθιάδος εἶπας ἢ
Καδμείας χθονός;

ΤΑΛΘΥΒΙΟΣ

κατ᾽ ἄνδρ᾽ ἑκάστη κοὐχ ὁμοῦ λελόγχατε.

ΕΚΑΒΗ

τίν᾽ ἄρα τίς ἔλαχε; τίνα πότμος εὐτυχὴς
245 Ἰλιάδων μένει;

ΤΑΛΘΥΒΙΟΣ

οἶδ᾽· ἀλλ᾽ ἕκαστα πυνθάνου, μὴ πάνθ᾽ ὁμοῦ.

ΕΚΑΒΗ

τοὐμὸν ⟨μὲν⟩ τίς ἄρ᾽ ἔλαχε τέκος, ἔνεπε,
τλάμονα Κασσάνδραν;

ΤΑΛΘΥΒΙΟΣ

ἐξαίρετόν νιν ἔλαβεν Ἀγαμέμνων ἄναξ.

---

[239] sic Diggle: τόδε τόδε φίλαι γυναῖκες (vel Τρῳάδες) C
[241] sic (post Hartung, qui posterius ἢ del.) Willink: τίνα ἢ
Θεσσαλίας πόλιν ἢ Φθιάδος C
[247] ⟨μὲν⟩ Willink: ⟨δὴ⟩ Nauck

HECUBA[14]

Dear women of Troy, this, this
is what I have been dreading for a long time!

TALTHYBIUS

You have now been assigned by lot to your masters, if that
is what you were afraid of.

HECUBA

Ah me! What city of Phthia or of Cadmus' land
do you mean?

TALTHYBIUS

You are each assigned to a different man, not all together.

HECUBA

Then who has been assigned to whom? Who of the women
   of Troy
has blessedness awaiting her?

TALTHYBIUS

I know the answers. But ask particulars, not everything at
once.

HECUBA

Tell me, who has won my daughter,
Cassandra the unblest?

TALTHYBIUS

King Agamemnon took her as his special prize.

14 Hecuba's words from here until 292 are sung. Talthybius'
replies are spoken.

ΕΚΑΒΗ

250 ἦ τᾷ Λακεδαιμονίᾳ νύμφᾳ
δούλαν; ὤμοι μοι.

ΤΑΛΘΥΒΙΟΣ

οὔκ, ἀλλὰ λέκτρων σκότια νυμφευτήρια.

ΕΚΑΒΗ

ἦ τὰν τοῦ Φοίβου παρθένον, ᾇ γέρας ὁ
χρυσοκόμας ἔδωκ᾽ ἄλεκτρον ζόαν;

ΤΑΛΘΥΒΙΟΣ

255 ἔρως ἐτόξευσ᾽ αὐτὸν ἐνθέου κόρης.

ΕΚΑΒΗ

ῥῖπτε, τέκνον, ζαθέους κλά-
δας καὶ ἀπὸ χροὸς ἐνδυ-
τῶν στεφέων ἱεροὺς στολμούς.

ΤΑΛΘΥΒΙΟΣ

οὐ γὰρ μέγ᾽ αὐτῇ βασιλικῶν λέκτρων τυχεῖν;

ΕΚΑΒΗ

260 τί δ᾽ ὁ νεοχμὸν ἀπ᾽ ἐμέθεν ἐλάβετε τέκος,
ποῦ μοι ⟨νῦν κυρεῖ⟩;

ΤΑΛΘΥΒΙΟΣ

Πολυξένην ἔλεξας ἢ τίν᾽ ἱστορεῖς;

ΕΚΑΒΗ

ταύταν· τῷ πάλος ἔζευξεν;

256-7 κλάδας J. Stanley: κληΐδας fere C
260 δ᾽ ὁ Tyrwhitt: δὲ τὸ C   261 ⟨νῦν κυρεῖ⟩ Diggle

40

HECUBA

To be a slave to the Spartan wife?
Oh the pain!

TALTHYBIUS

No: to share his bed in secret.

HECUBA

Phoebus Apollo's virgin, the one to whom
the god of golden hair gave the gift of unmated life?

TALTHYBIUS

Love for the inspired maiden has pierced his heart like an
arrow.

HECUBA

Cast away, my child, your holy laurel branches,
and from your body strip
the sacred garlands you wear!

TALTHYBIUS

What? Is it not a great thing for her to win a king's bed?

HECUBA

But what about the daughter you took from me last?
Where ⟨is she now⟩?

TALTHYBIUS

Do you mean Polyxena? Or whom are you asking about?

HECUBA

I mean her: to whom has the lot joined her?

ΤΑΛΘΥΒΙΟΣ

τύμβῳ τέτακται προσπολεῖν Ἀχιλλέως.

ΕΚΑΒΗ

265 ὤμοι ἐγώ· τάφῳ πρόσπολον ἐτεκόμαν.
ἀτὰρ τίς ὅδ᾽ ἢ νόμος ἢ
τί θέσμιον, ὦ φίλος, Ἑλλάνων;

ΤΑΛΘΥΒΙΟΣ

εὐδαιμόνιζε παῖδα σήν· ἔχει καλῶς.

ΕΚΑΒΗ

τί τόδ᾽ ἔλακες; ἆρά μοι ἀέλιον λεύσσει;

ΤΑΛΘΥΒΙΟΣ

270 ἔχει πότμος νιν, ὥστ᾽ ἀπηλλάχθαι πόνων.

ΕΚΑΒΗ

⟨αἰαῖ·⟩ τί δ᾽ ἁ τοῦ χαλκεομήστορος Ἕκτορος
δάμαρ,
Ἀνδρομάχα τάλαινα, τίν᾽ ἔχει τύχαν;

ΤΑΛΘΥΒΙΟΣ

καὶ τήνδ᾽ Ἀχιλλέως ἔλαβε παῖς ἐξαίρετον.

ΕΚΑΒΗ

275 ἐγὼ δὲ τῷ πρόσπολος ἁ τριτοβά-
μονος χερὶ δευομένα βάκτρου,
γεραιὸν κάρα;

ΤΑΛΘΥΒΙΟΣ

Ἰθάκης Ὀδυσσεὺς ἔλαχ᾽ ἄναξ δούλην σ᾽ ἔχειν.

TROJAN WOMEN

TALTHYBIUS

Her assignment is to serve the tomb of Achilles.

HECUBA

Ah me! My daughter serving a tomb!
But what custom,
what usage of the Greeks is this, pray?

TALTHYBIUS

Count your daughter blessed: it is well with her.

HECUBA

What is it you are saying? Does she still look on the light?

TALTHYBIUS

It is her fate to be released from trouble.

HECUBA

⟨Ah me!⟩ But what of the wife of Hector skilled in war,
poor Andromache? What is her fate?

TALTHYBIUS

Achilles' son has won her as a special prize.

HECUBA

And I, whom shall I serve,
I that need a staff for my hand and go about on three feet,
an old woman?

TALTHYBIUS

Odysseus, King of Ithaca, has won you to keep as his slave.

---

272 ⟨αἰαῖ⟩ cum metri tum sensus gratia Willink cl. *Hel.* 688
274 καὶ τήνδ'] κοίτην Burges
277 γεραιὸν κάρα Wecklein: γεραιῷ κάρᾳ C

EKABH

ἒ ἔ·
ἄρασσε κρᾶτα κούριμον, ἕλκ᾽ ὀνύχεσσι
280 δίπτυχον παρειάν.
ἰώ μοί μοι.
μυσαρῷ δολίῳ λέλογχα φωτὶ δουλεύειν,
πολεμίῳ δίκας, παρανόμῳ δάκει,
285 ὃς πάντα τἀκεῖθεν ἐνθάδ᾽ <ἀναστρέφει,
τὰ δ᾽> ἀντίπαλ᾽ αὖθις ἐκεῖσε διπτύχῳ γλώσσᾳ,
φίλα τὰ πρότερ᾽ ἄφιλα τιθέμενος πάλιν.
<αἰαῖ,> γοᾶσθ᾽, ὦ Τρῳάδες, με· βέβακα
290 δύσποτμος, οἴχομαι ἁ
τάλαινα, δυστυχεστάτῳ
προσέπεσον κλήρῳ.

ΧΟΡΟΣ

τὸ μὲν σὸν οἶσθα, πότνια· τὰς δ᾽ ἐμὰς τύχας
τίς ἆρ᾽ Ἀχαιῶν ἢ τίς Ἑλλήνων ἔχει;

ΤΑΛΘΥΒΙΟΣ

ἴτ᾽, ἐκκομίζειν δεῦρο Κασσάνδραν χρεὼν
295 ὅσον τάχιστα, δμῶες, ὡς στρατηλάτῃ
ἐς χεῖρα δούς νιν εἶτα τὰς εἰληγμένας
καὶ τοῖσιν ἄλλοις αἰχμαλωτίδων ἄγω.
ἔα· τί πεύκης ἔνδον αἴθεται σέλας;
πιμπρᾶσιν—ἢ τί δρῶσι—Τρῳάδες μυχούς,

285–6 <ἀναστρέφει> Diggle, <τὰ δ᾽> Wilamowitz
287 φίλα . . . ἄφιλα Seidler: ἄφιλα . . . φίλα C   πάλιν
Wilamowitz: πάντων C   289 <αἰαῖ> Willink

HECUBA

Ah, ah!
Strike the shorn head! Scratch with your nails
your two cheeks!
Ah me, ah me!
It is my lot to be a slave to a vile and treacherous man,
an enemy of justice, a lawless creature!
He ⟨twists⟩ everything from there to here
and back from here to there by his deceitful tongue,
making enmity where before there was friendship!
⟨Alas!⟩ Wail for me, women of Troy! I am gone,
ill-starred one, I am sped,
unhappy one, it is to the unluckiest
of lots that I have fallen!

CHORUS LEADER

You have learned your fate, my lady. But what dweller in
Achaea or Hellas[15] holds my fate in his hands?

TALTHYBIUS

Servants, go and bring Cassandra out here quickly so that
I may put her in our commander's hands and then bring
the allotted prisoners to the other Greeks.

*Servants approach the door of the skene. The gleam of fire
is seen within.*

But what is this? Why is the light of a pine torch gleam-
ing inside? Are the Trojan women burning their tents,

15 Possibly used in its narrower (and older) sense to denote ei-
ther a region of Thessaly or Northern Greece in contrast to the
Peloponnesus.

300 ὡς ἐξάγεσθαι τῆσδε μέλλουσαι χθονὸς
πρὸς Ἄργος, αὐτῶν τ᾽ ἐκπυροῦσι σώματα
θανεῖν θέλουσαι· κάρτα τοι τοὐλεύθερον
ἐν τοῖς τοιούτοις δυσλόφως φέρει κακά.
ἄνοιγ᾽ ἄνοιγε, μὴ τὸ ταῖσδε πρόσφορον
305 ἐχθρὸν δ᾽ Ἀχαιοῖς εἰς ἔμ᾽ αἰτίαν βάλῃ.

ΕΚΑΒΗ

οὐκ ἔστιν, οὐ πιμπρᾶσιν, ἀλλὰ παῖς ἐμὴ
μαινὰς θοάζει δεῦρο Κασσάνδρα δρόμῳ.

ΚΑΣΣΑΝΔΡΑ

στρ.

ἄνεχε, πάρεχε, φῶς φέρε· σέβω φλέγω—
ἰδοὺ ἰδού—
310 λαμπάσι ⟨σοι⟩ τόδ᾽ ἱερόν, Ὑμέναι᾽ ἄναξ·
⟨ἰώ,⟩ μακάριος ὁ γαμέτας·
μακαρία δ᾽ ἐγὼ βασιλικοῖς λέκτροις
κατ᾽ Ἄργος ἁ γαμουμένα.
Ὑμὴν ὦ Ὑμέναι᾽ Ὑμήν.
315 ἐπεὶ σύ, μᾶτερ, ⟨μάται᾽⟩
ἐν δάκρυσι καὶ γόοισι τὸν

308 φέρε Bothe ex t: φέρω C
309 ἰδοὺ ἰδού quae post ἄναξ 310 habent C huc trai. Hermann
310 ⟨σοι⟩ Willink: Ὑμέναι᾽ Willink: ὦ Ὑ- C
311 lac. indic. Diggle, ⟨ἰώ⟩ suppl. Willink
314 Ὑμέναι᾽ Ὑμήν Hermann cl. 331: Ὑμέναι᾽ ἄναξ C
315–6 ⟨μάται᾽⟩ ἐν Willink: ἐπὶ C

since they are about to be led off from this land to Argos,
and setting fire to their own bodies from a desire to die?
Or what are they doing? In circumstances like these free
spirits bridle at misfortune. Open up, open up, so that I
may not be blamed for an action that is to their advantage
but hateful to the Greeks!

Enter from the skene CASSANDRA *carrying a flaming torch
in either hand.*

HECUBA
It is not so: they are not setting anything on fire: my mad
daughter Cassandra is coming here on the run.

CASSANDRA
Raise it, bring it on, bring a light! I honor, I make gleam
  ⟨for you⟩
(see, see!)
with torch fire[16] this holy place, Lord Hymenaeus!
⟨Hurray!⟩ Blessed is the bridegroom,
blessed too am I, to a king's bed
in Argos wedded!
Hymen, O Hymenaeus, Hymen![17]
For you, mother,
in tears and groans ⟨foolishly⟩
keep lamenting

---

16 Cassandra's torches at one level are appropriate for mar-
riage (though at Greek marriages it was not the bride but her
mother who held the torch). At another level they may suggest an
Erinys (cf. 457), sometimes represented as brandishing torches,
as well as Hecate (see note on 323). Hymen or Hymenaeus is the
god of marriage.

17 The marriage cry addressed to Hymen.

θανόντα πατέρα πατρίδα τε
φίλαν καταστένουσ' ἔχεις,
ἐγὼ δ' ἐπὶ γάμοις ἐμοῖς
320 ἀναφλέγω πυρὸς φῶς
ἐς αὐγάν, ἐς αἴγλαν
διδοῦσ', ὦ Ὑμέναιε, σοί,
διδοῦσ', ὦ Ἑκάτα, φάος
παρθένων ἐπὶ λέκτροις
ἇ νόμος ἔχει.

ἀντ.

325 πάλλε πόδ' αἰθέριον ⟨ἄναγ'⟩ ἄναγε χορόν—
εὐᾶν εὐοῖ—
ὡς ἐπὶ πατρὸς ἐμοῦ μακαριωτάταις
τύχαις· ὁ χορὸς ὅσιος ⟨ὅσιος⟩.
ἄγε σὺ Φοῖβέ νιν· κατὰ σὸν ἐν δάφναις
330 ἀνάκτορον θυηπολῶ.
Ὑμὴν ὦ Ὑμέναι' Ὑμήν.
χόρευε, μᾶτερ, χόρευ',
ἄναγε, πόδα σὸν ἕλισσε τᾷδ'
ἐκεῖσε, μετ' ἐμέθεν ποδῶν
φέρουσα φιλτάταν βάσιν.
335 βόασον ὑμέναιον ὦ
μακαρίαις ἀοιδαῖς
ἰαχαῖς τε νύμφαν.
ἴτ', ὦ καλλίπεπλοι Φρυγῶν

---

325 ⟨ἄναγ'⟩ Hermann   328 ⟨ὅσιος⟩ Hermann
335 βόασον Diggle: βοάσατε τὸν fere C

my dead father and our dear country,
but I at my marriage
set alight this blaze of fire,
giving it for gleam, for glare
to you, O Hymenaeus,
and to you, O Hecate,[18]
for a maiden's marriage,
as custom ordains!

Lift your foot and shake it, ‹strike up,› strike up the dance
(Euhan! Euhoi!)
just as in my father's happiest days!
The dance is holy, ‹holy›:
do you, Phoebus, lead it. For crowned with laurels I serve
in your temple.
Hymen, O Hymenaeus, Hymen!
Dance, mother, dance,
lead off and whirl your foot this way
and that, joining with me
in the joyful step!
Shout the cry of Hymen
with songs and shouts of blessedness
to the bride!
Come, you daughters of Phrygia, with your lovely gowns,

[18] Hecate is an underworld goddess worshiped at night. She
bears a torch (*Helen* 569) and is associated with revenge (*Medea*
395-8, *Ion* 1048-57).

κόραι, μέλπετ᾽ ἐμῶν γάμων
340 τὸν πεπρωμένον εὐνᾷ
πόσιν ἐμέθεν.

ΧΟΡΟΣ

βασίλεια, βακχεύουσαν οὐ λήψῃ κόρην,
μὴ κοῦφον ἄρῃ βῆμ᾽ ἐς Ἀργείων στρατόν;

ΕΚΑΒΗ

Ἥφαιστε, δᾳδουχεῖς μὲν ἐν γάμοις βροτῶν,
ἀτὰρ λυγράν γε τήνδ᾽ ἀναιθύσσεις φλόγα
345 ἔξω τε μεγάλων ἐλπίδων. οἴμοι, τέκνον,
ὡς οὐχ ὑπ᾽ αἰχμῆς ⟨σ᾽⟩ οὐδ᾽ ὑπ᾽ Ἀργείου δορὸς
γάμους γαμεῖσθαι τούσδ᾽ ἐδόξαζόν ποτε.
παράδος ἐμοὶ φῶς· οὐ γὰρ ὀρθὰ πυρφορεῖς
μαινὰς θοάζουσ᾽, οὐδὲ σαῖς τύχαις, τέκνον,
350 σεσωφρόνηκας ἀλλ᾽ ἔτ᾽ ἐν ταὐτῷ μένεις.
ἐσφέρετε πεύκας, δάκρυά τ᾽ ἀνταλλάξατε
τοῖς τῆσδε μέλεσι, Τρῳάδες, γαμηλίοις.

ΚΑΣΣΑΝΔΡΑ

μῆτερ, πύκαζε κρᾶτ᾽ ἐμὸν νικηφόρον
καὶ χαῖρε τοῖς ἐμοῖσι βασιλικοῖς γάμοις·
355 καὶ πέμπε, κἂν μὴ τἀμά σοι πρόθυμά γ᾽ ᾖ,
ὤθει βιαίως· εἰ γὰρ ἔστι Λοξίας,
Ἑλένης γαμεῖ με δυσχερέστερον γάμον
ὁ τῶν Ἀχαιῶν κλεινὸς Ἀγαμέμνων ἄναξ.

339 μέλπετέ μοι γάμων Willink   346 ⟨σ᾽⟩ Musgrave
349 σαῖς τύχαις Heath: σ᾽ αἱ τύχαι C
350 σεσωφρόνηκας Nauck: -ήκας t: ἐσωφρονήκασ᾽ C

sing for me of the one destined
for my marriage bed,
my husband!

CHORUS LEADER

My queen, stop your delirious daughter before she steps
lightly down into the Argive army!

HECUBA

Hephaestus, you bear the torch when mortals marry, but
this gleam you now spread abroad is painful and far re-
moved from our high hopes. Ah me, my daughter, how
little did I think you would ever make a marriage like this at
the point of an Argive spear! Give me the flame! (*She re-
moves the torches from Cassandra's hands.*) You are not
right to carry a torch, mad and frenzied as you are, and you
have not been brought to your senses by your fate, my
child, but still remain in the same demented state.

Trojan women, take the torches indoors and in ex-
change for her wedding songs give her your tears!

*Two Trojan women receive the torches from Hecuba and
takes them indoors.*

CASSANDRA

Mother, crown my victorious head and rejoice at my royal
marriage! Escort me on my way, and if in your eyes I do
not seem eager, push me along by force! For if Loxias[19]
lives, Agamemnon, the glorious leader of the Greeks, will
win, in marrying me, a wife more disastrous than Helen!

---

[19] A name for Apollo as god of prophecy.

κτενῶ γὰρ αὐτὸν κἀντιπορθήσω δόμους
360 ποινὰς ἀδελφῶν καὶ πατρὸς λαβοῦσ᾽ ἐμοῦ.
ἀλλ᾽ αὖτ᾽ ἐάσω· πέλεκυν οὐχ ὑμνήσομεν,
ὃς ἐς τράχηλον τὸν ἐμὸν εἶσι χἀτέρων·
μητροκτόνους τ᾽ ἀγῶνας, οὓς οὑμοὶ γάμοι
θήσουσιν, οἴκων τ᾽ Ἀτρέως ἀνάστασιν.
365 πόλιν δὲ δείξω τήνδε μακαριωτέραν
ἢ τοὺς Ἀχαιούς, ἔνθεος μέν, ἀλλ᾽ ὅμως
τοσόνδε γ᾽ ἔξω στήσομαι βακχευμάτων·
οἳ διὰ μίαν γυναῖκα καὶ μίαν Κύπριν
θηρῶντες Ἑλένην μυρίους ἀπώλεσαν.
370 ὁ δὲ στρατηγὸς ὁ σοφὸς ἐχθίστων ὕπερ
τὰ φίλτατ᾽ ὤλεσ᾽, ἡδονὰς τὰς οἴκοθεν
τέκνων ἀδελφῷ δοὺς γυναικὸς οὕνεκα,
καὶ ταῦθ᾽ ἑκούσης κοὐ βίᾳ λελησμένης.
ἐπεὶ δ᾽ ἐπ᾽ ἀκτὰς ἤλυθον Σκαμανδρίους,
375 ἔθνησκον, οὐ γῆς ὅρι᾽ ἀποστερούμενοι
οὐδ᾽ ὑψίπυργον πατρίδ᾽· οὓς δ᾽ Ἄρης ἕλοι,
οὐ παῖδας εἶδον, οὐ δάμαρτος ἐν χεροῖν
πέπλοις συνεστάλησαν, ἐν ξένῃ δὲ γῇ
κεῖνται. τὰ δ᾽ οἴκοι τοῖσδ᾽ ὅμοι᾽ ἐγίγνετο·
⟨γυναῖκες ἄνδρας ἀλκίμους ἀπώλλυσαν⟩
380 χῆραί τ᾽ ἔθνησκον, οἱ δ᾽ ἄπαιδες ἐν δόμοις
ἄλλως τέκν᾽ ἐκθρέψαντες· οὐδὲ πρὸς τάφοις
ἔσθ᾽ ὅστις αὐτῶν αἷμα γῇ δωρήσεται.
[ἦ τοῦδ᾽ ἐπαίνου τὸ στράτευμ᾽ ἐπάξιον.

361 ἀλλ᾽ αὖτ᾽ Musgrave: ἄλλα τ᾽ C: ἀλλ᾽ αἶσχρ᾽ Parmentier

For I shall kill him and plunder his house, exacting revenge for my brothers and my father! But this subject I dismiss. I shall not sing of the ax that will enter my neck and that of others, or the matricidal struggles my marriage shall bring about, or the ruin of the house of Atreus.

Instead I shall show that this city of ours is more fortunate than Greece is: although I am possessed by the god, yet to this extent I will step aside from my frenzy. In their quest for Helen the Greeks lost countless lives for the sake of one woman and one passion. Their general, so clever a man, destroyed what he loved best for the sake of what he hated most, surrendering to his brother his own pleasure in his children for a woman's sake, and at that a woman who was abducted of her own free will, not forcibly.

When they came to the banks of the Scamander, they began to perish, though they had not been deprived of territory or of their homeland's high towers. Those whom Ares slew did not see their children and were not clothed for burial by the hands of their wives but lie buried in foreign earth. Matters at home were just as bad: ⟨wives were losing their valiant husbands⟩ and dying in widowhood, while others died childless in their houses, having reared children all for nothing. There is no one who near their tombs will give the earth an offering of blood. [This is the praise the army deserves. Better to say nothing of

---

380 ante h. v. aliquid excidisse putat Matthiae
381 ἄλλως Tyrwhitt: -οις C
383 del. Wilamowitz, 384–5 Reichenberger

σιγᾶν ἄμεινον τᾀσχρά, μηδὲ μοῦσά μοι
385 γένοιτ' ἀοιδὸς ἥτις ὑμνήσει κακά.]
    Τρῶες δὲ πρῶτον μέν, τὸ κάλλιστον κλέος,
ὑπὲρ πάτρας ἔθνησκον· οὓς δ' ἕλοι δόρυ,
νεκροί γ' ἐς οἴκους φερόμενοι φίλων ὕπο
ἐν γῇ πατρῴα περιβολὰς εἶχον χθονός,
390 χερσὶν περισταλέντες ὧν ἐχρῆν ὕπο·
ὅσοι δὲ μὴ θάνοιεν ἐν μάχῃ Φρυγῶν,
ἀεὶ κατ' ἦμαρ σὺν δάμαρτι καὶ τέκνοις
ᾤκουν, Ἀχαιοῖς ὧν ἀπῆσαν ἡδοναί.
    τὰ δ' Ἕκτορός σοι λύπρ' ἄκουσον ὡς ἔχει·
395 δόξας ἀνὴρ ἄριστος οἴχεται θανών,
καὶ τοῦτ' Ἀχαιῶν ἵξις ἐξεργάζεται·
εἰ δ' ἦσαν οἴκοι, χρηστὸς ἔλαθεν ἂν γεγώς.
Πάρις δ' ἔγημε τὴν Διός· γήμας δὲ μή,
σιγώμενον τὸ κῆδος εἶχ' ἂν ἐν δόμοις.
400   φεύγειν μὲν οὖν χρὴ πόλεμον ὅστις εὖ φρονεῖ·
εἰ δ' ἐς τόδ' ἔλθοι, στέφανος οὐκ αἰσχρὸς πόλει
καλῶς ὀλέσθαι, μὴ καλῶς δὲ δυσκλεές.
ὧν οὕνεκ' οὐ χρή, μῆτερ, οἰκτίρειν σε γῆν,
οὐ τἀμὰ λέκτρα· τοὺς γὰρ ἐχθίστους ἐμοὶ
405 καὶ σοὶ γάμοισι τοῖς ἐμοῖς διαφθερῶ.

ΧΟΡΟΣ
ὡς ἡδέως κακοῖσιν οἰκείοις γελᾷς
μέλπεις θ' ἃ μέλπους' οὐ σαφῆ δείξεις ἴσως.

388 del. Dobree   399 εἶχ' ἂν Burges: εἶχεν vel εἶδεν C
401 πόλει] πέλει Nauck

disgraceful matters: may my Muse not be a singer who hymns disaster.]

As for the Trojans, in the first place—their greatest glory—they died on behalf of their country. Those who were slain by the spear were carried into the house by their kin and were covered with earth in the land of their fathers, and those who ought to do so dressed them for burial. Any Phrygians who were not killed in battle lived day by day with their wives and children, a pleasure the Greeks were denied. As for Hector's fate, grievous in your eyes, hear how things stand. He perished after winning repute for the greatest valor, and it was the coming of the Greeks that brought this about. Had they stayed at home, his bravery would have gone unnoticed. Paris married Zeus's daughter, and had he not done so, he would have had a wife in his house no one talked of.

Now any man of sense ought to shun war. But if it comes to this, it is no shameful garland for a city to die a noble death, though dying ignobly is a disgrace. Therefore, mother, you ought not to pity our country or my marriage bed. With my marriage I shall destroy those you and I hate most.

CHORUS LEADER
How happily you smile at your own misfortunes and prophesy, and yet perhaps you will show that your prophecies are unreliable.

ΤΑΛΘΥΒΙΟΣ

εἰ μή σ᾽ Ἀπόλλων ἐξεβάκχευσεν φρένας,
οὔ τἂν ἀμισθὶ τοὺς ἐμοὺς στρατηλάτας
410 τοιαῖσδε φήμαις ἐξέπεμπες ἂν χθονός.
ἀτὰρ τὰ σεμνὰ καὶ δοκήμασιν σοφὰ
οὐδέν τι κρείσσω τῶν τὸ μηδὲν ἦν ἄρα.
ὁ γὰρ μέγιστος τῶν Πανελλήνων ἄναξ,
Ἀτρέως φίλος παῖς, τῆσδ᾽ ἔρωτ᾽ ἐξαίρετον
415 μαινάδος ὑπέστη· καὶ πένης μέν εἰμ᾽ ἐγώ,
ἀτὰρ λέχος γε τῆσδ᾽ ἂν οὐκ ἠτησάμην.
  καὶ σοῦ μέν (οὐ γὰρ ἀρτίας ἔχεις φρένας)
Ἀργεῖ᾽ ὀνείδη καὶ Φρυγῶν ἐπαινέσεις
ἀνέμοις φέρεσθαι παραδίδωμ᾽· ἕπου δέ μοι
420 πρὸς ναῦς, καλὸν νύμφευμα τῷ στρατηλάτῃ.
σὺ δ᾽, ἡνίκ᾽ ἄν σε Λαρτίου χρῄζῃ τόκος
ἄγειν, ἕπεσθαι· σώφρονος δ᾽ ἔσῃ λάτρις
γυναικός, ὥς φασ᾽ οἱ μολόντες Ἴλιον.

ΚΑΣΣΑΝΔΡΑ

[ἦ δεινὸς ὁ λάτρις. τί ποτ᾽ ἔχουσι τοὔνομα
425 κήρυκες, ἓν ἀπέχθημα πάγκοινον βροτοῖς,
οἱ περὶ τυράννους καὶ πόλεις ὑπηρέται;]
σὺ τὴν ἐμὴν φῂς μητέρ᾽ εἰς Ὀδυσσέως
ἥξειν μέλαθρα· ποῦ δ᾽ Ἀπόλλωνος λόγοι,
οἵ φασιν αὐτὴν εἰς ἔμ᾽ ἡρμηνευμένοι
430 αὐτοῦ θανεῖσθαι; τἄλλα δ᾽ οὐκ ὀνειδιῶ.

---

416 ἠτησάμην Naber: ἐκτησ- C   417 σοῦ Hermann: σοὶ C
424–6 ut huic loco alienos secl. Kovacs

TALTHYBIUS

If Apollo had not struck your wits awry, you would pay dearly for sending my generals from the land with such words.[20] But it seems that those who are looked up to and considered wise are in no way better than those of no account. The high commander of all the Greeks, Atreus' beloved son, has succumbed to a passion for this mad-woman, choosing her above all others. I may be a poor man, but I would never have asked to have her as my mistress.

As for you, since you are not right in your head, I give your taunts against the Argives and your encomiums of the Trojans to the winds to carry away. Follow me to the ships, a fine prize for our general's bed! (*to Hecuba*) And you, when the son of Laertes wants to take you away, follow him. You will be the servant of a virtuous woman: so say those who have come to Troy.

CASSANDRA

[What a clever fellow this servant is! Why are they called "heralds," these creatures all mortals hate, when they are merely lackeys bustling about tyrants and cities?] You claim that my mother will come to the palace of Odysseus. But where are the words of Apollo, communicated to me, that she will die here? I will not reproach her with the rest of her fate.[21]

---

20 Saying words of ill omen at the beginning of a journey was thought to be dangerous.

21 Hecuba was transformed into a dog and gave her name to the promontory Cynossema ("Dog's Grave"): see *Hecuba* 1258-74.

EURIPIDES

δύστηνος, οὐκ οἶδ᾽ οἷά νιν μένει παθεῖν·
ὡς χρυσὸς αὐτῷ τἀμὰ καὶ Φρυγῶν κακὰ
δόξει ποτ᾽ εἶναι. δέκα γὰρ ἐκπλήσας ἔτη
πρὸς τοῖσιν ἐνθάδ᾽ ἵξεται μόνος πάτραν
οὗ δὴ <στεναγμῶν ἄξι᾽ εὑρήσει κακά·
νόστου δ᾽ ἐπισχήσει νιν ἄγρυπνος φύλαξ
435 ἢ πρὸς> στενὸν δίαυλον ᾤκισται πέτραις,
δεινὴ Χάρυβδις, ὠμοβρώς τ᾽ ὀρειβάτης
Κύκλωψ, Λιγυστίς θ᾽ ἡ συῶν μορφώτρια
Κίρκη, θαλάσσης θ᾽ ἁλμυρᾶς ναυάγια,
λωτοῦ τ᾽ ἔρωτες, Ἡλίου θ᾽ ἁγναὶ βόες,
440 αἳ σαρκὶ φοινίαισιν ἤσουσίν ποτε
πικρὰν Ὀδυσσεῖ γῆρυν. ὡς δὲ συντέμω,
ζῶν εἶσ᾽ ἐς Ἅιδου κἀκφυγὼν λίμνης ὕδωρ
κάκ᾽ ἐν δόμοισι μυρί᾽ εὑρήσει μολών.

ἀλλὰ γὰρ τί τοὺς Ὀδυσσέως ἐξακοντίζω πόνους;
445 στεῖχ᾽ ὅπως τάχιστ᾽· ἐν Ἅιδου νυμφίῳ γημώμεθα.
ἦ κακὸς κακῶς ταφήσῃ νυκτός, οὐκ ἐν ἡμέρᾳ,
ὦ δοκῶν σεμνόν τι πράσσειν, Δαναϊδῶν ἀρχηγέτα.
κἀμέ τοι νεκρὸν φάραγγες γυμνάδ᾽ ἐκβεβλημένην
ὕδατι χειμάρρῳ ῥέουσαι νυμφίου πέλας τάφου
450 θηρσὶ δώσουσιν δάσασθαι, τὴν Ἀπόλλωνος λάτριν.
ὦ στέφη τοῦ φιλτάτου μοι θεῶν, ἀγάλματ᾽ εὔια,
χαίρετ᾽· ἐκλέλοιφ᾽ ἑορτάς, αἷς πάροιθ᾽ ἠγαλλόμην.

434 post h. v. lac. indic. Heath, post οὗ δὴ Kovacs
435 πέτραις Diggle: -ας C

58

Poor man, he does not know what suffering his fate holds in store for him. How golden will the Phrygians' misfortunes and mine one day seem to him! He will fill up the measure of ten years in addition to those he spent here and will reach his homeland all alone, where indeed ⟨he will find troubles worthy of his tears. But his homecoming will be delayed by the sleepless watchman who⟩ dwells on the cliffs beside the current's ebb and flow, the dread Charybdis, and by the mountaineer Cyclops who eats raw flesh, the Ligurian Circe who turns men to swine, shipwreck on the briny sea, longing for lotus, and the sacred cattle of the Sun, which with their bloody flesh shall one day utter to Odysseus an ominous sound he will not like.[22] To cut my story short, he will go down alive to Hades, and when he has escaped the sea water, he will go home to find countless troubles in his house.

But why do I hurl forth Odysseus' woes? Go with all speed! Let me marry my bridegroom in Hades! O general of the Greeks, man whose fortunes men think lofty, you will be buried in wretched state, wretch that you are, by night not day! And I, when I am cast out as a naked corpse, shall be given to the wild beasts to tear asunder by the gullies that flow in winter spate past my bridegroom's tomb, I, Apollo's servant. O garlands that belong to the god I love best, finery of divine inspiration, farewell! (*She throws her sacred emblems on the ground.*) I have left be-

----

22 Cf. *Odyssey* 12.394-5 where the spitted flesh of the cattle of the Sun begins to moo.

----

440 σαρξὶ φοινίαισιν Bothe: σάρκα φωνήεσσαν C
445 ἐν Heiland: ἐς C   γαμούμεθα Porson

EURIPIDES

ἴτ᾽ ἀπ᾽ ἐμοῦ χρωτὸς σπαραγμοῖς, ὡς ἔτ᾽ οὖσ᾽ ἁγνὴ
  χρόα
δῶ θοαῖς αὔραις φέρεσθαί σοι τάδ᾽, ὦ μαντεῖ᾽ ἄναξ.
455   ποῦ σκάφος τὸ τοῦ στρατηγοῦ; ποῖ πόδ᾽ ἐμβαί-
    νειν με χρή;
οὐκέτ᾽ ἂν φθάνοις ἂν αὔραν ἱστίοις καραδοκῶν,
ὡς μίαν τριῶν Ἐρινὺν τῆσδέ μ᾽ ἐξάξων χθονός.
χαῖρέ μοι, μῆτερ· δακρύσῃς μηδέν· ὦ φίλη πατρίς,
οἵ τε γῆς ἔνερθ᾽ ἀδελφοὶ χὠ τεκὼν ἡμᾶς πατήρ,
460   οὐ μακρὰν δέξεσθέ μ᾽· ἥξω δ᾽ ἐς νεκροὺς νικηφόρος
καὶ δόμους πέρσασ᾽ Ἀτρειδῶν, ὧν ἀπωλόμεσθ᾽ ὕπο.

ΧΟΡΟΣ

Ἑκάβης γεραιᾶς φύλακες, οὐ δεδόρκατε
δέσποιναν ὡς ἄναυδος ἐκτάδην πίτνει;
οὐκ ἀντιλήψεσθ᾽; ἦ μεθήσετ᾽, ὦ κακαί,
465   γραῖαν πεσοῦσαν; αἴρετ᾽ εἰς ὀρθὸν δέμας.

ΕΚΑΒΗ

ἐᾶτέ μ᾽ (οὔτοι φίλα τὰ μὴ φίλ᾽, ὦ κόραι)
κεῖσθαι πεσοῦσαν· πτωμάτων γὰρ ἄξια
πάσχω τε καὶ πέπονθα κἄτι πείσομαι.
ὦ θεοί· κακοὺς μὲν ἀνακαλῶ τοὺς συμμάχους,

455 πόδ᾽ Elmsley: ποτ᾽ C
457 Ἐρινύων Burges: cf. IT 931, 970, 1456
463 ἐκτάδην Verrall: εἰς Αΐδην C

---

23 Cassandra identifies herself with the spirits of vengeance who punish crimes, particularly against kindred and mostly at the behest of Zeus. Euripides here gives their number, usually un-

hind the festivals in which I once used to exult. Depart from my flesh as I tear you away, so that while I am still pure in body I may give you to the swift winds to carry to you, my prophetic lord!

Where is the general's ship? Where must I go on board? Now is not too soon for you to be on the lookout for a breeze for your sails, for in me you are taking from this land an Erinys, one of the three.[23] Farewell, mother! Do not weep. Dear fatherland, my brothers beneath the earth, and the father who begot us, you will receive me soon! I shall come to the land of the dead victorious, having sacked the house of the Atridae at whose hands we perished!

Exit by Eisodos A CASSANDRA, TALTHYBIUS, *and retinue. Hecuba collapses to the ground.*

CHORUS LEADER

You who keep watch over aged Hecuba, do you not see that your mistress has fallen outstretched upon the ground without a word? Will you not take hold of her? Will you leave an old woman where she has fallen, you worthless creatures? Raise her body upright!

HECUBA

Let me lie where I have fallen (for unwelcome help is not kindness, my daughters). Collapse is the proper response to what I have suffered, am suffering, and will suffer. O gods! To be sure, I am calling on allies that are faithless,

specified, as three. Cf. *Orestes* 408 and see also J. Diggle, *Studies on the Text of Euripides* (Oxford, 1981), p. 62, who, however, prefers a different explanation.

470 ὅμως δ' ἔχει τι σχῆμα κικλήσκειν θεούς,
ὅταν τις ἡμῶν δυστυχῆ λάβῃ τύχην.
πρῶτον μὲν οὖν μοι τἀγάθ' ἐξᾷσαι φίλον·
τοῖς γὰρ κακοῖσι πλείον' οἶκτον ἐμβαλῶ.
ἢ μὲν τύραννος κἀς τύραννν' ἐγημάμην,
475 κἀνταῦθ' ἀριστεύοντ' ἐγεινάμην τέκνα,
οὐκ ἀριθμὸν ἄλλως ἀλλ' ὑπερτάτους Φρυγῶν·
οὐ τοιάδ' οὔθ' Ἑλληνὶς οὐδὲ βάρβαρος
γυνὴ τεκοῦσα κομπάσειεν ἄν ποτε.
κἀκεῖνά τ' εἶδον δορὶ πεσόνθ' Ἑλληνικῷ
480 τρίχας τ' ἐτμήθην τάσδε πρὸς τύμβοις νεκρῶν,
καὶ τὸν φυτουργὸν Πρίαμον οὐκ ἄλλων πάρα
κλυοῦσ' ἔκλαυσα, τοῖσδε δ' εἶδον ὄμμασιν
αὐτὴ κατασφαγέντ' ἐφ' ἑρκείῳ πυρᾷ,
πόλιν θ' ἁλοῦσαν. ἃς δ' ἔθρεψα παρθένους
485 ἐς ἀξίωμα νυμφίων ἐξαίρετον,
ἄλλοισι θρέψασ' ἐκ χερῶν ἀφῃρέθην.
κοὔτ' ἐξ ἐκείνων ἐλπὶς ὡς ὀφθήσομαι
αὐτή τ' ἐκείνας οὐκέτ' ὄψομαί ποτε.
490 δούλη γυνὴ γραῦς Ἑλλάδ' εἰσαφίξομαι.
ἃ δ' ἐστὶ γήρᾳ τῷδ' ἀσυμφορώτατα,
τούτοις με προσθήσουσιν, ἢ θυρῶν λάτριν
κλῇδας φυλάσσειν, τὴν τεκοῦσαν Ἕκτορα,
ἢ σιτοποιεῖν, κἀν πέδῳ κοίτας ἔχειν
495 ῥυσοῖσι νώτοις, βασιλικῶν ἐκ δεμνίων,
τρυχηρὰ περὶ τρυχηρὸν εἱμένην χρόα
πέπλων λακίσματ', ἀδόκιμ' ὀλβίοις ἔχειν.
οἲ 'γὼ τάλαινα, διὰ γάμον μιᾶς ἕνα

62

yet nonetheless it is proper to invoke them when we suffer misfortune. My desire therefore is first to sing of my blessings. For in this way I shall make my woes seem the more to be pitied.

I was of royal blood and married into a royal house. There I gave birth to children of great excellence, no mere ciphers but preeminent among the Phrygians. No woman, Greek nor yet barbarian, could boast that she gave birth to their like. These sons I beheld slain by the Greek spear, and I cut my hair before the tombs of the dead. Their father, Priam, I did not lament from the report of others: I myself, with these eyes, saw him slaughtered at the household altar, saw too my city captured. The virgin daughters I raised to be deemed worthy of husbands of great station I raised for others' benefit, and they have been taken from me. I have no hope that I shall ever see them again or they me. Last, to put the capstone to my misfortunes, I shall go to Greece as an aged slave woman. They will assign me to tasks that ill befit my old age, either to keep watch over the keys as a doorkeeper, me who gave birth to Hector, or to make their bread. They will make me lay my aged back on the ground after sleeping in royal state, my broken body dressed in tattered rags, a disgrace for the prosperous to wear. Ah unhappy me, what sufferings I have and shall continue to have because of a single

---

474 ἦ μὲν τύραννος Elmsley: ἦμεν τύραννοι C
477 τοιάδ' οὔθ' Weil: Τρῳὰς οὐδ' C
479 fort. κἀκεῖν' ἐσεῖδον

γυναικὸς οἵων ἔτυχον ὧν τε τεύξομαι.
500 ὦ τέκνον, ὦ σύμβακχε Κασσάνδρα θεοῖς,
οἵαις ἔλυσας συμφοραῖς ἅγνευμα σόν.
σύ τ᾽, ὦ τάλαινα, ποῦ ποτ᾽ εἶ, Πολυξένη;
ὡς οὔτε μ᾽ ἄρσην οὔτε θήλεια σπορὰ
πολλῶν γενομένων τὴν τάλαιναν ὠφελεῖ.
505 τί δῆτά μ᾽ ὀρθοῦτ᾽; ἐλπίδων ποίων ὕπο;
ἄγετε τὸν ἁβρὸν δή ποτ᾽ ἐν Τροίᾳ πόδα,
νῦν δ᾽ ὄντα δοῦλον, στιβάδα πρὸς χαμαιπετῆ
πέτρινά τε δέμνι᾽, ὡς πεσοῦσ᾽ ἀποφθαρῶ
δακρύοις καταξανθεῖσα. τῶν δ᾽ εὐδαιμόνων
510 μηδένα νομίζετ᾽ εὐτυχεῖν, πρὶν ἂν θάνῃ.

ΧΟΡΟΣ

στρ.

ἀμφί μοι Ἴλιον, ὦ
Μοῦσα, καινῶν ὕμνων
ᾆσον σὺν δακρύοις ᾠδὰν ἐπικήδειον·
515 νῦν γὰρ μέλος ἐς Τροίαν ἰαχήσω,
τετραβάμονος ὡς ὑπ᾽ ἀπήνας
Ἀργείων ὀλόμαν τάλαινα δοριάλωτος,
ὅτ᾽ ἔλιπον ἵππον οὐράνια
520 βρέμοντα χρυσεοφάλαρον ἔνο-
πλον ἐν πύλαις Ἀχαιοί·
ἀνὰ δ᾽ ἐβόασεν λεὼς
Τρῳάδος ἀπὸ πέτρας σταθείς·
Ἴτ᾽, ὦ πεπαυμένοι πόνων,
525 τόδ᾽ ἱερὸν ἀνάγετε ξόανον

marriage of one woman!

My daughter Cassandra, you that shared in the gods' inspiration, what misfortunes brought you to end your chaste devotion to the god! And you, poor Polyxena, where are you? Neither male child nor female, of all I have given birth to, can help the poor woman that is me. So why do you try to raise me up? In hope of what? Lead me, who once walked so delicately in Troy but am now a slave, to my pallet on the ground and my stony bedding so that I may fall upon it and waste to death, worn down with weeping. Consider no prosperous man blessed until he dies.

Servants take Hecuba back to her pallet before the door of the skene.

CHORUS

Sing for me concerning Ilium,
O Muse, a new-made
ode of mourning accompanied by tears.
For now I shall sing a song of Troy,
how that Argive conveyance with four feet
wrought my destruction and wretched enslavement,
when the horse, reaching high heaven
with its clatter, decked with gold cheekpieces,
arms within, was left at the gates by the Achaeans.
The people shouted aloud
from where they stood on Troy's citadel,
"Come, you whose labors are over,
bring this holy statue

---

499 ὦν] ἔτι Broadhead   508 δέμνι' Dobree: κρήδεμν' C

65

Ἰλιάδι Διογενεῖ κόρᾳ.
τίς οὐκ ἔβα νεανίδων,
τίς οὐ γεραιὸς ἐκ δόμων;
κεχαρμένοι δ᾽ ἀοιδαῖς
530 δόλιον ἔσχον ἄταν.

ἀντ.

πᾶσα δὲ γέννα Φρυγῶν
πρὸς πύλας ὡρμάθη,
πεύκαν οὐρεῖαν, ξεστὸν λόχον Ἀργείων
535 καὶ Δαρδανίας ἄταν, θεᾷ δώσων,
χάριν ἄζυγος ἀμβροτοπώλου·
κλωστοῦ δ᾽ ἀμφιβόλοις λίνοιο, ναὸς ὡσεὶ
σκάφος κελαινόν, εἰς ἔδρανα
540 λάινα δάπεδά τε, φόνια πατρί-
δι, Παλλάδος θέσαν θεᾶς.
ἐπὶ δὲ πόνῳ καὶ χαρᾷ
νύχιον ἐπεὶ κνέφας παρῆν,
Λίβυς τε λωτὸς ἐκτύπει
545 Φρύγιά τε μέλεα, παρθένοι δ᾽
ἀέριον ἅμα κρότον ποδῶν
βοάν τ᾽ ἔμελπον εὔφρον᾽, ἐν
δόμοις δὲ παμφαὲς σέλας
πυρὸς μέλαιναν αἴγλαν
550 ἀντέδωκεν ὕπνου.

ἐπῳδ.

ἐγὼ δὲ τὰν ὀρεστέραν

533 πεύκαν οὐρεῖαν Dobree: πεύκᾳ ἐν οὐρείᾳ C

to Troy's Zeus-begotten daughter!"
Which of the girls did not go,
which of the old men, out of his house?
Rejoicing in song
they took for themselves ruin in disguise.

All of Phrygia's folk
rushed to the gates
to give this mountain pinewood, Greek ambush the adze
    had smoothed,
this ruin for Dardanus' land, to the goddess,
a gift to the maid of immortal horses.
With nooses of spun flax they brought it,
like the dark hull of a ship, to the temple of stone
and the precincts of the goddess Pallas,
precincts fatal to their country.
But when their labor and their joy
were overtaken by night's blackness,
the Libyan pipe sounded
and Phrygian tunes were played, and maidens
as they lifted their feet in dancing
sang a song of joy,
while within doors the blaze
of fire gave forth its sinister gleam
to banish sleep.

In that hour in honor of her of the wilds,

---

546 ἅμα Diggle: ἀνά C
550 ἀντέδωκεν ὕπνου Tyrrell: ἔδωκεν ὕπνῳ C

τότ᾽ ἀμφὶ μέλαθρα παρθένον
Διὸς κόραν ἐμελπόμαν
555 χοροῖσι· φοινία δ᾽ ἀνὰ
πτόλιν βοὰ κατέσχε Περ-
γάμων ἕδρας· βρέφη δὲ φίλι-
α περὶ πέπλους ἔβαλλε μα-
τρὶ χεῖρας ἐπτοημένας.
560 λόχου δ᾽ ἐξέβαιν᾽ Ἄρης,
κόρας ἔργα Παλλάδος.
σφαγαὶ δ᾽ ἀμφιβώμιοι
Φρυγῶν ἔν τε δεμνίοις
καράτομος ἐρημία
565 νεανίδων στέφανον ἔφερεν
Ἑλλάδι κουροτρόφον,
Φρυγῶν δὲ πατρίδι πένθος.

—Ἑκάβη, λεύσσεις τήνδ᾽ Ἀνδρομάχην
ξενικοῖς ἐπ᾽ ὄχοις πορθμευομένην;
570 παρὰ δ᾽ εἰρεσίᾳ μαστῶν ἔπεται
φίλος Ἀστυάναξ, Ἕκτορος ἶνις.
ποῖ ποτ᾽ ἀπήνης νώτοισι φέρῃ,
δύστηνε γύναι,
πάρεδρος χαλκέοις Ἕκτορος ὅπλοις
σκύλοις τε Φρυγῶν δοριθηράτοις,
575 οἷσιν Ἀχιλλέως παῖς Φθιώτας
στέψει ναοὺς ἀπὸ Τροίας;

556 κατέσχε Wilamowitz: κατεῖχε C

68

TROJAN WOMEN

Zeus's maiden daughter,
I was dancing about the temple,
when a murderous cry throughout the city
possessed the dwelling places of Pergamum.
Beloved young children threw frightened arms
about their mothers' skirts.
The war god was emerging from his ambush,
and this was Pallas' doing.
The slaughtering of Phrygians about the altars
and, in our beds, desolation wrought by the headsman's
    blade
brought a victory garland of young women
to Greece to bear them children,
but grief to the land of the Phrygians.

Enter by Eisodos B ANDROMACHE *and Astyanax, riding
on a wagon laden with Trojan spoils and accompanied by
guards.*

CHORUS LEADER

Hecuba, do you see Andromache here carried on an en-
emy wagon? Next to her heaving breast is her beloved
Astyanax, Hector's son. Where are you being taken on the
seat of a wagon, poor woman, sitting next to the bronze
armor of Hector and the spear-captured spoils of the
Phrygians, with which Achilles' son will deck the temples
of Phthia from Troy's store?

στρ. α

ΑΝΔΡΟΜΑΧΗ

Ἀχαιοὶ δεσπόται μ' ἄγουσιν.
οἴμοι.

ΕΚΑΒΗ
τί παιᾶν' ἐμὸν στενάζεις;

ΑΝΔΡΟΜΑΧΗ

αἰαῖ . . .

ΕΚΑΒΗ
. . . τῶνδ' ἀλγέων,
580   ὦ Ζεῦ, καὶ συμφορᾶς.
τέκεα, πρίν ποτ' ἦμεν.

ἀντ. α

ΑΝΔΡΟΜΑΧΗ

βέβακ' ὄλβος, βέβακε Τροία
τλάμων . . .

ΕΚΑΒΗ
. . . ἐμῶν τ' εὐγένεια παίδων.

ΑΝΔΡΟΜΑΧΗ

φεῦ φεῦ . . .

ΕΚΑΒΗ
φεῦ δῆτ' ἐμῶν
585   κακῶν· οἰκτρὰ τύχα
πόλεος, ἃ καπνοῦται.

TROJAN WOMEN

ANDROMACHE
My Achaean masters are taking me away!
Ah me!

HECUBA
My paean of sorrow, why do you make it yours?

ANDROMACHE
Alas!

HECUBA
Alas for these miseries,
O Zeus, and this woe!
My children, our life is over!

ANDROMACHE
Sped is blessedness, sped is Troy
the unblest . . .

HECUBA
. . . and also my noble sons!

ANDROMACHE
Alas!

HECUBA
Yes, alas for my
misfortunes! Pitiable is the fate
of the city, now a smoking ruin!

577–86 sic inter personas dispert. Willink: codices in stropha
οἴμοι, αἰαῖ, ὦ Ζεῦ, τέκεα Hecubae tribuunt, cetera Andromachae,
tum in antistropha Andromachae τλάμων, φεῦ φεῦ, κακῶν,
πόλεος, cetera Hecubae
580 fort. συμφορὰν

στρ. β

ΑΝΔΡΟΜΑΧΗ

μόλοις, ὦ πόσις μοι . . .

ΕΚΑΒΗ

βοᾷς τὸν παρ' Ἅιδα
παῖδ' ἐμόν; ὦ μέλεος,
590 σὺ δάμαρτος ἄλκαρ;

ἀντ. β

ΑΝΔΡΟΜΑΧΗ

σύ τοι, λῦμ' Ἀχαιῶν . . .

ΕΚΑΒΗ

τέκνων δή ποθ' ἁμῶν
πρεσβυγενὲς Πριάμῳ,
κόμισαί μ' ἐς Ἅιδαν.

στρ. γ

ΑΝΔΡΟΜΑΧΗ

595 οἵδε πόθοι μεγάλοι . . .

ΕΚΑΒΗ

σχέτλι' ⟨ὡς⟩ τάδε πάσχομεν ἄλγη.

ΑΝΔΡΟΜΑΧΗ

. . . οἰχομένας πόλεως . . .

ΕΚΑΒΗ

ἐπὶ δ' ἄλγεσιν ἄλγεα κεῖται.

ANDROMACHE

Come, my husband . . .

HECUBA

Do you call upon my son
in Hades? Poor man,
can you defend your wife?

ANDROMACHE

You, who once destroyed the Greeks . . .

HECUBA

Yes, eldest of my children
I bore to Priam,
bring me to Hades!

ANDROMACHE

Powerful are these longings . . .

HECUBA

And cruel are these pains we suffer!

ANDROMACHE

. . . for a city that has perished . . .

HECUBA

Woe lies on top of woe!

587–94 sic dispert. Willink: codices in stropha 587 et 590 Andromachae tribuunt, Hecubae cetera, tum antistropham totam Hecubae vel Andromachae   589 μέλεος Willink: μελέα C
  590 σὺ Kovacs: σᾶς C
  591 τοι Musgrave: τε ὦ C
  592 δή ποθ' Seidler: δέσποθ' C
  593 Πριάμῳ Musgrave: Πρίαμε C
  594 Ἄιδαν Kovacs: Ἄιδου C
  595 ⟨ὡς⟩ Kirchhoff

EURIPIDES

δυσφροσύναισι θεῶν, ὅτε σὸς γόνος ἔκφυγεν Ἅιδαν,
ὃς λεχέων στυγερῶν χάριν ὤλεσε πέργαμα Τροίας·
αἱματόεντα δὲ θεᾷ παρὰ Παλλάδι σώματα νεκρῶν
600 γυψὶ φέρειν τέταται, ζυγὰ δ' ἤνυσε δούλια Τροίᾳ.
ἀντ. γ

ΕΚΑΒΗ

ὦ πατρίς, ὦ μελέα . . .

ΑΝΔΡΟΜΑΧΗ

κατερειπομέναν σε δακρύω.

ΕΚΑΒΗ

. . . νῦν τέλος οἰκτρὸν ὁρᾷς.

ΑΝΔΡΟΜΑΧΗ

καὶ ἐμὸν δόμον ἔνθ' ἐλοχεύθην.

ΕΚΑΒΗ

ὦ τέκν', ἐρημόπολις μάτηρ ἀπολείπεται ὑμῶν.
οἷος ἰάλεμος <οἷος ὀδυρμός θ'> οἷά τε πένθη
605 δάκρυά τ' ἐκ δακρύων καταλείβεται <οἰκτρὰ κατ'
ὄσσων>
ἀμετέροισι δόμοις· ὁ θανὼν δ' ἐπιλάθεται ἀλγέων.

ΧΟΡΟΣ

ὡς ἡδὺ δάκρυα τοῖς κακῶς πεπραγόσιν
θρήνων τ' ὀδυρμοὶ μοῦσά θ' ἢ λύπας ἔχει.

601 κατερειπομέναν Jacobs: καταλειπ- C
604 lac. indic. et suppl. Hartung
605 lac. indic. Seidler, suppl. Heinsch

74

ANDROMACHE

. . . because of the malice the gods showed when your son
  escaped death,
a son who for the sake of a hateful marriage destroyed
  Troy's citadel.
Bloodied corpses of the slain are laid out next to the god-
  dess Pallas
for vultures to plunder, for it was she who brought the yoke
  of slavery upon Troy.

HECUBA

O unhappy fatherland . . .

ANDROMACHE

            I weep for you as you are being razed . . .

HECUBA

. . . now you behold the pitiable end.

ANDROMACHE

           . . . and weep for my home, where I gave birth.

HECUBA

My sons, your mother parts from you, a mother whose city
  is desolate!
What lamentation, ⟨what keening,⟩ what griefs,
what tears succeeding tears are shed ⟨from our eyes in
  pity⟩
over our house! But the dead forget their grief.

CHORUS LEADER

How sweet for those in misfortune are tears, the keening
of lamentations, and the song that has sorrow for its theme!

EURIPIDES

ΑΝΔΡΟΜΑΧΗ

610 ὦ μῆτερ ἀνδρὸς ὅς ποτ' Ἀργείων δορὶ
πλείστους διώλεσ' Ἕκτορος, τάδ' εἰσορᾷς;

ΕΚΑΒΗ

ὁρῶ τὰ τῶν θεῶν, ὡς τὰ μὲν πυργοῦσ' ἄνω
τὸ μηδὲν ὄντα, τὰ δὲ δοκοῦντ' ἀπώλεσαν.

ΑΝΔΡΟΜΑΧΗ

ἀγόμεθα λεία σὺν τέκνῳ· τὸ δ' εὐγενὲς
615 ἐς δοῦλον ἥκει, μεταβολὰς τοσάσδ' ἔχον.

ΕΚΑΒΗ

τὸ τῆς ἀνάγκης δεινόν· ἄρτι κἀπ' ἐμοῦ
βέβηκ' ἀποσπασθεῖσα Κασσάνδρα βίᾳ.

ΑΝΔΡΟΜΑΧΗ

φεῦ φεῦ·
ἄλλος τις Αἴας, ὡς ἔοικε, δεύτερος
παιδὸς πέφηνε σῆς. νοσεῖς δὲ χἄτερα.

ΕΚΑΒΗ

620 ὧν γ' οὔτε μέτρον οὔτ' ἀριθμός ἐστί μοι·
κακῷ κακὸν γὰρ εἰς ἅμιλλαν ἔρχεται.

ΑΝΔΡΟΜΑΧΗ

τέθνηκέ σοι παῖς πρὸς τάφῳ Πολυξένη
σφαγεῖσ' Ἀχιλλέως, δῶρον ἀψύχῳ νεκρῷ.

ΕΚΑΒΗ

οἲ 'γὼ τάλαινα. τοῦτ' ἐκεῖν' ὅ μοι πάλαι
625 Ταλθύβιος αἴνιγμ' οὐ σαφῶς εἶπεν σαφές.

76

ANDROMACHE

O mother of Hector, the man who once killed so many
Greeks with his spear, do you see this?

HECUBA

I see the work of the gods: they raise high what is nothing
and destroy what is esteemed.

ANDROMACHE

I am carried away as booty with my son: nobility has been
enslaved and has suffered so great a change!

HECUBA

Terrible is the force of necessity. Just now Cassandra has
gone away, torn from me by force.

ANDROMACHE

Ah me! It seems a second Ajax has appeared to take away
your daughter! But you have still other troubles.

HECUBA

Yes, I have troubles without measure or number! For one
disaster comes to compete with another.

ANDROMACHE

Your daughter Polyxena is dead, slain at the tomb of Achil-
les as a gift to a lifeless corpse.

HECUBA

O woe is me! This is the meaning of that riddle Talthybius
spoke so darkly and yet so truly!

ΑΝΔΡΟΜΑΧΗ

εἶδόν νιν αὐτή, κἀποβᾶσα τῶνδ᾽ ὄχων
ἔκρυψα πέπλοις κἀπεκοψάμην νεκρόν.

ΕΚΑΒΗ

αἰαῖ, τέκνον, σῶν ἀνοσίων προσφαγμάτων·
αἰαῖ μάλ᾽ αὖθις, ὡς κακῶς διόλλυσαι.

ΑΝΔΡΟΜΑΧΗ

630 ὄλωλεν ὡς ὄλωλεν· ἀλλ᾽ ὅμως ἐμοῦ
ζώσης γ᾽ ὄλωλεν εὐτυχεστέρῳ πότμῳ.

ΕΚΑΒΗ

οὐ ταὐτόν, ὦ παῖ, τῷ βλέπειν τὸ κατθανεῖν·
τὸ μὲν γὰρ οὐδέν, τῷ δ᾽ ἔνεισιν ἐλπίδες.

ΑΝΔΡΟΜΑΧΗ

[ὦ μῆτερ, ὦ τεκοῦσα, κάλλιστον λόγον
635 ἄκουσον, ὥς σοι τέρψιν ἐμβάλω φρενί.]
τὸ μὴ γενέσθαι τῷ θανεῖν ἴσον λέγω,
τοῦ ζῆν δὲ λυπρῶς κρεῖσσόν ἐστι κατθανεῖν.
ἀλγεῖ γὰρ οὐδὲν ⟨τῶν ἀγεννήτων πλέον
τεθνεώς τις, οὐδὲν⟩ τῶν κακῶν ᾐσθημένος·
ὁ δ᾽ εὐτυχήσας ἐς τὸ δυστυχὲς πεσὼν
640 ψυχὴν ἀλᾶται τῆς πάροιθ᾽ εὐπραξίας.
    κείνη δ᾽, ὁμοίως ὥσπερ οὐκ ἰδοῦσα φῶς,
τέθνηκε κοὐδὲν οἶδε τῶν αὑτῆς κακῶν.
ἐγὼ δὲ τοξεύσασα τῆς εὐδοξίας
λαχοῦσα πλεῖστον τῆς τύχης ἡμάρτανον.
645 ἃ γὰρ γυναιξὶ σῶφρον᾽ ἔσθ᾽ ηὑρημένα,
ταῦτ᾽ ἐξεμόχθουν Ἕκτορος κατὰ στέγας.

78

ANDROMACHE

I saw her myself and getting down from this wagon I covered her corpse with a garment and mourned for her.

HECUBA

Alas, my child, for your unhallowed slaughter! Alas, once more! How painful was your death!

ANDROMACHE

She died as she died. But her death is a happier lot than mine, who am alive.

HECUBA

My child, to die is not the same as to be alive. The one is nothing, but in the other there are hopes.

ANDROMACHE

[O mother, you who bore me, listen to a noble speech so that I may gladden your heart.] Not to be born is the same, I say, as to die, and to die is better than to live in pain. For ⟨one who is dead⟩ feels no ⟨more⟩ pain ⟨than those who have never been born⟩ since he has ⟨no⟩ sense of his troubles. But the man who enjoys good fortune and then falls into misery is distraught in mind because of his previous prosperity.

Polyxena, just as if she had never seen the light of day, has perished and knows nothing of her own misfortune. But I, though I aimed at a good name and hit that mark well, failed to hit good fortune. Everything that women have discovered of modest behavior I practiced diligently in the house of Hector. First, whether or not there is any-

---

634–5 del. Dindorf   638 lac. indic. Seidler
644 πλεῖστον Hartung ex Σ: πλεῖον C

πρῶτον μέν, ἔνθα (κἂν προσῇ κἂν μὴ προσῇ
ψόγος γυναιξίν) αὐτὸ τοῦτ᾽ ἐφέλκεται
κακῶς ἀκούειν, ἥτις οὐκ ἔνδον μένει,
650 τούτου παρεῖσα πόθον ἔμιμνον ἐν δόμοις·
ἔσω τε μελάθρων κομψὰ θηλειῶν ἔπη
οὐκ εἰσεφρούμην, τὸν δὲ νοῦν διδάσκαλον
οἴκοθεν ἔχουσα χρηστὸν ἐξήρκουν ἐμοί.
γλώσσης τε σιγὴν ὄμμα θ᾽ ἥσυχον πόσει
655 παρεῖχον· ἤδη δ᾽ ἅμ᾽ ἐχρῆν νικᾶν πόσιν,
κείνῳ τε νίκην ὧν ἐχρῆν παριέναι.
    καὶ τῶνδε κληδὼν ἐς στράτευμ᾽ Ἀχαϊκὸν
ἐλθοῦσ᾽ ἀπώλεσέν μ᾽· ἐπεὶ γὰρ ᾑρέθην,
Ἀχιλλέως με παῖς ἐβουλήθη λαβεῖν
660 δάμαρτα· δουλεύσω δ᾽ ἐν αὐθεντῶν δόμοις.
κεἰ μὲν παρώσασ᾽ Ἕκτορος φίλον κάρα
πρὸς τὸν παρόντα πόσιν ἀναπτύξω φρένα,
κακὴ φανοῦμαι τῷ θανόντι· τόνδε δ᾽ αὖ
στυγοῦσ᾽ ἐμαυτῆς δεσπόταις μισήσομαι.
665 καίτοι λέγουσιν ὡς μί᾽ εὐφρόνη χαλᾷ
τὸ δυσμενὲς γυναικὸς εἰς ἀνδρὸς λέχος·
ἀπέπτυσ᾽ αὐτὴν ἥτις ἄνδρα τὸν πάρος
καινοῖσι λέκτροις ἀποβαλοῦσ᾽ ἄλλον φιλεῖ.
ἀλλ᾽ οὐδὲ πῶλος ἥτις ἂν διαζυγῇ
670 τῆς συντραφείσης ῥᾳδίως ἕλκει ζυγόν.
καίτοι τὸ θηριῶδες ἄφθογγόν τ᾽ ἔφυ
ξυνέσει τ᾽ ἄχρηστον τῇ φύσει τε λείπεται.
    σὲ δ᾽, ὦ φίλ᾽ Ἕκτορ, εἶχον ἄνδρ᾽ ἀρκοῦντά μοι,
ξυνέσει γένει πλούτῳ τε κἀνδρείᾳ μέγαν,

thing blameworthy in a woman's conduct, the very fact that she goes out of the house draws criticism. I let go all longing for this and stayed in the house. I did not admit within my walls women with their clever talk but was content to have within myself a good teacher, my own mind. I kept my tongue quiet and my gaze tranquil before my husband. I knew where I ought to be the winner over my husband and where I should yield the victory to him.

When the report of this reached the Greek army, it was my undoing. For when I was taken captive, the son of Achilles wished to make me his wife: I shall be a slave in the house of people who have killed my own kin. If I put my love for Hector out of my mind and open my heart to my present husband, I shall appear disloyal to him who has died. But if I loathe my present husband, I shall incur the hatred of my own master. Yet they say that a single night dispels the hatred a woman feels for her bedmate. I reject with contempt a woman who casts her former husband aside because of a new connection and loves another. Why, not even a mare that has been separated from its companion bears the yoke easily. Yet a brute beast lacks speech and reason and is inferior to us in nature.

In you, beloved Hector, I possessed a husband that sufficed me, great in intelligence, in birth, in wealth, and

---

647 ἔνθα] ἔνδον Fecht
674 del. Paley

675 ἀκήρατον δέ μ᾽ ἐκ πατρὸς λαβὼν δόμων
πρῶτος τὸ παρθένειον ἐζεύξω λέχος.
καὶ νῦν ὄλωλας μὲν σύ, ναυσθλοῦμαι δ᾽ ἐγὼ
πρὸς Ἑλλάδ᾽ αἰχμάλωτος ἐς δοῦλον ζυγόν.
ἆρ᾽ οὐκ ἐλάσσω τῶν ἐμῶν ἔχει κακῶν
680 Πολυξένης ὄλεθρος, ἣν καταστένεις;
ἐμοὶ γὰρ οὐδ᾽ ὃ πᾶσι λείπεται βροτοῖς
ξύνεστιν ἐλπίς, οὐδὲ κλέπτομαι φρένας
πράξειν τι κεδνόν· ἡδὺ δ᾽ ἐστὶ καὶ δοκεῖν.

ΧΟΡΟΣ
ἐς ταὐτὸν ἥκεις συμφορᾶς· θρηνοῦσα δὲ
685 τὸ σὸν διδάσκεις μ᾽ ἔνθα πημάτων κυρῶ.

ΕΚΑΒΗ
αὐτὴ μὲν οὔπω ναὸς εἰσέβην σκάφος,
γραφῇ δ᾽ ἰδοῦσα καὶ κλυοῦσ᾽ ἐπίσταμαι.
ναῦται γάρ, ἢν μὲν μέτριος ᾖ χειμὼν φέρειν,
προθυμίαν ἔχουσι σωθῆναι πόνων,
690 ὁ μὲν παρ᾽ οἴαχ᾽, ὁ δ᾽ ἐπὶ λαίφεσιν βεβώς,
ὁ δ᾽ ἄντλον εἴργων ναός· ἢν δ᾽ ὑπερβάλῃ
πολὺς ταραχθεὶς πόντος, ἐνδόντες τύχῃ
παρεῖσαν αὑτοὺς κυμάτων δραμήμασιν.
οὕτω δὲ κἀγὼ πόλλ᾽ ἔχουσα πήματα
695 ἄφθογγός εἰμι καὶ παρεῖσ᾽ ἔχω στόμα·
νικᾷ γὰρ οὐκ θεῶν με δύστηνος κλύδων.
ἀλλ᾽, ὦ φίλη παῖ, τὰς μὲν Ἕκτορος τύχας
ἔασον· οὐ μὴ δάκρυά νιν σώσῃ τὰ σά.
τίμα δὲ τὸν παρόντα δεσπότην σέθεν,

in courage. You received me as a virgin from my father's house and were the first to yoke my maidenhood in love. And now you are dead, while I am going by ship to Greece as a captive to bear the yoke of slavery. Does not Polyxena's death, which you weep for, involve less misery than mine? I do not have hope as my companion, the thing that is left behind for all mortals, and I do not delude myself that I shall fare well, though even delusions are pleasant.

CHORUS

You have come into as much misfortune as I have. But as you lament your circumstances, you teach me where I stand in misery.

HECUBA

I myself have never gone on board a ship, but from seeing them in pictures and hearing reports of them I know about them. When sailors encounter a storm that is not too violent to bear, they show an eagerness to win their way out of their troubles to safety, one man standing by the steering oar, another by the sails, while a third keeps the bilge out of the ship. But if a heavy and agitated sea overwhelms them, they surrender to luck and yield themselves to the running of the waves. So too I, suffering so many misfortunes, am mute, letting my troubles go and holding my tongue. For the wave of misery sent by the gods overwhelms me.

But, dear daughter, think no longer of Hector's fate. Your tears cannot bring him back safe. Honor instead your present master, giving your husband the enticements of

---

688 ναῦται Diggle: ναύταις C   695 ἔχω Bothe: ἐῶ C

EURIPIDES

700 φίλον διδοῦσα δέλεαρ ἀνδρὶ σῶν τρόπων.
κἂν δρᾷς τάδ', ἐς τὸ κοινὸν εὐφρανεῖς φίλους
καὶ παῖδα τόνδε παιδὸς ἐκθρέψειας ἂν
Τροίᾳ μέγιστον ὠφέλημ', ἵν' οἵ ποτε
ἐκ σοῦ γενόμενοι παῖδες Ἴλιον πάλιν
705 κατοικίσειαν καὶ πόλις γένοιτ' ἔτι.
   ἀλλ' ἐκ λόγου γὰρ ἄλλος ἐκβαίνει λόγος,
τίν' αὖ δέδορκα τόνδ' Ἀχαικὸν λάτριν
στείχοντα καινῶν ἄγγελον βουλευμάτων;

ΤΑΛΘΥΒΙΟΣ
Φρυγῶν ἀρίστου πρίν ποθ' Ἕκτορος δάμαρ,
710 μή με στυγήσῃς· οὐχ ἑκὼν γὰρ ἀγγελῶ
Δαναῶν τε κοινὰ Πελοπιδῶν τ' ἀγγέλματα.

ΑΝΔΡΟΜΑΧΗ
τί δ' ἔστιν; ὥς μοι φροιμίων ἄρχῃ κακῶν.

ΤΑΛΘΥΒΙΟΣ
ἔδοξε τόνδε παῖδα . . . πῶς εἴπω λόγον;

ΑΝΔΡΟΜΑΧΗ
μῶν οὐ τὸν αὐτὸν δεσπότην ἡμῖν ἔχειν;

ΤΑΛΘΥΒΙΟΣ
715 οὐδεὶς Ἀχαιῶν τοῦδε δεσπόσει ποτέ.

ΑΝΔΡΟΜΑΧΗ
ἀλλ' ἐνθάδ' αὐτοῦ λείψανον Φρυγῶν λιπεῖν;

706 ἐκβάλλει Kovacs

84

your winning ways. If you do this, you will bring joy to all your friends in common and may raise to manhood my grandson here as Troy's greatest helper, so that sons one day born of your lineage may refound Ilium and it may become a city once again.

Enter TALTHYBIUS *with retinue by Eisodos A.*

But now a new subject arises after the old: what servant of the Achaeans is this I see coming to announce new edicts?

TALTHYBIUS

Wife of Hector, once the bravest of the Phrygians, do not hate me! It is against my will that I shall make my announcement from both the Greeks and the sons of Pelops in common!

ANDROMACHE

What is it? How ominous is the beginning of your speech!

TALTHYBIUS

It has been decreed that this child . . . how can I say it?

ANDROMACHE

. . . will not have the same master as we?

TALTHYBIUS

None of the Greeks shall ever be his master.

ANDROMACHE

Have you decided to leave him here as a sorry remnant of Troy?

ΤΑΛΘΥΒΙΟΣ

οὐκ οἶδ᾽ ὅπως σοι ῥᾳδίως εἴπω τάδε.

ΑΝΔΡΟΜΑΧΗ

ἐπήνεσ᾽ αἰδῶ, πλὴν ἐὰν λέγῃς καλά.

ΤΑΛΘΥΒΙΟΣ

κτενοῦσι σὸν παῖδ᾽, ὡς πύθῃ κακὸν μέγα.

ΑΝΔΡΟΜΑΧΗ

720   οἴμοι, γάμων τόδ᾽ ὡς κλύω μεῖζον κακόν.

ΤΑΛΘΥΒΙΟΣ

νικᾷ δ᾽ Ὀδυσσεὺς ἐν Πανέλλησιν λόγῳ . . .

ΑΝΔΡΟΜΑΧΗ

αἰαῖ μάλ᾽· οὐ γὰρ μέτρια πάσχομεν κακά.

ΤΑΛΘΥΒΙΟΣ

. . . λέξας ἀρίστου παῖδα μὴ τρέφειν πατρὸς . . .

ΑΝΔΡΟΜΑΧΗ

τοιαῦτα νικήσειε τῶν αὑτοῦ πέρι.

ΤΑΛΘΥΒΙΟΣ

725   ῥῖψαι δὲ πύργων δεῖν σφε Τρωικῶν ἄπο.
    ἀλλ᾽ ὡς γενέσθω, καὶ σοφωτέρα φανῇ·
    μήτ᾽ ἀντέχου τοῦδ᾽, εὐγενῶς δ᾽ ἄλγει κακοῖς,
    μήτε σθένουσα μηδὲν ἰσχύειν δόκει.

717 τάδε Wecklein: κακά C   718 καλά p: κακά L
725 δεῖν Jacobs: δεῖ C

TALTHYBIUS

I do not know how I am to tell you this easily.

ANDROMACHE

I approve of such hesitation unless you are telling good news.[24]

TALTHYBIUS

To tell you the terrible truth, they are going to kill your son.

ANDROMACHE

Ah, ah! This is worse news than even my marriage!

TALTHYBIUS

Odysseus won the day, speaking in the assembly of the Greeks . . .

ANDROMACHE

Ah, ah once more! The misfortunes I suffer are beyond all measure!

TALTHYBIUS

. . . telling them that they should not raise to manhood the son of a noble father . . .

ANDROMACHE

May some one be similarly persuasive concerning *his* sons!

TALTHYBIUS

. . . but should hurl him from the Trojan battlements.

But this is the way it must be if you are to show yourself wiser: do not hold on to him but nobly bear the pain of your misfortune. Since you are weak, do not suppose that

---

[24] If the reading adopted here is correct, Andromache echoes Theseus' sentiments at *Suppliant Women* 296. But the text is doubtful.

ἔχεις γὰρ ἀλκὴν οὐδαμῇ. σκοπεῖν δὲ χρή·
730 πόλις τ᾽ ὄλωλε καὶ πόσις, κρατῇ δὲ σύ,
ἡμεῖς δὲ πρὸς γυναῖκα μάρνασθαι μίαν
οἷοί τε. τούτων οὕνεκ᾽ οὐ μάχης ἐρᾶν
οὐδ᾽ αἰσχρὸν οὐδὲν οὐδ᾽ ἐπίφθονόν σε δρᾶν
οὐδ᾽ αὖ σ᾽ Ἀχαιοῖς βούλομαι ῥίπτειν ἀράς.
735 εἰ γάρ τι λέξεις ὧν χολώσεται στρατός,
οὔτ᾽ ἂν ταφείη παῖς ὅδ᾽ οὔτ᾽ οἴκτου τύχοι.
σιγῶσα δ᾽ εὖ τε τὰς τύχας κεκτημένη
τὸν τοῦδε νεκρὸν οὐκ ἄθαπτον ἂν λίποις
αὐτή τ᾽ Ἀχαιῶν πρευμενεστέρων τύχοις.

ΑΝΔΡΟΜΑΧΗ

740 ὦ φίλτατ᾽, ὦ περισσὰ τιμηθεὶς τέκνον,
θανῇ πρὸς ἐχθρῶν μητέρ᾽ ἀθλίαν λιπών.
ἡ τοῦ πατρὸς δέ σ᾽ εὐγένει᾽ ἀποκτενεῖ,
ἡ τοῖσιν ἄλλοις γίγνεται σωτηρία,
τὸ δ᾽ ἐσθλὸν οὐκ ἐς καιρὸν ἦλθέ σοι πατρός.
745 ὦ λέκτρα τἀμὰ δυστυχῆ τε καὶ γάμοι,
οἷς ἦλθον ἐς μέλαθρον Ἕκτορός ποτε,
οὐ σφάγιον ⟨υἱὸν⟩ Δαναΐδαις τέξουσ᾽ ἐμόν,
ἀλλ᾽ ὡς τύραννον Ἀσιάδος πολυσπόρου.
    ὦ παῖ, δακρύεις· αἰσθάνῃ κακῶν σέθεν;
750 τί μου δέδραξαι χερσὶ κἀντέχῃ πέπλων,
νεοσσὸς ὡσεὶ πτέρυγας ἐσπίτνων ἐμάς;
οὐκ εἶσιν Ἕκτωρ κλεινὸν ἁρπάσας δόρυ
γῆς ἐξανελθὼν σοὶ φέρων σωτηρίαν,
οὐ συγγένεια πατρός, οὐκ ἰσχὺς Φρυγῶν·

you have power. You have no one anywhere to defend you. Consider: your city and your husband are gone, and you are in the power of others, and we are strong enough to fight against a single woman. For these reasons I want you not to be enamored of a fight or to do anything either undignified or hateful or yet to hurl curses at the Greeks. If you say anything to anger the army, this boy might not receive the mercy of a burial. But if you keep still and bear your misfortunes well, you will not leave this boy's corpse behind unburied, and you yourself will win the favor of the Achaeans.

ANDROMACHE

O best beloved, O child most highly honored, you will be killed by our enemies and leave your poor mother behind! It is the nobility of your father that will be your undoing, a nobility which has been the salvation of others, and your father's bravery has turned out to be no benefit to you! O unhappy marriage bed and marriage of mine, by which I once came into the house of Hector, in order to give birth not to a sacrificial victim for the Greeks but rather a ruler over all of fertile Asia!

My child, you are weeping. Do you realize your misfortune? Why do you grasp me in your arms and hold fast to my clothing, falling like some young bird into the embrace of my wings? Hector will not come, glorious spear in hand, from the depths of earth to bring you rescue, nor will your father's kinsmen or the armed might of Troy. You will fall

---

737 ταῖς τύχαις κεχρημένη Hartung
742–3 del. Nauck   745–8 del. West
747 οὐ σφάγιον ⟨υἱὸν⟩ Nauck: οὐχ ὡς σφάγιον C

EURIPIDES

755 λυγρὸν δὲ πήδημ᾽ ἐς τράχηλον ὑψόθεν
πεσὼν ἀνοίκτως πνεῦμ᾽ ἀπορρήξεις σέθεν.
ὦ νέον ὑπαγκάλισμα μητρὶ φίλτατον,
ὦ χρωτὸς ἡδὺ πνεῦμα· διὰ κενῆς ἄρα
ἐν σπαργάνοις σε μαστὸς ἐξέθρεψ᾽ ὅδε,
760 μάτην δ᾽ ἐμόχθουν καὶ κατεξάνθην πόνοις.
νῦν, οὔποτ᾽ αὖθις, μητέρ᾽ ἀσπάζου σέθεν,
πρόσπιτνε τὴν τεκοῦσαν, ἀμφὶ δ᾽ ὠλένας
ἕλισσ᾽ ἐμοῖς νώτοισι καὶ στόμ᾽ ἅρμοσον.
ὦ βάρβαρ᾽ ἐξευρόντες Ἕλληνες κακά,
765 τί τόνδε παῖδα κτείνετ᾽ οὐδὲν αἴτιον;
ὦ Τυνδάρειον ἔρνος, οὔποτ᾽ εἶ Διός,
πολλῶν δὲ πατέρων φημί σ᾽ ἐκπεφυκέναι,
Ἀλάστορος μὲν πρῶτον, εἶτα δὲ Φθόνου,
Φόνου τε Θανάτου θ᾽ ὅσα τε γῆ τρέφει κακά,
770 οὐ γάρ ποτ᾽ αὐχῶ Ζηνὸς ἐκφῦναί σ᾽ ἐγώ,
πολλοῖσι κῆρα βαρβάροις Ἕλλησί τε.
ὄλοιο· καλλίστων γὰρ ὀμμάτων ἄπο
αἰσχρῶς τὰ κλεινὰ πεδί᾽ ἀπώλεσας Φρυγῶν.
⟨ἀλλ᾽⟩ ἄγετε φέρετε ῥίπτετ᾽, εἰ ῥίπτειν δοκεῖ·
775 δαίνυσθε τοῦδε σάρκας. ἔκ τε γὰρ θεῶν
διολλύμεσθα παιδί τ᾽ οὐ δυναίμεθ᾽ ἂν
θάνατον ἀρῆξαι. κρύπτετ᾽ ἄθλιον δέμας
καὶ ῥίπτετ᾽ ἐς ναῦς· ἐπὶ καλὸν γὰρ ἔρχομαι
ὑμέναιον, ἀπολέσασα τοὐμαυτῆς τέκνον.

ΧΟΡΟΣ
780 τάλαινα Τροία, μυρίους ἀπώλεσας

90

from on high, a baleful leap, and break your neck, pitiably cutting short your life's breath. O child that my arms have held when young, so dear to your mother, O sweet fragrance of your flesh! It was for nothing, it seems, that this breast of mine suckled you when you were in swaddling clothes, and all in vain was my labor and the pain of my toil! Now, and never again, kiss your mother, fall into my embrace, put your arms around me and press your lips against mine!

Greeks, devisers of barbaric cruelty, why do you kill this innocent boy? O offshoot of Tyndareus, never were you born from Zeus! I say it was many fathers who begot you, first the Avenging Spirit, then Envy, then Slaughter and Death and all the miseries the earth breeds! Never, I am certain, was Zeus your father, you who were death to so many barbarians and Greeks. A curse on you! From your fair eyes you brought foul ruin on the glorious plains of the Phrygians.

⟨So,⟩ come, Greeks, take and hurl him, if to hurl him is your will: feast on his flesh! For we are being destroyed by the gods, and we cannot ward off death from this child. Cover my wretched body and sling me into the ship! It is to a splendid marriage that I go, having lost my own child!

CHORUS

Poor Troy, countless are the folk you have lost because of

---

760 del. Valckenaer cl. *Med.* 1030
770 Ζηνὸς ἐκφῦναί Reiske: Ζῆνά γ᾽ ἐκφῦσαί C
774 ⟨ἀλλ᾽⟩ Hermann

μιᾶς γυναικὸς καὶ λέχους στυγνοῦ χάριν.

ΤΑΛΘΥΒΙΟΣ

ἄγε παῖ, φίλιον πρόσπτυγμα μεθεὶς
μητρὸς μογερᾶς, βαῖνε πατρῴων
πύργων ἐπ᾽ ἄκρας στεφάνας, ὅθι σοι
785 πνεῦμα μεθεῖναι ψῆφος ἐκράνθη.
λαμβάνετ᾽ αὐτόν. τὰ δὲ τοιάδε χρὴ
κηρυκεύειν ὅστις ἄνοικτος
καὶ ἀναιδείᾳ τῆς ἡμετέρας
γνώμης μᾶλλον φίλος ἐστίν.

ΕΚΑΒΗ

790 ὦ τέκνον, ὦ παῖ παιδὸς μογεροῦ,
συλώμεθα σὴν ψυχὴν ἀδίκως
μήτηρ κἀγώ. τί πάθω; τί σ᾽ ἐγώ,
δύσμορε, δράσω; τάδε σοι δίδομεν
πλήγματα κρατὸς στέρνων τε κόπους·
795 τῶνδε γὰρ ἄρχομεν. οἲ ᾽γὼ πόλεως,
οἴμοι δὲ σέθεν· τί γὰρ οὐκ ἔχομεν,
τίνος ἐνδέομεν μὴ οὐ πανσυδίᾳ
χωρεῖν ὀλέθρου διὰ παντός;

ΧΟΡΟΣ

στρ. α

μελισσοτρόφου Σαλαμῖνος ὦ βασιλεῦ Τελαμών,
800 νάσου περικύμονος οἰκήσας ἕδραν
τᾶς ἐπικεκλιμένας ὄχθοις ἱεροῖς, ἵν᾽ ἐλαίας
πρῶτον ἔδειξε κλάδον γλαυκᾶς Ἀθάνα,

one woman and one marriage bed!

TALTHYBIUS

Come, child, leave the loving embrace of your dear
mother, come to the high coronal of your father's towers
where it is decreed you must breathe your last. Take him!
(*Attendants take Astyanax from Andromache.*) Such her-
ald's errands had best be done by someone who is without
pity and is more inclined than I am to heartlessness.

*Exit TALTHYBIUS and retinue by Eisodos B, leading Asty-
anax, ANDROMACHE under guard by Eisodos A.*

HECUBA

My child, son of my luckless son, we are robbed of your life
unjustly, your mother and I. What am I to do? What can I
do for you, ill-starred one? Our gifts to you are these, to
strike our breasts and head: that much lies in our power!
Alas for my city, alas for you! What do we not have, what
more is needed for our utter and immediate destruction?

CHORUS

O Telamon, king of bee-nurturing Salamis,
who dwell in a wave-washed isle
that lies opposite the holy hill[25] where the shoot
of the gray-green olive was first revealed by Athena,

25 Athens.

---

788 ἡμετέρας Tyrwhitt: ὑμ- C

οὐράνιον στέφανον λιπαραῖσί ⟨τε⟩ κόσμον
  Ἀθάναις,
ἔβας ἔβας τῷ τοξοφόρῳ συναρι-
805 στεύων ἅμ' Ἀλκμήνας γόνῳ
Ἴλιον Ἴλιον ἐκπέρσων πόλιν ἁμετέραν
τὸ πάροιθεν ἀφ' Ἑλλάδος ⟨γᾶς⟩·

ἀντ. α

ὅθ' Ἑλλάδος ἄγαγε πρῶτον ἄνθος ἀτιζόμενος
810 πώλων, Σιμόεντι δ' ἐπ' εὐρείᾳ πλάταν
ἔσχασε ποντοπόρον καὶ ναύδετ' ἀνήψατο πρυμνῶν
καὶ χερὸς εὐστοχίαν ἐξεῖλε ναῶν,
Λαομέδοντι φόνον· κανόνων δὲ τυκίσματα Φοίβου
815 πυρὸς ⟨πυρὸς⟩ φοίνικι πνοᾷ καθελὼν
Τροίας ἐπόρθησε χθόνα.
δὶς δὲ δυοῖν πιτύλοιν τείχη πυρὶ Δαρδανίας
φονία κατέλυσεν αἰχμά.

στρ. β

820 μάταν ἄρ', ὦ χρυσέαις ἐν οἰνοχόαις ἁβρὰ βαίνων,
Λαομεδόντιε παῖ,
Ζηνὸς ἔχεις κυλίκων πλήρωμα, καλλίσταν λατρείαν.
825 ἁ δέ σε γειναμένα πυρὶ δαίεται·

---

803 ⟨τε⟩ Seidler
808 ἀφ' Ἑλλάδος ⟨γᾶς⟩ Hermann: ὅτ' ἔβας ἀφ' Ἑλλάδος C
809 ἀτιζόμενος Jackson: ἀτυζ- C   815 ⟨πυρὸς⟩ Meineke
817 πυρὶ Seidler: περὶ vel παρὰ C

---

26 Laomedon promised Heracles some horses given him by
Zeus if he would rescue his daughter Hesione, who was threat-

a heavenly garland and a glory for gleaming Athens,
you came, you came, sharing the great exploit,
with the bow-wielding son of Alcmene
to sack Ilium, Ilium, our city,
came long ago from Hellas.

Of Hellas he brought the finest flower, he who was cheated
of the promised horses, and at the Simois with its fair
    streams
he let go of his seagoing oars and tied cables to the sterns
and disembarked from his ships the skillful bowcraft
to bring death to Laomedon.[26] The stone work made to
    Phoebus' carpenter's rule
he destroyed with the ruddy blast of fire, ⟨fire,⟩
and ravaged the land of Troy.
Twice, in two attacks, the murderous spear has brought
    down
the walls of Dardania by fire.

It is for nought, son of Laomedon,[27]
you that go with delicate step amid the ewers of gold,
that you have the office of filling Zeus's cups, service most
    noble.
The land that gave you birth is burnt with fire,

ened by a sea monster sent by Poseidon. (Poseidon in his turn had
been cheated by Laomedon of his reward for building the walls of
Troy.) After Heracles rescued Hesione, Laomedon refused to
give him the horses. Although the Chorus evoke the sadness of
this earlier attack, it shows Troy's guilty past and helps to explain
her present fall. See Burnett 1977.
[27] Ganymede, abducted by Zeus to be the gods' cupbearer.

ἠιόνες δ' ἅλιαι
ἀχοῦσιν οἰωνὸς οἷ-
830 ον τέκνων ὕπερ βοᾷ,
ᾇ μὲν εὐνάς, ᾇ δὲ παῖδας,
ᾇ δὲ ματέρας γεραιάς.
τὰ δὲ σὰ δροσόεντα λουτρὰ
γυμνασίων τε δρόμοι
835 βεβᾶσι, σὺ δὲ πρόσωπα νεα-
ρὰ χάρισι παρὰ Διὸς θρόνοις
καλλιγάλανα τρέφεις· Πριάμοιο δὲ γαῖαν
Ἑλλὰς ὤλεσ' αἰχμά.

ἀντ. β

840 Ἔρως Ἔρως, ὃς τὰ Δαρδάνεια μέλαθρά ποτ' ἦλθες
οὐρανίδαισι μέλων,
ὡς τότε μὲν μεγάλως Τροίαν ἐπύργωσας, θεοῖσι
845 κῆδος ἀναψάμενος. τὸ μὲν οὖν Διὸς
οὐκέτ' ὄνειδος ἐρῶ·
τὸ τᾶς δὲ λευκοπτέρου
φίλιον Ἀμέρας βροτοῖς
850 φέγγος ὀλοὸν εἶδε γαίας,
εἶδε Περγάμων ὄλεθρον,
τεκνοποιὸν ἔχουσα τᾶσδε
γᾶς πόσιν ἐν θαλάμοις,
855 ὃν ἀστέρων τέθριππος ἔλα-
βε χρύσεος ὄχος ἀναρπάσας,

829 ἀχοῦσιν Fecht: ἴακχον vel ἴσχον C   829–30 οἰωνὸς
οἷον Hermann: οἶον οἰ- C   831 εὐνάς Seidler: εὐνάτορας C

while the sea beaches
utter such groan
as a bird makes for her young,
here for wives, here for children,
here for aged mothers.
The watering places where you bathed
and the race courses where you ran
are gone, while by the throne of Zeus
you keep that face, young in its charms,
in its beautiful serenity, though Priam's land
has been destroyed by the Greek spear.

Eros, Eros, who once visited the halls of Dardanus[28]
being much in the minds of the gods,
how greatly did you exalt Troy on that day, making
a marriage tie for her with the gods! It is no longer
Zeus that I reproach.
The light of Dawn, dear to mortals,[29]
Dawn the white-winged,
looked with baleful gleam upon the land's,
upon Pergamum's, destruction
though she had a husband from this land
in her bedchamber to sire her children.
A star chariot all golden
took him and snatched him up,

---

28 Son of Zeus and early king of Troy.
29 Eos, goddess of the dawn, fell in love with Tithonus, a son
of Laomedon, and took him up to heaven to be her husband.

849 φίλιον Ἀμέρας Murray: Ἀμέρας φίλιον fere C
850 γαίας Bothe et fort. Σ: γαῖαν C

ἐλπίδα γᾷ πατρίᾳ μεγάλαν· τὰ θεῶν δὲ
φίλτρα φροῦδα Τροίᾳ.

ΜΕΝΕΛΑΟΣ

860 ὦ καλλιφεγγὲς ἡλίου σέλας τόδε,
ἐν ᾧ δάμαρτα τὴν ἐμὴν χειρώσομαι
Ἑλένην· ὁ γὰρ δὴ πολλὰ μοχθήσας ἐγὼ
Μενέλαος ⟨αἰχμῇ καὶ κατασκήψας πόλιν
νῦν Ἑλλάδ'⟩ εἰμι καὶ στράτευμ' Ἀχαικόν.
ἦλθον δὲ Τροίαν οὐχ ὅσον δοκοῦσί με
865 γυναικὸς οὕνεκ', ἀλλ' ἐπ' ἄνδρ' ὃς ἐξ ἐμῶν
δόμων δάμαρτα ξεναπάτης ἐλήσατο.
κεῖνος μὲν οὖν δέδωκε σὺν θεοῖς δίκην
αὐτός τε καὶ γῆ δορὶ πεσοῦσ' Ἑλληνικῷ.
ἥκω δὲ τὴν Λάκαιναν (οὐ γὰρ ἡδέως
870 ὄνομα δάμαρτος ἥ ποτ' ἦν ἐμὴ λέγω)
ἄξων· δόμοις γὰρ τοῖσδ' ἐν αἰχμαλωτικοῖς
κατηρίθμηται Τρῳάδων ἄλλων μέτα.
οἵπερ γὰρ αὐτὴν ἐξεμόχθησαν δορὶ
κτανεῖν ἐμοί νιν ἔδοσαν, εἴτε μὴ κτανὼν
875 θέλοιμ' ἄγεσθαι πάλιν ἐς Ἀργείαν χθόνα.
ἐμοὶ δ' ἔδοξε τὸν μὲν ἐν Τροίᾳ μόρον
Ἑλένης ἐᾶσαι, ναυπόρῳ δ' ἄγειν πλάτῃ
Ἑλληνίδ' ἐς γῆν κᾆτ' ἐκεῖ δοῦναι κτανεῖν,
ποινὰς ὅσων τεθνᾶσ' ἐν Ἰλίῳ φίλοι.
880 ἀλλ' εἶα χωρεῖτ' ἐς δόμους, ὀπάονες,
κομίζετ' αὐτὴν τῆς μιαιφονωτάτης
κόμης ἐπισπάσαντες· οὔριοι δ' ὅταν

planting great hopes in his homeland. But the gods' love for Troy is fled and gone.

Enter MENELAUS with retinue by Eisodos A.

MENELAUS

O glorious light of day, this day in which I shall lay hands on my wife Helen: for I, Menelaus who endured so many toils ‹in war and overthrew the city of Troy, am now› going ‹to Greece,› and the Greek army with me! I have come to Troy not so much as men suppose for the sake of my wife as to find the man who cheated his host and took her as plunder from my house. Now he has paid the penalty—the gods be praised—himself and his land, which has fallen by the Greek spear. I have come to take the Spartan woman away (for I take no pleasure in speaking the name of the wife who was once mine). She is in this tent reserved for captives, numbered with the other women of Troy. Those who worked so hard with the spear to win her have given her to me to kill or, if I wish, to take her back alive to the land of Argos. I have decided not to kill Helen in Troy but to take her back by seagoing oar to Greece and then put her to death there as satisfaction for all those whose loved ones have been killed in Troy.

So come now, attendants, go into the tent, bring her out, dragging her by her murderous hair! When the wind

---

863 lac. post Μενέλαος indic. et suppl. West
879 ὅσοις Canter
881 τὴν μιαιφονωτάτην Paley

πνοαὶ μόλωσι, πέμψομέν νιν Ἑλλάδα.

ΕΚΑΒΗ

ὦ γῆς ὄχημα κἀπὶ γῆς ἔχων ἕδραν,
885 ὅστις ποτ' εἶ σύ, δυστόπαστος εἰδέναι,
Ζεύς, εἴτ' ἀνάγκη φύσεος εἴτε νοῦς βροτῶν,
προσηυξάμην σε· πάντα γὰρ δι' ἀψόφου
βαίνων κελεύθου κατὰ δίκην τὰ θνήτ' ἄγεις.

ΜΕΝΕΛΑΟΣ

τί δ' ἔστιν; εὐχὰς ὡς ἐκαίνισας θεῶν.

ΕΚΑΒΗ

890 αἰνῶ σε, Μενέλα', εἰ κτενεῖς δάμαρτα σήν.
ὁρᾶν δὲ τήνδε φεῦγε, μή σ' ἕλῃ πόθῳ.
αἱρεῖ γὰρ ἀνδρῶν ὄμματ', ἐξαιρεῖ πόλεις,
πίμπρησιν οἴκους· ὧδ' ἔχει κηλήματα.
ἐγώ νιν οἶδα καὶ σὺ χοἰ πεπονθότες.

ΕΛΕΝΗ

895 Μενέλαε, φροίμιον μὲν ἄξιον φόβου
τόδ' ἐστίν· ἐν γὰρ χερσὶ προσπόλων σέθεν
βίᾳ πρὸ τῶνδε δωμάτων ἐκπέμπομαι.
ἀτὰρ σχεδὸν μὲν οἶδά σοι στυγουμένη,
ὅμως δ' ἐρέσθαι βούλομαι· γνῶμαι τίνες
900 Ἕλλησι καὶ σοὶ τῆς ἐμῆς ψυχῆς πέρι;

ΜΕΝΕΛΑΟΣ

οὐκ εἰς ἀκριβὲς ἦλθεν, ἀλλ' ἅπας στρατὸς

891 ὁρᾶν Stanley: ὁρῶν C

sits for home, we will take her to Greece.

Some of Menelaus' retinue go into the skene.

HECUBA

You that support the earth and have your seat upon it, whoever you may be, so hard for human conjecture to find out, Zeus, whether you are the necessity of nature or the mind of mortal men, I address you in prayer! For proceeding on a silent path you direct all mortal affairs toward justice!

MENELAUS

What does this mean? How strange your prayer to the gods is!

HECUBA

I approve your intention, Menelaus, to kill your wife. But avoid looking at her lest she capture you with desire. For she captures the eyes of men, destroys their cities, and burns their houses. So powerful is the spell she creates, as you and I and others who have suffered know well.

Enter HELEN *from the* skene, *brought forth forcibly by Menelaus' attendants. She is splendidly dressed.*

HELEN

Menelaus, this is a worrisome beginning: by the hands of your servants I am forcibly brought out in front of this tent. But, although I am fairly certain that you hate me, I want to ask you: what decision has been made by you and the Greeks about my life?

MENELAUS

No clear decision was made: the whole army entrusted to

EURIPIDES

κτανεῖν ἐμοί σ' ἔδωκεν, ὅνπερ ἠδίκεις.

ΕΛΕΝΗ

ἔξεστιν οὖν πρὸς ταῦτ' ἀμείψασθαι λόγῳ,
ὡς οὐ δικαίως, ἢν θάνω, θανούμεθα;

ΜΕΝΕΛΑΟΣ

905 οὐκ ἐς λόγους ἐλήλυθ' ἀλλά σε κτενῶν.

ΕΚΑΒΗ

ἄκουσον αὐτῆς, μὴ θάνῃ τοῦδ' ἐνδεής,
Μενέλαε, καὶ δὸς τοὺς ἐναντίους λόγους
ἡμῖν κατ' αὐτῆς· τῶν γὰρ ἐν Τροίᾳ κακῶν
οὐδὲν κάτοισθα. συντεθεὶς δ' ὁ πᾶς λόγος
910 κτενεῖ νιν οὕτως ὥστε μηδαμοῦ φυγεῖν.

ΜΕΝΕΛΑΟΣ

σχολῆς τὸ δῶρον· εἰ δὲ βούλεται λέγειν,
ἔξεστι. τῶν σῶν δ' οὕνεχ', ὡς μάθῃ, λόγων
δώσω τόδ' αὐτῇ· τῆσδε δ' οὐ δώσω χάριν.

ΕΛΕΝΗ

ἴσως με, κἂν εὖ κἂν κακῶς δόξω λέγειν,
915 οὐκ ἀνταμείψῃ πολεμίαν ἡγούμενος.
ἐγὼ δ', ἅ σ' οἶμαι διὰ λόγων ἰόντ' ἐμοῦ
κατηγορήσειν, ἀντιθεῖσ' ἀμείψομαι
τοῖς σοῖσι †τἀμὰ καὶ τὰ σ'† αἰτιάματα.

    πρῶτον μὲν ἀρχὰς ἔτεκεν ἥδε τῶν κακῶν,
920 Πάριν τεκοῦσα· δεύτερον δ' ἀπώλεσεν
Τροίαν τε κἄμ' ὁ πρέσβυς οὐ κτανὼν βρέφος,

918 τἄμ' ἰσαίτατ' Pearson, τἀμὰ πάνδικ' Herwerden

102

me, the man you have wronged, the power to kill you.

HELEN

Am I permitted to argue against this decision, and show
that if I am killed it would be unjustly done?

MENELAUS

I have not come for arguments but to put you to death.

HECUBA

Hear her out, let her not die without this, Menelaus, and
give me the right to speak on the other side against her!
For you do not know the miseries we suffered in Troy.
When it has been put together, the entire account will kill
her: she will have nowhere to escape.

MENELAUS

To grant you this will require leisure, but if she wants to
speak, I give her permission. You should be clear, however,
that it is because of your plea that I will grant this to her. I
will not grant it for her sake.

HELEN

(addressing Menelaus) It may be that, whether I seem to
be talking sense or not, you will make no reply to me since
you consider me an enemy. As for me, the accusations I
think you will make in arguing against me I shall answer,
making most just accusations in reply to yours.

First, it was this woman who gave birth to the first cause
of our troubles when she bore Paris. Second, it was the old
man[30] who destroyed both Troy and me since he did not at

---

30 The reference is either to the old retainer in *Alexandros*,
who raised Alexandros/Paris as his own child instead of killing him
as he was ordered to do, or to Priam.

δαλοῦ πικρὸν μίμημ', Ἀλέξανδρον τότε.
ἐνθένδε τἀπίλοιπ' ἄκουσον ὡς ἔχει.
ἔκρινε τρισσὸν ζεῦγος ὅδε τριῶν θεῶν·
925 καὶ Παλλάδος μὲν ἦν Ἀλεξάνδρῳ δόσις
Φρυξὶ στρατηγοῦνθ' Ἑλλάδ' ἐξανιστάναι
Ἥρα δ' ὑπέσχετ' Ἀσιάδ' Εὐρώπης θ' ὅρους
τυραννίδ' ἕξειν, εἴ σφε κρίνειεν Πάρις·
Κύπρις δὲ τοὐμὸν εἶδος ἐκπαγλουμένη
930 δώσειν ὑπέσχετ', εἰ θεὰς ὑπερδράμοι
κάλλει. τὸν ἔνθεν δ' ὡς ἔχει σκέψαι λόγον·
νικᾷ Κύπρις θεάς, καὶ τοσόνδ' οὑμοὶ γάμοι
ὤνησαν Ἑλλάδ'· οὐ κρατεῖσθ' ἐκ βαρβάρων,
οὔτ' ἐς δόρυ σταθέντες, οὐ τυραννίδι.
935 ἃ δ' ηὐτύχησεν Ἑλλάς, ὠλόμην ἐγὼ
εὐμορφίᾳ πραθεῖσα, κὠνειδίζομαι
ἐξ ὧν ἐχρῆν με στέφανον ἐπὶ κάρα λαβεῖν.
    οὔπω με φήσεις αὐτὰ τἀν ποσὶν λέγειν,
ὅπως ἀφώρμησ' ἐκ δόμων τῶν σῶν λάθρᾳ.
940 ἦλθ' οὐχὶ μικρὰν θεὸν ἔχων αὑτοῦ μέτα
ὁ τῆσδ' ἀλάστωρ, εἴτ' Ἀλέξανδρον θέλεις
ὀνόματι προσφωνεῖν νιν εἴτε καὶ Πάριν·
ὅν, ὦ κάκιστε, σοῖσιν ἐν δόμοις λιπὼν
Σπάρτης ἀπῆρας νηὶ Κρησίαν χθόνα.
    εἶἑν.
945 οὐ σ', ἀλλ' ἐμαυτὴν τοὐπὶ τῷδ' ἐρήσομαι·
τί δὴ φρονοῦσά γ' ἐκ δόμων ἅμ' ἑσπόμην

922 τότε Lenting: ποτε C

the start kill the babe Alexandros, who so fatally resembled a torch.[31] Next, listen to what followed after that. This man judged the trio of goddesses. Pallas Athena's bribe to Alexandros was that he would lead the Phrygians in war and lay waste to Greece. Hera promised him that he would hold sway over both Asia and the bounds of Europe if he awarded her the victory. Cypris,[32] admiring my beauty, promised she would give me to him if she defeated the other goddesses in the beauty contest. Now hear how the story goes after that. Cypris defeated the other goddesses, and my relations with Paris benefitted Greece to this extent: you are not ruled by barbarians, either because of a battle or by usurpation.[33] But Hellas' good fortune was my ruin: I was sold because of my beauty, and I am reproached for something for which I should have received a garland on my head.

You will claim that I am not yet talking about the obvious point, how I slipped secretly from your house. He came with no small goddess at his side to help him, that spirit sent to ruin this woman, call him Paris or Alexandros as you like. This man, you worthless creature, you left in your house and took ship from Sparta to Crete!

Well then, in what follows I will question myself and not you. What was I thinking of that I left the house in

31 A reference to *Alexandros*: Hecuba, when pregnant with Alexandros, dreamt that she gave birth to a firebrand.

32 Aphrodite.

33 One or the other of these would have resulted from Athena's or Hera's victory in the contest.

ξένῳ, προδοῦσα πατρίδα καὶ δόμους ἐμούς;
τὴν θεὸν κόλαζε καὶ Διὸς κρείσσων γενοῦ,
ὃς τῶν μὲν ἄλλων δαιμόνων ἔχει κράτος,
950 κείνης δὲ δοῦλός ἐστι· συγγνώμη δ᾽ ἐμοί.

ἔνθεν δ᾽ ἔχοις ἂν εἰς ἔμ᾽ εὐπρεπῆ λόγον·
ἐπεὶ θανὼν γῆς ἦλθ᾽ Ἀλέξανδρος μυχούς,
χρῆν μ᾽, ἡνίκ᾽ οὐκ ἦν θεοπόνητά μου λέχη,
λιποῦσαν οἴκους ναῦς ἐπ᾽ Ἀργείων μολεῖν.
955 ἔσπευδον αὐτὸ τοῦτο· μάρτυρες δέ μοι
πύργων πυλωροὶ κἀπὸ τειχέων σκοποί,
οἳ πολλάκις μ᾽ ἐφηῦρον ἐξ ἐπάλξεων
πλεκταῖσιν ἐς γῆν σῶμα κλέπτουσαν τόδε.
[βίᾳ δ᾽ ὁ καινός μ᾽ οὗτος ἁρπάσας πόσις
960 Δηίφοβος ἄλοχον εἶχεν ἀκόντων Φρυγῶν.]
πῶς οὖν ἔτ᾽ ἂν θνήσκοιμ᾽ ἂν ἐνδίκως, πόσι,
⟨πῶς δ᾽ οὐχὶ πολλῷ μᾶλλον ἐλεηθεῖμεν ἂν⟩
πρὸς σοῦ δικαίως, ἣν ὁ μὲν βίᾳ γαμεῖ,
τὰ δ᾽ οἴκοθεν κεῖν᾽ ἀντὶ νικητηρίων
965 πικρῶς ἐδούλωσ᾽; εἰ δὲ τῶν θεῶν κρατεῖν
βούλῃ, τὸ χρῄζειν ἀμαθές ἐστί σου τόδε.

ΧΟΡΟΣ

βασίλει᾽, ἄμυνον σοῖς τέκνοισι καὶ πάτρᾳ
πειθὼ διαφθείρουσα τῆσδ᾽, ἐπεὶ λέγει
καλῶς κακοῦργος οὖσα· δεινὸν οὖν τόδε.

959-60 del. Wilamowitz
961 post h. v. lac. indic. Murray
964 ἐδούλωσ᾽ Dobree: ἐδούλευσ᾽ C

company with a stranger, abandoning my country and my home? Discipline the goddess and be stronger than Zeus! Zeus holds sway over all the other divinities but is a slave to her. So it is pardonable in me.

At this point you might raise a specious objection against me. When Alexandros died and went into the recesses of the earth and my marriage the gods had brought about was no more, I ought to have left my house and gone to the ships of the Argives. That is just what I attempted to do! As witnesses I cite the gatekeepers in the towers and the watchmen on the walls, who often discovered me trying to steal this body of mine by ropes let down from the battlements to the ground. [My new husband, Deiphobus, kept me as his wife by force, against the wishes of the Phrygians.] How then should I be justly put to death, dear husband, ‹how should I not much rather be› justly ‹pitied› by you, seeing that Paris married me by constraint, while my own situation³⁴ caused me painful slavery instead of a crown of victory? If you wish to defeat the gods, your desire is a foolish one.

CHORUS LEADER

My queen, come to the rescue of your children and country by destroying the persuasive force of her words: she speaks eloquently, although she is guilty, and that is a terrible thing.

---

³⁴ Or "my natural endowments," referring to her beauty, or possibly "my departure from home."

ΕΚΑΒΗ

ταῖς θεαῖσι πρῶτα σύμμαχος γενήσομαι
970 καὶ τήνδε δείξω μὴ λέγουσαν ἔνδικα.
ἐγὼ γὰρ Ἥραν παρθένον τε Παλλάδα
οὐκ ἐς τοσοῦτον ἀμαθίας ἐλθεῖν δοκῶ,
ὥσθ᾽ ἡ μὲν Ἄργος βαρβάροις ἀπημπόλα,
Παλλὰς δ᾽ Ἀθήνας Φρυξὶ δουλεύειν ποτέ·
975 οὐ παιδιαῖσι καὶ χλιδῇ μορφῆς πέρι
ἦλθον πρὸς Ἴδην. τοῦ γὰρ οὕνεκ᾽ ἂν θεὰ
Ἥρα τοσοῦτον ἔσχ᾽ ἔρωτα καλλονῆς;
πότερον ἀμείνον᾽ ὡς λάβῃ Διὸς πόσιν;
ἢ γάμον Ἀθηνᾶ θεῶν τινος θηρωμένη,
980 ἢ παρθενείαν πατρὸς ἐξῃτήσατο
φεύγουσα λέκτρα; μὴ ἀμαθεῖς ποίει θεὰς
τὸ σὸν κακὸν κοσμοῦσα, μὴ <οὐ> πείσῃς σοφούς.
    Κύπριν δ᾽ ἔλεξας (ταῦτα γὰρ γέλως πολύς)
ἐλθεῖν ἐμῷ ξὺν παιδὶ Μενέλεω δόμους.
985 οὐκ ἂν μένουσ᾽ ἂν ἥσυχός σ᾽ ἐν οὐρανῷ
αὐταῖς Ἀμύκλαις ἤγαγεν πρὸς Ἴλιον;
ἦν οὑμὸς υἱὸς κάλλος ἐκπρεπέστατος,
ὁ σὸς δ᾽ ἰδών νιν νοῦς ἐποιήθη Κύπρις·
τὰ μῶρα γὰρ πάντ᾽ ἐστὶν Ἀφροδίτη βροτοῖς,
990 καὶ τοὔνομ᾽ ὀρθῶς ἀφροσύνης ἄρχει θεᾶς.
ὃν εἰσιδοῦσα βαρβάροις ἐσθήμασιν
χρυσῷ τε λαμπρὸν ἐξεμαργώθης φρένας.
ἐν μὲν γὰρ Ἄργει σμίκρ᾽ ἔχουσ᾽ ἀνεστρέφου,
Σπάρτης δ᾽ ἀπαλλαχθεῖσα τὴν Φρυγῶν πόλιν
995 χρυσῷ ῥέουσαν ἤλπισας κατακλύσειν

HECUBA

First of all, I will become an ally of the goddesses and show that this woman's plea is unjust. I do not think that Hera or the virgin Pallas would be so foolish that the former would ever sell Argos to the barbarians and Pallas give Athens to the Phrygians as their subject. They did not go to Ida to engage in the frivolous extravagance of a beauty contest. Why should the goddess Hera conceive such a great desire to be beautiful? So that she could get a better husband than Zeus? Or was Athena looking for marriage with one of the gods, she who begged from her father the gift of maidenhood and fled from marriage? Do not make the gods foolish in an attempt to gloss over your own evil nature: you will not persuade the wise.

You claim that Cypris (the idea is hilarious) went with my son to the house of Menelaus. Could she not have stayed quietly in heaven and brought you to Ilium—and the whole city of Amyclae with you? My son was very handsome, and when you saw him your mind was turned into Cypris. For mortals call all acts of foolishness Aphrodite, and it is proper that the goddess' name begins with the word for folly.[35] You saw him resplendent in the golden raiment of the East, and your mind became utterly wanton. For in Argos you lived with small means, but you thought that by being quit of Sparta you would be able to flood the city of Troy, which is awash in gold, with your extravagance.

---

[35] It is implied that Aphrodite's name derives from *aphrosune*, folly.

---

975 οὐ Hartung: αἱ C   982 ⟨οὐ⟩ Seidler
985 σ' Hermann: γ' C

109

δαπάναισιν· οὐδ᾽ ἦν ἱκανά σοι τὰ Μενέλεω
μέλαθρα ταῖς σαῖς ἐγκαθυβρίζειν τρυφαῖς.

εἶεν· βίᾳ γὰρ παῖδα φῄς σ᾽ ἄγειν ἐμόν·
τίς Σπαρτιατῶν ᾔσθετ᾽; ἢ ποίαν βοὴν
1000 ἀνωλόλυξας, Κάστορος νεανίου
τοῦ συζύγου τ᾽ ἔτ᾽ ὄντος, οὐ κατ᾽ ἄστρα πω;

ἐπεὶ δὲ Τροίαν ἦλθες Ἀργεῖοί τέ σου
κατ᾽ ἴχνος, ἦν δὲ δοριπετὴς ἀγωνία,
εἰ μὲν τὰ τοῦδε κρείσσον᾽ ἀγγέλλοιτό σοι,
1005 Μενέλαον ᾔνεις, παῖς ὅπως λυποῖτ᾽ ἐμὸς
ἔχων ἔρωτος ἀνταγωνιστὴν μέγαν·
εἰ δ᾽ εὐτυχοῖεν Τρῶες, οὐδὲν ἦν ὅδε.
ἐς τὴν τύχην δ᾽ ὁρῶσα τοῦτ᾽ ἤσκεις, ὅπως
ἕποι᾽ ἅμ᾽ αὐτῇ, τῇ ἀρετῇ δ᾽ οὐκ ἤθελες.
1010 κἄπειτα πλεκταῖς σῶμα σὸν κλέπτειν λέγεις
πύργων καθιεῖσ᾽, ὡς μένουσ᾽ ἀκουσίως.
ποῦ δῆτ᾽ ἐλήφθης ἢ βρόχοις ἀρτωμένη
ἢ φάσγανον θήγουσ᾽, ἃ γενναία γυνὴ
δράσειεν ἂν ποθοῦσα τὸν πάρος πόσιν;
1015 καίτοι σ᾽ ἐνουθέτουν γε πολλὰ πολλάκις·
Ὦ θύγατερ, ἔξελθ᾽· οἱ δ᾽ ἐμοὶ παῖδες γάμους
ἄλλους γαμοῦσι, σὲ δ᾽ ἐπὶ ναῦς Ἀχαικὰς
πέμψω συνεκκλέψασα· καὶ παῦσον μάχης
Ἕλληνας ἡμᾶς τ᾽. ἀλλὰ σοὶ τόδ᾽ ἦν πικρόν.
1020 ἐν τοῖς Ἀλεξάνδρου γὰρ ὑβρίζειν δόμοις
καὶ προσκυνεῖσθαι βαρβάρων ὕπ᾽ ἤθελες·
μεγάλα γὰρ ἦν σοι. κἀπὶ τοῖσδε σὸν δέμας
ἐξῆλθες ἀσκήσασα κἄβλεψας πόσει

110

Menelaus' palace was not grand enough for your luxurious tastes to run riot in.

Well now. You say that my son took you by constraint. Who of the Spartan women heard this? What cry did you raise, with young Castor and his brother[36] still alive and not yet among the stars?

When you came to Troy and the Argives arrived following your track and there was a deadly battle, whenever you received news that Menelaus was winning, you praised him so that my son would feel grief because he had a great rival in love. But if the Trojans were successful, Menelaus was nothing. Keeping your eye on Fortune you made sure that you followed her and refused to follow goodness. And then you claim that you tried to steal yourself away with ropes, letting them down from the towers, as though you were staying against your will. Then when were you caught hanging yourself with a noose or sharpening a sword, actions which a noble woman would do if she longed for her former husband? And yet I often advised you, "Daughter, depart! My sons will make other marriages. I will help to conceal you and send you down to the Greek ships. Deliver both the Greeks and us from war." But this suggestion was unwelcome to you. You wanted to indulge your haughtiness in Alexandros' palace, you wanted the barbarians to make their obeisance before you. That was the great thing in your eyes. And after that have you come out dressed in

36 See note on line 133 above.

1000 ἀνωτότυξας Wecklein
1012 βρόχοις Burgesii amicus: -ους C
1020 ὑβρίζειν Lehrs: ὕβριζες C

τὸν αὐτὸν αἰθέρ᾽, ὦ κατάπτυστον κάρα;
1025 ἣν χρῆν ταπεινὴν ἐν πέπλων ἐρειπίοις,
φρίκῃ τρέμουσαν, κρᾶτ᾽ ἀπεσκυθισμένην
ἐλθεῖν, τὸ σῶφρον τῆς ἀναιδείας πλέον
ἔχουσαν ἐπὶ τοῖς πρόσθεν ἡμαρτημένοις.
Μενέλα᾽, ἵν᾽ εἰδῇς οἷ τελευτήσω λόγον,
1030 στεφάνωσον Ἑλλάδ᾽ ἀξίως τήνδε κτανὼν
σαυτοῦ, νόμον δὲ τόνδε ταῖς ἄλλαισι θὲς
γυναιξί, θνῄσκειν ἥτις ἂν προδῷ πόσιν.

ΧΟΡΟΣ

Μενέλαε, προγόνων τ᾽ ἀξίως δόμων τε σῶν
τεῖσαι δάμαρτα κἀφελοῦ πρὸς Ἑλλάδος
1035 ψόγον τὸ θῆλύ τ᾽, εὐγενὴς ἐχθροῖς φανείς.

ΜΕΝΕΛΑΟΣ

ἐμοὶ σὺ συμπέπτωκας ἐς ταὐτὸν λόγου,
ἑκουσίως τήνδ᾽ ἐκ δόμων ἐλθεῖν ἐμῶν
ξένας ἐς εὐνάς· χἠ Κύπρις κόμπου χάριν
λόγοις ἔνεισαι. βαῖνε λευστήρων πέλας
1040 πόνους τ᾽ Ἀχαιῶν ἀπόδος ἐν σμικρῷ μακροὺς
θανοῦσ᾽, ἵν᾽ εἰδῇς μὴ καταισχύνειν ἐμέ.

ΕΛΕΝΗ

μή, πρός σε γονάτων, τὴν νόσον τὴν τῶν θεῶν
προσθεὶς ἐμοὶ κτάνῃς με, συγγίγνωσκε δέ.

1033 τ᾽ ἀξίως Seidler: ἀξίως τε C

112

finery? Do you look on the same sky as your husband does, you execrable woman? You ought to have come humbly dressed in rags, trembling in fear and with shaven head, showing modesty rather than brazenness over your former misdeeds.

Menelaus, here, for your information, is the conclusion to which my speech is tending: crown Greece with glory by killing this woman, an act worthy of yourself! Establish this law for the rest of women: death to her who betrays her husband!

CHORUS LEADER

Menelaus, punish your wife in a manner worthy of your ancestors and your house and clear yourself of Greece's charge that you are not a man, showing yourself noble in the eyes of your adversaries!

MENELAUS

You have come to the same conclusion as I have, that it was of her own free will that she left my house for the bed of a stranger. Cypris was introduced into her story to allow her to boast. March off now to those who will stone you to death, and give satisfaction in a short time for the long labors of the Greeks, so that you may learn not to besmirch my honor!

HELEN

(*falling before Menelaus as a suppliant*) I beg you by your knees, do not attribute to me the malady sent by the gods and put me to death! Rather, forgive me!

113

ΕΚΑΒΗ

μηδ' οὓς ἀπέκτειν' ἥδε συμμάχους προδῷς·
1045 ἐγὼ πρὸ κείνων καὶ τέκνων σε λίσσομαι.

ΜΕΝΕΛΑΟΣ

παῦσαι, γεραιά· τῆσδε δ' οὐκ ἐφρόντισα.
λέγω δὲ προσπόλοισι πρὸς πρύμνας νεῶν
τήνδ' ἐκκομίζειν, ἔνθα ναυστολήσεται.

ΕΚΑΒΗ

μή νυν νεὼς σοὶ ταὐτὸν ἐσβήτω σκάφος.

ΜΕΝΕΛΑΟΣ

1050 τί δ' ἔστι; μεῖζον βρῖθος ἢ πάροιθ' ἔχει;

ΕΚΑΒΗ

οὐκ ἔστ' ἐραστὴς ὅστις οὐκ ἀεὶ φιλεῖ.

ΜΕΝΕΛΑΟΣ

ὅπως ἂν ἐκβῇ τῶν ἐρωμένων ὁ νοῦς.
ἔσται δ' ἃ βούλῃ· ναῦν γὰρ οὐκ ἐσβήσεται
ἐς ἥνπερ ἡμεῖς· καὶ γὰρ οὐ κακῶς λέγεις·
1055 ἐλθοῦσα δ' Ἄργος ὥσπερ ἀξία κακῶς
κακὴ θανεῖται καὶ γυναιξὶ σωφρονεῖν
πάσαισι θήσει. ῥᾴδιον μὲν οὐ τόδε·
ὅμως δ' ὁ τῆσδ' ὄλεθρος ἐς φόβον βαλεῖ
τὸ μῶρον αὐτῶν, κἂν ἔτ' ὦσ' ἐχθίονες.

1044 ante h. v. aliquid desiderat Wecklein, e.g. ⟨μέμνησ' ἃ
πᾶσαν Ἑλλάδ' εἴργασται κακά⟩
1059 αἰσχίονες Hermann

HECUBA

Do not betray the allies of yours this woman has killed! I
beg you for their sake and for that of my sons!

MENELAUS

Old woman, cease! I pay her no heed. To my servants I say,
Take her to the ships, and from there she will be conveyed
by sea!

HECUBA

Well, then, do not let her embark on the same vessel as
you.

MENELAUS

What is wrong? Is she heavier than she was?

HECUBA

All passionate lovers love for ever.

MENELAUS

That depends on the character of those they love. But I
shall do as you wish. She shall not go on board the same
ship with me. That, in fact, is not a bad suggestion. But
when she reaches Argos the wretch will die a wretched
death, as she deserves, and will cause all women to be
chaste. To be sure, this is not easy. But her death will make
foolish women afraid, though they be still more reprobate
than she is!

Exit HELEN and MENELAUS with retinue by Eisodos A.

ΧΟΡΟΣ

στρ. α

1060 οὕτω δὴ τὸν ἐν Ἰλίῳ
ναὸν καὶ θυόεντα βω-
μὸν προύδωκας Ἀχαιοῖς,
ὦ Ζεῦ, καὶ πελανῶν φλόγα
σμύρνας αἰθερίας τε κα-
1065 πνὸν καὶ Πέργαμον ἱερὰν
Ἰδαῖά τ᾽ Ἰδαῖα κισσοφόρα νάπη
χιόνι κατάρυτα ποταμίᾳ
τέρμονα τε †πρωτόβολον ἁλίῳ†,
1070 τὰν καταλαμπομέναν ζαθέαν θεράπναν;

ἀντ. α

φροῦδαί σοι θυσίαι χορῶν τ᾽
εὔφαμοι κέλαδοι κατ᾽ ὄρφ-
ναν τε παννυχίδες θεῶν,
χρυσέων τε ξοάνων τύποι
1075 Φρυγῶν τε ζάθεοι σελᾶ-
ναι συνδώδεκα πλήθει·
μέλει μέλει μοι τάδ᾽ εἰ φρονεῖς, ἄναξ,
οὐράνιον ἕδρανον ἐπιβεβὼς
αἰθέρα τε, πόλεος ὀλομένας
1080 ἃν πυρὸς αἰθομένα κατέλυσεν ὁρμά.

στρ. β

ὦ φίλος ὦ πόσι μοι,

1069 πρωτόβολον ἔῳ Wilamowitz (sed vide Diggle ad *Phaeth.*
64): πρόβολον ἁλίῳ Seidler

CHORUS

Did you, O Zeus, so lightly betray
your temple in Ilium and its incense-laden
altar to the Greeks,
the flame that arises from holy cakes,
the smoke of myrrh borne upon the air,
Pergamum the holy,
the vales of Ida, Ida, luxuriant with ivy,
watered with the stream of melted snow,
the boundary of earth first struck by the sun's rays,
an abode illuminated and holy?

Vanished are your sacrifices,
the lovely songs of choruses, and in the darkness
the all-night festivals of the gods,
your shapely golden statues
and the Phrygians' full-moon festivals,[37]
twelve in their number.
It matters, it matters to me whether you mark these things,
 lord,
as you sit aloft in the upper air
though the city has perished,
undone by the blazing onslaught of fire.

Ah dear husband,

---

[37] Others, following Parmentier (Budé edition, *ad loc.*), take
σελᾶναι to be sacrificial cakes, shaped like moons: see Athenaeus
489D and Euripides fr. 350.

σὺ μὲν φθίμενος ἀλαίνεις
1085 ἄθαπτος ἄνυδρος, ἐμὲ δὲ πόντιον σκάφος
ᾆσσον πτεροῖσι πορεύσει
ἱππόβοτον Ἄργος, †ἵνα τείχεα†
λάινα Κυκλώπι᾽ οὐράνια νέμονται.
τέκνων δὲ πλῆθος ἐν πύλαις
1090 δάκρυσι κατάροον ἀσθενῆ βοὰν βοᾷ·
Μᾶτερ, ὤμοι, μόναν δή μ᾽ Ἀχαιοὶ κομί-
ζουσι σέθεν ἀπ᾽ ὀμμάτων
κυανέαν ἐπὶ ναῦν,
1095 εἶθ᾽ ἁλίαισι πλάταις
ἢ Σαλαμῖν᾽ ἱερὰν
ἢ δίπορον κορυφὰν
Ἴσθμιον, ἔνθα πύλας
Πέλοπος ἔχουσιν ἕδραι.

ἀντ. β

1100 εἶθ᾽ ἀκάτου Μενέλα
μέσον πέλαγος ἰούσας,
δίπαλτον ἱερὸν ἀνὰ μέσον πλατᾶν πέσοι
Δῖον κεραυνοφαὲς πῦρ,
1105 Ἰλιόθεν ὅτε με πολυδάκρυον
Ἑλλάδι λάτρευμα γᾶθεν ἐξορίζει,
χρύσεα δ᾽ ἔνοπτρα, παρθένων
χάριτας, ἔχουσα τυγχάνει Διὸς κόρα·
1110 μηδὲ γαῖάν ποτ᾽ ἔλθοι Λάκαιναν πατρῷ-

1086 ᾆσσον Hermann: ἀίσσον C
1087 fort. ἵν᾽ ἐρύματα

118

you wander in death
unburied and with no lustral water, while I by ship seagoing
with flashing oars shall be taken
to horse-pasturing Argos, where men dwell in walls
of stone, Cyclopean, heaven-high.
The throng of children in the gates,
awash with tears, cry their weak cry,
"Mother, ah mother, the Achaeans take me by myself
away from your eyes
down to their dark ship,
and then with seagoing oar
either to holy Salamis
or to the peak of the Isthmus
with its two sea paths, where stand the gates
to Pelops' home!"

O that when Menelaus' ship
is crossing the open sea
in the midst of his oars might fall the hurled
lightning blaze of Zeus
as he takes me in tears from the land of Ilium
as a slave to Greece
while Zeus's daughter holds her golden mirror,
the delight of maidens!
May he never reach the land of Sparta

1090 κατάροον post Meridor Willink: κατάορα C   ἀσθενῆ
βοὰν Paley: στένει βοᾷ C
1095 εἶθ' ἁλίαισι Musgrave: ἐν ἁλ- vel ἐναλ- C
1104 Δῖον Schenkl: Αἰγαῖον C
1105 πολυδάκρυον Bothe: πολύδακρυν C

119

ὅν τε θάλαμον ἑστίας,
μηδὲ πόλιν Πιτάνας
χαλκόπυλόν τε θεάν,
δύσγαμον αἶσχος ἔχων
1115 Ἑλλάδι τᾷ μεγάλᾳ
καὶ Σιμοεντιάσιν
μέλεα πάθεα ῥοαῖσιν.

—ἰὼ ἰώ,
καίν’ ⟨ἐκ⟩ καινῶν μεταβάλλουσαι
χθονὶ συντυχίαι. λεύσσετε Τρώων
1120 τόνδ’ Ἀστυάνακτ’ ἄλοχοι μέλεαι
νεκρόν, ὃν πύργων δίσκημα πικρὸν
Δαναοὶ κτείναντες ἔχουσιν.

ΤΑΛΘΥΒΙΟΣ
Ἑκάβη, νεὼς μὲν πίτυλος εἷς λελειμμένος
λάφυρα τἀπίλοιπ’ Ἀχιλλείου τόκου
1125 μέλλει πρὸς ἀκτὰς ναυστολεῖν Φθιώτιδας·
αὐτὸς δ’ ἀνῆκται Νεοπτόλεμος, καινάς τινας
Πηλέως ἀκούσας συμφοράς, ὥς νιν χθονὸς
Ἄκαστος ἐκβέβληκεν, ὁ Πελίου γόνος.
οὗ θᾶσσον οὕνεκ’, οὐ χάριν μονῆς ἔχων,
1130 φροῦδος, μετ’ αὐτοῦ δ’ Ἀνδρομάχη, πολλῶν ἐμοὶ
δακρύων ἀγωγός, ἡνίκ’ ἐξώρμα χθονός,
πάτραν τ’ ἀναστένουσα καὶ τὸν Ἕκτορος

1113 θεάν Musgrave: θεᾶς θάλαμον C
1114 ἔχων Wilamowitz: ἑλὼν C

or his ancestral hearth,
or the city of Pitana,
or the goddess of the brazen gate![38]
He has her as wife
who shamed mighty Greece by her evil marriage
and upon the streams of Simois
brought grievous woes.

Enter by Eisodos B TALTHYBIUS *with attendants carrying the body of Astyanax upon the shield of Hector.*

CHORUS LEADER
Ah, ah! Our land's fortunes undergo one woeful change after another! Look, unhappy wives of the Trojans, at the dead Astyanax! The Greeks have killed him, hurling him hatefully from the tower!

TALTHYBIUS
Hecuba, the oars of one last ship are about to carry the rest of the spoils belonging to Achilles' son back to the shores of Phthia. Neoptolemus himself has already set sail, having heard that Peleus has suffered a new misfortune: Pelias' son Acastus has driven him from the country. Therefore, not having the pleasure of tarrying, he has gone off in haste, and Andromache with him. She wrung many tears from my eyes as she set out from the land lamenting for her country and saying farewell to the tomb of Hector.

---

[38] Pitana is a district of Sparta, and the goddess of the brazen gate is Athena Chalkeoikos, worshiped on the Spartan acropolis.

1118 ⟨ἐκ⟩ Wilamowitz
1129 οὐ Bothe: ἤ C

τύμβον προσεννέπουσα. καί σφ᾿ ᾐτήσατο
θάψαι νεκρὸν τόνδ᾿, ὃς πεσὼν ἐκ τειχέων
1135 ψυχὴν ἀφῆκεν Ἕκτορος τοῦ σοῦ γόνος·
φόβον τ᾿ Ἀχαιῶν, χαλκόνωτον ἀσπίδα
τήνδ᾿, ἣν πατὴρ τοῦδ᾿ ἀμφὶ πλεύρ᾿ ἐβάλλετο,
μή νιν πορεῦσαι Πηλέως ἐφ᾿ ἑστίαν
μηδ᾿ ἐς τὸν αὐτὸν θάλαμον οὗ νυμφεύσεται
1140 [μήτηρ νεκροῦ τοῦδ᾿ Ἀνδρομάχη, λύπας ὁρᾶν],
ἀλλ᾿ ἀντὶ κέδρου περιβόλων τε λαΐνων
ἐν τῇδε θάψαι παῖδα· σὰς δ᾿ ἐς ὠλένας
δοῦναι, πέπλοισιν ὡς περιστείλῃς νεκρὸν
στεφάνοις θ᾿, ὅση σοι δύναμις, ὡς ἔχει τὰ σά·
1145 ἐπεὶ βέβηκε καὶ τὸ δεσπότου τάχος
ἀφείλετ᾿ αὐτὴν παῖδα μὴ δοῦναι τάφῳ.
    ἡμεῖς μὲν οὖν, ὅταν σὺ κοσμήσῃς νέκυν,
γῆν τῷδ᾿ ἐπαμπισχόντες ἀροῦμεν δόρυ·
σὺ δ᾿ ὡς τάχιστα πρᾶσσε τἀπεσταλμένα.
1150 ἑνὸς μὲν οὖν μόχθου σ᾿ ἀπαλλάξας ἔχω·
Σκαμανδρίους γὰρ τάσδε διαπερῶν ῥοὰς
ἔλουσα νεκρὸν κἀπένιψα τραύματα.
    ἀλλ᾿ εἶμ᾿ ὀρυκτὸν τῷδ᾿ ἀναρρήξων τάφον,
ὡς σύντομ᾿ ἡμῖν τἀπ᾿ ἐμοῦ τε κἀπὸ σοῦ
1155 ἐς ἓν ξυνελθόντ᾿ οἴκαδ᾿ ὁρμήσῃ πλάτην.

ΕΚΑΒΗ
θέσθ᾿ ἀμφίτορνον ἀσπίδ᾿ Ἕκτορος πέδῳ,
λυπρὸν θέαμα κοὐ φίλον λεύσσειν ἐμοί.
    ὦ μεῖζον᾿ ὄγκον δορὸς ἔχοντες ἢ φρενῶν,

She begged Neoptolemus that this dead child, who was hurled from the walls and breathed his last, the son of your Hector, be buried. She begged him also not to bring this bronze-backed shield, the Achaeans' terror, which this boy's father used to hold against his side, to the home of Peleus or to take it into the same chamber where she will become his bride [the mother of this dead boy, Andromache, so as to see grief], but to bury the boy in it instead of a cedar coffin and a stone tomb. She asked him to put it into your hands so that with funeral clothes and garlands you may deck out the corpse as well as you can in your present circumstances. For she is gone, and her master's haste has prevented her from burying the boy.

When you have adorned the body, we for our part will cover it in earth and then set sail. Do you carry out your orders as quickly as possible. I have freed you from one bit of toil: as I was crossing the Scamander River here, I bathed the body and washed the blood from its wounds.

So, now I shall go and dig a grave so that your actions and mine, joined together, may quickly send our vessel on its way.

HECUBA

Put the rimmed shield of Hector on the ground, a sight that is painful, not dear, for me to look on!

Talthybius' men put the shield with Astyanax's body on the ground and depart with TALTHYBIUS *by Eisodos A.*

O Achaeans, whose spears are more massive than your

1140 del. Herwerden, Paley   1148 ἀροῦμεν Burges: αἴρ- C

τί τόνδ', Ἀχαιοί, παῖδα δείσαντες φόνον
1160 καινὸν διειργάσασθε; μὴ Τροίαν ποτὲ
πεσοῦσαν ὀρθώσειεν; οὐδὲν ἦτ' ἄρα,
ὅθ' Ἕκτορος μὲν εὐτυχοῦντος ἐς δόρυ
διωλλύμεσθα μυρίας τ' ἄλλης χερός,
πόλεως δ' ἁλούσης καὶ Φρυγῶν ἐφθαρμένων
1165 βρέφος τοσόνδ' ἐδείσατ'· οὐκ αἰνῶ φόβον,
ὅστις φοβεῖται μὴ διεξελθὼν λόγῳ.

ὦ φίλταθ', ὥς σοι θάνατος ἦλθε δυστυχής.
εἰ μὲν γὰρ ἔθανες πρὸ πόλεως ἥβης τυχὼν
γάμων τε καὶ τῆς ἰσοθέου τυραννίδος,
1170 μακάριος ἦσθ' ἄν, εἴ τι τῶνδε μακάριον·
νῦν <δ'> αὔτ' ἰδὼν μὲν γνούς τε σῇ ψυχῇ, τέκνον,
†οὐκ οἶσθ', ἐχρήσω δ' οὐδὲν ἐν δόμοις ἔχων†.

δύστηνε, κρατὸς ὥς σ' ἔκειρεν ἀθλίως
τείχη πατρῷα, Λοξίου πυργώματα,
1175 ὃν πόλλ' ἐκήπευσ' ἡ τεκοῦσα βόστρυχον
φιλήμασίν τ' ἔδωκεν, ἔνθεν ἐκγελᾷ
ὀστέων ῥαγέντων φόνος, ἵν' αἰσχρὰ μὴ στέγω.
ὦ χεῖρες, ὡς εἰκοὺς μὲν ἡδείας πατρὸς
κέκτησθ', ἐν ἄρθροις δ' ἔκλυτοι πρόκεισθέ μοι.
1180 ὦ πολλὰ κόμπους ἐκβαλών, φίλον στόμα,
ὄλωλας, ἐψεύσω μ', ὅτ' ἐσπίπτων λέχος,
Ὦ μῆτερ, ηὔδας, ἦ πολύν σοι βοστρύχων
πλόκαμον κεροῦμαι πρὸς τάφον θ' ὁμηλίκων
κώμους ἐπάξω, φίλα διδοὺς προσφθέγματα.

1171 <δ'> Reiske   σὰ (sc. ὄντα) Munro

brains, why did you fear this boy and commit so strange a murder? Was it so that he would never raise up Troy that has fallen? Then it is clear you Greeks are worthless. When Hector was successful on the field of battle and with him countless other spear-hands, we were still being killed. Yet when the city was taken and the Trojans destroyed, you are so afraid of this child. I do not praise fear when it is someone's unreasoning terror.

Dear child, what an unlucky death was yours! If you had attained manhood and marriage and godlike kingship and been killed defending the city, you would have been blessed, if blessedness lies in any of these things. As it is, though you are aware that you have seen these things and known them in your imagination, my child, you are unable to get the enjoyment of them for yourself.

Poor child, how terribly your father's walls, fortifications Apollo built, have shorn those curls upon your head which I so often tended, so often smothered with kisses! That is where, with your bones shattered, the blood now appears in a smiling gash, to speak the ugly truth plainly. O hands, how sweet is your resemblance to your father's hands, but now you lie all slackened in your joints! You often uttered grand promises, dear lips, but now you have perished, and it was a cheat when you used to fling yourself into my bed and say, "Grandmother, I shall cut a great lock of curls for you and bring gatherings of my agemates to your tomb and speak loving words of farewell!" For now

---

1172 fort. σύνοισθα (Hartung), χρῆσθαι δ' οὐδὲν ἐν δόμοις ἔχων   1177 στέγω Diggle: λέγω C
1184 ἐπάξω Nauck: ἀπ- C

1185 σὺ δ᾽ οὐκ ἔμ᾽, ἀλλ᾽ ἐγὼ σὲ τὸν νεώτερον,
γραῦς ἄπολις ἄτεκνος, ἄθλιον θάπτω νεκρόν.
οἴμοι, τὰ πόλλ᾽ ἀσπάσμαθ᾽ αἵ τ᾽ ἐμαὶ τροφαὶ
ὕπνοι τε κοινοὶ φροῦδά μοι. τί καί ποτε
γράψειεν ἄν σε μουσοποιὸς ἐν τάφῳ;

1190 Τὸν παῖδα τόνδ᾽ ἔκτειναν Ἀργεῖοί ποτε
δείσαντες; αἰσχρὸν τοὐπίγραμμά γ᾽ Ἑλλάδι.
ἀλλ᾽ οὖν πατρῴων οὐ λαχὼν ἕξεις ὅμως
ἐν ᾗ ταφήσῃ χαλκόνωτον ἰτέαν.

ὦ καλλίπηχυν Ἕκτορος βραχίονα
1195 σῴζουσ᾽, ἄριστον φύλακ᾽ ἀπώλεσας σέθεν.
ὡς ἡδὺς ἐν πόρπακι σῷ κεῖται τύπος
ἴτυός τ᾽ ἐν εὐτόρνοισι περιδρόμοις ἱδρώς,
ὃν ἐκ μετώπου πολλάκις πόνους ἔχων
ἔσταζεν Ἕκτωρ προστιθεὶς γενειάδι.

1200 φέρετε, κομίζετ᾽ ἀθλίῳ κόσμον νεκρῷ
ἐκ τῶν παρόντων· οὐ γὰρ ἐς κάλλος τύχας
δαίμων δίδωσιν· ὧν δ᾽ ἔχω, λήψῃ τάδε.

θνητῶν δὲ μῶρος ὅστις εὖ πράσσειν δοκῶν
βέβαια χαίρει· τοῖς τρόποις γὰρ αἱ τύχαι,
1205 ἔμπληκτος ὡς ἄνθρωπος, ἄλλοτ᾽ ἄλλοσε
πηδῶσι, †κοὐδεὶς αὐτὸς εὐτυχεῖ ποτε†.

ΧΟΡΟΣ
καὶ μὴν πρόχειρον αἵδε σοι σκυλευμάτων
Φρυγίων φέρουσι κόσμον ἐξάπτειν νεκρῷ.

1188 τε κοινοὶ Munro: τ᾽ ἐκεῖνοι C
1203–4 πράσσων δοκεῖ . . . χαίρειν Bothe

you are not burying me but I am burying you, who are younger, I an old woman with no city or children and you an unlucky corpse. Ah me, those countless kisses, my care for you, the slumbers we shared, all are gone for nought! What could a poet write upon your tomb? "This child the Argives killed upon a time—in terror"? The epitaph brings disgrace upon Greece. Yet though you lost your patrimony, you will still have your father's bronze-backed shield, in which you will be buried.

O shield that preserved Hector's fair arm, you have lost your best guardian! How lovely is the mark of his body upon your strap and the sweat on your well-turned rim, sweat which Hector often in his toil dripped from his forehead as he pressed you against his chin! Come, all of you, bring adornment for this poor dead boy from what you have! Our fate does not allow us to be lavish. But from my store this is what you shall receive.

That man is a fool who imagines he is firmly prosperous and is glad. For in its very nature fortune, like a crazed man, leaps now in one direction, now in another, and the same man is never fortunate forever.

Atttendants of Hecuba bring from the tent adornment for Astyanax' body.

CHORUS LEADER

See, these women are bringing you from the spoils of Troy some ready adornment to deck the corpse.

1206 κοὔποθ' αὐτὸς εὐτυχὴς ἀεί Barthold
1207 πρόχειρον Wecklein: πρὸ χειρῶν C

127

ΕΚΑΒΗ

ὦ τέκνον, οὐχ ἵπποισι νικήσαντά σε
1210 οὐδ' ἥλικας τόξοισιν, οὓς Φρύγες νόμους
τιμῶσιν, †οὐκ ἐς πλησμονὰς θηρώμενοι†,
μήτηρ πατρός σοι προστίθησ' ἀγάλματα
τῶν σῶν ποτ' ὄντων· νῦν δέ σ' ἡ θεοστυγὴς
ἀφείλεθ' Ἑλένη, πρὸς δὲ καὶ ψυχὴν σέθεν
1215 ἔκτεινε καὶ πάντ' οἶκον ἐξαπώλεσεν.

ΧΟΡΟΣ

ἒ ἔ, φρενῶν
ἔθιγες ἔθιγες, ὦ μέγας ἐμοί ποτ' ὢν
ἀνάκτωρ πόλεως.

ΕΚΑΒΗ

ἃ δ' ἐν γάμοισι χρῆν σε προσθέσθαι χροΐ
Ἀσιατίδων γήμαντα τὴν ὑπερτάτην,
1220 Φρύγια πέπλων ἀγάλματ' ἐξάπτω χροός.
σύ τ', ὦ ποτ' οὖσα καλλίνικε μυρίων
μῆτερ τροπαίων, Ἕκτορος φίλον σάκος,
στεφανοῦ· θανῇ γὰρ οὐ θανοῦσα σὺν νεκρῷ·
ἐπεὶ σὲ πολλῷ μᾶλλον ἢ τὰ τοῦ σοφοῦ
1225 κακοῦ τ' Ὀδυσσέως ἄξιον τιμᾶν ὅπλα.

ΧΟΡΟΣ

αἰαῖ αἰαῖ·
πικρὸν ὄδυρμα γαῖά σ', ὦ
τέκνον, δέξεται.
στέναζε, μᾶτερ . . .

1211 τιμῶσι, νείκους Eden   1212 προστίθημ' Herwerden

Hecuba adorns the body of Astyanax.

HECUBA

Child, it is not for a victory in horsemanship or bowcraft over your agemates—practices the Phrygians honor from a desire to sate the spirit of rancor[39]—that I, your father's mother, place these adornments on you from what was once your own wealth. In reality, the god-detested Helen has taken it all away and in addition has destroyed your life and utterly ruined the entire house.

CHORUS

Ah, ah! My heart
you have touched, have touched, you who were once in my eyes
the city's lord![40]

HECUBA

The Phrygian finery you should have put on for your marriage, as you wed the noblest princess of Asia, I put about your body. And you, beloved shield of Hector, that were once glorious mother of countless victories, receive this garland! For you shall perish with this dead boy, and yet you do not die. It is far better to honor you than the arms of the clever but cowardly Odysseus.

CHORUS

Ah, ah!
As a bitter object of lamentation the earth
shall receive you, my child.
Utter aloud, mother, the groan . . .

---

39 I translate Eden's attractive but uncertain conjecture.
40 The etymology of his name is "lord of the city."

ΕΚΑΒΗ

αἰαῖ.

ΧΟΡΟΣ

1230 νεκρῶν ἴακχον.

ΕΚΑΒΗ

οἴμοι.

ΧΟΡΟΣ

οἴμοι δῆτα σῶν ἀλάστων κακῶν.

ΕΚΑΒΗ

τελαμῶσιν ἕλκη τὰ μὲν ἐγώ σ᾽ ἰάσομαι,
τλήμων ἰατρός, ὄνομ᾽ ἔχουσα, τἄργα δ᾽ οὔ·
τὰ δ᾽ ἐν νεκροῖσι φροντιεῖ πατὴρ σέθεν.

ΧΟΡΟΣ

1235 ἄρασσ᾽ ἄρασσε κρᾶτα πιτύ-
λους διδοῦσα χειρός,
ἰώ μοί μοι.

ΕΚΑΒΗ

ὦ φίλταται γυναῖκες . . .

ΧΟΡΟΣ

†Ἑκάβη, σὰς† ἔνεπε· τίνα θροεῖς αὐδάν;

ΕΚΑΒΗ

1240 †οὐκ ἦν ἄρ᾽ ἐν θεοῖσι† πλὴν οὑμοὶ πόνοι
Τροία τε πόλεων ἔκκριτον μισουμένη,

1235 κρᾶτα Bothe, Seidler: χειρὶ κρᾶτα C

HECUBA

Ah me!

CHORUS

. . . of lament for the dead!

HECUBA

Alas!

CHORUS

Yes, alas for your miseries none may forget!

HECUBA

With constricting bands I shall treat some of your wounds, a poor physician, having the name of doctor but not the work. The others your father will care for in the Underworld.

CHORUS

Strike, strike your heads,
moving your hands in rhythm!
Ah me!

HECUBA

O dearest women . . .

CHORUS

Hecuba, tell us: what is it you are uttering?

HECUBA

The gods, as we now see, had nothing in view but my misery and their hatred of Troy beyond all other cities. Our

---

1238-9 fort. lacuna laborant hi vv.
1239 θαρσήσασ᾽ Hermann: σιγώσαις Willink
1240 fort. οὐκ ἦν ἄρ᾽ ⟨οὐδ⟩ὲν θεοῖσι

μάτην δ' ἐβουθυτοῦμεν. εἰ δὲ μὴ θεὸς
ἔστρεψε τἄνω περιβαλὼν κάτω χθονός,
ἀφανεῖς ἂν ὄντες οὐκ ἂν ὑμνήθημεν ἂν
1245 μούσαις ἀοιδὰς δόντες ὑστέρων βροτῶν.
   χωρεῖτε, θάπτετ' ἀθλίῳ τύμβῳ νεκρόν·
ἔχει γὰρ οἷα δεῖ γε νερτέρων στέφη.
δοκῶ δὲ τοῖς θανοῦσι διαφέρειν βραχὺ
εἰ πλουσίων τις τεύξεται κτερισμάτων·
1250 κενὸν δὲ γαύρωμ' ἐστὶ τῶν ζώντων τόδε.

ΧΟΡΟΣ

ἰὼ ἰώ·
μελέα μῆτερ, ἢ τὰς μεγάλας
ἐλπίδας ἐν σοὶ κατέκναψε βίου.
μέγα δ' ὀλβισθεὶς ὡς ἐκ πατέρων
ἀγαθῶν ἐγένου
1255 δεινῷ θανάτῳ διόλωλας.
ἔα ἔα·
τίνας Ἰλιάσιν τούσδ' ἐν κορυφαῖς
λεύσσω φλογέας δαλοῖσι χέρας
διερέσσοντας; μέλλει Τροίᾳ
καινόν τι κακὸν προσέσεσθαι.

ΤΑΛΘΥΒΙΟΣ

1260 αὐδῶ λοχαγοῖς, οἳ τέταχθ' ἐμπιμπράναι
Πριάμου τόδ' ἄστυ, μηκέτ' ἀργοῦσαν φλόγα
ἐν χειρὶ σῴζειν ἀλλὰ πῦρ ἐνιέναι,
ὡς ἂν κατασκάψαντες Ἰλίου πόλιν
στελλώμεθ' οἴκαδ' ἄσμενοι Τροίας ἄπο.

sacrificing was for nothing. But if the divinity had not over-turned things, putting what was above ground below, we would have been unknown and not have been sung of, nor provided a theme for song to the Muses of men to come.

Go, bury the dead boy in his wretched grave! For he has all the funeral adornment that he needs. I think it makes little difference to the dead whether they get a lavish funeral. That is merely idle display by the living.

Attendants carry the body of Astyanax off by Eisodos B.

CHORUS LEADER

Ah, ah! Unhappy mother, whose high hopes for your life have been wrecked! You, child, though greatly blessed in your noble birth, have perished by a terrible death!

But look! Who are these men I see on the heights of Troy waving hands that gleam with torches? Some new disaster is about to be added to Troy's woes.

Enter by Eisodos A TALTHYBIUS with retinue.

TALTHYBIUS

(*shouting to men imagined on the city wall behind the* skene) Captains, who have been assigned to burn this city of Priam, no longer keep the flame idle in your hands but hurl it, so that when we have destroyed Ilium we may set off for home with glad hearts!

1242 δὲ μὴ Stephanus: δ' ἡμᾶς C   1244 ὑμνηθεῖμεν Hermann   1245 ὑστέρων Wecklein: ὑστέραν C
1252 ἐν Porson: ἐπὶ C   1256 τούσδ' Lenting: ταῖσδ' C

133

1265　ὑμεῖς δ᾽, ἵν᾽ αὐτὸς λόγος ἔχῃ μορφὰς δύο,
χωρεῖτε, Τρώων παῖδες, ὀρθίαν ὅταν
σάλπιγγος ἠχὼ δῶσιν ἀρχηγοὶ στρατοῦ,
πρὸς ναῦς Ἀχαιῶν, ὡς ἀποστέλλησθε γῆς.
σύ τ᾽, ὦ γεραιὰ δυστυχεστάτη γύναι,
1270　ἕπου. μεθήκουσίν σ᾽ Ὀδυσσέως πάρα
οἵδ᾽, ᾧ σε δούλην κλῆρος ἐκπέμπει πάτρας.

ΕΚΑΒΗ

οἲ ᾽γὼ τάλαινα· τοῦτο δὴ τὸ λοίσθιον
καὶ τέρμα πάντων τῶν ἐμῶν ἤδη κακῶν·
ἔξειμι πατρίδος, πόλις ὑφάπτεται πυρί.
1275　ἀλλ᾽, ὦ γεραιὲ πούς, ἐπίσπευσον μόλις,
ὡς ἀσπάσωμαι τὴν ταλαίπωρον πόλιν.
ὦ μεγάλα δή ποτ᾽ ἀμπνέουσ᾽ ἐν βαρβάροις
Τροία, τὸ κλεινὸν ὄνομ᾽ ἀφαιρήσῃ τάχα.
πιμπρᾶσί σ᾽, ἡμᾶς δ᾽ ἐξάγουσ᾽ ἤδη χθονὸς
1280　δούλας· ἰὼ θεοί. καὶ τί τοὺς θεοὺς καλῶ;
καὶ πρὶν γὰρ οὐκ ἤκουσαν ἀνακαλούμενοι.
φέρ᾽ ἐς πυρὰν δράμωμεν· ὡς κάλλιστά μοι
σὺν τῇδε πατρίδι κατθανεῖν πυρουμένῃ.

ΤΑΛΘΥΒΙΟΣ

ἐνθουσιᾷς, δύστηνε, τοῖς σαυτῆς κακοῖς.
1285　ἀλλ᾽ ἄγετε, μὴ φείδεσθ᾽· Ὀδυσσέως δὲ χρὴ
ἐς χεῖρα δοῦναι τήνδε καὶ πέμπειν γέρας.

στρ. α

ΕΚΑΒΗ

ὀτοτοτοτοῖ.

But as for you, daughters of Troy, so that my one order may have two parts, when the leaders of the expedition sound a shrill trumpet blast, depart for the Achaean ships so that you may leave the country. And you, old woman most unfortunate, follow me. These men have come from Odysseus to fetch you, for the allotment has made you his slave as it sends you from your homeland.

HECUBA

Ah unhappy me! This is the endpoint of all my sufferings! I am leaving my country, and my city is being set ablaze! So, aged feet, hasten with halting tread so that I may say farewell to this unlucky city.

Troy, who were once so proud among the barbarian peoples, soon you will be deprived of your famous name! They are burning you, and they lead us away from the land as slaves. Hear me, you gods! But why do I call upon the gods? They did not listen before when we called upon them.

Come let us rush into the pyre! It is noblest to die together with this land of ours as it burns!

TALTHYBIUS

You are out of your mind, poor woman, with your misfortune. (*to his retinue*) Come take her, no delaying. You must hand her over to Odysseus, delivering him his prize.

HECUBA

O woe!

1269 δ' Blaydes, fort. recte
1273 τῶν ἐμῶν ἤδη Musgrave: ἤδη τ- ἐ- C

Κρόνιε, πρύτανι Φρύγιε, γενέτα
[πάτερ, ἀνάξια τῆς Δαρδάνου]
1290 γονᾶς, τάδ᾽ οἷα πάσχομεν δέδορκας;

ΧΟΡΟΣ
δέδορκεν, ἁ δὲ μεγαλόπολις
ἄπολις ὄλωλεν οὐδ᾽ ἔτ᾽ ἔστι Τροία.

ἀντ. α

ΕΚΑΒΗ
ὀτοτοτοτοῖ.
1295 λέλαμπεν Ἰλίοιο περ-
γάμων τε πυρὶ τέραμν᾽ ἄκρα τε τειχέων.

ΧΟΡΟΣ
πτέρυγι δὲ καπνὸς ὥς τις οὐ-
ρίᾳ πεσοῦσα δορὶ καταφθίνει γᾷ.
1300 [μαλερὰ μέλαθρα πυρὶ κατάδρομα
δαΐῳ τε λόγχᾳ.]

στρ. β

ΕΚΑΒΗ
ἰὼ γᾶ τρόφιμε τῶν ἐμῶν τέκνων.

ΧΟΡΟΣ
ἒ ἔ.

ΕΚΑΒΗ
ὦ τέκεα, κλύετε, μάθετε ματρὸς αὐδάν.

ΧΟΡΟΣ
ἰαλέμῳ τοὺς θανόντας ἀπύεις.

Son of Kronos, lord of Phrygia, father
of our race, do you see what things we suffer?

CHORUS

He sees. But the great city
is now no city and has perished. Troy is no more.

HECUBA

O woe!
The houses and high peak of Ilium and its fortress
are glowing with flame!

CHORUS

Like smoke upon a following breeze
our land, fallen to the spear, wastes away.
[The wild dwellings are overrun by fire
and by the spear of the enemy.]

HECUBA

O land, nurse of my children!

CHORUS

Alas!

HECUBA

My children, hear, listen to your mother's voice!

CHORUS

It is the dead you address with your cry of lament.

1289 secl. Willink   1295 Ἰλίοιο Willink: Ἴλιος C
1296 πυρὶ Willink post Diggle, scholiorum silentio fretus: πυρὶ
καταίθεται C   τέραμν' Hartung: τέραμνα καὶ πόλις C
1298–9 οὐρίᾳ Wilamowitz: οὐρανίᾳ C
1300-1 secl. Diggle   1303 τέκεα West: τέκνα C

ΕΚΑΒΗ

1305 γεραιά γ' ἐς πέδον μέλεα
τιθεῖσα καὶ χερσὶ γαῖ-
αν κτυποῦσα δισσαῖς.

ΧΟΡΟΣ

διάδοχά σοι γόνυ τίθημι γαίᾳ
τοὺς ἐμοὺς καλοῦσα νέρ-
θεν ἀθλίους ἀκοίτας.

ΕΚΑΒΗ

1310 ἀγόμεθα φερόμεθ' . . .

ΧΟΡΟΣ

ἄλγος ἄλγος βοᾷς.

ΕΚΑΒΗ

. . . δούλειον ὑπὸ μέλαθρον.

ΧΟΡΟΣ

ἐκ πάτρας γ' ἐμᾶς.

ΕΚΑΒΗ

ἰὼ ἰώ, Πρίαμε Πρίαμε,
σὺ μὲν ὀλόμενος ἄταφος ἄφιλος
ἄτας ἐμᾶς ἄιστος εἶ.

ΧΟΡΟΣ

1315 μέλας γὰρ ὄσσε κατεκάλυ-
ψε θάνατος ὅσιος ἀνοσίοις σφαγαῖσιν.

1305 γ' Seidler: τ' C   1305–6 μέλεα τιθεῖσα West: τ- μ- C
1307 διάδοχά Dindorf: -όν C
1316 ἀνοσίοις L. Dindorf: -αις C

HECUBA

Yes, as I let my aged limbs sink to the ground
and strike the earth
with my two hands.

*Hecuba beats the ground with her hands. The Chorus go
down upon their knees.*

CHORUS

Taking up your lament I kneel upon the earth
and call up from below
my poor husband.

HECUBA

We are taken away, borne off . . .

CHORUS

It is grief, grief, that you utter!

HECUBA

. . . to a house of slavery!

CHORUS

Yes, away from my homeland!

HECUBA

Oh, oh, Priam, Priam!
You have perished without a grave, without a friend,
and have no knowledge of my destruction!

CHORUS

Yes, for in blackness his eyes are covered
by death the holy, amid unholy slaughter.

ἀντ. β

ΕΚΑΒΗ

ἰὼ θεῶν μέλαθρα καὶ πόλις φίλα . . .

ΧΟΡΟΣ

ἒ ἔ.

ΕΚΑΒΗ

. . . τὰν φόνιον ἔχετε φλόγα δορός τε λόγχαν.

ΧΟΡΟΣ

τάχ᾽ ἐς φίλαν γᾶν πεσεῖσθ᾽ ἀνώνυμοι.

ΕΚΑΒΗ

1320 κόνις δ᾽ ἴσα καπνῷ πτέρυγι
πρὸς αἰθέρ᾽ ἄιστον οἴ-
κων ἐμῶν με θήσει.

ΧΟΡΟΣ

ὄνομα δὲ γᾶς ἀφανὲς εἶσιν· ἄλλᾳ δ᾽
ἄλλο φροῦδον, οὐδ᾽ ἔτ᾽ ἔ-
στιν ἁ τάλαινα Τροία.

ΕΚΑΒΗ

1325 ἐμάθετ᾽, ἐκλύετε;

ΧΟΡΟΣ

περγάμων ⟨γε⟩ κτύπον.

ΕΚΑΒΗ

ἔνοσις ἅπασαν ἔνοσις . . .

1320 καπνοῦ Seidler

HECUBA

O temples of the gods and city I love . . .

CHORUS

Alas!

HECUBA

. . . your fate is the murderous flame and the spear point!

CHORUS

Soon you will fall down to the beloved earth and be without a name.

HECUBA

Dust, like smoke winging
to the sky, shall take away the thought
of my home.

CHORUS

The land's name shall be wiped out! In one place
one thing, in another another vanishes away,
and poor Troy is no more!

HECUBA

Did you mark, did you hear?

CHORUS

Yes, the crashing of the towers.

HECUBA

With quaking, quaking the whole . . .

1320–1 αἰθέρ᾽ ᾆσσουσ᾽ ἄοικον δόμων West
1325 ⟨γε⟩ Seidler

ΧΟΡΟΣ

ἐπικλύζει πόλιν.

ΕΚΑΒΗ

ἰὼ ⟨ἰώ⟩, τρομερὰ τρομερὰ
μέλεα, φέρετ᾽ ἐμὸν ἴχνος· ἴτ᾽ ἐπὶ
1330 δούλειον ἀμέραν βίου.

ΧΟΡΟΣ

ἰὼ τάλαινα πόλις· ὅμως
δὲ πρόφερε πόδα σὸν ἐπὶ πλάτας Ἀχαιῶν.

1326 ἐπικλύζει Burges: -κλύσει C
1327 ⟨ἰώ⟩ Kirchhoff

CHORUS

>. . . city is overrun.

HECUBA

Oh, ⟨oh,⟩ trembling trembling
limbs, march me forward! Go to
your life's day of slavery!

CHORUS

Alas, unhappy city! Yet
go forward now to the ships of the Achaeans.

Exit by Eisodos A HECUBA, TALTHYBIUS *with retinue,
and* CHORUS.

IPHIGENIA AMONG THE
TAURIANS

INTRODUCTION

To most modern readers, a tragedy with a happy ending is a contradiction in terms: if promised a tragedy we expect to see a play like *Oedipus* or *Hamlet,* in which the characters we have come to care about are dead or in misery at the end of the play. In antiquity there was no such firm expectation, and tragic poets not rarely produced as *tragoidiai* plays where the sympathetic characters, after a harrowing escape, reach safety and the prospect of lasting happiness. In the fifth century *tragoidia,* unlike "tragedy" in English, meant a dramatic representation of the deeds of heroes of myth, in contrast to a *komoidia* (comedy), which is about ordinary characters in the present day. (The only dramatizations of myth that fall outside the category *tragoidia* are satyr plays like *Cyclops.*) In his *Poetics* Aristotle cites *Iphigenia among the Taurians* almost as many times as he cites *Oedipus the King* to show what a tragic dramatist can and should do.

In Aristotle's view, the tragic dramatist tries to generate in his audience the tragic emotions of pity and fear by means of a *pathos,* a deed of violence, usually between close kin. In a play like *Oedipus* this deed of violence has taken place before the opening of the play, and Oedipus discovers that it was his father whom he killed on the road to Thebes. This discovery or recognition (*anagnorisis*) brings about a *peripeteia* or swift change of fortune as Oedipus realizes that he has committed a horrible crime and is the most unblest of men. But Aristotle recognizes that there is another way to achieve the tragic emotions: dramatize a situation in which the deed of violence between kin is on the point of happening but is in the end avoided. Though Aristotle says very little about the "metaphysics" of tragedy, the world view it exhibits, the common element in the two kinds of *tragoidia* would seem to be that both sorts of play demonstrate the radical uncertainty of human life, the limitations of mortal knowledge, and man's dependence on the power of the gods.

In a play like *Oedipus* we see the malignity of Apollo, who is determined to bring to an end the cursed race of Laius and whose management of circumstances known to him but not to the characters is breathtakingly cruel. In the other sort of play the gods operate, overtly or covertly, to bring about rescue and blessing for the principal characters. That is what happens in *Iphigenia among the Taurians*.

The story of the sacrifice of Agamemnon's daughter Iphigenia to Artemis to calm the adverse winds holding the Greek fleet at Aulis was either unknown to or (more likely) suppressed by Homer, who mentions Agamemnon's three daughters, Chrysothemis, Laodice, and Iphianassa as still alive in the ninth year of the Trojan War. It first appears (in extant works) in Aeschylus' *Agamemnon*, where the Chorus describe the terrible choice of Agamemnon (be a "deserter" and call off the expedition or sacrifice his daughter) and the ruinous consequences the sacrifice had for him in the hatred of his wife Clytaemestra. Other tragic poets, including both Sophocles in his *Electra* and Euripides in his

147

Electra and *Iphigenia at Aulis*, allude to or dramatize this version of the story.

But there was early on a different version. In the lost *Cypria*, a poem of the so-called Epic Cycle (seventh or sixth century B.C.), Artemis spirits Iphigenia away to the land of the Taurians (the modern Crimea), where she makes her immortal. (There are indications that Iphigenia was originally the name of a goddess, identified with Artemis herself. We will see that there is a cult of her in Attica.) This is the version Euripides adopts, though he makes her not a goddess but the priestess of the Taurian Artemis. She serves the goddess by consecrating for sacrifice any foreigners who land in this region. We know from Herodotus 4.103 that the Taurians performed human sacrifice to a goddess they called The Virgin.

It was probably Euripides who connected this story of Iphigenia with the end of the troubles of the house of Atreus, the house of her father Agamemnon. Orestes, son of Agamemnon and brother of Iphigenia, had killed his mother Clytaemestra in obedience to an oracle of Apollo. In Aeschylus' version of this story, adopted elswhere by Euripides, Orestes, pursued by the Erinyes, is acquitted by the court of the Areopagus in Athens and returns to Argos to rule in peace, unmolested by the Erinyes. In *Iphigenia among the Taurians* he is still being pursued by some of the Erinyes who are not satisfied with the verdict, and Apollo prophesies that he will win final release only if he goes to the land of the Taurians, steals the statue of Artemis, and takes it to a new home in Greece. So in obedience to Apollo Orestes, whom Iphigenia has not seen since he was a baby, sails to the Taurian land, is captured by the Taurians, and is on the point of being sacrificed by the

Greek priestess when a chance series of events causes him to learn that the woman is his sister. He reveals himself, and the two form and carry out a plot for escaping from the land of the Taurians with the statue.

In both *Oedipus* and *Iphigenia* Apollo has a crucial role, and in both the god brings about the result he desires by surprising means. In *Oedipus* Apollo foretells to Oedipus that he will kill his father and marry his mother. Oedipus, in order to avoid this result, leaves his supposed father and mother, Polybus and Merope, in Corinth and sets out on the road on which his father is traveling and where he will kill him, a road that will lead him to Thebes and marriage with his mother. Just before his discovery of the truth, it looks to him and to Jocasta as if the oracle to him and another to Laius that he would be killed by his son have failed to come true. But in two swift scenes the awful truth is brought to light. In *Iphigenia* Apollo is acting to save, not to ruin, but here too up until near the end it seems that his oracular pronouncement has led Orestes astray. Unable to steal the statue, captured and brought as a prisoner to the temple of Artemis, and on the point of being sacrificed, he concludes that Apollo has betrayed him and that his death is inevitable. But when he learns that the priestess is his sister, in an instant he sees that the hand of heaven has been at work.

At the end of the play the goddess Athena appears to assure the escape of Orestes, Iphigenia, and the Greek women of the Chorus. As the gods at the ends of Euripides' plays frequently do, she connects the events of the play with the religious observances of the poet's own day. There was a cult of Artemis Tauropolos in the Attic deme of Halai where a kind of mock human sacrifice took place at the yearly festival: the neck of a man was grazed so as to draw blood. This, says Athena, is in memory of Orestes' near sacrifice. Rites in honor of Iphigenia will also be celebrated at the Attic deme of Brauron. Thus the Athenians are reminded by their own rituals of the radical insecurity of human life dramatized by the play they have just seen.

SELECT BIBLIOGRAPHY

Editions

E. B. England (London, 1883).

M. Platnauer (Oxford, 1938).

D. Sansone (Leipzig, 1981).

M. Cropp (Warminster, forthcoming).

Literary Criticism

E. A. Belfiore, "Aristotle and Iphigenia," in *Essays on Aristotle's Poetics*, ed. A. O. Rorty (Princeton, 1992), pp. 359-77.

A. P. Burnett, *Catastrophe Survived: Euripides' Plays of Mixed Reversal* (Oxford, 1971), pp. 47-75.

D. Kovacs, "The End of the *Iphigenia in Tauris*," forthcoming.

D. Sansone, "The Sacrifice-Motif in Euripides' *IT*," *TAPA* 105 (1975), 283-95.

Cedric H. Whitman, *Euripides and the Full Circle of Myth* (Cambridge, Mass., 1974), pp. 1-34.

ΙΦΙΓΕΝΕΙΑ	IPHIGENIA, daughter of Agamemnon, sister of Orestes
ΟΡΕΣΤΗΣ	ORESTES, son of Agamemnon and Clytaemestra
ΠΥΛΑΔΗΣ	PYLADES, Orestes' friend
ΧΟΡΟΣ	CHORUS of Greek women, slaves of Iphigenia
ΒΟΥΚΟΛΟΣ	HERDSMAN
ΘΟΑΣ	THOAS, King of the Taurians
ΑΓΓΕΛΟΣ	Servant of Thoas as MESSENGER
ΑΘΗΝΑ	ATHENA

A Note on Staging

The *skene* represents the temple of Artemis in the land of the Taurians. Eisodos A leads to the seashore, Eisodos B to the palace of Thoas.

ΙΦΙΓΕΝΕΙΑ Η ΕΝ ΤΑΥΡΟΙΣ

ΙΦΙΓΕΝΕΙΑ

Πέλοψ ὁ Ταντάλειος ἐς Πῖσαν μολὼν
θοαῖσιν ἵπποις Οἰνομάου γαμεῖ κόρην,
ἐξ ἧς Ἀτρεὺς ἔβλαστεν· Ἀτρέως δὲ παῖς
Μενέλαος Ἀγαμέμνων τε· τοῦ δ' ἔφυν ἐγώ,
5 τῆς Τυνδαρείας θυγατρὸς Ἰφιγένεια παῖς,
ἣν ἀμφὶ δίνας ἃς θάμ' Εὔριπος πυκναῖς
αὔραις ἑλίσσων κυανέαν ἅλα στρέφει
ἔσφαξεν Ἑλένης οὕνεχ', ὡς δοκεῖ, πατὴρ
Ἀρτέμιδι κλειναῖς ἐν πτυχαῖσιν Αὐλίδος.
10 ἐνταῦθα γὰρ δὴ χιλίων νεῶν στόλον
Ἑλληνικὸν συνήγαγ' Ἀγαμέμνων ἄναξ,
τὸν καλλίνικον στέφανον Ἰλίου θέλων
λαβεῖν Ἀχαιοῖς τούς θ' ὑβρισθέντας γάμους
Ἑλένης μετελθεῖν, Μενέλεῳ χάριν φέρων.

6 δίνας Monk: δίναις L
13 Ἀχαιοῖς Lenting: -οὺς L

---

1 Oenomaus, king of Pisa in the northern Peloponnese, chal-
lenged his daughter's suitors to a race in which they rode off with
the daughter and he killed them if they could not outrace his

IPHIGENIA AMONG THE
TAURIANS

Enter IPHIGENIA *from the* skene, *which represents the temple of Artemis in the Tauric Chersonese. Nearby is an altar from whose top edge hang either the weapons or the skulls of the goddess' victims.*

IPHIGENIA

Pelops the son of Tantalus went to Pisa and with his swift horses won as his bride the daughter of Oenomaus. [1] She gave birth to Atreus, whose sons in turn were Menelaus and Agamemnon. It is from this last that I was begotten, I, Iphigenia, daughter of Tyndareus' daughter Clytaemestra. Near the eddies which the Euripus with its frequent breezes sets rolling, churning up the dark-blue sea, my father sacrificed me—so it is believed—to Artemis for Helen's sake in the famous clefts of Aulis.

It was there that King Agamemnon had gathered together the Greek fleet, a thousand strong, desiring to win for the Achaeans the glorious crown of victory over Troy and to gratify Menelaus by punishing the outrage done to

chariot. In one version of the story, Pelops succeeds by trickery, bribing Oenomaus' charioteer to replace his lynch pins with ones of wax.

15 δεινῇ δ᾽ ἀπλοίᾳ πνευμάτων τ᾽ οὐ τυγχάνων
ἐς ἔμπυρ᾽ ἦλθε, καὶ λέγει Κάλχας τάδε·
ᾮ τῆσδ᾽ ἀνάσσων Ἑλλάδος στρατηγίας,
Ἀγάμεμνον, οὐ μὴ ναῦς ἀφορμίσῃς χθονὸς
πρὶν ἂν κόρην σὴν Ἰφιγένειαν Ἄρτεμις
20 λάβῃ σφαγεῖσαν· ὅ τι γὰρ ἐνιαυτὸς τέκοι
κάλλιστον, ηὔξω φωσφόρῳ θύσειν θεᾷ.
παῖδ᾽ οὖν ἐν οἴκοις σὴ Κλυταιμήστρα δάμαρ
τίκτει—τὸ καλλιστεῖον εἰς ἔμ᾽ ἀναφέρων—
ἣν χρή σε θῦσαι. καί μ᾽ Ὀδυσσέως τέχναις
25 μητρὸς παρείλοντ᾽ ἐπὶ γάμοις Ἀχιλλέως.
ἐλθοῦσα δ᾽ Αὐλίδ᾽ ἡ τάλαιν᾽ ὑπὲρ πυρᾶς
μεταρσία ληφθεῖσ᾽ ἐκαινόμην ξίφει.
ἀλλ᾽ ἐξέκλεψεν ἔλαφον ἀντιδοῦσά μου
Ἄρτεμις Ἀχαιοῖς, διὰ δὲ λαμπρὸν αἰθέρα
30 πέμψασά μ᾽ ἐς τήνδ᾽ ᾤκισεν Ταύρων χθόνα,
οὗ γῆς ἀνάσσει βαρβάροισι βάρβαρος
Θόας, ὃς ὠκὺν πόδα τιθεὶς ἴσον πτεροῖς
ἐς τοὔνομ᾽ ἦλθε τόδε ποδωκείας χάριν.
ναοῖσι δ᾽ ἐν τοῖσδ᾽ ἱερέαν τίθησί με·
35 ὅθεν νόμοισιν οἷσιν ἥδεται θεὰ
Ἄρτεμις ἑορτῆς, τοὔνομ᾽ ἧς καλὸν μόνον
(τὰ δ᾽ ἄλλα σιγῶ, τὴν θεὸν φοβουμένη),
[θύω γὰρ ὄντος τοῦ νόμου καὶ πρὶν πόλει]

---

15 δεινῇ . . . ἀπλοίᾳ Rauchenstein: δεινῆς . . . ἀπλοίας L
18 ἀφορμίσῃς Kirchhoff: -ίσῃ L
35 νόμοισιν οἷσιν Herwerden: νόμοισι τοῖσιδ᾽ L

154

his marriage with Helen. But sailing was bad and he did not get the right winds and, when he turned to burnt offerings,[2] Calchas told him, "Agamemnon, lord of Hellas' high command, never will you unmoor your ships from this land until Artemis receives your daughter Iphigenia as her slaughtered victim. You vowed to the light-bearing goddess[3] that you would sacrifice the fairest thing the year brought forth. Well, your wife Clytaemestra is mother of a child in your house," said he, giving the title of fairest to me, "and you must sacrifice her." They took me from my mother to be married to Achilles: this was Odysseus' ruse. But when I reached Aulis, they held me aloft in my misery over the sacrificial hearth and put me to the sword. Yet Artemis stole me away, giving the Greeks a deer in my place. Conveying me through the bright heaven she settled me here in the land of the Taurians, where Thoas rules, barbarian king of a barbarian folk. (He came into his name[4] because of his swift-footedness, for he runs with the speed of wings.) In this temple she has made me priestess. And therefore in accordance with the custom in which the goddess Artemis delights, the custom of the feast whose name alone is fair (its other aspects I pass over in silence for fear of the goddess) [I sacrifice, since this was also formerly the

[2] I. e. divination by the burning of entrails.

[3] Artemis is called "light-bearing" because she carries torches when she hunts at night. The vow to her was made in the year of Iphigenia's birth.

[4] Thoas is here derived from θοός, "swift."

---

38 del. Koechly

ὃς ἂν κατέλθῃ τήνδε γῆν Ἕλλην ἀνὴρ
40 κατάρχομαι μέν, σφάγια δ᾿ ἄλλοισιν μέλει
[ἄρρητ᾿ ἔσωθεν τῶνδ᾿ ἀνακτόρων θεᾶς].
  ἃ καινὰ δ᾿ ἥκει νὺξ φέρουσα φάσματα
λέξω πρὸς αἰθέρ᾿, εἴ τι δὴ τόδ᾿ ἔστ᾿ ἄκος.
ἔδοξ᾿ ἐν ὕπνῳ τῆσδ᾿ ἀπαλλαχθεῖσα γῆς
45 οἰκεῖν ἐν Ἄργει, παρθενῶσι δ᾿ ἐν μέσοις
εὕδειν, χθονὸς δὲ νῶτα σεισθῆναι σάλῳ,
φεύγειν δὲ κἄξω στᾶσα θριγκὸν εἰσιδεῖν
δόμων πίτνοντα, πᾶν δ᾿ ἐρείψιμον στέγος
βεβλημένον πρὸς οὖδας ἐξ ἄκρων σταθμῶν.
50 μόνος δ᾿ ἐλείφθη στῦλος, ὡς ἔδοξέ μοι,
δόμων πατρῴων, ἐκ δ᾿ ἐπικράνων κόμας
ξανθὰς καθεῖναι, φθέγμα δ᾿ ἀνθρώπου λαβεῖν,
κἀγὼ τέχνην τήνδ᾿ ἣν ἔχω ξενοκτόνον
τιμῶσ᾿ ὑδραίνειν αὐτὸν ὡς θανούμενον,
55 κλαίουσα. τοὔναρ δ᾿ ὧδε συμβάλλω τόδε·
τέθνηκ᾿ Ὀρέστης, οὗ κατηρξάμην ἐγώ.
στῦλοι γὰρ οἴκων παῖδές εἰσιν ἄρσενες,
θνῄσκουσι δ᾿ οὓς ἂν χέρνιβες βάλωσ᾿ ἐμαί.
[οὐδ᾿ αὖ συνάψαι τοὔναρ ἐς φίλους ἔχω·
60 Στροφίῳ γὰρ οὐκ ἦν παῖς, ὅτ᾿ ὠλλύμην ἐγώ.]
  νῦν οὖν ἀδελφῷ βούλομαι δοῦναι χοὰς
ἀποῦσ᾿ ἀπόντι (ταῦτα γὰρ δυναίμεθ᾿ ἄν)
σὺν προσπόλοισιν, ἃς ἔδωχ᾿ ἡμῖν ἄναξ

41 del. Monk
45 παρθενῶσι... μέσοις Markland: παρθένοισι... μέσαις L

custom for the city], I consecrate as victim any Greek who comes to this land, but the slaying is the concern of others [, secret sacrifices within this temple of the goddess].

This night has brought strange visions with it, and I shall tell them to the upper air, if that is indeed any cure for them.[5] I dreamt that I had escaped from this land and lived in Argos, and that as I slept within my maiden chamber the flat expanse of earth began to heave and roll. I fled the house and, when I stood outside, I saw the cornice of the palace topple and all the house, from its column tops down, cast in ruins to the ground. Only one pillar of my ancestral home, it seemed, was left standing, and from its capital it seemed to grow a head of blond hair and to take on human speech. And I, honoring this office I have of killing foreigners, sprinkled it with water to consign it to death, weeping as I did so. This is how I interpret the dream: Orestes is dead—it is he I consecrated for sacrifice—for the pillars of a house are its male children, and those who are sprinkled by my lustral basin are killed. [I cannot refer the dream to relatives, for Strophius had no son when I went to my death.]

Now therefore I want to pour libations as absent sister to my absent brother: this lies in my power. I shall do so with my servants, the Greek women the king gave me. But

5 In ancient belief telling a bad dream to the air at dawn might avert what it portended.

59-60 del. Monk
62 ἀποῦσ᾽ ἀπόντι Badham: παροῦσα παντὶ L

Ἑλληνίδας γυναῖκας. ἀλλ᾽ ἐξ αἰτίας
65 οὔπω τινὸς πάρεισιν· εἰμ᾽ ἔσω δόμων
ἐν οἷσι ναίω τῶνδ᾽, ἀνακτόρων θεᾶς.

ΟΡΕΣΤΗΣ

ὅρα, φυλάσσου μή τις ἐν στίβῳ βροτῶν.

ΠΥΛΑΔΗΣ

ὁρῶ, σκοποῦμαι δ᾽ ὄμμα πανταχῇ στρέφων.

ΟΡΕΣΤΗΣ

Πυλάδη, δοκεῖ σοι μέλαθρα ταῦτ᾽ εἶναι θεᾶς,
70 ἔνθ᾽ Ἀργόθεν ναῦν ποντίαν ἐστείλαμεν;

ΠΥΛΑΔΗΣ

ἔμοιγ᾽, Ὀρέστα· σοὶ δὲ συνδοκεῖν χρεών.

ΟΡΕΣΤΗΣ

καὶ βωμός, Ἕλλην οὗ καταστάζει φόνος;

ΠΥΛΑΔΗΣ

ἐξ αἱμάτων γοῦν ξάνθ᾽ ἔχει θριγκώματα.

ΟΡΕΣΤΗΣ

θριγκοῖς δ᾽ ὑπ᾽ αὐτοῖς σκῦλ᾽ ὁρᾷς ἠρτημένα;

ΠΥΛΑΔΗΣ

75 τῶν κατθανόντων γ᾽ ἀκροθίνια ξένων.
ἀλλ᾽ ἐγκυκλοῦντ᾽ ὀφθαλμὸν εὖ σκοπεῖν χρεών.

ΟΡΕΣΤΗΣ

ὦ Φοῖβε, ποῖ μ᾽ αὖ τήνδ᾽ ἐς ἄρκυν ἤγαγες

73 θριγκώματα Ruhnken: τριχώ- L
77 τήνδ᾽] fort. τίνα δ᾽

for some reason they have not arrived: I will go back into this house in which I dwell, the goddess' temple.

Exit IPHIGENIA *into the* skene. *Enter* ORESTES *and* PYLADES *by Eisodos A.*

ORESTES
Look carefully to see whether there is anyone on the path.

PYLADES
I'm looking, casting my glance in all directions.

ORESTES
Pylades, do you think this is the goddess' temple, goal of our sea journey from Argos?

PYLADES
I do, Orestes, and you should think so too.

ORESTES
And is this the altar where Greek blood is shed?

PYLADES
Well, its top is blood-stained.

ORESTES
But right under the top, do you see trophies hanging?

PYLADES
Yes, dedicated spoil of foreigners who have been killed.[6] But we must look carefully all around.

ORESTES
O Phoebus, where have you brought me this time by your

---

6 Either Greek weapons or skulls hang from the altar's sides.

χρήσας, ἐπειδὴ πατρὸς αἷμ' ἐτεισάμην
μητέρα κατακτάς; διαδοχαῖς δ' Ἐρινύων
80 ἠλαυνόμεσθα φυγάδες ἔξεδροι χθονὸς
δρόμους τε πολλοὺς ἐξέπλησα καμπίμους·
ἐλθὼν δέ σ' ἠρώτησα πῶς τροχηλάτου
μανίας ἂν ἔλθοιμ' ἐς τέλος πόνων τ' ἐμῶν
[οὓς ἐξεμόχθουν περιπολῶν καθ' Ἑλλάδα]·
85 σὺ δ' εἶπας ἐλθεῖν Ταυρικῆς μ' ὅρους χθονός,
ἔνθ' Ἄρτεμίς σοι σύγγονος βωμοὺς ἔχει,
λαβεῖν τ' ἄγαλμα θεᾶς, ὅ φασιν ἐνθάδε
ἐς τούσδε ναοὺς οὐρανοῦ πεσεῖν ἄπο·
λαβόντα δ' ἢ τέχναισιν ἢ τύχῃ τινί,
90 κίνδυνον ἐκπλήσαντ', Ἀθηναίων χθονὶ
δοῦναι (τὸ δ' ἐνθένδ' οὐδὲν ἐρρήθη πέρα)
καὶ ταῦτα δράσαντ' ἀμπνοὰς ἕξειν πόνων.
ἥκω δὲ πεισθεὶς σοῖς λόγοισιν ἐνθάδε
ἄγνωστος ἐς γῆν ἄξενον. σὲ δ' ἱστορῶ,
95 Πυλάδη (σὺ γάρ μοι τοῦδε συλλήπτωρ πόνου),
τί δρῶμεν; ἀμφίβληστρα γὰρ τοίχων ὁρᾷς
ὑψηλά· πότερα κλιμάκων προσαμβάσεις
ἐμβησόμεσθα; πῶς ἂν οὖν λάθοιμεν ἄν;
ἢ χαλκότευκτα κλῇθρα λύσαντες μοχλοῖς
100 ὧδ' οἶκον ἔσιμεν; ἢν δ' ἀνοίγοντες πύλας
ληφθῶμεν ἐσβάσεις τε μηχανώμενοι,
θανούμεθ'. ἀλλὰ πρὶν θανεῖν νεὼς ἔπι
φεύγωμεν, ᾗπερ δεῦρ' ἐναυστολήσαμεν.

oracles, into what net, since I avenged my father's murder by killing my mother? I was driven from my country as an exile by successive attacks of Erinyes, and many are the circling laps in the race I have run. When I came and asked you how I might reach the end of this whirling madness and my labors, [which I performed wandering about Hellas,] you commanded me to go to the land of the Taurians, where Artemis your sister has an altar, and to take the goddess' statue, which they say fell from the sky into this temple here. You told me to take it either by guile or by some stroke of luck and, when I had completed my dangerous task, to give it to the land of Athens (my orders went no further than this): when I had done so I would receive rest from my labors. Persuaded by your words I have come here as a stranger to this hostile land. But, Pylades, I ask your opinion (for you share this labor with me), what are we to do? You see that the walls on all sides are high. Shall we climb up on ladders? Then how can we avoid being seen? Or shall we pry the bronze doors open with crowbars and thus enter the temple? But if we are caught opening the doors and breaking in, we will be put to death. Rather, before we are killed let's get away on the ship that brought us here!

---

78 ἐπεὶ γὰρ Markland, tum δ'
79 del. Blomfield   84 del. Markland cl. 1455
86 σοι Kirchhoff: σὺ L
87 οὑνθάδε Markland
94 ἄγνωστος Gaisford: -ον L
97 κλιμάκων Kayser: δωμάτων L
98 λάθοιμεν Sallier: μάθ- L
100 ὧδ' οἶκον ἔσιμεν post Badham (ὧδ'... ἔσιμεν) Maehly: ὧν οὐδὲν ἴσμεν L   ante h. v. lac. indic. Holzner

EURIPIDES

ΠΥΛΑΔΗΣ

φεύγειν μὲν οὐκ ἀνεκτὸν οὐδ᾽ εἰώθαμεν,
105 τὸν τοῦ θεοῦ δὲ χρησμὸν οὐκ ἀτιστέον·
ναοῦ δ᾽ ἀπαλλαχθέντε κρύψωμεν δέμας
κατ᾽ ἄντρ᾽ ἃ πόντος νοτίδι διακλύζει μέλας
νεὼς ἄπωθεν, μή τις εἰσιδὼν σκάφος
βασιλεῦσιν εἴπῃ κᾆτα ληφθῶμεν βίᾳ.
110 ὅταν δὲ νυκτὸς ὄμμα λυγαίας μόλῃ,
τολμητέον τοι ξεστὸν ἐκ ναοῦ λαβεῖν
ἄγαλμα πάσας προσφέροντε μηχανάς.
†ὅρα δέ γ᾽ εἴσω τριγλύφων ὅποι κενὸν
δέμας καθεῖναι†· τοὺς πόνους γὰρ ἀγαθοὶ
115 τολμῶσι, δειλοὶ δ᾽ εἰσὶν οὐδὲν οὐδαμοῦ.
οὔτοι μακρὸν μὲν ἤλθομεν κώπῃ πόρον
ἐκ τερμάτων δὲ νόστον ἀροῦμεν πάλιν.

ΟΡΕΣΤΗΣ

ἀλλ᾽ εὖ γὰρ εἶπας, πειστέον· χωρεῖν χρεὼν
ὅποι χθονὸς κρύψαντε λήσομεν δέμας.
120 οὐ γὰρ τὸ τοῦ θεοῦ γ᾽ αἴτιος γενήσομαι
πεσεῖν ἄχρηστον θέσφατον· τολμητέον.
μόχθος γὰρ οὐδεὶς τοῖς νέοις σκῆψιν φέρει.

ΧΟΡΟΣ

εὐφαμεῖτ᾽, ὦ

---

105 οὐκ ἀτιστέον Valckenaer: οὐ κακιστέον L
113-4 post 113 lac. indicandam suspicatus est Platnauer: sed
fort. ὅρα δέ μ᾽ εἴσω τριγλύφων ‹εἰ χρὴ περᾶν / ἀναβάντα
κεράμων τ᾽ ἐξελόνθ᾽› ὅπῃ κενὸν / δέμας καθεῖναι

PYLADES

Running away is not to be endured and is not our custom,
and we must not dishonor the god's oracle. Let's leave the
temple and hide ourselves in a cave washed by the spray of
dark seawater far from the ship. Otherwise someone see-
ing the ship might tell the authorities, and then we would
be taken captive. But when the face of murky night ap-
pears, we must be bold and take the polished statue from
the temple by any means we can. Look, there might be a
way to let ourselves down beyond the triglyphs.[7] The brave
meet challenges, while cowards are never good for any-
thing. We have not rowed such a long way only to reach our
destination and go back home again.

ORESTES

Well, your advice is good, and I must take it. We must go
where we can hide ourselves. It will not be because of me
that the god's oracle is unfulfilled. We must show courage:
no amount of work gives the young an excuse to shirk.

Exit ORESTES *and* PYLADES *by Eisodos A. Enter from
the temple* IPHIGENIA *with attendants and by Eisodos B
Iphigenia's Greek serving women as* CHORUS.

CHORUS

Keep holy silence,

[7] Text uncertain.

116-7 Pyladae contin. Hardion: Orestae trib. L: eosdem
Pyladae tributos post 105 trai. Camper, del. Dindorf

120 αἴτιος γενήσομαι Heath: -ον -σεται L, quibus servatis τὸ
τοῦδέ γ᾽ Weil

πόντου δισσὰς συγχωρούσας
125 πέτρας ἀξείνου ναίοντες.

ἰὼ παῖ τᾶς
Λατοῦς, Δίκτυνν᾽ οὐρεία,
πρὸς σὰν αὐλάν, εὐστύλων
ναῶν χρυσήρεις θριγκούς,
130 ὁσίας ὅσιον πόδα παρθένιον
κληδούχου δούλα πέμπω,
Ἑλλάδος εὐίππου πύργους
καὶ τείχη χόρτων τ᾽ εὐδένδρων
135 ἐξαλλάξασ᾽ Εὐρώπαν,
πατρῴων οἴκων ἕδρας.
ἔμολον· τί νέον; τίνα φροντίδ᾽ ἔχεις;
τί με πρὸς ναοὺς ἄγαγες ἄγαγες,
ὦ παῖ τοῦ τᾶς Τροίας πύργους
140 ἐλθόντος κλεινᾷ σὺν κώπᾳ
χιλιοναύτᾳ μυριοτευχοῦς
⟨στρατιᾶς ταγοῦ τοῦ πρεσβυγενοῦς
τῶν⟩ Ἀτρειδᾶν τῶν κλεινῶν;

ΙΦΙΓΕΝΕΙΑ
ἰὼ δμωαί,

125 ἀξείνου Markland: εὐξείνου L
126 ἰὼ olim Hermann: ὦ L   130 ὁσίας ὅσιον πόδα
παρθένιον Seidler: πόδα π- ὅσιον ὁσίας L: πόδα π- ζάθεον
ζαθέας Wecklein   135 εὔροιαν Willink
141 μυριοτευχοῦς Seidler: -χοις L
142 ante h. v. lac. indic. et suppl. Hermann

164

all who dwell by the clashing rocks
of the Hostile Sea![8]

Daughter of Leto,
Dictynna of the mountains,
to your court with its lovely
pillars and gilded cornice
I walk in holy procession on maiden feet,
servant of your holy temple warder,
I who have left behind the towers and ramparts
of Hellas, land of lovely horses,
and Europe with its fields well wooded,
where stands my ancestral home.
I am here: what is amiss? What worries you?
Why have you brought me, brought me to the temple,
O daughter of him who came to Troy's towers
with a glorious armada
of a thousand ships, ⟨leader of an army⟩
of ten thousand panoplies, ⟨eldest born⟩
of the glorious sons of Atreus?

IPHIGENIA

O servants,

---

[8] The Greek name for what we call the Black Sea was "the
Euxine Sea," *euxeinos* meaning "friendly to foreigners," perhaps
an attempt to placate a place that was notoriously hostile to strangers. This play avoids the euphemistic name and refers throughout
to "the Hostile Sea" (*axeinos*). The clashing rocks, called Symplegades ("Clashers") or Kuaneai ("Dark Rocks"), were supposed to
guard the entrance to the Bosporus and smash all entering ships.

δυσθρηνήτοις ὡς θρήνοις
145 ἔγκειμαι, τᾶς οὐκ εὐμούσου
μολπᾶς ἀλύροις ἐλέγοις, αἰαῖ,
ἐν κηδείοις οἴκτοισιν·
ἆταί μοι συμβαίνουσ᾽ ἆται,
σύγγονον ἀμὸν κατακλαιομένᾳ,
150 οἵαν ἰδόμαν ὄψιν ὀνείρων
νυκτός, τᾶς ἐξῆλθ᾽ ὄρφνα.
ὀλόμαν ὀλόμαν·
οὐκ εἴσ᾽ οἶκοι πατρῷοι·
155 οἴμοι <μοι> φροῦδος γέννα.
φεῦ φεῦ τῶν Ἄργει μόχθων.
ἰὼ δαῖμον,
μόνον ὅς με κασίγνητον συλᾷς
Ἅιδᾳ πέμψας, ᾧ τάσδε χοὰς
160 μέλλω κρατῆρά τε τὸν φθιμένων
ὑγραίνειν γαίας ἐν νώτοις
παγάς τ᾽ οὐρειᾶν ἐκ μόσχων
Βάκχου τ᾽ οἰνηρὰς λοιβὰς
165 ξουθᾶν τε πόνημα μελισσᾶν,
ἃ νεκροῖς θελκτήρια χεῖται.
ἀλλ᾽ ἔνδος μοι πάγχρυσον
τεῦχος καὶ λοιβὰν Ἅιδα.
170 ὦ κατὰ γαίας Ἀγαμεμνόνιον
θάλος, ὡς φθιμένῳ τάδε σοι πέμπω.

---

146 μολπᾶς Bothe: μ- βοὰν L
148 ἆταί Diggle: αἴ L

166

in what painful lamentations
am I enmeshed, in elegies that no lyre accompanies
and the muses do not love, alas,
amid the keening of grief!
It is disaster, disaster that has come upon me,
and I mourn for my brother:
such is the dream vision I saw
in the night whose darkness has just departed!
I am undone, undone:
my ancestral house is no more!
Ah, ah, my family is gone!
Oh the troubles in Argos!
Cruel fate,
you stripped me of my only brother
and sent him to Hades! To him these libations,
this mixing bowl for the dead,
I shall pour upon the earth's expanse:
the milk of young cows of the mountains,
the wine libation of Bacchus,
and honey made by the toil of tawny bees.
All these are poured out to soothe the dead.
(*to her attendant*) Give me the vessel of pure gold,
the libation for Hades.
(*pouring the libation*) Scion of Agamemnon beneath the
    earth,
I send you these libations as one who has perished.

---

149 κατακλαιομένα Elmsley: κ- ζωᾶς L
155 ⟨μοι⟩ Hermann
158 μόνον ὅς με Bothe: ὃς τὸν μόνον με L
161 ὑγραίνειν Blaydes: ὑδρ- L
166 χεῖται Nauck: κεῖται L

167

δέξαι δ'· οὐ γὰρ πρὸς τύμβον σοι
ξανθὰν χαίταν, οὐ δάκρυ' οἴσω.
175 τηλόσε γὰρ δὴ σᾶς ἀπενάσθην
πατρίδος καὶ ἐμᾶς, ἔνθα δοκήμασι
κεῖμαι σφαχθεῖσ' ἁ τλάμων.

ΧΟΡΟΣ
ἀντιψάλμους ᾠδὰς ὕμνων τ'
180 Ἀσιητᾶν σοι βάρβαρον ἀχάν,
δέσποιν', ἐξαυδάσω <'γώ>,
τὰν ἐν θρήνοισιν μοῦσαν
νέκυσιν μέλεον, τὰν ἐν μολπαῖς
185 Ἅιδας ὑμνεῖ δίχα παιάνων.
οἴμοι, τῶν Ἀτρειδᾶν οἴκων
ἔρρει φῶς σκῆπτρόν <τ'>, οἴμοι
[πατρῴων οἴκων]·
ἦν ἐκ τῶν εὐόλβων Ἄργει
190 βασιλέων <τᾶς νῦν ἄτας> ἀρχά,
μόχθος δ' ἐκ μόχθων ᾄσσει,
δινευούσαις ἵπποισιν <ἐπεὶ>
πταναῖς ἀλλάξας ἐξ ἕδρας
ἱερὸν <μετέβασ'> ὄμμ' αὐγᾶς
195 Ἅλιος, ἄλλοτε δ' ἄλλα προσέβα
χρυσέας ἀρνὸς μελάθροις ὀδύνα,

176 δοκήμασι Porson: δοκίμα L
181 <'γώ> Willink
187 σκῆπτρόν <τ'> Burges: σκήπτρων L
188 del. Hartung

168

Receive them, for I shall not bring to your tomb
my yellow tresses or my tears.
Far from your fatherland and mine
I have been taken where, it is thought,
I lie in luckless slaughter.

CHORUS

Songs antiphonal to yours and the foreign
clamor of Asian hymns
to you, mistress, shall I intone,
music for the dead amid dirges,
the unblessed tunes which Hades sings
(no paean these) among his songs.
Ah me, the light of the house of the Atridae
and its scepter have perished, ah me
[of my ancestral home]!
From the blessed kings in Argos
⟨this disaster⟩ took its beginning,
and trouble from trouble came,
⟨ever since⟩ with his whirling winged steeds
Helios changed from its station
the sun's holy radiant face,
and now at one time, now at another there came to the
    house
woe from the golden lamb,

---

189 ἦν Murray: τίν' L
190 ⟨τᾶς νῦν ἄτας⟩ Diggle
192 ⟨ἐπεὶ⟩ Wecklein
193 ἀλλάξας Musgrave: -ξας δ' L
194 ⟨μετέβασ'⟩ Paley
195 ἄλλοτε Platnauer: ἄλλοις L

†φόνος ἐπὶ φόνῳ ἄχεα ἄχεσιν†·
ἔνθεν τῶν πρόσθεν δμαθέντων
200 ἐκβαίνει ποινὰ Τανταλιδᾶν
εἰς οἴκους, σπεύδει δ' ἀσπούδαστ'
ἐπὶ σοὶ δαίμων ⟨δυσδαίμων⟩.

ΙΦΙΓΕΝΕΙΑ

ἐξ ἀρχᾶς μοι δυσδαίμων
δαίμων· ⟨ἐκ⟩ τᾶς ματρὸς ζώνας
205 ⟨λύσεως⟩ καὶ νυκτὸς κείνας
λόχιαι στερρὰν παιδείαν
Μοῖραι ξυντείνουσι θεαί,
⟨οἵαν ἄρ' ἔχω μοῖραν, ἀρίστων⟩
ἁ μναστευθεῖσ' ἐξ Ἑλλάνων·
ἃν πρωτόγονον θάλος ἐν θαλάμοις
210 Λήδας ἁ τλάμων κούρα
σφάγιον πατρῴᾳ λώβᾳ
καὶ θῦμ' οὐκ εὐγάθητον
τέκεν ἔκτρεφεν, ⟨εἶτ'⟩ ἀκταιὰν
ἱππείοις ἐν δίφροισι

197 fort. φόνοι ἀμφὶ φόνοις   ἄχθεα τ' ἄχθεσιν Musgrave
v. del. Hartung
  200 sic Monk: Τανταλιδᾶν ἐκβαίνει ποινά γ' L
  202 ⟨δυσδαίμων⟩ Mekler   204 ⟨ἐκ⟩ Willink
  205 ⟨λύσεως⟩ Willink   κείνας Willink: κ- ἐξ ἀρχᾶς L
  206 λόχιαι Hermann: -χείαν L
  208 ante h. v. lac. indic. Seidler, suppl. Willink
  213 τέκεν ἔκτρεφεν Kovacs: ἔτεκεν ἔτρεφεν L   ⟨εἶτ'⟩
ἀκταιὰν Willink: εὐκταίαν L

170

slaughter upon slaughter, grief upon grief.[9]
Hence from those long dead sons
of Tantalus breaks out affliction
against the house, and not to be pushed forward are the
    designs
against you that your ⟨ill-starred⟩ fate is hastening on.

IPHIGENIA

From the beginning my fate
has been ill-starred. From the night
my mother ⟨loosed⟩ her maiden girdle
the Fates that look on childbirth have spun out for me
a harsh bringing up!
⟨What a fate I have,⟩ I who was wooed
by ⟨the noblest⟩ of the Greeks!
Me as the first-born in her chamber
Leda's ill-fated daughter
bore, nurtured as a victim for my father to misuse
and a beast for sacrifice
in which there is no joy. ⟨Then⟩ on the sandy
shore of Aulis they set me down

---

9 The allusion is to the quarrel of Atreus and Thyestes. Atreus
had been proclaimed king by a divinely sent portent, a golden
lamb brought to him by Pan. Thyestes seduced Atreus' wife and
stole the lamb, but when Atreus was about to be banished, the sun,
to show that the kingship belonged to him, changed course, rising
in the east and setting in the west as it does now. (Other sources
say that the sun changed course in horror at Atreus' revenge: he
killed Thyestes' children and served them to him at a banquet.)

215 ψαμάθων Αὐλίδος ἐπέβασαν
νύμφαν μ', οἴμοι, δύσνυμφον
τῷ τᾶς Νηρέως κούρας, αἰαῖ.
νῦν δ' ἀξείνου πόντου ξείνα
συγχόρτους οἴκους ναίω,
220 ἄγαμος ἄτεκνος ἄπολις ἄφιλος,
οὐ τὰν Ἄργει μέλπουσ' Ἥραν
οὐδ' ἱστοῖς ἐν καλλιφθόγγοις
κερκίδι Παλλάδος Ἀτθίδος εἰκὼ
⟨καὶ⟩ Τιτάνων ποικίλλουσ', ἀλλ'
225 αἱμορράντῳ δυσφόρμιγγι
ξείνων ῥαίνουσ' ἄτᾳ βωμούς,
οἰκτράν τ' αἰαζόντων αὐδὰν
οἰκτρόν τ' ἐκβαλλόντων δάκρυον.
καὶ νῦν κείνων μέν μοι λάθα,
230 τὸν δ' Ἄργει δμαθέντ' ἀγκλαίω
σύγγονον, ὃν ἔλιπον ἐπιμαστίδιον,
ἔτι βρέφος, ἔτι νέον, ἔτι θάλος
ἐν χερσὶν ματρὸς πρὸς στέρνοις τ'
235 Ἄργει σκηπτοῦχον Ὀρέσταν.

ΧΟΡΟΣ

καὶ μὴν ὅδ' ἀκτὰς ἐκλιπὼν θαλασσίους
βουφορβὸς ἥκει σημανῶν τί σοι νέον.

---

216 νύμφαν μ' post Scaliger (νύμφαν) England: νύμφαιον L
219 συγχόρτους Köchly: δυσχ- L
224 ⟨καὶ⟩ Tyrwhitt   225 αἱμορράντῳ Madvig: -ων L
δυσφόρμιγγι Tyrwhitt: -ιγγα L

from the horse-drawn chariot
to be bride ill-wed—ah me!—
to the Nereid's son, oh woe!
And now as a stranger I dwell in a house
that borders on the Hostile Sea,
with no husband, children, city, or friend.
I do not sing in honor of Hera at Argos
or weave with my shuttle upon the sounding loom
the likeness of Athenian Pallas
and the Titans in colors various: no,
with blood-stained death of foreign men,
death no lyre accompanies, I stain the altars,
men who wail their piteous cry
and shed their piteous tear.
And now I no longer think of these:
it is the one dead in Argos that I weep for,
my brother, whom I left at his mother's breast,
still a tender shoot, a young babe,
in the arms and embrace of his mother,
Orestes, Argos' scepter-bearing king.

Enter a HERDSMAN *by Eisodos A.*

CHORUS LEADER

But see! A herdsman has come from the seashore to bring
you news.

---

226 ῥαίνουσ᾿ Maehly: αἱμάσσουσ᾿ L   ἄτᾳ Tyrwhitt: -αν L
227-8 αὐδὰν / οἰκτρόν τ᾿ Tyrwhitt: οὐδ᾿ ἄνοικτρόν τ᾿ L
230 δμαθέντ᾿ ἀγκλαίω Weil: δμαθέντα κλαίω L
231 fort. λίπον
236-7 del. Willink cl. 333–5

EURIPIDES

ΒΟΥΚΟΛΟΣ

Ἀγαμέμνονός τε καὶ Κλυταιμήστρας τέκνον,
ἄκουε καινῶν ἐξ ἐμοῦ κηρυγμάτων.

ΙΦΙΓΕΝΕΙΑ

240 τί δ' ἔστι τοῦ παρόντος ἔκπλησσον λόγου;

ΒΟΥΚΟΛΟΣ

ἥκουσιν ἐς γῆν, κυανέας Συμπληγάδας
πλάτῃ φυγόντες, δίπτυχοι νεανίαι,
θεᾷ φίλον πρόσφαγμα καὶ θυτήριον
Ἀρτέμιδι. χέρνιβας δὲ καὶ κατάργματα
245 οὐκ ἂν φθάνοις ἂν εὐτρεπῆ ποιουμένη.

ΙΦΙΓΕΝΕΙΑ

ποδαποί; τίνος γῆς σχῆμ' ἔχουσιν οἱ ξένοι;

ΒΟΥΚΟΛΟΣ

Ἕλληνες· ἐν τοῦτ' οἶδα κοὐ περαιτέρω.

ΙΦΙΓΕΝΕΙΑ

οὐδ' ὄνομ' ἀκούσας οἶσθα τῶν ξένων φράσαι;

ΒΟΥΚΟΛΟΣ

Πυλάδης ἐκλῄζεθ' ἅτερος πρὸς θατέρου.

ΙΦΙΓΕΝΕΙΑ

250 τῷ ξυζύγῳ δὲ τοῦ ξένου τί τοὔνομ' ἦν;

240 γόου Lenting
241 κυανέας Συμπληγάδας Bentley: -έαν -άδα L
246 σχῆμ' Monk: ὄνομ' L
250 τῷ ξυζύγῳ Elmsley: τοῦ -ου L

174

HERDSMAN

Daughter of Agamemnon and Clytaemestra, listen to this strange report from me.

IPHIGENIA

What is startling about what you have to say?

HERDSMAN

Two young men, escaping the dark Symplegades[10] in their ship, have arrived in the country, a welcome sacrifice and offering to the goddess Artemis. It is high time to get ready the means of purifying and consecrating.[11]

IPHIGENIA

From where have they come? What country's garb do the strangers wear?

HERDSMAN

They are Greek. I know this but nothing more.

IPHIGENIA

Have you heard the strangers' names? Can you tell me them?

HERDSMAN

One of them called the other Pylades.

IPHIGENIA

The foreigner's friend—what was he called?

10 See above on line 125.

11 At the beginning of a sacrifice water was sprinkled on victim and participants and the victim was consecrated by being sprinkled with barley corns and having hairs cut from its head with a sacrificial knife. See *Electra* 773-843 for a full description of the rite.

EURIPIDES

ΒΟΥΚΟΛΟΣ

οὐδεὶς τόδ᾽ οἶδεν· οὐ γὰρ εἰσηκούσαμεν.

ΙΦΙΓΕΝΕΙΑ

ποῦ δ᾽ εἴδετ᾽ αὐτοὺς κἀντυχόντες εἵλετε;

ΒΟΥΚΟΛΟΣ

ἄκραις ἐπὶ ῥηγμῖσιν ἀξένου πόρου.

ΙΦΙΓΕΝΕΙΑ

καὶ τίς θαλάσσης βουκόλοις κοινωνία;

ΒΟΥΚΟΛΟΣ

255   βοῦς ἤλθομεν νίψοντες ἐναλίᾳ δρόσῳ.

ΙΦΙΓΕΝΕΙΑ

ἐκεῖσε δὴ ᾽πάνελθε, ποῦ νιν εἵλετε
τρόπῳ θ᾽ ὁποίῳ· τοῦτο γὰρ μαθεῖν θέλω.
[χρόνιοι γὰρ ἥκουσ᾽· οὐδέ πω βωμὸς θεᾶς
Ἑλληνικαῖσιν ἐξεφοινίχθη ῥοαῖς.]

ΒΟΥΚΟΛΟΣ

260   ἐπεὶ τὸν ἐκρέοντα διὰ Συμπληγάδων
βοῦς ὑλοφορβοὺς πόντον εἰσεβάλλομεν,
ἦν τις διαρρὼξ κυμάτων πολλῷ σάλῳ
κοιλωπὸς ἀγμός, πορφυρευτικαὶ στέγαι.
ἐνταῦθα δισσοὺς εἶδέ τις νεανίας
265   βουφορβὸς ἡμῶν, κἀνεχώρησεν πάλιν
ἄκροισι δακτύλοισι πορθμεύων ἴχνος.
ἔλεξε δ᾽· Οὐχ ὁρᾶτε; δαίμονές τινες
θάσσουσιν οἵδε. θεοσεβὴς δ᾽ ἡμῶν τις ὢν
ἀνέσχε χεῖρε καὶ προσηύξατ᾽ εἰσιδών·

HERDSMAN

No one knows: we did not catch his name.

IPHIGENIA

Where did you see them, come upon and capture them?

HERDSMAN

Where the surf of the Hostile Sea breaks.

IPHIGENIA

What do herdsmen have to do with the sea?

HERDSMAN

We came to bathe our oxen in seawater.

IPHIGENIA

Go back in your tale: where and how did you catch them?
That is what I want to know. [For they have come after a
long time. And the altar of the goddess has not yet been
reddened with Greek blood.]

HERDSMAN

We were putting our forest-grazing oxen into the sea that
flows out through the Symplegades. There is a hollow cave
there, made by the constant beating of the waves, a place
where murex-fishers take shelter. Here a herdsman of our
company saw two young men and returned hurrying on
tiptoe. He said, "Don't you see? There are deities sitting
over there!" One of our number , a god-fearing man, lifted
up his hands in prayer and as he looked at them said, "Son

---

252 ποῦ Musgrave: πῶς L   256 ποῦ Bothe: πῶς L
258-9 del. Monk   οὐδέ πω] οἶδ᾽ ἐπεὶ Seidler
260 ἐκρέοντα Elmsley: εἰσρ- L
265 κἀνεχώρησεν Blomfield: κἀπ- L
269 χεῖρε Markland: -α L

270　ὦ ποντίας παῖ Λευκοθέας, νεῶν φύλαξ,
　　δέσποτα Παλαῖμον, ἵλεως ἡμῖν γενοῦ,
　　εἴτ᾽ οὖν ἐπ᾽ ἀκταῖς θάσσετον Διοσκόρω,
　　ἢ Νηρέως ἀγάλμαθ᾽, ὃς τὸν εὐγενῆ
　　ἔτικτε πεντήκοντα Νηρῄδων χορόν.
275　ἄλλος δέ τις μάταιος, ἀνομίᾳ θρασύς,
　　ἐγέλασεν εὐχαῖς, ναυτίλους δ᾽ ἐφθαρμένους
　　θάσσειν φάραγγ᾽ ἔφασκε τοῦ νόμου φόβῳ,
　　κλυόντας ὡς θύοιμεν ἐνθάδε ξένους.
　　ἔδοξε δ᾽ ἡμῶν εὖ λέγειν τοῖς πλείοσιν,
280　θηρᾶν τε τῇ θεῷ σφάγια τἀπιχώρια.
　　κἂν τῷδε πέτραν ἅτερος λιπὼν ξένοιν
　　ἔστη κάρα τε διετίναξ᾽ ἄνω κάτω
　　κἀνεστέναξεν ὠλένας τρέμων ἄκρας,
　　μανίαις ἀλαίνων, καὶ βοᾷ, Κυνωπίδα,
285　Πυλάδη, δέδορκας τήνδε; τήνδε δ᾽ οὐχ ὁρᾷς
　　Ἅιδου δράκαιναν ὥς με βούλεται κτανεῖν
　　δειναῖς ἐχίδναις εἰς ἔμ᾽ ἐστομωμένη;
　　ἡ ᾽κ γειτόνων δὲ πῦρ πνέουσα καὶ φόνον
　　πτεροῖς ἐρέσσει, μητέρ᾽ ἀγκάλαις ἐμὴν
290　ἔχουσα, πέτρινον ὄγκον, ὡς ἐπεμβάλῃ.
　　οἴμοι, κτενεῖ με· ποῖ φύγω; παρῆν δ᾽ ὁρᾶν
　　οὐ ταῦτα μορφῆς σχήματ᾽, ἀλλ᾽ †ἠλλάσσετο†
　　φθογγάς τε μόσχων καὶ κυνῶν ὑλάγματα,
　　ἅφασκ᾽ Ἐρινύων ἱέναι μιμήματα.

[284] κυνωπίδα Nauck: κυναγὸς ὡς L
[288] ἡ ᾽κ γειτόνων δὲ Jackson: ἤδ᾽ ἐκ χιτώνων L
[290] ὄγκον Heimsoeth: ὄχθον L

of the sea goddess Leukothea, lord Palaemon, guardian of ships, be merciful to us! Or perhaps you are the Dioscuri that sit upon this shore, or darling boys of Nereus, who begot the noble chorus of the fifty Nereids!"[12] But another, a foolish fellow, bold in his irreverence, laughed at these prayers and said it was shipwrecked sailors sitting in the cave for fear of our law since they had heard that we sacrifice foreigners here. What he said made sense to most of us, and we decided to hunt down victims for the goddess as our custom here demands.

Meanwhile one of the two strangers left the cliff and stood shaking his head this way and that. He groaned aloud, his hands trembled, and in his mad delirium he shouted, "Pylades, don't you see this hound-faced one? Don't you see how this hellish dragon, fringed with terrible vipers, tries to kill me? And next to her another, breathing out fire and gore, beats her wings and holds my mother in her arms, a mass of stone, to hurl at me! Ah, she will kill me! Where can I escape to?" But none of these apparitions was there to see: he mistook the lowing of cattle and the barking of dogs, noises he claimed were uttered by what seemed like Erinyes.

---

[12] According to the myth dramatized by Euripides in his *Ino*, Palaemon and Leucothea are sea gods who were previously the mortal Melicertes and his mother Ino. The god-fearing man first identifies the two with Palaemon and an unnamed companion, second with the twin sons of Zeus, Castor and Polydeuces, and third with grandsons of Nereus, sons of one of the Nereids.

---

292 ταῦτα Markland: ταὐτὰ L   294 ἄφασκ' Badham: ἆς
φᾶσ' L   Ἐρινύων Kovacs cl. 931, 970, 1456: -νῦς L

295   ἡμεῖς δὲ συσταλέντες, ὡς θανουμένου,
    σιγῇ καθήμεθ'· ὁ δὲ χερὶ σπάσας ξίφος,
    μόσχους ὀρούσας ἐς μέσας λέων ὅπως,
    παίει σιδήρῳ λαγόνας ἐς πλευράς ⟨θ'⟩ ἱείς,
    δοκῶν Ἐρινῦς θεὰς ἀμύνεσθαι τάδε,
300   ὥσθ' αἱματηρὸν πέλαγος ἐξανθεῖν ἁλός.
    κἂν τῷδε πᾶς τις, ὡς ὁρᾷ βουφόρβια
    πίπτοντα καὶ πορθούμεν', ἐξωπλίζετο,
    κόχλους τε φυσῶν συλλέγων τ' ἐγχωρίους·
    πρὸς εὐτραφεῖς γὰρ καὶ νεανίας ξένους
305   φαύλους μάχεσθαι βουκόλους ἡγούμεθα.
    πολλοὶ δ' ἐπληρώθημεν οὐ μακρῷ χρόνῳ.
    πίπτει δὲ μανίας πίτυλον ὁ ξένος μεθείς,
    στάζων ἀφρῷ γένειον· ὡς δ' ἐσείδομεν
    προύργου πεσόντα, πᾶς ἀνὴρ εἶχεν πόνον
310   βάλλων ἀράσσων. ἅτερος δὲ τοῖν ξένοιν
    ἀφρόν τ' ἀπέψη σώματός τ' ἐτημέλει
    πέπλων τε προυκάλυπτεν εὐπήνους ὑφάς,
    καραδοκῶν μὲν τἀπιόντα τραύματα,
    φίλον δὲ θεραπείαισιν ἄνδρ' εὐεργετῶν.
315   ἔμφρων δ' ἀνᾴξας ὁ ξένος πεσήματος
    ἔγνω κλύδωνα πολεμίων προσκείμενον
    [καὶ τὴν παροῦσαν συμφορὰν αὑτοῖν πέλας]
    ᾤμωξέ θ'· ἡμεῖς δ' οὐκ ἀνίεμεν πέτροις
    βάλλοντες, ἄλλος ἄλλοθεν προσκείμενοι.
320   οὗ δὴ τὸ δεινὸν παρακέλευσμ' ἠκούσαμεν·
    Πυλάδη, θανούμεθ'· ἀλλ' ὅπως θανούμεθα
    κάλλισθ'· ἕπου μοι, φάσγανον σπάσας χερί.

We, for our part, drew back and crouched down in silence, expecting him to die. But he unsheathed his sword and, rushing into the midst of the cattle like a lion, thrust and stabbed their flanks and ribs, thinking that by so doing he was warding off the Erinyes. The sea swell flowered blood red. Thereupon, seeing that our herds were being cut down and ravaged, we all armed ourselves and blew on conch shells to summon those who lived nearby. We thought that herdsmen were no match in a fight for these strapping young strangers. Before long a large number of us had gathered. But the foreigner ceased from his mad fit and fell down, foam dripping from his chin. When we saw him fall so advantageously for us, we all exerted ourselves in pelting and striking him. But the other foreigner wiped the foam from his face, protected his body, and shielded him with the thick weave of his garments, anticipating the blows as they fell and helping his friend with loving attentions. Then the stranger, now in his senses, leapt up from his fall, and when he realized that a threatening wave of enemies was attacking them [and that the present calamity was near them], he groaned. But we did not stop pelting them with stones, attacking them from all sides.

Here we heard that terrible exhortation: "Pylades, we are going to die: see that we die a most glorious death! Draw your sword and follow me!" When we saw our foes'

295 θανουμένου Wilamowitz: -οι L   298 ⟨θ'⟩ Reiske

299 del. West

300 ὥσθ' Markland: ὡς L

306 οὐ Nauck: ἐν L

309 εἶχεν Heiland: ἔσχεν L

317 del. Bothe

ὡς δ᾽ εἴδομεν δίπαλτα πολεμίων ξίφη,
φυγῇ λεπαίας ἐξεπίμπλαμεν νάπας.
325 ἀλλ᾽, εἰ φύγοι τις, ἄτεροι προσκείμενοι
ἔβαλλον αὐτούς· εἰ δὲ τούσδ᾽ ὠσαίατο,
αὖθις τὸ νῦν ὑπεῖκον ἤρασσεν πέτροις.
ἀλλ᾽ ἦν ἄπιστον· μυρίων γὰρ ἐκ χερῶν
οὐδεὶς τὰ τῆς θεοῦ θύματ᾽ ηὐτύχει βαλών.
330 μόλις δέ νιν τόλμῃ μὲν οὐ χειρούμεθα,
κύκλῳ δὲ περιβαλόντες ἐξεκόψαμεν
πέτροισι χειρῶν φάσγαν᾽, ἐς δὲ γῆν γόνυ
καμάτῳ καθεῖσαν. πρὸς δ᾽ ἄνακτα τῆσδε γῆς
κομίζομέν νιν. ὁ δ᾽ ἐσιδὼν ὅσον τάχος
335 ἐς χέρνιβάς τε καὶ σφαγεῖ᾽ ἔπεμπέ σοι.
    εὔχου δὲ τοιάδ᾽ ὦ νεᾶνί σοι ξένων
σφάγια παρεῖναι· κἂν ἀναλίσκῃς ξένους
τοιούσδε, τὸν σὸν Ἑλλὰς ἀποτείσει φόνον
δίκας τίνουσα τῆς ἐν Αὐλίδι σφαγῆς.

ΧΟΡΟΣ

340 θαυμάστ᾽ ἔλεξας τὸν φανένθ᾽, ὅστις ποτὲ
Ἕλληνος ἐκ γῆς πόντον ἦλθεν ἄξενον.

ΙΦΙΓΕΝΕΙΑ

εἶέν· σὺ μὲν κόμιζε τοὺς ξένους μολών,
τὰ δ᾽ ἐνθάδ᾽ ἡμεῖς ὅσια φροντιούμεθα.
    ὦ καρδία τάλαινα, πρὶν μὲν ἐς ξένους
345 γαληνὸς ἦσθα καὶ φιλοικτίρμων ἀεί,

331 ἐξεκόψαμεν Bothe: ἐξεκλέψ- L
337 ξένους] fort. νέους

182

two brandished swords, we fled and crowded into the stony gulleys. But when some of us fled, others ran up to the men and pelted them. When the men drove them off, those who had just run away came back and pounded the men with stones. Yet it was astonishing: out of the countless hands that threw, not one succeeded in hitting the goddess' victims. With difficulty we subdued them, though it was not by our bravery: we surrounded them and knocked the swords from their hands with our stones, and they sank to their knees exhausted. We brought them to our country's king, and he took one look and proceeded to send them to you with all speed to be consecrated and slaughtered.

Lady, foreign victims like these are what you should pray to receive. If you kill foreigners like these, Greece will be punished for your murder, paying the penalty for your sacrifice at Aulis.

CHORUS LEADER

Strange is the story you tell of this man, whoever he is, that has turned up, coming from Greece to the Hostile Sea.

IPHIGENIA

Well then: go and bring the strangers, and I shall attend to what ritual prescribes here.

Exit HERDSMAN *by Eisodos A.*

O my woe-laden heart! Till now you were mild and full of pity toward foreigners and gave your meed of tears to

---

340 μανένθ' Kaehler, Lakon
343 ὅσια Reiske: οἷα L

ἐς θοὐμόφυλον ἀναμετρουμένη δάκρυ,
Ἕλληνας ἄνδρας ἡνίκ' ἐς χέρας λάβοις.
νῦν δ' ἐξ ὀνείρων οἶσιν ἠγριώμεθα
[δοκοῦσ' Ὀρέστην μηκέθ' ἥλιον βλέπειν]
350 δύσνουν με λήψεσθ', οἵτινές ποθ' ἥκετε.
[καὶ τοῦτ' ἄρ' ἦν ἀληθές, ἠσθόμην, φίλαι·
οἱ δυστυχεῖς γὰρ τοῖσιν εὐτυχεστέροις
αὐτοὶ κακῶς πράξαντες οὐ φρονοῦσιν εὖ.]
ἀλλ' οὔτε πνεῦμα Διόθεν ἦλθε πώποτε,
355 οὐ πορθμίς, ἥτις διὰ πέτρας Συμπληγάδας
Ἑλένην ἐπήγαγ' ἐνθάδ', ἥ μ' ἀπώλεσεν,
Μενέλεών θ', ἵν' αὐτοὺς ἀντετιμωρησάμην,
τὴν ἐνθάδ' Αὖλιν ἀντιθεῖσα τῆς ἐκεῖ,
οὗ μ' ὥστε μόσχον Δαναΐδαι χειρούμενοι
360 ἔσφαζον, ἱερεὺς δ' ἦν ὁ γεννήσας πατήρ.
  οἴμοι (κακῶν γὰρ τῶν τότ' οὐκ ἀμνημονῶ),
ὅσας γενείου χεῖρας ἐξηκόντισα
[γονάτων τε τοῦ τεκόντος, ἐξαρτωμένη],
λέγουσα τοιάδ'· Ὦ πάτερ, νυμφεύομαι
365 νυμφεύματ' αἰσχρὰ πρὸς σέθεν· μήτηρ δ' ἐμὲ
σέθεν κατακτείνοντος Ἀργεῖαί τε νῦν
ὑμνοῦσιν ὑμεναίοισιν, αὐλεῖται δὲ πᾶν
μέλαθρον· ἡμεῖς δ' ὀλλύμεσθα πρὸς σέθεν.
Ἅιδης ἐκεῖνος ἦν ἄρ', οὐχ ὁ Πηλέως,
370 ὅν μοι προτείνας πόσιν ἐν ἁρμάτων ὄχοις
ἐς αἱματηρὸν γάμον ἐπόρθμευσας δόλῳ.
  ἐγὼ δὲ λεπτῶν ὄμμα διὰ καλυμμάτων
ἔχουσ' ἀδελφὸν οὔτ' ἀνειλόμην χεροῖν,

your fellow Greeks whenever you took any as your prisoners. But now because of the dreams that have made me savage [thinking that Orestes no longer looks upon the sun], you who have arrived here will find me unkind. [It is quite true, I have learned, my friends, that the unlucky in their own misfortune feel no goodwill toward those more fortunate.] But no breeze from Zeus has come, no ship, to bring Helen through the Symplegades—Helen who caused my death—and Menelaus, so that I might take vengeance on them, making an Aulis here to match the one in Greece. There the Greeks took me in their grasp like a calf and slit my throat, and the slayer was the father who begot me.

Ah me (for I cannot forget the pain of that day), how many times did I reach my hand out to touch my father's chin [and, as I clung to them, his knees,] uttering words such as these: "O father, I am given in marriage by you—a marriage of shame! Now, even as you are killing me, my mother and the Argive women are singing the wedding song for me, and the whole house resounds with piping! And yet it is death I receive at your hands! The husband you promised me in the chariot as you ferried me deceitfully to my blood-stained marriage was Hades, not the son of Peleus!"

Hiding my eyes behind a veil of fine cloth I did not take my little brother up in my arms (and now he is dead), did

---

349 del. Nauck   351-3 del. F. W. Schmidt
356 ἐπήγαγ᾽ Haupt: ἀπ- L   363 del. West
365 ἐμὲ Reiske: ἐμὴ L   369 ἐκεῖνος Haslam: Ἀχιλλεύς L
370 προτείνας Badham: προσεῖπας L   ⟨μ᾽⟩ ὄχοις Bothe
373 οὔτ᾽ ἀνειλόμην Tyrwhitt: τοῦτον εἱλ- L

ὃς νῦν ὄλωλεν, οὐ κασιγνήτῃ στόμα
375 συνῆψ᾽ ὑπ᾽ αἰδοῦς, ὡς ἰοῦσ᾽ ἐς Πηλέως
μέλαθρα· πολλὰ δ᾽ ἀπεθέμην ἀσπάσματα
ἐς αὖθις, ὡς ἥξουσ᾽ ἐς Ἄργος αὖ πάλιν.
ὦ τλῆμον, εἰ τέθνηκας, ἐξ οἵων καλῶν
ἔρρεις, Ὀρέστα, καὶ πατρὸς ζηλωμάτων.
380 τὰ τῆς θεοῦ δὲ μέμφομαι σοφίσματα,
ἥτις βροτῶν μὲν ἤν τις ἅψηται φόνου,
ἢ καὶ λοχείας ἢ νεκροῦ θίγῃ χεροῖν,
βωμῶν ἀπείργει, μυσαρὸν ὡς ἡγουμένη,
αὐτὴ δὲ θυσίαις ἥδεται βροτοκτόνοις.
385 οὐκ ἔσθ᾽ ὅπως ἔτεκεν ἂν ἡ Διὸς δάμαρ
Λητὼ τοσαύτην ἀμαθίαν. ἐγὼ μὲν οὖν
τὰ Ταντάλου θεοῖσιν ἑστιάματα
ἄπιστα κρίνω, παιδὸς ἡσθῆναι βορᾷ,
τοὺς δ᾽ ἐνθάδ᾽, αὐτοὺς ὄντας ἀνθρωποκτόνους,
390 ἐς τὴν θεὸν τὸ φαῦλον ἀναφέρειν δοκῶ·
οὐδένα γὰρ οἶμαι δαιμόνων εἶναι κακόν.

ΧΟΡΟΣ

στρ. α
κυάνεαι κυανέας σύνοδοι θαλάσσας,
ἵν᾽ οἶστρος †ὁ πετόμενος Ἀργόθεν†
395 ἄξενον ἐπ᾽ οἶδμα διεπέρασε ⟨πόντου⟩
Ἀσιήτιδα γαῖαν Εὐρώπας διαμείψας·

378 καλῶν Reiske: κακῶν L   382 del. Badham
393 κυάνεαι κυανέας Willink: -αι -αι L
394 ἵν᾽ Hermann: ἣν L   fort. Ἀργόθεν συθεὶς

not kiss my sister. Shame[13] prevented me, for I thought I was going to the house of Peleus. Many were the embraces I put off until later since I thought I would return to Argos again. O poor Orestes, if you are dead, how great is the fortune, how great the enviable lot of your father, you have left behind!

I do not approve of the goddess' cleverness. Any mortal who has had contact with blood or childbirth or a corpse she keeps from her altars, deeming him unclean. Yet she herself takes pleasure in human sacrifice! Impossible that Zeus's bride Leto could have given birth to such a foolish creature. Now just as I find it incredible that the gods at Tantalus' feast enjoyed the flesh of his son, so I believe that people here, themselves murderous, ascribe their own fault to the goddess. None of the gods, I think, is wicked.

CHORUS

Dark confluences of the dark sea,
where the gadfly[14] that flew from Argos
passed over the wave of the Hostile Sea
to Asia's land, leaving Europe behind:

[13] A sheltered Greek girl would feel inhibition at leaving her virginal life for the public spectacle of a wedding and her sexual initiation.

[14] Io, priestess of Hera, was beloved by Zeus, who turned her into a heifer to disguise her from Hera. Hera in jealousy had her pursued by a gadfly from Greece by way of Asia to Egypt where she became the mother of Epaphus (the bull god Apis). The strait is called Bosporus (Cow-ford; cf. Oxford) in honor of Io's crossing.

395 ἄξενον Markland: εὔξεινον L   ⟨πόντου⟩ Schoene

τίνες ποτ᾽ ἄρα τὸν εὔυδρον δονακόχλοον

400 λιπόντες Εὐρώταν ἢ ῥεύματα σεμνὰ Δίρκας
ἔβασαν ἔβασαν ἄμεικτον αἶαν, ἔνθα κούρᾳ
Δίᾳ τέγγει

405 βωμοὺς καὶ περικίονας
ναοὺς αἷμα βρότειον;

ἀντ. α

ἢ ῥοθίοις εἰλατίνας δικρότοισι κώπας
†ἔπλευσαν ἐπὶ πόντια κύματα†

410 νάιον ὄχημα λινοπόροις ⟨σὺν⟩ αὔραις,
φιλόπλουτον ἄμιλλαν αὔξοντες μελάθροισιν;
φίλα γὰρ ἐλπὶς †γένετ᾽ ἐπὶ πήμασι βροτῶν†

415 ἄπληστος ἀνθρώποις, ὄλβου βάρος οἳ φέρονται
πλάνητες ἐπ᾽ οἶδμα πόλεις τε βαρβάρους περῶντες,
κοινᾷ δόξᾳ·

420 γνώμα δ᾽ οἷς μὲν ἄκαιρος ὄλ-
βου, τοῖς δ᾽ ἐς μέσον ἥκει.

στρ. β

πῶς τὰς συνδρομάδας πέτρας,
πῶς Φινηΐδας αὖ πολύ-
πνους ἀκτὰς ἐπέρασαν;

425 ⟨ἢ⟩ παρ᾽ ἄλιον αἰγιαλὸν ἐπ᾽ Ἀμφιτρί-
τας ῥοθίῳ δραμόντες,

---

399 δονακόχλοον Elmsley: -χλοα L
407 εἰλατίνας … κώπας Reiske: -οις … -αις L
409 fort. πόντι᾽ ἐπὶ κύματ᾽ (vel ἐφ᾽ ἅλια κύματ᾽) ἤλασαν
410 ⟨σὺν⟩ Wecklein

who can they be then who left the reeds and plentiful
    water
of the Eurotas or the august streams of Dirce
and came, came, to the savage land where for the
    maiden
daughter of Zeus
the altars and colonnaded temples are drenched
in human blood?

Have they with plashing of pine oars on either side
driven over the sea wave
their ship chariot accompanied by linen-wafting breezes
in eager quest of growing wealth for their houses?
Hope is enticing, and for their hurt
it comes insatiable to men who strive to win a weight of
    riches
by wandering over the sea to barbarian cities,
pursuing a common fancy.
To some the thought of wealth proves untimely,
while for others it hits the mark of moderation.

How did they pass the clashing rocks,
how the windy shores
of Phineus?
Did they run near the beach
by the billows of Amphitrite,

---

414 φίλα γὰρ ἐλπίς γ᾽, ἐπί τε πήμασιν βροτῶν Murray: φιλεῖ
γὰρ ἐλπίς γ᾽ ἔτ᾽ ἐπὶ πήμασιν βρύειν Willink
    423 αὖ πολύπνους Willink: ἀύπνους L
    425 ⟨ἢ⟩ Willink

ὅπου πεντήκοντα κορᾶν
Νηρέως ⟨ᾠδαῖσι⟩ χοροὶ
μέλπουσιν ἐγκυκλίοις·
430   ⟨ἢ⟩ πλησιστίοισι πνοαῖς
συριζόντων κατὰ πρύ-
μναν †εὐναίων† πηδαλίων
αὔραισιν νοτίαις
ἢ πνεύμασι Ζεφύρου,
435   τὰν πολυόρνιθον ἐπ᾽ αἶ-
αν, Λευκὰν ἀκτάν, Ἀχιλῆ-
ος δρόμους καλλισταδίους,
ἄξεινον κατὰ πόντον;

ἀντ. β

εἴθ᾽ εὐχαῖσιν δεσποσύνοις
440   Λήδας ⟨τάνδ᾽⟩ Ἑλένα φίλα
παῖς ἐλθοῦσα τύχοι γᾶν,
Τρωιάδα λιποῦσα πόλιν, ἵν᾽ ἀμφὶ χαί-
ταν δρόσον αἱματηρὰν
ἑλιχθεῖσα λαιμοτόμῳ
445   δεσποίνας χειρὶ θάνοι
ποινὰς δοῦσ᾽ ἀντιπάλους.
ἡδίσταν δ᾽ ἂν ἀγγελίαν
δεξαίμεθ᾽, Ἑλλάδος ἐκ
γᾶς πλωτήρων εἴ τις ἔβα,

428 Νηρέως ⟨ᾠδαῖσι⟩ Willink: Νηρηίδων L
430 ⟨ἢ⟩ Bergk   432 εὐπαγῶν Herwerden
439 δεσποσύνοις Markland: -νας L

190

where the chorus of fifty daughters
of Nereus sing
⟨their songs⟩ in a circle?
⟨Or⟩ with breezes that fill the sail,
their well-made steering oar
humming at the stern
with southerly breeze
or the breath of the Zephyr,
did they make for the bird-thronged shore,
Whitestrand,[15] where Achilles
has his lovely racing ground
by the shore of the Hostile Sea?

O that by my mistress' prayers
Leda's beloved daughter Helen
would come to ⟨this⟩ land
leaving Troy's city behind,
and here with crimson dew
encircling her head she would die
by my lady's throat-cutting hand,
paying the penalty she owes.
But sweetest of all would it be
if we heard news that from Hellas
some sailor has come

15 Achilles, after his death, was transported to Leuke Akte on
the Black Sea: see *Andromache* 1259-62.

---

440 ⟨τάνδ'⟩ Willink
441 γᾶν Willink: τὰν L
445 θάνοι Seidler: -ῃ L: cf. *Hip.* 734
447 ἡδίσταν δ' ἂν Musgrave, Seidler: ἥδιστ' ἂν τήνδ' L

450 δουλείας ἐμέθεν
δειλαίας παυσίπονος·
⟨κἂν⟩ γὰρ ὀνείροισι κυροί-
η 'ν δόμοις πόλει τε πατρῴ-
ᾳ τερπνῶν ὕμνων ἀπολαύ-
455 ειν, κοινὰν χάριν ὄλβου.

—ἀλλ' οἵδε χέρας δεσμοῖς δίδυμοι
συνερεισθέντες χωροῦσι, νέον
πρόσφαγμα θεᾶς· σιγᾶτε, φίλαι·
τὰ γὰρ Ἑλλήνων ἀκροθίνια δὴ
460 ναοῖσι πέλας τάδε βαίνει,
οὐδ' ἀγγελίας ψευδεῖς ἔλακεν
βουφορβὸς ἀνήρ.
ὦ πότνι', εἴ σοι τάδ' ἀρεσκόντως
πόλις ἥδε τελεῖ,
465 δέξαι θυσίας, ἃς ὁ παρ' ἡμῖν
νόμος οὐχ ὁσίας ἀναφαίνει.

ΙΦΙΓΕΝΕΙΑ
εἶέν·
τὰ τῆς θεοῦ μὲν πρῶτον ὡς καλῶς ἔχῃ
φροντιστέον μοι. μέθετε τῶν ξένων χέρας,
ὡς ὄντες ἱεροὶ μηκέτ' ὦσι δέσμιοι.
470 ναοῦ δ' ἔσω στείχοντες εὐτρεπίζετε

452 ⟨κἂν⟩ Herwerden
452-3 ὀνείροισι Fritzsche: ὀνείρασι L   κυροίη 'ν post
Hartung ('ν) Kovacs: συμβαίην L

to end the toil
of my wretched slavery.
Even in my dreams may I have
the joy of singing gladdening hymns
in the house and city of my fathers,
a delight in blessedness all may share in!

Enter ORESTES and PYLADES bound, led by servants.

CHORUS LEADER

But here come the two men with their hands bound
together, a fresh sacrifice for the goddess. Keep silence,
my friends! The finest offering of Greece draws near to our
temple. It was no false message our cowherd bore. Re-
vered goddess, if it is pleasing in your sight that the city
does these things, receive the sacrifices which the law in
our country declares to be unholy.

IPHIGENIA

Well, then, my first thought must be that the goddess'
property is well taken care of. Release the strangers' hands
so that being consecrate they may go unchained.[16] (*The
servants release their hands.*) Go into the temple and pre-

---

[16] It was customary for sacrificial victims to wander loose in
the precinct of a temple before they were sacrificed.

454–5 ἀπολαύειν Aldina: ἀπόλαυσιν L
455 ὄλβου Dupuy: ὄλβα L: ὄρφνας Morel
458 post θεᾶς 461-2 (οὐδ' . . . ἀνήρ) trai. Elmsley
466 ὁσίας Bergk: ὁσίας Ἕλλησι διδοὺς L

ἃ χρὴ 'πὶ τοῖς παροῦσι καὶ νομίζεται.
  φεῦ·
τίς ἆρα μήτηρ ἡ τεκοῦσ' ὑμᾶς ποτε
πατήρ τ'; ἀδελφὴ δ', εἰ γεγῶσα τυγχάνει,
οἵων στερεῖσα διπτύχων νεανιῶν
475 ἀνάδελφος ἔσται. τὰς τύχας τίς οἶδ' ὅτῳ
τοιαίδ' ἔσονται; πάντα γὰρ τὰ τῶν θεῶν
ἐς ἀφανὲς ἕρπει κοὐδὲν οἶδ' οὐδεὶς κακὸν
⟨ὁπηνίχ' ἥξει χὠπόθεν κἀφ' ὅντινα⟩.
ἡ γὰρ τύχη παρήγαγ' ἐς τὸ δυσμαθές.
  πόθεν ποθ' ἥκετ', ὦ ταλαίπωροι ξένοι;
480 ὡς διὰ μακροῦ μὲν τήνδ' ἐπλεύσατε χθόνα,
μακρὸν δ' ἀπ' οἴκων χρόνον ἔσεσθε δὴ κάτω.

ΟΡΕΣΤΗΣ

τί ταῦτ' ὀδύρῃ κἀπὶ τοῖς μέλουσι νῶν
κακοῖς σὲ λυπεῖς, ἥτις εἶ ποτ', ὦ γύναι;
οὔτοι νομίζω σοφόν, ὃς ἂν μέλλων κτανεῖν
485 οἴκτῳ τὸ δεῖμα τοὐλέθρου νικᾶν θέλῃ,
οὐδ' ὅστις Ἅιδην ἐγγὺς ὄντ' οἰκτίζεται
σωτηρίας ἄνελπις· ὡς δύ' ἐξ ἑνὸς
κακὼ συνάπτει· μωρίαν τ' ὀφλισκάνει
θνῄσκει θ' ὁμοίως· τὴν τύχην δ' ἐᾶν χρεών.
490 ἡμᾶς δὲ μὴ θρήνει σύ· τὰς γὰρ ἐνθάδε
θυσίας ἐπιστάμεσθα καὶ γιγνώσκομεν.

---

473 δ' Markland: τ' L   477 post h.v. lac. indic. et suppl.
Bruhn   478 del. Hirzel
    481 ἔσεσθε δὴ Dobree: ἔσεσθ' ἀεὶ L

pare what is needful and customary for the business at hand.

Exit some of the servants into the temple.

Ah me! What mother was yours and what father? And your sister, if you happen to have one—of what a pair of young men will she be bereft! Who knows to whom fortunes like these will come? All that the gods dispense is obscure in its outcome, and where trouble is concerned no one knows ⟨when it will come or from what quarter or to whom⟩. Fortune leads us into perplexity.

Where have you come from, unhappy strangers? Long is the sea journey you have traveled to come here, and long will be your sojourn in the Underworld far from home.

ORESTES
Why make this lament and vex yourself over troubles that are our affair, woman, whoever you are? I do not think it clever if someone about to kill a man tries to overcome his fear of death by expressions of pity. Foolish too is the man who bewails the near approach of Hades though he has no hope of life: he makes double misfortune out of single since he is reproached as a fool but dies all the same. We should let our fate be. As for us, do not weep for our misfortune. We understand perfectly well the sacrifices practiced here.

---

482 μέλουσι Kvíčala: μέλλ- L
483 κακοῖς σὲ Housman: κακοῖσι L
484 κτανεῖν Seidler: θανεῖν L
486 οὐδ' Hermann: οὐχ L
487 ἐξ] ἀνθ' Wecklein

ΙΦΙΓΕΝΕΙΑ

πότερος ἄρ᾽ ὑμῶν †ἐνθάδ᾽ ὠνομασμένος†
Πυλάδης κέκληται; τόδε μαθεῖν πρῶτον θέλω.

ΟΡΕΣΤΗΣ

ὅδ᾽, εἴ τι δή σοι τοῦτ᾽ ἐν ἡδονῇ μαθεῖν.

ΙΦΙΓΕΝΕΙΑ

495   ποίας πολίτης πατρίδος Ἕλληνος γεγώς;

ΟΡΕΣΤΗΣ

τί δ᾽ ἂν μαθοῦσα τόδε πλέον λάβοις, γύναι;

ΙΦΙΓΕΝΕΙΑ

πότερον ἀδελφὼ μητρός ἐστον ἐκ μιᾶς;

ΟΡΕΣΤΗΣ

φιλότητί γ᾽· ἐσμὲν δ᾽ οὐ κασιγνήτω γένει.

ΙΦΙΓΕΝΕΙΑ

σοὶ δ᾽ ὄνομα ποῖον ἔθεθ᾽ ὁ γεννήσας πατήρ;

ΟΡΕΣΤΗΣ

500   τὸ μὲν δίκαιον Δυστυχὴς καλοίμεθ᾽ ἄν.

ΙΦΙΓΕΝΕΙΑ

οὐ τοῦτ᾽ ἐρωτῶ· τοῦτο μὲν δὸς τῇ τύχῃ.

ΟΡΕΣΤΗΣ

504   τὸ σῶμα θύσεις τοὐμόν, οὐχὶ τοὔνομα.

ΙΦΙΓΕΝΕΙΑ

503   τί δὲ φθονεῖς τοῦτ᾽; ἢ φρονεῖς οὕτω μέγα;

IPHIGENIA
Which of you is called Pylades? That is the first thing I
want to know.

ORESTES
He is, if it gives you any pleasure to learn this.

IPHIGENIA
Of what Greek city is he a citizen?

ORESTES
What good does it do you, lady, to learn this?

IPHIGENIA
Are you brothers from a single mother?

ORESTES
Yes, in affection. But we are not brothers by birth.

IPHIGENIA
And you, what name did your father give you?

ORESTES
In justice my name might be Ill-starred.

IPHIGENIA
That is not my question. You may give that answer to your
fortune.

ORESTES
You will sacrifice my body, not my name.

IPHIGENIA
But why grudge me this? Are you so proud?

---

492 ὄνομ' ἐπωνομασμένος Diggle
498 γένει Koechly: γύναι L
500 Δυστυχὴς Barthold: δυστυχεῖς L
502 et 504 inter se trai. Barthold

ΟΡΕΣΤΗΣ

502 ἀνώνυμοι θανόντες οὐ γελώμεθ᾽ ἄν.

ΙΦΙΓΕΝΕΙΑ

505 οὐδ᾽ ἂν πόλιν φράσειας ἥτις ἐστί σοι;

ΟΡΕΣΤΗΣ

ζητεῖς γὰρ οὐδὲν κέρδος ὡς θανουμένῳ.

ΙΦΙΓΕΝΕΙΑ

χάριν δὲ δοῦναι τήνδε κωλύει τί σε;

ΟΡΕΣΤΗΣ

τὸ κλεινὸν Ἄργος πατρίδ᾽ ἐμὴν ἐπεύχομαι.

ΙΦΙΓΕΝΕΙΑ

πρὸς θεῶν, ἀληθῶς, ὦ ξέν᾽, εἶ κεῖθεν γεγώς;

ΟΡΕΣΤΗΣ

510 ἐκ τῶν Μυκηνῶν ⟨γ᾽⟩, αἵ ποτ᾽ ἦσαν ὄλβιαι.

ΙΦΙΓΕΝΕΙΑ

515 καὶ μὴν ποθεινός γ᾽ ἦλθες ἐξ Ἄργους μολών.

ΟΡΕΣΤΗΣ

516 οὔκουν ἐμαυτῷ γ᾽· εἰ δὲ σοί, σὺ τοῦθ᾽ ὅρα.

ΙΦΙΓΕΝΕΙΑ

511 φυγὰς ⟨δ᾽⟩ ἀπῆρας πατρίδος ἢ ποίᾳ τύχῃ;

ΟΡΕΣΤΗΣ

φεύγω τρόπον γε δή τιν᾽ οὐχ ἑκὼν ἑκών.

510 ⟨γ᾽⟩ Monk
515-16 post 510 trai. Platnauer
511 ⟨δ᾽⟩ Scaliger

ORESTES

If I die nameless I cannot be made a laughingstock.

IPHIGENIA

Will you not even tell me your city?

ORESTES

No: your question holds no profit for a man who is about to die.

IPHIGENIA

But what prevents you from granting me the answer as a favor?

ORESTES

I claim Argos the glorious as my home.

IPHIGENIA

In the gods' name, stranger, are you really from there?

ORESTES

Yes, from Mycenae, which once was flourishing.

IPHIGENIA

Your coming here from Argos is much longed for.

ORESTES

Not by me. If by you, that is your affair.

IPHIGENIA

Did you leave your country as an exile? Or what happened to you?

ORESTES

A sort of exile, both constrained and voluntary.

ΙΦΙΓΕΝΕΙΑ

ἆρ' ἄν τί μοι φράσειας ὧν ἐγὼ θέλω;

ΟΡΕΣΤΗΣ

514 ὡς ἐν παρέργῳ τῆς ἐμῆς δυσπραξίας.

ΙΦΙΓΕΝΕΙΑ

517 Τροίαν ἴσως οἶσθ', ἧς ἁπανταχοῦ λόγος.

ΟΡΕΣΤΗΣ

ὡς μήποτ' ὤφελόν γε μηδ' ἰδὼν ὄναρ.

ΙΦΙΓΕΝΕΙΑ

φασίν νιν οὐκέτ' οὖσαν οἴχεσθαι δορί.

ΟΡΕΣΤΗΣ

520 ἔστιν γὰρ οὕτως οὐδ' ἄκραντ' ἠκούσατε.

ΙΦΙΓΕΝΕΙΑ

Ἑλένη δ' ἀφῖκται δῶμα Μενέλεω πάλιν;

ΟΡΕΣΤΗΣ

ἥκει, κακῶς γ' ἐλθοῦσα τῶν ἐμῶν τινι.

ΙΦΙΓΕΝΕΙΑ

καὶ ποῦ 'στι; κἀμοὶ γάρ τι προυφείλει κακόν.

ΟΡΕΣΤΗΣ

Σπάρτῃ ξυνοικεῖ τῷ πάρος ξυνευνέτῃ.

ΙΦΙΓΕΝΕΙΑ

525 ὦ μῖσος εἰς Ἕλληνας, οὐκ ἐμοὶ μόνη.

ΟΡΕΣΤΗΣ

ἀπέλαυσα κἀγὼ δή τι τῶν κείνης γάμων.

IPHIGENIA

Will you tell me something I wish to hear?

ORESTES

Yes: this adds but little to my troubles.

IPHIGENIA

Perhaps you know of Troy, talked of everywhere.

ORESTES

Oh would that I did not, even in dreams!

IPHIGENIA

They say that it has perished, destroyed by war.

ORESTES

That is so: it is no idle tale you heard.

IPHIGENIA

Has Helen come back to the house of Menelaus?

ORESTES

She has come, a calamitous return for one of my family.

IPHIGENIA

And where is she? To me too she owes a debt for grief she caused.

ORESTES

She lives in Sparta with her former husband.

IPHIGENIA

Hateful creature in Greece's eyes, not only in mine!

ORESTES

I too have reaped some benefit of her marriage.

EURIPIDES

ΙΦΙΓΕΝΕΙΑ

νόστος δ' Ἀχαιῶν ἐγένεθ', ὡς κηρύσσεται;

ΟΡΕΣΤΗΣ

ὡς πάνθ' ἅπαξ με συλλαβοῦσ' ἀνιστορεῖς.

ΙΦΙΓΕΝΕΙΑ

πρὶν γὰρ θανεῖν σε, τοῦδ' ἐπαυρέσθαι θέλω.

ΟΡΕΣΤΗΣ

530   ἔλεγχ', ἐπειδὴ τοῦδ' ἐρᾷς· λέξω δ' ἐγώ.

ΙΦΙΓΕΝΕΙΑ

Κάλχας τις ἦλθε μάντις ἐκ Τροίας πάλιν;

ΟΡΕΣΤΗΣ

ὄλωλεν, ὡς ἦν ἐν Μυκηναίοις λόγος.

ΙΦΙΓΕΝΕΙΑ

ὦ πότνι', ὡς εὖ. τί γὰρ ὁ Λαέρτου γόνος;

ΟΡΕΣΤΗΣ

οὔπω νενόστηκ' οἶκον, ἔστι δ', ὡς λόγος.

ΙΦΙΓΕΝΕΙΑ

535   ὄλοιτο, νόστου μήποτ' ἐς πάτραν τυχών.

ΟΡΕΣΤΗΣ

μηδὲν κατεύχου· πάντα τἀκείνου νοσεῖ.

ΙΦΙΓΕΝΕΙΑ

Θέτιδος δ' ὁ τῆς Νηρῇδος ἔστι παῖς ἔτι;

ΟΡΕΣΤΗΣ

οὐκ ἔστιν· ἄλλως λέκτρ' ἔγημ' ἐν Αὐλίδι.

IPHIGENIA

And have the Greeks come home, as is reported?

ORESTES

So many questions you ask all together!

IPHIGENIA

Before you die I want to gain this benefit.

ORESTES

Ask on, since your heart is set on it: I will answer.

IPHIGENIA

Did a prophet called Calchas return from Troy?

ORESTES

He's dead, was the report in Mycenae.

IPHIGENIA

Goddess, my thanks! What of Laertes' son?

ORESTES

They say he is alive but not returned.

IPHIGENIA

Death take him! May he never get back home!

ORESTES

No need for your curses: his fortunes all are bad.

IPHIGENIA

Is the son of Nereid Thetis still alive?

ORESTES

He is dead: the marriage he made in Aulis was for nought.

---

533 εὖ. τί Musgrave: ἔστι L

ΙΦΙΓΕΝΕΙΑ

δόλια γάρ, ὡς ἴσασιν οἱ πεπονθότες.

ΟΡΕΣΤΗΣ

540 τίς εἶ ποθ'; ὡς εὖ πυνθάνῃ τἀφ' Ἑλλάδος.

ΙΦΙΓΕΝΕΙΑ

ἐκεῖθέν εἰμι· παῖς ἔτ' οὖσ' ἀπωλόμην.

ΟΡΕΣΤΗΣ

ὀρθῶς ποθεῖς ἄρ' εἰδέναι τἀκεῖ, γύναι.

ΙΦΙΓΕΝΕΙΑ

τί δ' ὁ στρατηγός, ὅν λέγουσ' εὐδαιμονεῖν;

ΟΡΕΣΤΗΣ

τίς; οὐ γὰρ ὅν γ' ἐγᾦδα τῶν εὐδαιμόνων.

ΙΦΙΓΕΝΕΙΑ

545 Ἀτρέως ἐλέγετο δή τις Ἀγαμέμνων ἄναξ.

ΟΡΕΣΤΗΣ

οὐκ οἶδ'· ἄπελθε τοῦ λόγου τούτου, γύναι.

ΙΦΙΓΕΝΕΙΑ

μὴ πρὸς θεῶν, ἀλλ' εἴφ', ἵν' εὐφρανθῶ, ξένε.

ΟΡΕΣΤΗΣ

τέθνηχ' ὁ τλήμων, πρὸς δ' ἀπώλεσέν τινα.

ΙΦΙΓΕΝΕΙΑ

τέθνηκε; ποίᾳ συμφορᾷ; τάλαιν' ἐγώ.

ΟΡΕΣΤΗΣ

550 τί δ' ἐστέναξας τοῦτο; μῶν προσῆκέ σοι;

539 ἴσασιν Nauck: φασὶν L

204

IPHIGENIA

Deceitful marriage, as they know who endured it.

ORESTES

Who are you? How good your questions about Greek affairs are!

IPHIGENIA

I come from there. I was lost while still a child.

ORESTES

No wonder then you long to know of events there, lady.

IPHIGENIA

What about the general who they say is prosperous?

ORESTES

Who is that? The general I know is not one of the blessed.

IPHIGENIA

A son of Atreus, one King Agamemnon, was so called.

ORESTES

I do not know. Leave this topic, lady.

IPHIGENIA

I beg you by the gods, no! Tell me and make me happy, stranger!

ORESTES

The poor man is dead, but he has caused the ruin of someone else.

IPHIGENIA

Dead? Of what did he die? Ah poor me!

ORESTES

Why do you weep at this news? Surely he was no relation of yours?

ΙΦΙΓΕΝΕΙΑ

τὸν ὄλβον αὐτοῦ τὸν πάροιθ᾽ ἀναστένω.

ΟΡΕΣΤΗΣ

δεινῶς γὰρ ἐκ γυναικὸς οἴχεται σφαγείς.

ΙΦΙΓΕΝΕΙΑ

ὦ πανδάκρυτος ἡ κτανοῦσα χὠ θανών.

ΟΡΕΣΤΗΣ

παῦσαί νυν ἤδη μηδ᾽ ἐρωτήσῃς πέρα.

ΙΦΙΓΕΝΕΙΑ

555   τοσόνδε γ᾽, εἰ ζῇ τοῦ ταλαιπώρου δάμαρ.

ΟΡΕΣΤΗΣ

οὐκ ἔστι· παῖς νιν ὃν ἔτεκ᾽ αὐτὸς ὤλεσεν.

ΙΦΙΓΕΝΕΙΑ

ὦ συνταραχθεὶς οἶκος. ὡς τί δὴ θέλων;

ΟΡΕΣΤΗΣ

πατρὸς θανόντος τήνδε τιμωρούμενος.

ΙΦΙΓΕΝΕΙΑ

φεῦ·
ὡς εὖ κακὸν δίκαιον ἐξεπράξατο.

ΟΡΕΣΤΗΣ

560   ἀλλ᾽ οὐ τὰ πρὸς θεῶν εὐτυχεῖ δίκαιος ὤν.

ΙΦΙΓΕΝΕΙΑ

λείπει δ᾽ ἐν οἴκοις ἄλλον Ἀγαμέμνων γόνον;

ΟΡΕΣΤΗΣ

λέλοιπεν Ἠλέκτραν γε παρθένον μίαν.

IPHIGENIA

I weep for the good fortune he once had.

ORESTES

As you should: his was a dreadful death, slaughtered by his
wife.

IPHIGENIA

O pitiable, both the slayer and the slain!

ORESTES

Halt there then: question me no further!

IPHIGENIA

Just one thing more: is the poor man's wife still alive?

ORESTES

No: she was killed by her very own son.

IPHIGENIA

O house in utter turmoil! For what reason?

ORESTES

He took revenge on her for his father's murder.

IPHIGENIA

Ah! What a good deed, this righteous crime he committed!

ORESTES

Yet the gods do not bless him for all his righteousness.

IPHIGENIA

Did Agamemnon leave behind another child in his house?

ORESTES

Yes, one unmarried daughter, Electra.

---

556 ἔτεκ᾽ αὐτὸς Markland: ἔτεχ᾽ οὗτος L
559 ἐξεπράξατο Elmsley: εἰσ- L

ΙΦΙΓΕΝΕΙΑ

τί δέ; σφαγείσης θυγατρὸς ἔστι τις λόγος;

ΟΡΕΣΤΗΣ

οὐδείς γε, πλὴν θανοῦσαν οὐχ ὁρᾶν φάος.

ΙΦΙΓΕΝΕΙΑ

565 τάλαιν' ἐκείνη χὠ κτανὼν αὐτὴν πατήρ.

ΟΡΕΣΤΗΣ

κακῆς γυναικὸς χάριν ἄχαριν ἀπώλετο.

ΙΦΙΓΕΝΕΙΑ

ὁ τοῦ θανόντος δ' ἔστι παῖς Ἄργει πατρός;

ΟΡΕΣΤΗΣ

ἔστ', ἄθλιός γε, κοὐδαμοῦ καὶ πανταχοῦ.

ΙΦΙΓΕΝΕΙΑ

ψευδεῖς ὄνειροι, χαίρετ'· οὐδὲν ἦτ' ἄρα.

ΟΡΕΣΤΗΣ

570 οὐδ' οἱ σοφοί γε δαίμονες κεκλημένοι
πτηνῶν ὀνείρων εἰσὶν ἀψευδέστεροι.
[πολὺς ταραγμὸς ἔν τε τοῖς θείοις ἔνι
κἀν τοῖς βροτείοις· ἐν δὲ λυπεῖται μόνον,
ὃς οὐκ ἄφρων ὢν μάντεων πεισθεὶς λόγοις
575 ὄλωλεν ὡς ὄλωλε τοῖσιν εἰδόσιν.]

ΧΟΡΟΣ

φεῦ φεῦ· τί δ' ἡμεῖς οἵ τ' ἐμοὶ γεννήτορες;
ἆρ' εἰσίν; ἆρ' οὐκ εἰσί; τίς φράσειεν ἄν;

572-5 del. Cropp, 570-5 suspectos habet Diggle

IPHIGENIA

Does anyone still speak of the daughter who was sacrificed?

ORESTES

No, save that she is dead and does not look on the light.

IPHIGENIA

Poor daughter, poor too the father who killed her!

ORESTES

She died for the wretched sake of a wicked woman.

IPHIGENIA

The murdered man's son, is he still alive in Argos?

ORESTES

He lives, unhappy man, both nowhere and everywhere.

IPHIGENIA

Farewell, false dreams! I see now you were worthless!

ORESTES

And the gods, who are called wise, are no more truthful than winged dreams. [There is much confusion in the divine and in the mortal realm. Only one grief has he who though no fool yet trusted the words of seers and died the death that those who know realize he died.]

CHORUS LEADER

Ah, ah! What about us? What about our parents? Are they alive or dead? Who can tell us?

---

574 ὃς Monk: ὅτ’ L

ΙΦΙΓΕΝΕΙΑ

ἀκούσατ'· ἐς γὰρ δή τιν' ἥκομεν λόγον,
ὑμῖν τ' ὄνησιν, ὦ ξένοι, σπεύδουσ' ἅμα
580 κἀμοί. τὸ δ' εὖ μάλιστα τῇδε γίγνεται,
εἰ πᾶσι ταὐτὸν πρᾶγμ' ἀρεσκόντως ἔχει.
θέλοις ἄν, εἰ σώσαιμί σ', ἀγγεῖλαί τί μοι
πρὸς Ἄργος ἐλθὼν τοῖς ἐμοῖς ἐκεῖ φίλοις,
δέλτον τ' ἐνεγκεῖν, ἥν τις οἰκτίρας ἐμὲ
585 ἔγραψεν αἰχμάλωτος, οὐχὶ τὴν ἐμὴν
φονέα νομίζων χεῖρα, τοῦ νόμου δ' ὕπο
θνήσκειν, τὰ τῆς θεοῦ τάδε δίκαι' ἡγούμενος;
οὐδένα γὰρ εἶχον ὅστις ἀγγείλαι μολὼν
ἐς Ἄργος αὖθις τάς ‹τ'› ἐμὰς ἐπιστολὰς
590 πέμψειε σωθεὶς τῶν ἐμῶν φίλων τινί.
σὺ δ' (εἶ γάρ, ὡς ἔοικας, οὐχὶ δυσμενὴς
καὶ τὰς Μυκήνας οἶσθα χοὺς ἐγὼ φιλῶ)
σώθητι κεῖσε, μισθὸν οὐκ αἰσχρὸν λαβών,
κούφων ἕκατι γραμμάτων σωτηρίαν.
595 οὗτος δ', ἐπείπερ πόλις ἀναγκάζει τάδε,
θεᾷ γενέσθω θῦμα χωρισθεὶς σέθεν.

ΟΡΕΣΤΗΣ

καλῶς ἔλεξας τἄλλα πλὴν ἕν, ὦ ξένη·
τὸ γὰρ σφαγῆναι τόνδ' ἐμοὶ βάρος μέγα.
ὁ ναυστολῶν γάρ εἰμ' ἐγὼ τὰς συμφοράς,
600 οὗτος δὲ συμπλεῖ τῶν ἐμῶν μόχθων χάριν.
οὔκουν δίκαιον ἐπ' ὀλέθρῳ τῷ τοῦδ' ἐμὲ
χάριν τίθεσθαι καὐτὸν ἐκδῦναι κακῶν.

IPHIGENIA

Listen! I have come upon a plan: I am trying to benefit you, strangers, and at the same time myself. That is the best result, when the same course of action is pleasing to everyone. *(to Orestes)* If I spared your life, would you be willing to bring news to those I love in Argos and to deliver a tablet? A prisoner took pity and wrote it for me since he did not think that mine was the murderous hand but that it was the law that killed him, this being the goddess' idea of right. I had no one who might bear a message back to Argos and, his life being spared, convey my letters to someone of my kin. But you, it seems, are not ill-disposed and you know Mycenae and those I love: win your way safely there and get no shabby wage, your life for carrying a light letter. But since the city requires it, let this man be separated from you and sacrificed to the goddess.

ORESTES

Your proposal is good except for one thing, stranger. The sacrifice of this man would be a great weight upon me. I am the one with the cargo of misfortune in his hold, and he has sailed with me to share my troubles. It is not right, therefore, for me to do you a good turn and escape from trouble

---

579 σπεύδουσ' Musgrave: σπουδῆς L
580 τῆδε Heimsoeth: γ' οὕτω L
587 τάδε Pierson: ταῦτα L   ἡγούμενος Hermann: -μένης L
588-90 del. Dindorf
589 ⟨τ'⟩ Bothe
591 οὐχὶ Diggle: οὔτε L
592 ἐγὼ Markland: κἀγὼ L   φιλῶ Musgrave: θέλω L
593 κεῖσε Heimsoeth: καὶ σὺ L

ἀλλ᾽ ὡς γενέσθω· τῷδε μὲν δέλτον δίδου·
πέμψει γὰρ Ἄργος, ὥστε σοι καλῶς ἔχειν·
605 ἡμᾶς δ᾽ ὁ χρῄζων κτεινέτω. τὰ τῶν φίλων
αἴσχιστον ὅστις καταβαλὼν ἐς ξυμφορὰς
αὐτὸς σέσωται. τυγχάνει δ᾽ ὅδ᾽ ὢν φίλος,
ὃν οὐδὲν ἧσσον ἢ ᾽μὲ φῶς ὁρᾶν θέλω.

ΙΦΙΓΕΝΕΙΑ

ὦ λῆμ᾽ ἄριστον, ὡς ἀπ᾽ εὐγενοῦς τινος
610 ῥίζης πέφυκας τοῖς φίλοις τ᾽ ὀρθῶς φίλος.
τοιοῦτος εἴη τῶν ἐμῶν ὁμοσπόρων
ὅσπερ λέλειπται. καὶ γὰρ οὐδ᾽ ἐγώ, ξένοι,
ἀνάδελφός εἰμι, πλὴν ὅσ᾽ οὐχ ὁρῶσά νιν.
ἐπεὶ δὲ βούλῃ ταῦτα, τόνδε πέμψομεν
615 δέλτον φέροντα, σὺ δὲ θανῇ· πολλὴ δέ τις
προθυμία σε τοῦδ᾽ ἔχουσα τυγχάνει.

ΟΡΕΣΤΗΣ

θύσει δὲ τίς με καὶ τὰ δεινὰ τλήσεται;

ΙΦΙΓΕΝΕΙΑ

ἐγώ· θεᾶς γὰρ τήνδε προστροπὴν ἔχω.

ΟΡΕΣΤΗΣ

ἄζηλον, ὦ νεᾶνι, κοὐκ εὐδαίμονα.

ΙΦΙΓΕΝΕΙΑ

620 ἀλλ᾽ εἰς ἀνάγκην κείμεθ᾽, ἣν φυλακτέον.

ΟΡΕΣΤΗΣ

αὐτὴ ξίφει κτείνουσα θῆλυς ἄρσενας;

myself at the cost of his death. Rather, this is what should be done: give him the tablet. He will take it to Argos, so that all will be well with you. As for me, let him who wants kill me. It is vile for a man to hurl his friends into disaster while saving his own life. This man happens to be a friend, and I desire that he should look on the light no less than I.

IPHIGENIA
O valiant heart, from what noble stock you have come, and how true a friend you are to your friends! May he of my kin who is still left to me be like you! For in fact, strangers, I also have a brother, have him in all but seeing him. But since this is your wish, I will send this man with the tablet and you shall be killed. For some reason you are very eager for this.

ORESTES
Who will do the dread deed of sacrificing me?

IPHIGENIA
I will: this is the service I render to the goddess.

ORESTES
An unenviable and unhappy one, lady.

IPHIGENIA
But I am under compulsion and must perform it.

ORESTES
Will you, a woman, yourself kill a man with the sword?

---

619 ἄζηλον Bothe: ἄζηλά γ᾽ L
621 κτείνουσα Π: θύουσα L

ΙΦΙΓΕΝΕΙΑ

οὔκ, ἀλλὰ χαίτην ἀμφὶ σὴν χερνίψομαι.

ΟΡΕΣΤΗΣ

ὁ δὲ σφαγεὺς τίς, εἰ τάδ᾽ ἱστορεῖν με χρή;

ΙΦΙΓΕΝΕΙΑ

ἔσω δόμων τῶνδ᾽ εἰσὶν οἷς μέλει τάδε.

ΟΡΕΣΤΗΣ

625 τάφος δὲ ποῖος δέξεταί μ᾽, ὅταν θάνω;

ΙΦΙΓΕΝΕΙΑ

πῦρ ἱερὸν ἔνδον χάσμα τ᾽ εὐρωπὸν πέτρας.

ΟΡΕΣΤΗΣ

φεῦ·
πῶς ἄν μ᾽ ἀδελφῆς χεὶρ περιστείλειεν ἄν;

ΙΦΙΓΕΝΕΙΑ

μάταιον εὐχήν, ὦ τάλας, ὅστις ποτ᾽ εἶ,
ηὔξω· μακρὰν γὰρ βαρβάρου ναίει χθονός.
630 οὐ μήν, ἐπειδὴ τυγχάνεις Ἀργεῖος ὤν,
ἀλλ᾽ ὧν γε δυνατὸν οὐδ᾽ ἐγὼ ᾽λλείψω χάριν.
πολύν τε γάρ σοι κόσμον ἐνθήσω τάφῳ,
ξανθῷ τ᾽ ἐλαίῳ σῶμα σὸν <χρίσω καλῶς
καὶ συμπυρωθὲν Βακχίῳ> κατασβέσω,
καὶ τῆς ὀρείας ἀνθεμόρρυτον γάνος
635 ξουθῆς μελίσσης ἐς πυρὰν βαλῶ σέθεν.
   ἀλλ᾽ εἶμι δέλτον τ᾽ ἐκ θεᾶς ἀνακτόρων
οἴσω· τὸ μέντοι δυσμενὲς μή μούγκαλῇς,
φυλάσσετ᾽ αὐτούς, πρόσπολοι, δεσμῶν ἄτερ.

IPHIGENIA

No, I will pour lustral water about your head.

ORESTES

Who will do the killing, if I may ask?

IPHIGENIA

There are people in this temple whose business this is.

ORESTES

What kind of burial will I get when I have been killed?

IPHIGENIA

There is a sacred fire inside and a broad cleft in the cliff.

ORESTES

Ah me! How I wish my sister's hand would deck my corpse!

IPHIGENIA

Poor man, whoever you are, your wish is in vain! She dwells far off from this barbarian land. But since you are an Argive, I shall not omit such service as I can give. I will deck your burial with plentiful adornment, ⟨richly anoint⟩ your body with tawny olive oil and extinguish ⟨your ashes with wine,⟩ and on the spot where your body was burned I shall pour fragrant honey from tawny mountain bees.

Well, I will go now and bring the tablet from the goddess' temple. Yet, so that you may not charge me with ill-will, (*to the servants*) guard them without fetters, servants.

---

631 'λλείψω Markland: λείψω L

633 inter σὸν et κατασβέσω lac. indic. Jackson

637 μοὐγκαλῆς post Kirchhoff Jackson: μου λάβης L

ἴσως <δ᾽> ἄελπτα τῶν ἐμῶν φίλων τινὶ
640 πέμψω πρὸς Ἄργος, ὃν μάλιστ᾽ ἐγὼ φιλῶ,
καὶ δέλτος αὐτῷ ζῶντας οὓς δοκεῖ θανεῖν
λέγουσ᾽ ἀπίστους ἡδονὰς ἀπαγγελεῖ.

ΧΟΡΟΣ
κατολοφύρομαι σὲ τὸν χερνίβων
645 ῥανίσι μελόμενον <μέλεον> αἱμακταῖς.

ΟΡΕΣΤΗΣ
οἶκτος γὰρ οὐ ταῦτ᾽, ἀλλὰ χαίρετ᾽, ὦ ξέναι.

ΧΟΡΟΣ
σὲ δὲ τύχας μάκαρος, ὦ νεανία,
σεβόμεθ᾽, ἐς πάτραν ὅτι πόδ᾽ ἐμβάσῃ.

ΠΥΛΑΔΗΣ
650 ἄζηλά τοι φίλοισι, θνῃσκόντων φίλων.

ΧΟΡΟΣ
ὦ σχέτλιοι πομπαί, φεῦ φεῦ,
<δύο> διολλῦσαι·
αἰαῖ αἰαῖ πότερος ὁ μᾶλλον <τλάμων>;
655 ἔτι γὰρ ἀμφίλογα δίδυμα μέμονε φρήν,
σὲ πάρος ἢ σ᾽ ἀναστενάξω γόοις.

ΟΡΕΣΤΗΣ
Πυλάδη, πέπονθας ταὐτὸ πρὸς θεῶν ἐμοί;

639 <δ᾽> Diggle
645 <μέλεον> Monk
646 ἀλλ᾽ οὐ γὰρ οἶκτος ταῦτα Weil
647 σὲ δέ, νεανία, τύχας μάκαρος, ὦ Diggle

Perhaps the news I shall send to the one I love best at
Argos will be unlooked for, and the tablet, telling him that
one he thought dead is alive, will bring him joy he can
scarcely believe.

Exit IPHIGENIA *into the* skene.

CHORUS
I lament for you, ⟨unhappy man,⟩
destined for the deadly drops of the lustral basin.

ORESTES
This does not call for tears: ladies, farewell!

CHORUS
But you, young man, we honor for your blessed fortune:
you will set foot on your native soil.

PYLADES
No enviable thing for a friend to do when his friend is
being killed.

CHORUS
O cruel the sending, ah me,
that slays ⟨two men⟩!
Ah, ah, which of the two is more ⟨luckless⟩?
The impulse of my mind is twofold and wavering:
is it you or you that I should first weep for?

ORESTES
Pylades, in heaven's name do you feel the same as I do?

---

649 πόδ᾽ Elmsley: ποτ᾽ L   ἐμβάσῃ Seidler: ἐπεμ- L
650 τοι Burges: τοῖς L
652 ⟨δύο⟩ Bothe
654 μᾶλλον Musgrave: μέλλων L   ⟨τλάμων⟩ Willink

EURIPIDES

ΠΥΛΑΔΗΣ

οὐκ οἶδ'· ἐρωτᾷς οὐ λέγειν ἔχοντά με.

ΟΡΕΣΤΗΣ

660   τίς ἐστὶν ἡ νεᾶνις; ὡς Ἑλληνικῶς
ἀνήρεθ' ἡμᾶς τούς τ' ἐν Ἰλίῳ πόνους
νόστον τ' Ἀχαιῶν τόν τ' ἐν οἰωνοῖς σοφὸν
Κάλχαντ' Ἀχιλλέως τ' ὄνομα, καὶ τὸν ἄθλιον
Ἀγαμέμνον' ὡς ᾤκτιρ' ἀνηρώτα τέ με
665   γυναῖκα παῖδάς τ'. ἔστιν ἡ ξένη γένος
ἐκεῖθεν Ἀργεία τις· οὐ γὰρ ἄν ποτε
δέλτον τ' ἔπεμπε καὶ τάδ' ἐξεμάνθανεν,
ὡς κοινὰ πράσσουσ', Ἄργος εἰ πράσσει καλῶς.

ΠΥΛΑΔΗΣ

ἔφθης με μικρόν· ταὐτὰ δὲ φθάσας λέγεις,
670   πλὴν ἕν· τὰ γάρ τοι βασιλέων παθήματα
ἴσασι πάντες ὧν ἐπιστροφή τις ᾖ.
    ἀτὰρ διῆλθον χἅτερον λόγον τινά.

ΟΡΕΣΤΗΣ

τίν'; ἐς τὸ κοινὸν δοὺς ἄμεινον ἂν μάθοις.

ΠΥΛΑΔΗΣ

αἰσχρὸν θανόντος σοῦ βλέπειν ἡμᾶς φάος·
675   κοινῇ τ' ἔπλευσα δεῖ τε καὶ κοινῇ θανεῖν.
καὶ δειλίαν γὰρ καὶ κάκην κεκτήσομαι
Ἄργει τε Φωκέων τ' ἐν πολυπτύχῳ χθονί,
δόξω δὲ τοῖς πολλοῖσι (πολλοὶ γὰρ κακοί)
προδοὺς σεσῶσθαί σ' αὐτὸς εἰς οἴκους μόνος

PYLADES

You ask the question, but I cannot answer.

ORESTES

Who is the young woman? How Greek were her questions
to us about the troubles in Troy, the homecoming of the
Achaeans, Calchas skilled in the omens of birds, and the
fame of Achilles! What pity she showed for Agamemnon,
and what questions she asked me about his wife and chil-
dren! The woman must, I suppose, be from there, an
Argive by birth. Otherwise she would not be sending a
letter there, nor would she have asked her questions as if
she too prospered whenever Argos did.

PYLADES

You anticipate me and have taken the very words from my
mouth except for one thing: the sufferings of kings are
known to all who have paid any heed.

But there is another thing I have thought of.

ORESTES

What is that? If you share your thought, you will know it
better.

PYLADES

It is disgraceful for me to look on the light with you dead.
Just as I sailed on a common voyage with you, so ought I to
die with you. Otherwise I shall get a reputation for coward-
ice in Argos and the glens of Phocis. The many will think
(evil as they are) that I came home safely by myself be-

---

670 τοι Hermann: τῶν L   672 διῆλθον Porson: -ῆλθε L
675 τε West: με L
679 σεσῶσθαί σ᾽ Elmsley: σε σώζεσθ᾽ L

680 ἦ καὶ φονεύσας ἐπὶ νοσοῦσι δώμασιν
ῥάψαι μόρον σοι σῆς τυραννίδος χάριν,
ἔγκληρον ὡς δὴ σὴν κασιγνήτην γαμῶν.
ταῦτ᾽ οὖν φοβοῦμαι καὶ δι᾽ αἰσχύνης ἔχω,
κοὐκ ἔσθ᾽ ὅπως οὐ χρὴ συνεκπνεῦσαί μέ σοι
685 καὶ συσφαγῆναι καὶ πυρωθῆναι δέμας,
φίλον γεγῶτα καὶ φοβούμενον ψόγον.

ΟΡΕΣΤΗΣ

εὔφημα φώνει· τἀμὰ δεῖ φέρειν κακά,
ἁπλᾶς δὲ λύπας ἐξόν, οὐκ οἴσω διπλᾶς.
ὃ γὰρ σὺ λυπρὸν κἀπονείδιστον λέγεις,
690 ταῦτ᾽ ἔστιν ἡμῖν, εἴ σε συμμοχθοῦντ᾽ ἐμοὶ
κτενῶ· τὸ μὲν γὰρ εἰς ἔμ᾽ οὐ κακῶς ἔχει,
πράσσονθ᾽ ἃ πράσσω πρὸς θεῶν, λῦσαι βίον.
σὺ δ᾽ ὄλβιός τ᾽ εἶ καθαρά τ᾽, οὐ νοσοῦντ᾽, ἔχεις
μέλαθρ᾽, ἐγὼ δὲ δυσσεβῆ καὶ δυστυχῆ·
695 σωθεὶς δέ, παῖδας ἐξ ἐμῆς ὁμοσπόρου
κτησάμενος, ἣν ἔδωκά σοι δάμαρτ᾽ ἔχειν,
<σύ τ᾽ ἂν τὸ λοιπὸν βίον ἔχοις εὐδαίμονα>
ὄνομά τ᾽ ἐμοῦ γένοιτ᾽ ἄν, οὐδ᾽ ἄπαις δόμος
πατρῷος οὑμὸς ἐξαλειφθείη ποτ᾽ ἄν.
ἀλλ᾽ ἕρπε καὶ ζῆ καὶ δόμους οἴκει πατρός.
700 ὅταν δ᾽ ἐς Ἑλλάδ᾽ ἱππιόν τ᾽ Ἄργος μόλῃς,
πρὸς δεξιᾶς σε τῆσδ᾽ ἐπισκήπτω τάδε·
τύμβον τε χῶσον κἀπίθες μνημεῖά μου,
καὶ δάκρυ᾽ ἀδελφὴ καὶ κόμας δότω τάφῳ.
ἄγγελλε δ᾽ ὡς ὄλωλ᾽ ὑπ᾽ Ἀργείας τινὸς

cause I abandoned you or even that with your house in trouble I plotted your death to win your throne, being married to your sister, who would be the heiress. These things make me afraid and ashamed, and it is surely right for me to breathe my last, be slaughtered, and cremated with you since I am your friend and stand in fear of censure.

ORESTES

No more shocking words! I must endure my own misfortunes. Since I can bear one set of griefs, I will not bear two. What you have called painful and blameworthy applies also to me if I cause your death when you have shared my troubles. For my part, it is no misfortune for me to lose my life, given the fortunes the gods have sent me. But you are prosperous, and you have a house that is pure, not diseased, while mine is godless and unblest. If you come safely back and get children from my sister, whom I have given you as your wife, ⟨you could live henceforth a happy life,⟩ and my name will be preserved and my father's house will not lack descendants and be blotted out. So go and live and take care of the house of your father. But this I beg of you by your right hand: when you come to Greece and to horse-pasturing Argos, pile up a burial mound for me and put my memorial upon it. Let my sister give to my tomb the gift of her tears and cut hair. Proclaim to all that I

680-1 φονεῦσαί σ᾽ . . . ῥάψας Bergk
687 κακά] ἐμέ Porson
692 λῦσαι Schenkl: λήσειν L
697 num ante h. v. aliquid exciderit dubitat Diggle
701 σοι Hartung
702 μου Monk: μοι L

705 γυναικὸς ἀμφὶ βωμὸν ἁγνισθεὶς φόνῳ.
καὶ μὴ προδῷς μου τὴν κασιγνήτην ποτέ,
ἔρημα κήδη καὶ δόμους ὁρῶν πατρός.
καὶ χαῖρ'· ἐμῶν γὰρ φίλτατόν σ' ηὗρον φίλων,
ὦ συγκύναγε καὶ συνεκτραφεὶς ἐμοί,
710 ὦ πόλλ' ἐνεγκὼν τῶν ἐμῶν ἄχθη κακῶν.

ἡμᾶς δ' ὁ Φοῖβος μάντις ὢν ἐψεύσατο·
τέχνην δὲ θέμενος ὡς προσώταθ' Ἑλλάδος
ἀπήλασ', αἰδοῖ τῶν πάρος μαντευμάτων.
ᾧ πάντ' ἐγὼ δοὺς τἀμὰ καὶ πεισθεὶς λόγοις,
715 μητέρα κατακτὰς αὐτὸς ἀνταπόλλυμαι.

ΠΥΛΑΔΗΣ

ἔσται τάφος σοι, καὶ κασιγνήτης λέχος
οὐκ ἂν προδοίην, ὦ τάλας, ἐπεί σ' ἐγὼ
θανόντα μᾶλλον ἢ βλέπονθ' ἔξω φίλον.
ἀτὰρ τὸ τοῦ θεοῦ σ' οὐ διέφθορέν γέ πω
720 μάντευμα· καίτοι κἀγγὺς ἕστηκας φόνου.
ἀλλ' ἔστιν, ἔστιν ἡ λίαν δυσπραξία
λίαν διδοῦσα μεταβολάς, ὅταν τύχῃ.

ΟΡΕΣΤΗΣ

σίγα· τὰ Φοίβου δ' οὐδὲν ὠφελεῖ μ' ἔπη·
γυνὴ γὰρ ἥδε δωμάτων ἔξω περᾷ.

ΙΦΙΓΕΝΕΙΑ

725 ἀπέλθεθ' ὑμεῖς καὶ παρευτρεπίζετε
τἄνδον μολόντες τοῖς ἐφεστῶσι σφαγῇ.

719 σ'... γέ Nauck: γ'... σέ L
720 κἀγγὺς Erfurdt: γ' ἐγγὺς L

perished at the hand of an Argive woman, consecrated for death at the altar. And never desert my sister: my father's house, yours by marriage, is destitute. Farewell! My fellow huntsman who grew up with me and bore so much of the burden of my misfortunes, in you I have found the dearest of my friends!

It was the prophet Apollo who deceived me: by a cunning trick he drove me as far as possible from Hellas, in shame at his earlier prophecies. I gave my all to him, trusted his words, and killed my mother, but now in recompense I am perishing myself.

PYLADES

You shall have a burial, and I shall never desert the bed of your sister, poor man: I shall hold you a dearer friend in death than in life. But the god's oracle has not killed you yet, though you certainly stand near to being slaughtered. Still, dependably true it is that extreme misfortune often-times begets extreme change.

Enter IPHIGENIA *carrying a tablet.*

ORESTES

Enough! Phoebus' words do me no good: here comes the woman out of the house.

IPHIGENIA

(*to the servants*) Leave me: go inside and help those in charge of the sacrifice to prepare things. (*The remaining servants go into the temple.*)

223

δέλτου μὲν αἵδε πολύθυροι διαπτυχαί,
ξένοι, πάρεισιν· ἃ δ' ἐπὶ τοῖσδε βούλομαι
ἀκοῦσατ'. οὐδεὶς αὐτὸς ἐν πόνοις ⟨τ'⟩ ἀνὴρ
730 ὅταν τε πρὸς τὸ θάρσος ἐκ φόβου πέσῃ.
ἐγὼ δὲ ταρβῶ μὴ ἀπονοστήσας χθονὸς
θῆται παρ' οὐδὲν τὰς ἐμὰς ἐπιστολὰς
ὁ τήνδε μέλλων δέλτον εἰς Ἄργος φέρειν.

ΟΡΕΣΤΗΣ

τί δῆτα βούλῃ; τίνος ⟨ἐπήκοος λόγου
θαρσεῖν ἔχοις ἂν ὢν⟩ ἀμηχανεῖς πέρι;

ΙΦΙΓΕΝΕΙΑ

735 ὅρκον δότω μοι τάσδε πορθμεύσειν γραφὰς
πρὸς Ἄργος, οἷσι βούλομαι πέμψαι φίλων.

ΟΡΕΣΤΗΣ

ἦ κἀντιδώσεις τῷδε τοὺς αὐτοὺς λόγους;

ΙΦΙΓΕΝΕΙΑ

τί χρῆμα δράσειν ἢ τί μὴ δράσειν; λέγε.

ΟΡΕΣΤΗΣ

ἐκ γῆς ἀφήσειν μὴ θανόντα βαρβάρου.

ΙΦΙΓΕΝΕΙΑ

740 δίκαιον εἶπας· πῶς γὰρ ἀγγείλειεν ἄν;

ΟΡΕΣΤΗΣ

ἦ καὶ τύραννος ταῦτα συγχωρήσεται;

---

729 ⟨τ'⟩ Koechly
734 post τίνος lac. indic. Kovacs
738 fort. delendus: cf. Med. 748

Here is the tablet with its many leaves, strangers. Hear what I further desire. No man stays the same both when he is in trouble and when he has passed from fear to hope. I am afraid that the intended bearer of my letter to Argos may make light of my command to him once he has left this land.

ORESTES

So what is it you desire? What ⟨word can give you confidence where⟩ you are perplexed?

IPHIGENIA

Let him give me an oath that he will carry this tablet to Argos to those loved ones I want to send it to.

ORESTES

Will you make the same kind of oath to him?

IPHIGENIA

To do what or not to do what? You must say.

ORESTES

That you will release him alive from this barbarian land.

IPHIGENIA

That is only fair: otherwise how could he deliver the message?

ORESTES

Will the king go along with this?

ΙΦΙΓΕΝΕΙΑ

ναί.

πείσω σφε, καὐτὴ ναὸς ἐσβήσω σκάφος.

ΟΡΕΣΤΗΣ

ὄμνυ· σὺ δ᾽ ἔξαρχ᾽ ὅρκον ὅστις εὐσεβής.

ΙΦΙΓΕΝΕΙΑ

δώσειν λέγειν χρὴ τήνδε τοῖς ἐμοῖς φίλοις.

ΠΥΛΑΔΗΣ

745 τοῖς σοῖς φίλοισι γράμματ᾽ ἀποδώσω τάδε.

ΙΦΙΓΕΝΕΙΑ

κἀγὼ σὲ σώσω κυανέας ἔξω πέτρας.

ΠΥΛΑΔΗΣ

τίν᾽ οὖν ἐπόμνυς τοισίδ᾽ ὅρκιον θεῶν;

ΙΦΙΓΕΝΕΙΑ

Ἄρτεμιν, ἐν ἧσπερ δώμασιν τιμὰς ἔχω.

ΠΥΛΑΔΗΣ

ἐγὼ δ᾽ ἄνακτά γ᾽ οὐρανοῦ σεμνὸν Δία.

ΙΦΙΓΕΝΕΙΑ

750 εἰ δ᾽ ἐκλιπὼν τὸν ὅρκον ἀδικοίης ἐμέ;

ΠΥΛΑΔΗΣ

ἄνοστος εἴην· τί δὲ σύ, μὴ σώσασά με;

ΙΦΙΓΕΝΕΙΑ

μήποτε κατ᾽ Ἄργος ζῶσ᾽ ἴχνος θείην ποδός.

744 δώσειν Bothe: δώσω L

226

IPHIGENIA

Yes. I will persuade him. I will put the man on board ship
myself.

ORESTES

(*to Pylades*) Take the oath. (*to Iphigenia*) And you dictate
to him as piety enjoins.

IPHIGENIA

You must say that you will give this to my loved ones.

PYLADES

I will deliver this letter to your loved ones.

IPHIGENIA

And I shall convey you safely past the Dark Rocks.

PYLADES

Which of the gods do you invoke to witness this oath?

IPHIGENIA

Artemis, in whose temple I hold office.

PYLADES

And I call on Zeus, the august king of heaven.

IPHIGENIA

And what should happen if you break your oath and wrong
me?

PYLADES

May I never reach home! And what should happen to you if
you do not save me?

IPHIGENIA

May I never live to set foot on the soil of Argos!

ΠΥΛΑΔΗΣ

ἄκουε δή νυν ὃν παρήλθομεν λόγον.

ΙΦΙΓΕΝΕΙΑ

ἀλλ᾽ εὐθὺς ἔστω κοινός, ἢν καλῶς ἔχῃ.

ΠΥΛΑΔΗΣ

755 ἐξαίρετόν μοι δὸς τόδ᾽, ἤν τι ναῦς πάθῃ
χἠ δέλτος ἐν κλύδωνι χρημάτων μέτα
ἀφανὴς γένηται, σῶμα δ᾽ ἐκσώσω μόνον,
τὸν ὅρκον εἶναι τόνδε μηκέτ᾽ ἔμπεδον.

ΙΦΙΓΕΝΕΙΑ

ἀλλ᾽ οἶσθ᾽ ὃ δράσω (πολλὰ γὰρ πολλῶν κυρεῖ)·
760 τἀνόντα κἀγγεγραμμέν᾽ ἐν δέλτου πτυχαῖς
λόγῳ φράσω σοι πάντ᾽ ἀπαγγεῖλαι φίλοις.
ἐν ἀσφαλεῖ γάρ· ἢν μὲν ἐκσώσῃς γραφήν,
αὐτὴ φράσει σιγῶσα τἀγγεγραμμένα·
ἢν δ᾽ ἐν θαλάσσῃ γράμματ᾽ ἀφανισθῇ τάδε,
765 τὸ σῶμα σώσας τοὺς λόγους σώσεις ἐμοί.

ΠΥΛΑΔΗΣ

καλῶς ἔλεξας τῶν τε σῶν ἐμοῦ θ᾽ ὕπερ.
σήμαινε δ᾽ ᾧ χρὴ τάσδ᾽ ἐπιστολὰς φέρειν
πρὸς Ἄργος ὅ τι τε χρὴ κλυόντα σοῦ λέγειν.

ΙΦΙΓΕΝΕΙΑ

769 ἄγγελλ᾽ Ὀρέστῃ, παιδὶ τἀγαμέμνονος· . . .

ΠΥΛΑΔΗΣ

780 ὦ θεοί.

PYLADES

But listen, here is a consideration we overlooked.

IPHIGENIA

Well, let it be shared at once if it is a good one.

PYLADES

Allow me this exception: if something happens to the ship,
and the letter along with the cargo is lost and I save only
myself, let the oath no longer be binding.

IPHIGENIA

Well, here is what I shall do (for more precautions mean
more success): all that is contained in the folds of the tablet
I shall tell you in words so that you can tell my loved ones.
That way lies safety. If you keep the tablet unharmed, all by
itself it will silently communicate what it contains. But if
this letter is lost at sea, by saving yourself you also will save
my message for me.

PYLADES

Your suggestion is good, both for you and for me. So tell me
to whom in Argos I should bring this letter and what I
should report from your lips.

IPHIGENIA

Bear this message to Orestes, son of Agamemnon: . . .

PYLADES

O gods!

---

754 εὐθὺς ἔστω κοινός Markland (κοινός) et Fix cl. 673: αὖτις
ἔσται καινὸς L
765 ἐμοί] ὁμοῦ Badham
766 τε σῶν Haupt: θεῶν L
779-81 mutato ordine post 769 trai. Jackson

EURIPIDES

ΙΦΙΓΕΝΕΙΑ

τί τοὺς θεοὺς ἀνακαλεῖς ἐν τοῖς ἐμοῖς;

ΠΥΛΑΔΗΣ

781   οὐδέν· πέραινε δ'· ἐξέβην γὰρ ἄλλοσε.

ΙΦΙΓΕΝΕΙΑ

779   . . . Ὀρέσθ' (ἵν' αὖθις ὄνομα δὶς κλύων μάθῃς),
770   ἡ 'ν Αὐλίδι σφαγεῖσ' ἐπιστέλλει τάδε
ζῶσ' Ἰφιγένεια, τοῖς ἐκεῖ δ' οὐ ζῶσ' ἔτι . . .

ΟΡΕΣΤΗΣ

ποῦ δ' ἔστ' ἐκείνη; κατθανοῦσ' ἥκει πάλιν;

ΙΦΙΓΕΝΕΙΑ

ἥδ' ἦν ὁρᾷς σύ· μὴ λόγων ἔκπλησσέ με.
. . . Κόμισαί μ' ἐς Ἄργος, ὦ σύναιμε, πρὶν θανεῖν,
775   ἐκ βαρβάρου γῆς καὶ μετάστησον θεᾶς
σφαγίων, ἐφ' οἷσι ξενοφόνους τιμὰς ἔχω . . .

ΟΡΕΣΤΗΣ

Πυλάδη, τί λέξω; ποῦ ποτ' ὄνθ' ηὑρήμεθα;

ΙΦΙΓΕΝΕΙΑ

778   . . . ἢ σοῖς ἀραία δώμασιν γενήσομαι.
782   τάχ' οὖν ἐρωτῶν σ' εἰς ἄπιστ' ἀφίξεται·
λέγ' οὕνεκ' ἔλαφον ἀντιδοῦσά μου θεὰ
Ἄρτεμις ἔσωσέ μ', ἣν ἔθυσ' ἐμὸς πατήρ,
785   δοκῶν ἐς ἡμᾶς ὀξὺ φάσγανον βαλεῖν,

IPHIGENIA

Why do you call on the gods in the middle of my message?

PYLADES

It was nothing; go on: my mind was elsewhere.

IPHIGENIA

. . . "Orestes" (I say it twice so you will remember it), "here are the words of her who was slain at Aulis, Iphigenia, who is alive though to people there she is dead: . . ."

ORESTES

Where is she? Has she come back from the grave?

IPHIGENIA

It is she whom you see. Do not distract me from my message. " . . . Before you die, brother, fetch me home to Argos from this barbarian land! Take me away from the goddess' sacrifices where it is my office to kill foreigners . . ."

ORESTES

Pylades, what am I to say? Where in the world do we find ourselves?

IPHIGENIA

" . . . or I shall be a curse upon your house!" Perhaps in questioning you he will become incredulous. Tell him then that Artemis saved my life by putting a doe in my place, and it was this that my father sacrificed, thinking that it was into me that he had plunged his sharp sword, and that she

---

773 λόγων Seidler: -οις L

782 Iphigeniae trib. Markland: Pyladae L   ἀφίξεται
Burges: -ομαι L

784 fort. ἔθυ'   785 fort. delendus

ἐς τήνδε δ᾽ ᾤκισ᾽ αἶαν. αἵδ᾽ ἐπιστολαί,
τάδ᾽ ἐστὶ τὰν δέλτοισιν ἐγγεγραμμένα.

ΠΥΛΑΔΗΣ

ὦ ῥᾳδίοις ὅρκοισι περιβαλοῦσά με,
κάλλιστα δ᾽ ὀμόσασ᾽, οὐ πολὺν σχήσω χρόνον,
790   τὸν δ᾽ ὅρκον ὃν κατώμοσ᾽ ἐμπεδώσομεν.
ἰδού, φέρω σοι δέλτον ἀποδίδωμί τε,
Ὀρέστα, τῆσδε σῆς κασιγνήτης πάρα.

ΟΡΕΣΤΗΣ

δέχομαι· παρεὶς δὲ γραμμάτων διαπτυχὰς
τὴν ἡδονὴν πρῶτ᾽ οὐ λόγοις αἱρήσομαι.
795   ὦ φιλτάτη μοι σύγγον᾽, ἐκπεπληγμένος
ὅμως σ᾽ ἀπίστῳ περιβαλὼν βραχίονι
ἐς τέρψιν εἶμι, πυθόμενος θαυμάστ᾽ ἐμοί.

ΙΦΙΓΕΝΕΙΑ

ξέν᾽, οὐ δικαίως τῆς θεοῦ τὴν πρόσπολον
χραίνεις ἀθίκτοις περιβαλὼν πέπλοις χέρα.

ΟΡΕΣΤΗΣ

800   ὦ συγκασιγνήτη τε κἀκ ταὐτοῦ πατρὸς
Ἀγαμέμνονος γεγῶσα, μή μ᾽ ἀποστρέφου,
ἔχουσ᾽ ἀδελφόν, οὐ δοκοῦσ᾽ ἕξειν ποτέ.

ΙΦΙΓΕΝΕΙΑ

ἐγώ σ᾽ ἀδελφὸν τὸν ἐμόν; οὐ παύσῃ λέγων;
τό τ᾽ Ἄργος αὐτοῦ μεστὸν ἥ τε Ναυπλία.

796 σ᾽ ἀπίστῳ Markland: ἀπιστῶ L
798n Ἰφ. Monk: Χο. L

caused me to dwell in this country. Those are my commands, and that is the content of the tablets.

PYLADES

Lady, you have bound me with an easy oath and have taken a most noble one yourself! I shall not long delay but will make good the oath I have sworn! (*He hands the letter to Orestes.*) Here, Orestes, I bring you a letter from your sister here and put it in your hands.

ORESTES

I accept. I will not trouble to open the letter but will choose first a pleasure not of words but of deeds. Sister I love best, stunned though I am, with scarce believing arms, I yet come to the pleasure of your embrace. These are wonders I have heard.

He makes to embrace Iphigenia. She moves to avoid the embrace.

IPHIGENIA

Stranger, it is not right for you to defile the servant of the goddess, putting your arms about her inviolate clothing!

ORESTES

Sister, born from the same father Agamemnon, do not turn away from me: you have your brother though you never expected to have him again!

IPHIGENIA

I have my brother? Won't you stop this talk? It is Argos and Nauplia that hold him.

---

803 ἔχω Diggle   804 τ᾽ Bothe: δ᾽ L

ΟΡΕΣΤΗΣ

805 οὐκ ἔστ᾽ ἐκεῖ σός, ὦ τάλαινα, σύγγονος.

ΙΦΙΓΕΝΕΙΑ

ἀλλ᾽ ἡ Λάκαινα Τυνδαρίς σ᾽ ἐγείνατο;

ΟΡΕΣΤΗΣ

Πέλοπός γε παιδὶ παιδός, οὗ 'κπέφυκ᾽ ἐγώ.

ΙΦΙΓΕΝΕΙΑ

τί φής; ἔχεις τι τῶνδέ μοι τεκμήριον;

ΟΡΕΣΤΗΣ

ἔχω· πατρῴων ἐκ δόμων τι πυνθάνου.

ΙΦΙΓΕΝΕΙΑ

810 οὐκοῦν λέγειν μὲν χρὴ σέ, μανθάνειν δ᾽ ἐμέ;

ΟΡΕΣΤΗΣ

λέγοιμ᾽ ἂν ἀκοῇ πρῶτον Ἠλέκτρας τάδε·
Ἀτρέως Θυέστου τ᾽ οἶσθα γενομένην ἔριν;

ΙΦΙΓΕΝΕΙΑ

ἤκουσα· χρυσῆς ἀρνὸς ἦν νείκη πέρι.

ΟΡΕΣΤΗΣ

ταῦτ᾽ οὖν ὑφήνασ᾽ οἶσθ᾽ ἐν εὐπήνοις ὑφαῖς;

ΙΦΙΓΕΝΕΙΑ

815 ὦ φίλτατ᾽, ἐγγὺς τῶν ἐμῶν χρίμπτῃ φρενῶν.

806 ἦ Monk
807 γε Elmsley: τε L   οὗ 'κπέφυκ᾽ Elmsley: ἐκπ- L
811 ἀκοῇ Reiske: ἄκουε L
813 ἦν νείκη Mekler, Radermacher: ἡνίκ᾽ ἦν L
815 χρίμπτῃ Wecklein: κάμπτῃ L

ORESTES

Poor woman, your brother is not there.

IPHIGENIA

But did the Spartan daughter of Tyndareus bear you?

ORESTES

Yes, to Pelops' grandson, my father.

IPHIGENIA

What? Do you have some proof of this for me?

ORESTES

I have: ask me something about our father's house.

IPHIGENIA

Should you not rather speak, while I listen?

ORESTES

I will tell you first what I heard from Electra. Do you know
of the strife that occurred between Atreus and Thyestes?

IPHIGENIA

I have heard about it: the quarrel concerned a golden
lamb.[17]

ORESTES

Then do you remember weaving this tale upon cloth of fine
thread?

IPHIGENIA

Dear man, how near you touch my memory!

[17] See above on line 198.

ΟΡΕΣΤΗΣ

εἰκώ τ᾽ ἐν ἱστοῖς ἡλίου μετάστασιν;

ΙΦΙΓΕΝΕΙΑ

ὕφηνα καὶ τόδ᾽ εἶδος εὐμίτοις πλοκαῖς.

ΟΡΕΣΤΗΣ

καὶ λούτρ᾽ ἐς Αὖλιν μητρὸς ἀδέξω πάρα;

ΙΦΙΓΕΝΕΙΑ

οἶδ᾽· οὐ γὰρ ὁ γάμος ἐσθλὸς ὤν μ᾽ ἀφείλετο.

ΟΡΕΣΤΗΣ

820 τί γάρ; κόμας σὰς μητρὶ δοῦσα σῇ φέρειν;

ΙΦΙΓΕΝΕΙΑ

μνημεῖά γ᾽ ἀντὶ σώματος τοὐμοῦ τάφῳ.

ΟΡΕΣΤΗΣ

ἃ δ᾽ εἶδον αὐτός, τάδε φράσω τεκμήρια·
Πέλοπος παλαιὰν ἐν δόμοις λόγχην πατρός,
ἣν χερσὶ πάλλων παρθένον Πισάτιδα
825 ἐκτήσαθ᾽ Ἱπποδάμειαν, Οἰνόμαον κτανών,
ἐν παρθενῶσι τοῖσι σοῖς κεκρυμμένην.

ΙΦΙΓΕΝΕΙΑ

ὦ φίλτατ᾽, οὐδὲν ἄλλο, φίλτατος γὰρ εἶ,

818 ἀδέξω Kirchhoff: ἀνεδέξω L
819 οὐ] εἰ Semitelos   μ᾽ ἀφείλετο in susp. voc. Diggle

---

18 Both bride and groom were given a ritual bath by their mothers on the day of their wedding.

ORESTES

And do you remember weaving the story of the sun's change of course?

IPHIGENIA

This story too I wove in the lovely tapestry.

ORESTES

And do you remember the bath you received from your mother to prepare you for Aulis?[18]

IPHIGENIA

I do. The goodness of the marriage has not effaced this memory.

ORESTES

What then? Do you remember sending a lock of your hair to your mother?

IPHIGENIA

Yes, as a memorial for my tomb in place of my body.[19]

ORESTES

And now I will tell you for proof these things I saw myself: I saw the ancient spear of Pelops our ancestor in the house—which he brandished when he killed Oenomaus and won the maid of Pisa, Hippodamia—hidden in your bedroom.

Orestes and Iphigenia embrace.

IPHIGENIA

O dearest man, for that, and nothing else, is what you are,

---

[19] Presumably when she learned she was to die and would not be buried in Argos.

ἔχω σ’, Ὀρέστα, τηλύγετον ⟨σύμενον⟩
830 χθονὸς ἀπο⟨πρὸ⟩ πατρίδος Ἀργόθεν, ὦ φίλος.

ΟΡΕΣΤΗΣ

κἀγώ σε τὴν θανοῦσαν, ὡς δοξάζεται.

ΙΦΙΓΕΝΕΙΑ

κατὰ δὲ δάκρυα, κατὰ δὲ γόος ἅμα χαρᾷ
τοὐμὸν νοτίζει βλέφαρον.

ΟΡΕΣΤΗΣ

ὡσαύτως δ’ ἐμόν.

ΙΦΙΓΕΝΕΙΑ

τότ’ ἔτι βρέφος
835 ἔλιπον ἀγκάλαισι νεαρὸν τροφοῦ
νεαρὸν ἐν δόμοις.

ΟΡΕΣΤΗΣ

ὦ κρεῖσσον ἢ λόγοισιν εὐτυχῶν ἐγώ.

ΙΦΙΓΕΝΕΙΑ

⟨ὦ⟩ ψυχά, τί φῶ; θαυμάτων
840 πέρα καὶ λόγου πρόσω τάδ’ ἀπέβα.

ΟΡΕΣΤΗΣ

τὸ λοιπὸν εὐτυχοῖμεν ἀλλήλων μέτα.

829-30 ⟨σύμενον⟩ et ἀπο⟨πρὸ⟩ Diggle   830 φίλος] φάος
Willink   832 δάκρυα Bothe: δάκρυ L   832-3 κατὰ . . .
βλέφαρον Iphigeniae, cetera Orestae trib. Lee: Orestae contin. L
  833 τοὐμὸν Lee: τὸ σὸν L
  834 τότ’ ἔτι Matthiae: τὸ δέ τι L
  837n Ορ. Willink: Iphigeniae contin. L

IPHIGENIA AMONG THE TAURIANS

I hold you, Orestes, ‹sped› far
from your homeland of Argos, dear brother!

ORESTES
And I hold you, who were thought to be dead!

IPHIGENIA
Along with my joy a tear, a sob
bedews my face!

ORESTES
And mine as well!

IPHIGENIA
At that time still a babe
I left you in the arms of your nurse,
newborn in the palace.

ORESTES
O how great is my good fortune, greater than words can
    tell!

IPHIGENIA
O my soul, what am I to say? These events
surpass wonder and beggar speech!

ORESTES
From now on may we enjoy good fortune together!

---

837 fort. ἢ λέγοι τις, cl. *Hip.* 1186, *Andr.* 929   ἐγώ Willink,
monente Diggle: ἐμοῦ L   839 ‹ὦ› Monk   τύχα Cropp
840 ἀπέβα Reiske: ἐπ- L   τάδ᾽ ἀπέβα πρόσω Willink

239

ΙΦΙΓΕΝΕΙΑ

ἄτοπον ἡδονὰν ἔλαβον, ὦ φίλαι·
δέδοικα δ' ἐκ χερῶν με μὴ πρὸς αἰθέρα
ἀμπταμένα φύγῃ·
845 ἰὼ Κυκλωπὶς ἑστία· ἰὼ πατρίς,
Μυκήνα φίλα,
χάριν ἔχω ζόας, χάριν ἔχω τροφᾶς,
ὅτι μοι συνομαίμονα τόνδε δόμοις
ἐξεθρέψω φάος.

ΟΡΕΣΤΗΣ

850 γένει μὲν εὐτυχοῦμεν, ἐς δὲ συμφοράς,
ὦ σύγγον', ἡμῶν δυστυχὴς ἔφυ βίος.

ΙΦΙΓΕΝΕΙΑ

ἐγᾦδ' ἁ μέλεος, οἶδ', ὅτε φάσγανον
δέρᾳ 'φῆκέ μοι μελεόφρων πατήρ.

ΟΡΕΣΤΗΣ

855 οἴμοι. δοκῶ γὰρ οὐ παρών σ' ὁρᾶν ἐκεῖ.

ΙΦΙΓΕΝΕΙΑ

ἀνυμέναιος, ⟨ὦ⟩ σύγγον', Ἀχιλλέως
ἐς κλισίαν λέκτρων δόλιον ἀγόμαν·
860 παρὰ δὲ βωμὸν ἦν δάκρυα καὶ γόοι.
φεῦ φεῦ χερνίβων ἐκεί⟨νων· οἴμοι⟩.

844 ἀμπταμένα Seidler: -ος L   845 Κυκλωπὶς ἑστία
Hermann: -πίδες ἑστίαι L   852 ἐγᾦδ' ἁ Seidler: ἐγὼ L
854 'φῆκέ Elmsley: θῆκέ L   856 ⟨ὦ⟩ Bothe
859 δόλιον Hartung: -ίαν ὅτ' L
861 ἐκεί⟨νων· οἴμοι⟩ Jackson

IPHIGENIA AMONG THE TAURIANS

IPHIGENIA

How strange is the pleasure I have received, my friends!
I am afraid that out of my hands to heaven
it may take wing and flee!
O hearth built by the Cyclopes, O homeland,
dear Mycenae,
I feel gratitude for his life, for his nurture,
that you raised to manhood this brother of mine
to be a beacon to the house!

ORESTES

In our ancestry we are blessed, sister, but in its chances our
life has been unblessed.

IPHIGENIA

I remember it, I remember it well, I the ill-starred one,
when my ill-starred father put the knife to my throat!

ORESTES

Ah me! Though I was not present, I seem to see you there!

IPHIGENIA

It was with no wedding song, dear brother,
that I was brought to the false marriage bed of Achilles!
Next to the altar were tears and sobs.
Ah, those dread lustrations! ‹Ah me›!

ΟΡΕΣΤΗΣ

ᾤμωξα κἀγὼ τόλμαν ἣν ἔτλη πατήρ.

ΙΦΙΓΕΝΕΙΑ

ἀπάτορ᾽ ἀπάτορα πότμον ἔλαχον.

865 ἄλλα δ᾽ ἐξ ἄλλων κυρεῖ
867 δαίμονος τύχᾳ τινός.

ΟΡΕΣΤΗΣ

866 εἰ σόν γ᾽ ἀδελφόν, ὦ τάλαιν᾽, ἀπώλεσας.

ΙΦΙΓΕΝΕΙΑ

ὦ μελέα δεινᾶς τόλμας. δείν᾽ ἔτλαν,
870 ὤμοι, δείν᾽ ἔτλαν, σύγγονε. παρὰ δ᾽ ὀλίγον
ἀπέφυγες ὄλεθρον ἀνόσιον ἐξ ἐμᾶν
δαϊχθεὶς χερῶν.
ἁ δ᾽ ἐποῦσ᾽ αὖ τίς τελευτά;
875 τίς τύχα μοι συγκυρήσει;
τίνα σοι ⟨τίνα σοι⟩ πόρον εὑρομένα
πάλιν ἀπὸ πόλεως ἀνδροφόνου πέμψω
πατρίδ᾽ ἐς Ἀργείαν,
880 πρὶν ἐπὶ ξίφος αἵματι σῷ πελάσαι;
τόδ᾽ ⟨ἤδη⟩ τόδε σόν, ὦ μελέα ψυχά,
χρέος ἀνευρίσκειν.
πότερον κατὰ χέρσον, οὐχὶ
885 ναΐᾳ ἀλλὰ ποδῶν ῥιπᾷ;

---

867 ante 866 trai. et cum Seidler Iphigeniae trib. Monk:
Orestae trib. L   870 ὤμοι, δείν᾽ ἔτλαν Willink: δ- ἔ- ὤ- L
874 ἐποῦσ᾽ αὖ τίς Willink: ἐπ᾽ αὐτοῖσι τίς L
875 συγκυρήσει Bothe: συγχωρήσει L

IPHIGENIA AMONG THE TAURIANS

ORESTES

I too lament for our father's heartless deed.

IPHIGENIA

Fatherless, fatherless was the fate that was mine!
But now new things follow upon old
by the stroke of some heavenly power.

ORESTES

Poor woman, what if you had killed your brother?

IPHIGENIA

O how unblessed was I in my dread resolve! Dread
    things I dared,
ah me, dread things, my brother, and barely
did you escape the unholy fate
of slaughter at my hands.
But as for what follows, where will it end?
What fate shall come upon me?
What means, ⟨what means,⟩ shall I find to send you
from this murderous land
to your Argive home
before the sword goes after your blood?
This ⟨now⟩, this is your task, poor soul,
to discover.
Shall it be by land, with no ship
but with rhythmic tread of feet?

---

876 ⟨τίνα σοι⟩ Diggle   877 ἀνδροφόνου Sansone: ἀπὸ
φόνου L   881 ⟨ἤδη⟩ Willink
885 ναίᾳ Willink: ναὶ L: νάϊος Badham

EURIPIDES

θανάτῳ πελάσεις ἄρα, βάρβαρα φῦλα
καὶ δι᾽ ὁδοὺς ἀνόδους στείχων·
διὰ κυανέας ⟨γε⟩ μὰν
890   στενοπόρου πέτρας μακρὰ κέλευθα να-
ΐοισιν δρασμοῖς.
τάλαιν᾽ ⟨ἐγὼ⟩ τάλαιν᾽, ⟨αἰαῖ⟩·
895   τίς ἂν οὖν τάδ᾽ ἄνοι θεὸς ἢ βροτὸς ἢ
τί †τῶν ἀδοκήτων
πόρον ἄπορον† ἐξανύσας,
δυοῖν τλαμόνοιν Ἀτρείδαιν φανεῖ
κακῶν ἔκλυσιν;

ΧΟΡΟΣ

900   ἐν τοῖσι θαυμαστοῖσι καὶ μύθων πέρα
τάδ᾽ εἶδον αὐτὴ κοὐ κλυοῦσ᾽ ἀπ᾽ ἀγγέλων.

ΠΥΛΑΔΗΣ

τὸ μὲν φίλους ἐλθόντας εἰς ὄψιν φίλων,
Ὀρέστα, χειρῶν περιβολὰς εἰκὸς λαβεῖν·
λήξαντα δ᾽ οἴκτων κἀπ᾽ ἐκεῖν᾽ ἐλθεῖν χρεών,
905   ὅπως τὸ κλεινὸν ὄμμα τῆς σωτηρίας
λαβόντες ἐκ γῆς βησόμεσθα βαρβάρου.
[σοφῶν γὰρ ἀνδρῶν ταῦτα, μὴ ᾽κβάντας τύχης,
καιρὸν λαβόντας, ἡδονὰς ἄλλας λαβεῖν.]

---

889 ⟨γε⟩ Willink   894 ⟨ἐγὼ⟩ Diggle   ⟨αἰαῖ⟩ Willink
895 ἄνοι Mekler: ἂν ἦ L
896-7 τί ⟨μέσον τούτων⟩ ἀδόκητ᾽ ἀπόρων πόρον ἐξανύσας
(vel -σαν, Mekler) Willink
898 τλαμόνοιν Tucker: τοῖν μόνοιν L

244

Then you court death, going through
barbarous tribes by trackless paths.
But through the Dark
Rocks, the narrow way, is a long journey
by seafaring flight.
O luckless, luckless ‹me! Ah ah›!
What god, then, or what mortal,
or what that lies between shall find
the unhoped for way out of perplexity[20]
and reveal to the luckless children of Atreus
release from their troubles?

CHORUS LEADER

This is miraculous and beyond words! And I have seen it
with my eyes, not heard it by report!

PYLADES

When loved ones meet loved ones, Orestes, it is natural for
them to embrace. But we must stop these tearful words
and come to the question how we shall see salvation's glori-
ous face and escape from this barbarous country. [It is the
part of wise men not to depart from their fortune, to seize
the opportunity, and to win other pleasures.]

---

[20] I translate Willink's conjectural restoration of this corrupt
passage.

---

[901] κοὺ Bothe: καὶ L   ἀπ᾽ ἀγγέλων Hermann: ἀπαγγελῶ
L   [902] τὸ μὲν] εἶέν Markland   post h. v. lac. indicare paene
malit Diggle
[906] βλέποντες Page
[907-8] del. L. Dindorf

ΟΡΕΣΤΗΣ

καλῶς ἔλεξας· τῇ τύχῃ δ᾽ οἶμαι μέλειν
910 τοῦδε ξὺν ἡμῖν· ἢν δέ τις πρόθυμος ᾖ,
σπεύδειν τὸ θεῖον μᾶλλον εἰκότως ἔχει.

ΙΦΙΓΕΝΕΙΑ

οὐ μή μ᾽ ἐπίσχῃς οὐδ᾽ ἀποστήσεις λόγου,
πρῶτον πυθέσθαι τίνα ποτ᾽ Ἠλέκτρα πότμον
εἴληχε βιότου· φίλα γάρ ἐστι ταῦτ᾽ ἐμοί.

ΟΡΕΣΤΗΣ

915 τῷδε ξυνοικεῖ βίον ἔχουσ᾽ εὐδαίμονα.

ΙΦΙΓΕΝΕΙΑ

οὗτος δὲ ποδαπὸς καὶ τίνος πέφυκε παῖς;

ΟΡΕΣΤΗΣ

Στρόφιος ὁ Φωκεὺς τοῦδε κλήζεται πατήρ.

ΙΦΙΓΕΝΕΙΑ

ὁ δ᾽ ἐστί γ᾽ Ἀτρέως θυγατρός, ὁμογενὴς ἐμός;

ΟΡΕΣΤΗΣ

ἀνεψιός γε, μόνος ἐμοὶ σαφὴς φίλος.

ΙΦΙΓΕΝΕΙΑ

920 οὐκ ἦν τόθ᾽ οὗτος ὅτε πατὴρ ἔκτεινέ με.

ΟΡΕΣΤΗΣ

οὐκ ἦν· χρόνον γὰρ Στρόφιος ἦν ἄπαις τινά.

ΙΦΙΓΕΝΕΙΑ

χαῖρ᾽ ὦ πόσις μοι τῆς ἐμῆς ὁμοσπόρου.

ORESTES

Your advice is good. And I think fortune cares for this
result as much as we do. When someone makes an effort
himself, it is likely that the gods too will show more zeal.

IPHIGENIA

You will not hinder me or keep me from asking first how
Electra is faring. That question is dear to my heart.

ORESTES

She is married to this man and lives a blessed life.

IPHIGENIA

But where does he come from? Whose son is he?

ORESTES

His father is called Strophius the Phocian.

IPHIGENIA

And is he not also son of Atreus' daughter and kin to me?

ORESTES

Yes, your cousin, and my only true friend.

IPHIGENIA

He was not yet born when my father sacrificed me.

ORESTES

No: Strophius was childless for some time.

IPHIGENIA

Greetings, husband of my sister!

---

⁹¹¹ σπεύδειν Rauchenstein: σθένειν L

⁹¹² οὐ μή Elmsley: οὐδέν L   ἐπίσχῃς . . . ἀποστήσεις
Monk: ἐπίσχῃ γ᾽ . . . ἀποστήσῃ L

⁹¹⁴ ἐστι ταῦτ᾽ Markland: ἔσται πάντ᾽ L

EURIPIDES

ΟΡΕΣΤΗΣ

κἀμός γε σωτήρ, οὐχὶ συγγενὴς μόνον.

ΙΦΙΓΕΝΕΙΑ

τὰ δεινὰ δ᾽ ἔργα πῶς ἔτλης μητρὸς πέρι;

ΟΡΕΣΤΗΣ

925   σιγῶμεν αὐτά· πατρὶ τιμωρῶν ἐμῷ.

ΙΦΙΓΕΝΕΙΑ

ἡ δ᾽ αἰτία τίς ἀνθ᾽ ὅτου κτείνει πόσιν;

ΟΡΕΣΤΗΣ

ἔα τὰ μητρός· οὐδὲ σοὶ κλυεῖν καλόν.

ΙΦΙΓΕΝΕΙΑ

σιγῶ· τὸ δ᾽ Ἄργος πρὸς σὲ νῦν ἀποβλέπει;

ΟΡΕΣΤΗΣ

Μενέλαος ἄρχει· φυγάδες ἐσμὲν ἐκ πάτρας.

ΙΦΙΓΕΝΕΙΑ

930   οὔ που νοσοῦντας θεῖος ὕβρισεν δόμους;

ΟΡΕΣΤΗΣ

931   οὔκ, ἀλλ᾽ Ἐρινύων δεῖμά μ᾽ ἐκβάλλει χθονός.

ΙΦΙΓΕΝΕΙΑ

934   ἔγνωκα· μητρός ⟨σ᾽⟩ οὔνεκ᾽ ἠλάστρουν θεαί.

ΟΡΕΣΤΗΣ

935   ὥσθ᾽ αἱματηρὰ στόμι᾽ ἐπεμβαλεῖν ἐμοί.

934-5 post 931 trai. Monk
934 ⟨σ᾽⟩ Markland

ORESTES

Yes, and my savior, not only my kinsman.

IPHIGENIA

But how could you do those terrible deeds against our mother?

ORESTES

Let us not speak of them: I was avenging my father.

IPHIGENIA

But what was her reason for killing her husband?

ORESTES

Let be your mother's deeds: not even for you is it right to hear about them.

IPHIGENIA

I say nothing. But does Argos now look to you as its ruler?

ORESTES

Menelaus is king. I am exiled from my country.

IPHIGENIA

Surely our uncle has not done violence to our ailing house?

ORESTES

No: it was fear of the Erinyes that exiled me.

IPHIGENIA

I understand: the goddesses drove you out because of our mother.

ORESTES

Yes, and they forced their bloody bit into my mouth.

ΙΦΙΓΕΝΕΙΑ

932 ταῦτ' ἄρ' ἐπ' ἀκταῖς κἀνθάδ' ἠγγέλθης μανείς.

ΟΡΕΣΤΗΣ

933 ὤφθημεν οὐ νῦν πρῶτον ὄντες ἄθλιοι.

ΙΦΙΓΕΝΕΙΑ

936 τί γάρ ποτ' ἐς γῆν τήνδ' ἐπόρθμευσας πόδα;

ΟΡΕΣΤΗΣ

Φοίβου κελευσθεὶς θεσφάτοις ἀφικόμην.

ΙΦΙΓΕΝΕΙΑ

τί χρῆμα δρᾶσαι; ῥητὸν ἢ σιγώμενον;

ΟΡΕΣΤΗΣ

λέγοιμ' ἄν· ἀρχαὶ δ' αἵδε μοι πολλῶν πόνων·
940 ἐπεὶ τὰ μητρὸς ταῦθ' ἃ σιγῶμεν κακὰ
ἐς χεῖρας ἦλθε, μεταδρομαῖς Ἐρινύων
ἠλαυνόμεσθα φυγάδες ἐμμανῆ πόδα,
ἔστ' εἰς Ἀθήνας δή μ' ἔπεμψε Λοξίας,
δίκην παρασχεῖν ταῖς ἀνωνύμοις θεαῖς.
945 ἔστιν γὰρ ὁσία ψῆφος, ἣν Ἄρει ποτὲ
Ζεὺς εἵσατ' ἔκ του δὴ χερῶν μιάσματος.
ἐλθὼν δ' ἐκεῖσε πρῶτα μέν μ' οὐδεὶς ξένων
ἑκὼν ἐδέξαθ' ὡς θεοῖς στυγούμενον·
οἳ δ' ἔσχον αἰδῶ, ξένια μονοτράπεζά μοι
950 παρέσχον, οἴκων ὄντες ἐν ταὐτῷ στέγει,

938 δρᾶσαι Elmsley: δράσειν L
942-3 ἐμμανῆ πόδα, / ἔστ' εἰς ... δή μ' Weil: ἔνθεν μοι πόδα /
ἐς τὰς ... δή γ' L

IPHIGENIA

So that is the madness they said you suffered from here on the shore.

ORESTES

This is not the first time I have been seen in misery.

IPHIGENIA

But why in the world did you journey to this land?

ORESTES

I came under orders from Phoebus' oracles.

IPHIGENIA

Orders to do what? Can it be revealed or not?

ORESTES

I will tell you: this was the beginning of many troubles for me. When the wrongs against my mother that I do not describe had polluted my hands, the Erinyes pursued me as I fled headlong on my delirious course until Loxias sent me to Athens to stand trial before the nameless goddesses. There is a holy court, which Zeus established for Ares as a result of some uncleanness of hand.[21] When I came there, at first none of my guest-friends was willing to receive me, believing me to be detested by the gods. But those who felt pity for me provided guest fare for me by myself, though they were under the same roof with me. They contrived for

---

[21] The Areopagus was the court in charge of murder cases. In legend it was first convened to try Ares for the murder of Poseidon's son Halirrothius, who had raped Ares' daughter.

σιγῇ δ' ἐτεκτήναντ' ἀπρόσφθεγκτόν μ', ὅπως
δαιτός τ' ὀναίμην πώματός τ' αὐτῶν δίχα,
ἐς δ' ἄγγος ἴδιον ἴσον ἅπασι Βακχίου
μέτρημα πληρώσαντες εἶχον ἡδονήν.

955 κἀγὼ 'ξελέγξαι μὲν ξένους οὐκ ἠξίουν,
ἤλγουν δὲ σιγῇ κἀδόκουν οὐκ εἰδέναι,
μέγα στενάζων οὕνεκ' ἦ μητρὸς φονεύς.
κλύω δ' Ἀθηναίοισι τἀμὰ δυστυχῆ
τελετὴν γενέσθαι, κἄτι τὸν νόμον μένειν,

960 χοῆρες ἄγγος Παλλάδος τιμᾶν λεών.
    ὡς δ' εἰς Ἄρειον ὄχθον ἧκον, ἐς δίκην
ἔστην, ἐγὼ μὲν θάτερον λαβὼν βάθρον,
τὸ δ' ἄλλο πρέσβειρ' ἥπερ ἦν Ἐρινύων.
εἰπὼν ⟨δ'⟩ ἀκούσας θ' αἵματος μητρὸς πέρι,

965 Φοῖβός μ' ἔσωσε μαρτυρῶν, ἴσας δέ μοι
ψήφους διηρίθμησε Παλλὰς ὠλένῃ·
νικῶν δ' ἀπῆρα φόνια πειρατήρια.
ὅσαι μὲν οὖν ἕζοντο πεισθεῖσαι δίκῃ
ψῆφον παρ' αὐτὴν ἱερὸν ὡρίσαντ' ἔχειν·

970 ὅσαι δ' Ἐρινύων οὐκ ἐπείσθησαν νόμῳ,
δρόμοις ἀνιδρύτοισιν ἠλάστρουν μ' ἀεί,
ἕως ἐς ἁγνὸν ἦλθον αὖ Φοίβου πέδον.
καὶ πρόσθεν ἀδύτων ἐκταθείς, νῆστις βορᾶς,
ἐπώμοσ' αὐτοῦ βίον ἀπορρήξειν θανών,

951-2 post 954 trai. Schoene   951 ἀπρόσφθεγκτόν Her-
mann: ἀπόφθ- L   952 τ' ὀναίμην Housman: γενοίμην L
962 ἔστην Bothe: τ' ἔστην L   964 ⟨δ'⟩ Elmsley

me to be addressed by no one, in silence, so that I might eat and drink apart from them. To all they gave an equal measure of wine in separate vessels and thus took their pleasure. I did not wish to take my hosts to task: I grieved silently and pretended not to notice, groaning aloud because I was a matricide. But I hear that for the Athenians my troubles have become a ritual: even now the custom remains in force that Pallas' folk honor the three-quart pitcher.[22]

When I came to the hill of Ares, I stood my trial, I standing on one platform and the eldest of the Erinyes on the other. When I had been accused of my mother's death and had answered, Phoebus saved me by giving evidence, and with her hand Pallas counted out for me equal numbers of votes. Having won the deadly contest I departed. Those Erinyes who sat in judgment and were persuaded by the verdict marked out for their possession a sanctuary right next to the court. But those who were not persuaded by the law pursued me continually on unresting feet until I came again to the holy precincts of Phoebus. I lay stretched out upon the ground before his temple, taking no food, and swore that I would break my life's thread in death there on the spot unless Phoebus, who had de-

---

[22] At the Anthesteria, an annual festival of wine and flowers, one day was called Choes, "the Pitchers." Everyone brought his own wine in a separate jug, and drinking contests were held.

966-7 Παλλάς· ὧδε δὴ / νικῶν [δ'] Kvíčala   ὠλένη def.
Boeghold, *AJA* 93 (1989), 81-3, ellipsim non aeque: cui si mederi
vis, fort. Παλλάς, ‹ὧν ἄπο / φόνου μ' ἔδειξε μητρὸς ὅσιον›
ὠλένη

975 εἰ μή με σώσει Φοῖβος, ὅς μ' ἀπώλεσεν.
ἐντεῦθεν αὐδὴν τρίποδος ἐκ χρυσοῦ λακὼν
Φοῖβός μ' ἔπεμψε δεῦρο, διοπετὲς λαβεῖν
ἄγαλμ' Ἀθηνῶν τ' ἐγκαθιδρῦσαι χθονί.
ἀλλ' ἥνπερ ἡμῖν ὥρισεν σωτηρίαν

980 σύμπραξον· ἢν γὰρ θεᾶς κατάσχωμεν βρέτας,
μανιῶν τε λήξω καὶ σὲ πολυκώπῳ σκάφει
στείλας Μυκήναις ἐγκαταστήσω πάλιν.
    ἀλλ', ὦ φιληθεῖσ', ὦ κασίγνητον κάρα,
σῶσον πατρῷον οἶκον, ἔκσωσον δ' ἐμέ·

985 ὡς τἄμ' ὄλωλε πάντα καὶ τὰ Πελοπιδῶν,
οὐράνιον εἰ μὴ ληψόμεθα θεᾶς βρέτας.

ΧΟΡΟΣ

δεινή τις ὀργὴ δαιμόνων ἐπέζεσεν
ἐς Ταντάλειον σπέρμα διὰ πόνων τ' ἄγει.

ΙΦΙΓΕΝΕΙΑ

τὸ μὲν πρόθυμον, πρίν σε δεῦρ' ἐλθεῖν, ἔχω

990 Ἄργει γενέσθαι καὶ σέ, σύγγον', εἰσιδεῖν.
θέλω δ' ἅπερ σύ, σέ τε μεταστῆσαι πόνων
νοσοῦντά τ' οἶκον, οὐχὶ τῷ κτανόντι με
θυμουμένη, πατρῷον ὀρθῶσαι †θέλω†·
σφαγῆς τε γὰρ σῆς χεῖρ' ἀπαλλάξαιμεν ἂν

995 σώσαιμί τ' οἴκους. τὴν θεὸν δ' ὅπως λάθω
δέδοικα καὶ τύραννον· ἡνίκ' ἂν κενὰς
κρηπῖδας εὕρῃ λαΐνας ἀγάλματος,
πῶς οὐ θανοῦμαι; τίς δ' ἔνεστί μοι λόγος;
ἀλλ', εἰ μὲν ἔστι, τοῦθ' ὅπως γενήσεται,

stroyed me, saved my life. Then uttering speech from his golden tripod Phoebus sent me here to take the statue that fell from the sky and set it up in the land of Athens. So help to bring about the salvation he ordained for me. If I get hold of the goddess's statue, I will not only cease from my madness but will also take you on my many-oared ship and settle you once more in Mycenae.

Dear and much beloved sister, save your father's house, save me! All is lost for me and Pelops' descendants unless I get hold of the goddess' statue that fell from the skies.

CHORUS LEADER

Some dread wrath divine has boiled up against the race of Tantalus and dogs them with misfortune!

IPHIGENIA

Even before you came here, brother, I was eager to be in Argos and to see you. Your wish is also mine, to rescue you from your troubles. I feel no anger at the man who killed me and want to restore the troubled house of our fathers. By rescuing you I would keep my hand from shedding your blood and also save our house. But I am afraid the goddess and the king will notice: when he finds the stone pedestal with no statue on it, how will I escape death? What plea can I make? Yet if there is a way that this can happen and

---

976 λακὼν Scaliger: λαβὼν L
988 ἐς Stadtmueller: τὸ L
993 πάλιν Markland cl. S. *Ant.* 163
998 πῶς Bothe: πῶς δ' L
999 ἔστι . . . ὅπως Lenting: ἔν τι . . . ὁμοῦ L

1000 ἄγαλμά τ' οἴσεις κἄμ' ἐπ' εὐπρύμνου νεὼς
ἄξεις, τὸ κινδύνευμα γίγνεται καλόν·
τούτου δὲ χωρισθεῖσ' ἐγὼ μὲν ὄλλυμαι,
σὺ δ' ἂν τὸ σαυτοῦ θέμενος εὖ νόστου τύχοις.
οὐ μήν τι φεύγω γ', οὐδέ σ' εἰ θανεῖν χρεὼν

1005 σώσασαν· οὐ γὰρ ἀλλ' ἀνὴρ μὲν ἐκ δόμων
θανὼν ποθεινός, τὰ δὲ γυναικὸς ἀσθενῆ.

ΟΡΕΣΤΗΣ

οὐκ ἂν γενοίμην σοῦ τε καὶ μητρὸς φονεύς·
ἅλις τὸ κείνης αἷμα· κοινόφρων δὲ σοὶ
καὶ ζῶν θέλοιμ' ἂν καὶ θανὼν λαχεῖν ἴσον.

1010 ἄξω δέ σ', ἤνπερ καὐτὸς ἐντεῦθεν περῶ
πρὸς οἶκον, ἢ σοῦ κατθανὼν μενῶ μέτα.
γνώμης δ' ἄκουσον· εἰ πρόσαντες ἦν τόδε
Ἀρτέμιδι, πῶς ἂν Λοξίας ἐθέσπισεν
κομίσαι μ' ἄγαλμα θεᾶς πόλισμ' ἐς Παλλάδος,
⟨πῶς δ' ἐς νεών με σφάγιον εἴασεν μολεῖν⟩

1015 καὶ σὸν πρόσωπον εἰσιδεῖν; ἅπαντα γὰρ
συνθεὶς τάδ' εἰς ἓν νόστον ἐλπίζω λαβεῖν.

ΙΦΙΓΕΝΕΙΑ

πῶς οὖν γένοιτ' ἂν ὥστε μήθ' ἡμᾶς θανεῖν
λαβεῖν θ' ἃ βουλόμεσθα; τῇδε γὰρ νοσεῖ
νόστος πρὸς οἴκους, ἡ δὲ βούλησις πάρα.

ΟΡΕΣΤΗΣ

1020 ἆρ' ἂν τύραννον διολέσαι δυναίμεθ' ἄν;

1000 οἴσεις] εἰ σὺ Weil

256

that you can take the statue and me on your well-built ship,
the risk would be a noble one. But if I fail in this, then I am
dead, though you might set your own trouble to rights and
get safely home. Well, I do not shrink from this, even if I
must die for saving your life. No, when the house loses a
male, his loss is felt, but a woman's loss is of little effect.

ORESTES

I will not be your murderer as well as my mother's! Her
blood is enough! Ours is a single purpose, and I mean to
share equally with you in life and in death. If indeed I man-
age to get home myself, I will bring you there; otherwise I
will die and remain here with you. But hear a thought I
have had: if this were contrary to Artemis' will, why would
Loxias have commanded me to take the goddess' statue to
the city of Pallas, ⟨and why would he have allowed me to
be brought as a sacrificial victim to the temple⟩ and to see
your face? So putting all these facts together I have con-
fidence we shall get home.

IPHIGENIA

How then can we get what we want and avoid being killed?
That is where the trouble lies for our journey home: we do
not lack the will.

ORESTES

Could we kill the king?

1004-5 σ᾽ . . . σώσασαν Kirchhoff: μ᾽ . . . σώσασά σ᾽ L
1009 ζῶν Musgrave: ζῆν L   1010-11 del. Dindorf
1010 ἐντεῦθεν περῶ Seidler: ἐνταυθοῖ πέσω L
1014 post h. v. lac. indic. Koechly
1015 ἅπαντ᾽ ἄρα exspectares
1019 ἥδε βούλευσις Markland

ΙΦΙΓΕΝΕΙΑ

δεινὸν τόδ᾽ εἶπας, ξενοφονεῖν ἐπήλυδας.

ΟΡΕΣΤΗΣ

ἀλλ᾽, εἰ σὲ σώσει κἀμέ, κινδυνευτέον.

ΙΦΙΓΕΝΕΙΑ

οὐκ ἂν δυναίμην· τὸ δὲ πρόθυμον ᾔνεσα.

ΟΡΕΣΤΗΣ

τί δ᾽ εἴ με ναῷ τῷδε κρύψειας λάθρᾳ;

[ΙΦΙΓΕΝΕΙΑ

1025 ὡς δὴ σκότον λαβόντες ἐκσωθεῖμεν ἄν;

ΟΡΕΣΤΗΣ

κλεπτῶν γὰρ ἡ νύξ, τῆς δ᾽ ἀληθείας τὸ φῶς.]

ΙΦΙΓΕΝΕΙΑ

εἴσ᾽ ἔνδον ἱεροῦ φύλακες, οὓς οὐ λήσομεν.

ΟΡΕΣΤΗΣ

οἴμοι, διεφθάρμεσθα· πῶς σωθεῖμεν ἄν;

ΙΦΙΓΕΝΕΙΑ

ἔχειν δοκῶ μοι καινὸν ἐξεύρημά τι.

ΟΡΕΣΤΗΣ

1030 ποῖόν τι; δόξης μετάδος, ὡς κἀγὼ μάθω.

ΙΦΙΓΕΝΕΙΑ

ταῖς σαῖς ἀνίαις χρήσομαι σοφίσμασιν.

1025-6 del. Markland
1027 ἱεροῦ Dobree: ἱεροὶ L
1031 σοφίσματι West

258

IPHIGENIA

Foreigners murdering their hosts? A dangerous idea!

ORESTES

But if it will save your life and mine, we must run the risk.

IPHIGENIA

I could not do it, though I praise your enterprising spirit.

ORESTES

But suppose you hide me in this temple.

[IPHIGENIA

You mean we could win safety by taking darkness for a cover?

ORESTES

Yes, for night belongs to thieves, while daylight belongs to truthfulness.]

IPHIGENIA

There are guards inside the shrine: we could not escape their notice.

ORESTES

Oh, we are done for! How can we get away safely?

IPHIGENIA

I think I have hit on a new idea!

ORESTES

What is it? Share it with me so that I may know it too.

IPHIGENIA

I shall make use of your woes as a clever ruse.

ΟΡΕΣΤΗΣ

δειναὶ γὰρ αἱ γυναῖκες εὑρίσκειν τέχνας.

ΙΦΙΓΕΝΕΙΑ

φονέα σε φήσω μητρὸς ἐξ Ἄργους μολεῖν.

ΟΡΕΣΤΗΣ

χρῆσαι κακοῖσι τοῖς ἐμοῖς, εἰ κερδανεῖς.

ΙΦΙΓΕΝΕΙΑ

1035 ὡς οὐ θέμις σε λέξομεν θύειν θεᾷ . . .

ΟΡΕΣΤΗΣ

τίν' αἰτίαν ἔχουσ'; ὑποπτεύω τι γάρ.

ΙΦΙΓΕΝΕΙΑ

. . . οὐ καθαρὸν ὄντα· τὸ δ' ὅσιον δώσω φόνῳ.

ΟΡΕΣΤΗΣ

τί δῆτα μᾶλλον θεᾶς ἄγαλμ' ἁλίσκεται;

ΙΦΙΓΕΝΕΙΑ

πόντου σε πηγαῖς ἁγνίσαι βουλήσομαι.

ΟΡΕΣΤΗΣ

1040 ἔτ' ἐν δόμοισι βρέτας ἐφ' ᾧ πεπλεύκαμεν.

ΙΦΙΓΕΝΕΙΑ

κἀκεῖνο νίψειν, σοῦ θιγόντος ὥς, ἐρῶ.

ΟΡΕΣΤΗΣ

ποῖ δῆτα; πόντου νοτερὸν εἶ παρ' ἔκβολον;

1033-4 del. Czwalina   1035 σε Reiske: γε L
1036 ἔχονθ' Reiske   1040 ἐφ' ὃ πεπλεύκαμεν βρέτας
Wecklein   1041 νίψειν Madvig: νίψαι L

ORESTES

Well, women are clever at inventing subterfuges.

IPHIGENIA

I shall say that you have come from Argos as your mother's slayer.

ORESTES

Make use of my troubles if it will do you any good.

IPHIGENIA

I shall say that it is not lawful to sacrifice you to the goddess . . .

ORESTES

What reason will you allege? I have some inkling of your meaning.

IPHIGENIA

. . . as being unclean. I will sacrifice only what is pure.

ORESTES

How does this help us to capture the goddess' statue?

IPHIGENIA

I shall ask permission to purify you with seawater.

ORESTES

The statue we sailed here to get is still in the temple.

IPHIGENIA

I will say I mean to wash that too—since you touched it.

ORESTES

Where will you take it? Will you go to some sea-washed promontory?

1042 εἰ παρ' Reiske: εἶπας L

ΙΦΙΓΕΝΕΙΑ

οὗ ναῦς χαλινοῖς λινοδέτοις ὁρμεῖ σέθεν.

ΟΡΕΣΤΗΣ

σὺ δ᾽ ἤ τις ἄλλος ἐν χεροῖν οἴσει βρέτας;

ΙΦΙΓΕΝΕΙΑ

1045   ἐγώ· θιγεῖν γὰρ ὅσιόν ἐστ᾽ ἐμοὶ μόνῃ.

ΟΡΕΣΤΗΣ

Πυλάδης δ᾽ ὅδ᾽ ἡμῖν ποῦ τετάξεται πόνου;

ΙΦΙΓΕΝΕΙΑ

ταὐτὸν χεροῖν σοὶ λέξεται μίασμ᾽ ἔχων.

ΟΡΕΣΤΗΣ

λάθρᾳ δ᾽ ἄνακτος ἢ εἰδότος δράσεις τάδε;

ΙΦΙΓΕΝΕΙΑ

1049   πείσασα μύθοις· οὐ γὰρ ἂν λάθοιμί γε.
1051   σοὶ δὴ μέλειν χρὴ τἄλλ᾽ ὅπως ἕξει καλῶς.

ΟΡΕΣΤΗΣ

1050   καὶ μὴν νεώς γε πίτυλος εὐήρης πάρα.
1052   ἑνὸς μόνου δεῖ, τάσδε συγκρύψαι τάδε.
ἀλλ᾽ ἀντίαζε καὶ λόγους πειστηρίους
εὕρισκ᾽· ἔχει τοι δύναμιν εἰς οἶκτον γυνή.
1055   τὰ δ᾽ ἄλλ᾽ ἴσως ἂν πάντα συμβαίη καλῶς.

ΙΦΙΓΕΝΕΙΑ

ὦ φίλταται γυναῖκες, εἰς ὑμᾶς βλέπω,
καὶ τἄμ᾽ ἐν ὑμῖν ἐστιν ἢ καλῶς ἔχειν
ἢ μηδὲν εἶναι καὶ στερηθῆναι πάτρας

IPHIGENIA

Yes, where your ship is anchored on flaxen hawsers.

ORESTES

Will you or someone else carry the statue in your arms?

IPHIGENIA

I will: only I am allowed to touch it.

ORESTES

And what will be Pylades' role in this business?

IPHIGENIA

I will say he has the same taint as you.

ORESTES

Will you do these things with or without the king's knowledge?

IPHIGENIA

I will talk to him and win his assent. It would be impossible to conceal this from him. But you must take care that all else is in order.

ORESTES

Well, my fine-oared ship stands ready. But one thing is still needed: these women must keep this a secret. Find words of persuasion and entreat them: a woman has power to arouse pity. Perhaps all else will then go well.

IPHIGENIA

Dearest women, I look to you. My fate is in your hands—whether I prosper, or am ruined and deprived of my coun-

---

1044 σὺ δ' ἤ τις Jacobs: σοὶ δὴ τίς L
1050-1 inter se trai. Koechly   1055 del. Monk

263

φίλου τ᾽ ἀδελφοῦ φιλτάτης τε συγγόνου.
1060 καὶ πρῶτα μέν μοι τοῦ λόγου τάδ᾽ ἀρχέτω·
γυναῖκές ἐσμεν, φιλόφρον ἀλλήλαις γένος
σῴζειν τε κοινὰ πράγματ᾽ ἀσφαλέσταται.
σιγήσαθ᾽ ἡμῖν καὶ συνεκπονήσατε
φυγάς. καλόν τοι γλῶσσ᾽ ὅτῳ πιστὴ παρῇ.
1065 ὁρᾶτε δ᾽ ὡς τρεῖς μία τύχη τοὺς φιλτάτους
ἢ γῆς πατρῴας νόστος ἢ θανεῖν ἔχει.
σωθεῖσα δ᾽, ὡς ἂν καὶ σὺ κοινωνῇς τύχης,
σώσω σ᾽ ἐς Ἑλλάδ᾽. ἀλλὰ πρός σε δεξιᾶς
σὲ καὶ σ᾽ ἱκνοῦμαι, σὲ δὲ φίλης παρηίδος,
1070 γονάτων τε καὶ τῶν ἐν δόμοισι φιλτάτων
[μητρὸς πατρός τε καὶ τέκνων ὅτῳ κυρεῖ].
τί φατε; τίς ὑμῶν φησιν ἢ τίς οὐ θέλειν—
φθέγξασθε—ταῦτα; μὴ γὰρ αἰνουσῶν λόγους
ὄλωλα κἀγὼ καὶ κασίγνητος τάλας.

ΧΟΡΟΣ

1075 θάρσει, φίλη δέσποινα, καὶ σῴζου μόνον·
ὡς ἔκ γ᾽ ἐμοῦ σοι πάντα σιγηθήσεται
(ἴστω μέγας Ζεύς) ὧν ἐπισκήπτεις πέρι.

ΙΦΙΓΕΝΕΙΑ

ὄναισθε μύθων καὶ γένοισθ᾽ εὐδαίμονες.
σὸν ἔργον ἤδη καὶ σὸν ἐσβαίνειν δόμους·
1080 ὡς αὐτίχ᾽ ἥξει τῆσδε κοίρανος χθονός,
θυσίαν ἐλέγξων εἰ κατείργασται ξένων.
ὦ πότνι᾽, ἥπερ μ᾽ Αὐλίδος κατὰ πτυχὰς

1059 φιλτάτης Bothe: -ου L   1064 πιστὴ Bothe: πίστις L

264

try, my dear brother, and beloved sister. Let my plea begin here: we are women, and our sex wish each other well and are most firm in defending our common interests. Keep our secret and help us make our escape. It is a noble thing to have a loyal tongue in one's head. See how these three loved ones are joined in a single fate, either to reach their fatherland again or to die. Furthermore, so that you too may share my good fortune, if I get home I will bring you safely to Greece. So I beg you—and you and you—by your right hand and your dear cheek and knees and by your nearest and dearest at home [mother and father and any children you have]! What do you say? Who agrees to this and who refuses? Tell me! If you reject my plea, both I and my poor brother are dead.

CHORUS LEADER

Courage, dear mistress! Just get safely home! For, as Zeus is my witness, I will keep the secret you ask me to keep.

IPHIGENIA

May your good words be rewarded and may you find happiness!

(*to Orestes and Pylades*) It is your task now, and yours, to go into the temple. The king of this land will soon be coming to see whether the sacrifice of foreigners has been carried out.

O lady who in the glens of Aulis saved me from the mur-

1066 νόστος Valckenaer: -ον L
1071 del. Dindorf: etiam 1070 del. Cropp
1072 θέλειν Musgrave: -ει L
1081 ἐλέγξων Markland: -γχων L

δεινῆς ἔσωσας ἐκ πατροκτόνου χερός,
σῶσόν με καὶ νῦν τούσδε τ'· ἢ τὸ Λοξίου

1085 οὐκέτι βροτοῖσι διὰ σ' ἐτήτυμον στόμα.
ἀλλ' εὐμενὴς ἔκβηθι βαρβάρου χθονὸς
ἐς τὰς Ἀθήνας· καὶ γὰρ ἐνθάδ' οὐ πρέπει
ναίειν, παρόν σοι πόλιν ἔχειν εὐδαίμονα.

ΧΟΡΟΣ

στρ. α

ὄρνις ἃ παρὰ πετρίνας

1090 πόντου δειράδας ἀλκυὼν
ἔλεγον οἶτον ἀείδεις,
εὐξύνετον ξυνετοῖς βοάν,
ὅτι πόσιν κελαδεῖς ἀεὶ μολπαῖς,
ἐγώ σοι παραβάλλομαι

1095 θρηνοῦσ', ἄπτερος ὄρνις,
ποθοῦσ' Ἑλλάνων ἀγόρους,
ποθοῦσ' Ἄρτεμιν λοχίαν,
ἃ παρὰ Κύνθιον ὄχθον οἰ-
κεῖ φοίνικά θ' ἁβροκόμαν

1100 δάφναν τ' εὐερνέα καὶ
γλαυκᾶς θαλλὸν ἱερὸν ἐλαί-
ας, Λατοῦς ὠδῖνι φίλον,
λίμναν θ' εἱλίσσουσαν ὕδωρ

1083 ἐκ χερὸς παιδοκτόνου Bothe: ἐκ τεκνοκτόνου χερός
Herwerden   v. suspectum habet Diggle
1091 οἰκτρὸν Barnes
1095 θρηνοῦσ' Reiske: θρήνους L
1102 ὠδῖνι Portus: -να L   φίλον Markland: -αν L

derous hand of my father, save me now as well, and these men too! Otherwise it will be your fault that mortals no longer regard Loxias as a true prophet. So in kindness depart from this barbarian land and go to Athens. It is not fitting that you should dwell here when you can live in a blessed city.

Exit into the skene IPHIGENIA, ORESTES, *and* PYLADES.

CHORUS
Halcyon bird, that by the rocky
cliffs at the sea's edge
sing sadly of your fate,
a cry that makes plain to those with ears to hear
that you sing without surcease for your husband:[23]
I, a bird with no wings,
vie with you in lamentation,
longing for the Greeks' gathering places,
longing for Artemis, goddess of childbed,
who dwells by the Cynthian hill
and the date palm with its tender tresses
and the lovely slip of laurel
and the sacred shoot of the gray-green olive,
dear to Leto's offspring,
and the lake that swirls its water

---

[23] Myth told of a devoted human pair Alcyone and Ceyx. Alcyone, turned into the halcyon, laments the loss of her husband.

κύκλιον, ἔνθα κύκνος μελῳ-
1105 δὸς Μούσας θεραπεύει.

ἀντ. α

ὦ πολλαὶ δακρύων λιβάδες,
αἳ παρηίδας εἰς ἐμὰς
ἔπεσον, ἀνίκα πύργων
ὀλομένων ἐν ναυσὶν ἔβαν
1110 πολεμίων ἐρετμοῖσι καὶ λόγχαις·
ζαχρύσου δὲ δι᾽ ἐμπολᾶς
νόστον βάρβαρον ἦλθον,
ἔνθα τᾶς ἐλαφοκτόνου
θεᾶς ἀμφίπολον κόραν
1115 παῖδ᾽ Ἀγαμεμνονίαν λατρεύ-
ω βωμούς τ᾽ οὐ μηλοθύτας,
ζηλοῦσα τὸν διὰ παν-
τὸς δυσδαίμον᾽· ἐν γὰρ ἀνάγ-
καις οὐ κάμνει, σύντροφος ᾧ
1120 μεταβάλῃ δυσδαιμονία·
τὸ δὲ μετ᾽ εὐτυχίαν κακοῦ-
σθαι θνατοῖς βαρὺς αἰών.

στρ. β

καὶ σὲ μέν, πότνι᾽, Ἀργεία
πεντηκόντερος οἶκον ἄξει·
1125 συρίζων θ᾽ ὁ κηρόδετος
Πανὸς οὐρείου κάλαμος
κώπαις ἐπιθωύξει,

1104 κύκλιον Seidler: κύκνειον L
1116 τ᾽ οὐ Musgrave: τοὺς L

in a circle, where the melodious swan
renders his service to the Muses.

Ah, how many are the tear drops
that fell down upon my cheeks
when, my city's walls
destroyed, I was brought on a ship
by the oars and spears of the enemy!
Sold for much money
I reached my barbarian home
where I attend the maiden
daughter of Agamemnon, who serves
the hind-slaying goddess,
and attend the altars where no sheep are sacrificed.
How fortunate I hold the man
who is luckless throughout his life! In hard necessity
he feels no pain, whose constant companion
has been shifting misery.
But to come to grief after blessedness
is a heavy fate for mortals.

You, lady, shall be borne homeward
on an Argive ship with fifty rowers,
and the wax-bound reed pipe
of Pan, the mountain god,
will give the beat to the oars,

1117 ζηλοῦσα τὸν Bothe: ζηλοῦσ᾽ ἄταν L
1119 κάμνει Milton: -εις L   ᾧ Madvig: ὤν L
1120 μεταβάλῃ Willink: -βάλλει L
1125 κηρόδετος Porson: -δέτας L
1126 Πανὸς οὐρείου κάλαμος Diggle: κ- οὐ- Πανὸς L

ὁ Φοῖβός θ᾽ ὁ μάντις ἔχων
κέλαδον ἑπτατόνου λύρας
1130 ἀείδων ἄξει λιπαρὰν
εὖ σ᾽ Ἀθηναίων ἐπὶ γᾶν.
ἐμὲ δ᾽ αὐτοῦ †λιποῦσα
βήσῃ ῥοθίοις πλάταις†,
1135 ἀέρι δ᾽ ἱστί᾽ ⟨ἐπὶ⟩ πρότονον κατὰ
πρῷραν ὑπὲρ στόλον ἐκπετάσουσι πόδες
ναὸς ὠκυπόμπου.

ἀντ. β

λαμπροὺς ἱπποδρόμους βαίην,
ἔνθ᾽ εὐάλιον ἔρχεται πῦρ·
1140 οἰκείων δ᾽ ὑπὲρ θαλάμων
ἐν νώτοις ἀμοῖς πτέρυγας
λήξαιμι θοάζουσα·
χοροῖς δ᾽ ἐνσταίην, ὅθι καὶ
παρθένος εὐδοκίμων δόμων,
1145 παρὰ πόδ᾽ εἱλίσσουσα φίλας
ματρός, ἡλίκων θιάσοις
ἐς ἁμίλλας χαρίτων
ἁβροπλούτου τε χλιδᾶς
1150 εἰς ἔριν ὀρνυμένα, πολυποίκιλα

1131 εὖ σ᾽ Bothe: ἐς L   1132-3 αὐτοῦ ⟨προ⟩λιποῦσ᾽ /
ἀ⟨πο⟩βάσῃ ῥοθίοις [πλάταις] post Hermann (⟨προ-⟩) et
Schoene (⟨ἀπο-⟩) et Bergk ([πλάταις]) Willink
    1135 ἱστί᾽ ⟨ἐπὶ⟩ πρότονον post Fix (⟨ἐπὶ⟩) et Bergk
(πρότονον) Willink: ἱστία πρότονοι L

while Phoebus the prophet, holding
the loud-sounding seven-stringed lyre,
sings and leads you in safety
to the gleaming land of Athens.
Me you shall leave here
and fare over the waves,
as in the breeze the sailyards spread out the sails
against the forestay, over the bows and beyond the prow
of the swift-sailing ship.

Would that I could tread the gleaming track
where the sun goes with his lovely light!
But above my own chamber
the wings on my back
would cease to beat.
May I take my place in the choruses where once
as maiden of illustrious family
near my dear mother I whirled in dance,
and competing in grace
with the throngs of my agemates
and vying with them in the luxury
born of soft-living wealth I put on

1136 πόδες Seidler: πόδα L: πνοαὶ Bruhn
1141 ἐν νώτοις ἀμοῖς πτέρυγας Fritzsche: π- ἐν ν- ἀ- L
1143 δ' ἐνσταίην Platnauer: δὲ σταίην L
1144 δόμων Koechly: γάμων L
1146 θιάσοις Lachmann: -ους L
1149 ἀβροπλούτου τε χλιδᾶς England (χλιδᾶς Markland, τε
Weil): ἀβροπλούτοιο χαίτας L

φάρεα καὶ πλοκάμους περιβαλλομένα
γένυσιν ἐσκίαζον.

ΘΟΑΣ

ποῦ 'σθ' ἡ πυλωρὸς τῶνδε δωμάτων γυνὴ
Ἑλληνίς; ἤδη τῶν ξένων κατήρξατο;
1155 [ἀδύτοις ἐν ἁγνοῖς σῶμα λάμπονται πυρί;]

ΧΟΡΟΣ

ἥδ' ἐστίν, ἥ σοι πάντ', ἄναξ, ἐρεῖ σαφῶς.

ΘΟΑΣ

ἔα·
τί τόδε μεταίρεις ἐξ ἀκινήτων βάθρων,
Ἀγαμέμνονος παῖ, θεᾶς ἄγαλμ' ἐν ὠλέναις;

ΙΦΙΓΕΝΕΙΑ

ἄναξ, ἔχ' αὐτοῦ πόδα σὸν ἐν παραστάσιν.

ΘΟΑΣ

1160 τί δ' ἔστιν, Ἰφιγένεια, καινὸν ἐν δόμοις;

ΙΦΙΓΕΝΕΙΑ

ἀπέπτυσ'· Ὁσίᾳ γὰρ δίδωμ' ἔπος τόδε.

ΘΟΑΣ

τί φροιμιάζῃ νεοχμόν; ἐξαύδα σαφῶς.

1152 γέννας Markland
1155 del. Page

272

a veil of many hues and let down my tresses
to shade my cheek.

Enter by Eisodos B THOAS *with retinue.*

THOAS
Where is the Greek woman who keeps the gates of this
temple? Has she consecrated the strangers by now? [Are
their bodies blazing with fire in the inmost sanctuary?]

Enter from the skene IPHIGENIA *carrying the statue of
Artemis in her arms.*

CHORUS
Here she is, my lord. She will answer all your questions
reliably.

THOAS
But what is this? Daughter of Agamemnon, why do you
take the goddess' statue in your arms from its immovable
plinth?

IPHIGENIA
My lord, stop right there in the vestibule!

THOAS
But what has happened in the temple, Iphigenia?

IPHIGENIA
(*spitting as if to avert an evil omen*) Pah! There, the de-
mands of Holiness are satisfied!

THOAS
What strange business do your words portend? Tell me
plainly.

273

EURIPIDES

ΙΦΙΓΕΝΕΙΑ

οὐ καθαρά μοι τὰ θύματ᾽ ἠγρεύσασθ᾽, ἄναξ.

ΘΟΑΣ

τί τοὐκδιδάξαν τοῦτό σ᾽; ἢ δόξαν λέγεις;

ΙΦΙΓΕΝΕΙΑ

1165 βρέτας τὸ τῆς θεοῦ πάλιν ἕδρας ἀπεστράφη.

ΘΟΑΣ

αὐτόματον, ἤ νιν σεισμὸς ἔστρεψε χθονός;

ΙΦΙΓΕΝΕΙΑ

αὐτόματον· ὄψιν δ᾽ ὀμμάτων ξυνήρμοσεν.

ΘΟΑΣ

ἡ δ᾽ αἰτία τίς; ἢ τὸ τῶν ξένων μύσος;

ΙΦΙΓΕΝΕΙΑ

ἥδ᾽, οὐδὲν ἄλλο· δεινὰ γὰρ δεδράκατον.

ΘΟΑΣ

1170 ἀλλ᾽ ἦ τιν᾽ ἔκανον βαρβάρων ἀκτῆς ἔπι;

ΙΦΙΓΕΝΕΙΑ

οἰκεῖον ἦλθον τὸν φόνον κεκτημένοι.

ΘΟΑΣ

τίν᾽; εἰς ἔρον γὰρ τοῦ μαθεῖν πεπτώκαμεν.

ΙΦΙΓΕΝΕΙΑ

μητέρα κατειργάσαντο κοινωνῷ ξίφει.

ΘΟΑΣ

Ἄπολλον, οὐδ᾽ ἐν βαρβάροις ἔτλη τις ἄν.

IPHIGENIA

The victims you caught for me, my lord, were unclean.

THOAS

What told you this for sure? Or is it a guess?

IPHIGENIA

The goddess' statue turned away from where it stood.

THOAS

On its own? Or did an earthquake turn it?

IPHIGENIA

On its own. And it also closed its eyes.

THOAS

What was the cause? The uncleanness of the foreigners?

IPHIGENIA

That and that only. They have done unspeakable deeds.

THOAS

Did they kill a barbarian on the beach, then?

IPHIGENIA

They arrived with blood of their own already upon them.

THOAS

What blood? I am eager to hear.

IPHIGENIA

With collaborating swords they killed their mother.

THOAS

Apollo! Not even a barbarian would have dared to do that!

1174 ἔτλη Gaisford: τόδ' ἔτλη L

ΙΦΙΓΕΝΕΙΑ

1175 πάσης διωγμοῖς ἠλάθησαν Ἑλλάδος.

ΘΟΑΣ

ἦ τῶνδ᾽ ἔκατι δῆτ᾽ ἄγαλμ᾽ ἔξω φέρεις;

ΙΦΙΓΕΝΕΙΑ

σεμνόν γ᾽ ὑπ᾽ αἰθέρ᾽, ὡς μεταστήσω φόνου.

ΘΟΑΣ

μίασμα δ᾽ ἔγνως τοῖν ξένοιν ποίῳ τρόπῳ;

ΙΦΙΓΕΝΕΙΑ

ἤλεγχον, ὡς θεᾶς βρέτας ἀπεστράφη πάλιν.

ΘΟΑΣ

1180 σοφήν σ᾽ ἔθρεψεν Ἑλλάς, ὡς ἤσθου καλῶς.

ΙΦΙΓΕΝΕΙΑ

καὶ μὴν καθεῖσαν δέλεαρ ἡδύ μοι φρενῶν.

ΘΟΑΣ

τῶν Ἀργόθεν τι φίλτρον ἀγγέλλοντέ σοι;

ΙΦΙΓΕΝΕΙΑ

τὸν μόνον Ὀρέστην ἐμὸν ἀδελφὸν εὐτυχεῖν.

ΘΟΑΣ

ὡς δή σφε σώσαις ἡδοναῖς ἀγγελμάτων;

ΙΦΙΓΕΝΕΙΑ

1185 καὶ πατέρα γε ζῆν καὶ καλῶς πράσσειν ἐμόν.

1181 μὴν Monk: νῦν L
1183 fort. Ὀρέστην ⟨γ᾽⟩

IPHIGENIA

All Greece has driven them into exile.

THOAS

So this is the reason you are bringing the statue out of doors?

IPHIGENIA

Yes, under the holy sky, to cleanse it from blood.

THOAS

How did you learn of the foreigners' taint?

IPHIGENIA

I questioned them when the goddess' statue recoiled.

THOAS

Greece has raised in you a clever girl! Such keen observation!

IPHIGENIA

What is more, they told me a pleasant story to entice my heart.

THOAS

Reporting some news from Argos to charm you?

IPHIGENIA

Yes, that my only brother Orestes was prospering.

THOAS

So you'd spare them, no doubt, in joy at their report.

IPHIGENIA

Yes: and they also said that my father was alive and flourishing.

ΘΟΑΣ

σὺ δ' ἐς τὸ τῆς θεοῦ γ' ἐξένευσας εἰκότως.

ΙΦΙΓΕΝΕΙΑ

πᾶσάν γε μισοῦσ' Ἑλλάδ', ἥ μ' ἀπώλεσεν.

ΘΟΑΣ

τί δῆτα δρῶμεν, φράζε, τοῖν ξένοιν πέρι;

ΙΦΙΓΕΝΕΙΑ

τὸν νόμον ἀνάγκη τὸν προκείμενον σέβειν.

ΘΟΑΣ

1190   οὔκουν ἐν ἔργῳ χέρνιβες ξίφος τε σόν;

ΙΦΙΓΕΝΕΙΑ

ἁγνοῖς καθαρμοῖς πρῶτά νιν νίψαι θέλω.

ΘΟΑΣ

πηγαῖσιν ὑδάτων ἢ θαλασσίᾳ δρόσῳ;

ΙΦΙΓΕΝΕΙΑ

θάλασσα κλύζει πάντα τἀνθρώπων κακά.

ΘΟΑΣ

ὁσιώτεροι γοῦν τῇ θεῷ πέσοιεν ἄν.

ΙΦΙΓΕΝΕΙΑ

1195   καὶ τἀμά γ' οὕτω μᾶλλον ἂν καλῶς ἔχοι.

ΘΟΑΣ

οὔκουν πρὸς αὐτὸν ναὸν ἐκπίπτει κλύδων;

ΙΦΙΓΕΝΕΙΑ

ἐρημίας δεῖ· καὶ γὰρ ἄλλα δράσομεν.

THOAS
But you, naturally, inclined to the goddess' side.

IPHIGENIA
Yes: I hate all Hellas since it destroyed me.

THOAS
Tell me then: what are we to do about the foreigners?

IPHIGENIA
We must respect our established custom.

THOAS
So why are your basin and sword still idle?

IPHIGENIA
First I want to wash and purify them.

THOAS
With water from a spring or the sea?

IPHIGENIA
The sea washes all human ills away.

THOAS
Then they would be more acceptable victims for the goddess.

IPHIGENIA
Yes, and my situation would be better.

THOAS
Doesn't the sea wave wash up against the very temple?

IPHIGENIA
I need a deserted place: I shall do other things as well.

1194 ὁσιώτεροι Tournier: -ον L

ΘΟΑΣ

ἄγ᾽ ἔνθα χρῄζεις· οὐ φιλῶ τἄρρηθ᾽ ὁρᾶν.

ΙΦΙΓΕΝΕΙΑ

ἁγνιστέον μοι καὶ τὸ τῆς θεοῦ βρέτας.

ΘΟΑΣ

1200 εἴπερ γε κηλὶς ἔβαλέ νιν μητροκτόνος.

ΙΦΙΓΕΝΕΙΑ

οὐ γάρ ποτ᾽ ἄν νιν ἠράμην βάθρων ἄπο.

ΘΟΑΣ

1202 δίκαιος ηὐσέβεια καὶ προμηθία.
1214 ὡς εἰκότως σε πᾶσα θαυμάζει πόλις.

ΙΦΙΓΕΝΕΙΑ

1203 οἶσθά νυν ἅ μοι γενέσθω.

ΘΟΑΣ

σὸν τὸ σημαίνειν τάδε.

ΙΦΙΓΕΝΕΙΑ

δεσμὰ τοῖς ξένοισι πρόσθες.

ΘΟΑΣ

ποῖ δέ σ᾽ ἐκφύγοιεν ἄν;

ΙΦΙΓΕΝΕΙΑ

1205 πιστὸν Ἑλλὰς οἶδεν οὐδέν.

ΘΟΑΣ

ἴτ᾽ ἐπὶ δεσμά, πρόσπολοι.

1214 huc trai. Markland   1203 τάδε Diggle: τόδε L

THOAS

Go wherever you like: I do not wish to see forbidden things.

IPHIGENIA

I must also purify the goddess' statue.

THOAS

Yes, if it has been touched by the taint of matricide.

IPHIGENIA

It has: otherwise I would not have taken it from its pedestal.

THOAS

Your piety and forethought are quite proper. It is not surprising that the whole city admires you.

IPHIGENIA

Here is what should be done for me.

THOAS

It is yours to say.

IPHIGENIA

Put shackles on the foreigners.

THOAS

But where could they go to escape from you?

IPHIGENIA

Hellas is utterly untrustworthy.

THOAS

Servants, go fetch shackles!

Servants go into the skene.

ΙΦΙΓΕΝΕΙΑ

κἀκκομιζόντων γε δεῦρο τοὺς ξένους . . .

ΘΟΑΣ

ἔσται τάδε.

ΙΦΙΓΕΝΕΙΑ

. . . κρᾶτα κρύψαντες πέπλοισιν.

ΘΟΑΣ

ἡλίου πρόσθεν φλογός.

ΙΦΙΓΕΝΕΙΑ

σῶν τέ μοι σύμπεμπ' ὀπαδῶν.

ΘΟΑΣ

οἵδ' ὁμαρτήσουσί σοι.

ΙΦΙΓΕΝΕΙΑ

καὶ πόλει πέμψον τιν' ὅστις σημανεῖ . . .

ΘΟΑΣ

ποίας τύχας;

ΙΦΙΓΕΝΕΙΑ

1210 . . . ἐν δόμοις μίμνειν ἅπαντας.

ΘΟΑΣ

μὴ συναντῶσιν φόνῳ;

ΙΦΙΓΕΝΕΙΑ

μυσαρὰ γὰρ τὰ τοιάδ' ἐστί.

1206 γε Elmsley: δὲ L

IPHIGENIA

Yes, and let them bring the foreigners here . . .

THOAS

It shall be so.

IPHIGENIA

. . . covering their heads with garments.

THOAS

To shield the sun's rays from taint.[24]

IPHIGENIA

Send some of your servants with me.

THOAS

These will accompany you.

IPHIGENIA

And send someone to the city to tell them . . .

THOAS

Tell them of what?

IPHIGENIA

. . . to remain indoors, all of them.

THOAS

To avoid contact with shed blood?

IPHIGENIA

Yes, for such things carry a taint.

---

[24] Those polluted with bloodshed veiled their faces so as not to pollute the upper air and the all-seeing sun: cf. *Heracles* 1231-2 and Sophocles, *Oedipus the King* 1424-8.

ΘΟΑΣ

στεῖχε καὶ σήμαινε σύ . . .

ΙΦΙΓΕΝΕΙΑ

. . . μηδέν᾽ εἰς ὄψιν πελάζειν.

ΘΟΑΣ

εὖ γε κηδεύεις πόλιν.

ΙΦΙΓΕΝΕΙΑ

1213   καὶ φίλων γ᾽ οὓς δεῖ μάλιστα.

ΘΟΑΣ

τοῦτ᾽ ἔλεξας εἰς ἐμέ.

ΙΦΙΓΕΝΕΙΑ

1215   σὺ δὲ μένων αὐτοῦ πρὸ ναῶν τῇ θεῷ . . .

ΘΟΑΣ

τί χρῆμα δρῶ;

ΙΦΙΓΕΝΕΙΑ

. . . ἅγνισον πυρσῷ μέλαθρον.

ΘΟΑΣ

καθαρὸν ὡς μόλῃς πάλιν.

ΙΦΙΓΕΝΕΙΑ

ἡνίκ᾽ ἂν δ᾽ ἔξω περῶσιν οἱ ξένοι . . .

ΘΟΑΣ

τί χρή με δρᾶν;

ΙΦΙΓΕΝΕΙΑ

. . . πέπλον ὀμμάτων προθέσθαι.

THOAS

You there, go and tell them . . .

IPHIGENIA

. . . that no one should come and see.

THOAS

How well you care for the city!

IPHIGENIA

Yes, and for those of my loved ones I should most care for.

THOAS

You say this with me in mind!

IPHIGENIA

But you, remain here before the temple and for the goddess . . .

THOAS

What shall I do?

IPHIGENIA

. . . purify the temple with a torch.

THOAS

So that it may be pure for your return.

IPHIGENIA

When the foreigners come outside . . .

THOAS

What must I do?

IPHIGENIA

. . . cover your eyes with your cloak.

1213 οὓς δεῖ Badham: οὐδεὶς L
1216 πυρσῷ Reiske: χρυσῷ L

ΘΟΑΣ

μὴ παλαμναίους βλέπω.

ΙΦΙΓΕΝΕΙΑ

ἦν δ' ἄγαν δοκῶ χρονίζειν . . .

ΘΟΑΣ

τοῦδ' ὅρος τίς ἐστί μοι;

ΙΦΙΓΕΝΕΙΑ

1220 . . . θαυμάσῃς μηδέν.

ΘΟΑΣ

τὰ τῆς θεοῦ πρᾶσσ' ἐπὶ σχολῆς καλῶς.

ΙΦΙΓΕΝΕΙΑ

εἰ γὰρ ὡς θέλω καθαρμὸς ὅδε πέσοι.

ΘΟΑΣ

συνεύχομαι.

ΙΦΙΓΕΝΕΙΑ

τούσδ' ἄρ' ἐκβαίνοντας ἤδη δωμάτων ὁρῶ ξένους
καὶ θεᾶς κόσμους νεογνούς τ' ἄρνας, ὡς φόνῳ
    φόνον
μυσαρὸν ἐκνίψω, σέλας τε λαμπάδων τά τ' ἄλλ'
    ὅσα
1225 προυθέμην ἐγὼ ξένοισι καὶ θεᾷ καθάρσια.
ἐκποδὼν δ' αὐδῶ πολίταις τοῦδ' ἔχειν μιάσματος,
εἴ τις ἢ ναῶν πυλωρὸς χεῖρας ἁγνεύει θεοῖς
ἢ γάμον στείχει συνάψων ἢ τόκοις βαρύνεται·
φεύγετ', ἐξίστασθε, μή τῳ προσπέσῃ μύσος τόδε.

THOAS

So that I may not see those who are stained with blood.

IPHIGENIA

But if I seem to be gone a long time . . .

THOAS

How shall I measure this?

IPHIGENIA

. . . do not be surprised.

THOAS

Perform the goddess' business thoroughly and at leisure.

IPHIGENIA

May this purification come out as I wish!

THOAS

Amen!

Enter from the skene *Orestes and Pylades, their heads covered, and servants bringing sacrificial animals, torches, and shackles.*

IPHIGENIA

I see the foreigners coming out of the house and the finery for the goddess. And there are newborn lambs, with whose blood I shall wash away the tainting bloodshed, and torches and everything else I asked for to purify the foreigners and the goddess. To the citizens I say, stay out of the way of the taint, whether you are a guardian of temples who keeps his hands pure before the gods or are about to be married or are with child! Run, get out of the way, so that the pollution may not alight on any of you!

1218 παλαμναίους βλέπω Bauer: παλαμναῖον λάβω L

1230   ὦ Διὸς Λητοῦς τ᾽ ἄνασσα παρθέν᾽, ἢν νίψω φόνον
τῶνδε καὶ θύσωμεν οὗ χρή, καθαρὸν οἰκήσεις
  δόμον,
εὐτυχεῖς δ᾽ ἡμεῖς ἐσόμεθα. τἄλλα δ᾽ οὐ λέγουσ᾽
  ὅμως
τοῖς τὰ πλείον᾽ εἰδόσιν θεοῖς σοί τε σημαίνω, θεά.

ΧΟΡΟΣ

στρ.

  εὔπαις ὁ Λατοῦς γόνος,
1235   ὅν ποτε Δηλιάσιν καρποφόροις γυάλοις
  ⟨ἔτικτε⟩ χρυσοκόμαν,
  ἐν κιθάρᾳ σοφόν, ὅστ᾽ ἐπὶ τόξων
  εὐστοχίᾳ γάνυται· φέρε ⟨δ᾽⟩ ἵνιν
1240   ἀπὸ δειράδος εἰναλίας
  λοχεία κλεινὰ λιποῦσα τὰν
  ματέρ᾽ ἀστάκτων ὑδάτων,
  ⟨συμ⟩βακχεύουσαν Διονύ-
  σῳ Παρνάσιον κορυφάν,
1245   ὅθι ποικιλόνωτος οἰνωπὸς δράκων,
  σκιερᾷ κάτεχ᾽ ἄλσος εὔφυλλον δάφνᾳ,
  γᾶς πελώριον τέρας, ἄμφεπε ⟨τε⟩ χθόνιον ⟨ἕδραν⟩.
1250   ἔτι νιν ἔτι βρέφος, ἔτι φίλας
  ἐπὶ ματέρος ἀγκάλαισι θρώσκων

   1236 ⟨ἔτικτε⟩ Paley   χρυσοκόμαν Musgrave: χ- Φοῖβον L
   1237 ὅστ᾽ Burges: ἅ τ᾽ L
   1239 φέρε ⟨δ᾽⟩ ἵνιν Kirchhoff: φέρει νιν L
   1241-2 τὰν ματέρ᾽ ἀστάκτων ὑδάτων post Jacobs (ματέρ᾽)
  Sansone: ἀ- μάτηρ ὑ- τ- L

O maiden goddess, daughter of Zeus and Leto, if I wash
away these men's blood guilt and sacrifice where I must,
you will dwell in a pure house, and we shall be blessed by
fortune! My other thoughts I do not say but hint them to
the gods' greater knowledge and to you, goddess.

Exit IPHIGENIA, *Orestes, Pylades, and servants by Eisodos
A,* THOAS *into the* skene.

CHORUS

How comely a son is Leto's child,
whom once in Delos' fruitful glens
⟨she bore,⟩ the god of golden hair,
skilled in the lyre, who delights
in his bow's unerring aim. She took her son
from the cliff by the sea,
leaving the famed place of her childbed,
to the mother of gushing waters,
the peak of Parnassus,
that leaps in ecstatic dance with Dionysus.
There a dark-visaged dragon with speckled back
held in thrall the rich laurel-shaded grove—
a monstrous portent brought forth by Earth—and
    ranged the oracular shrine.
Though still a child, still
frolicking in the arms of your dear mother,

1243 ⟨συμ⟩βακχεύουσαν Diggle

1246 κάτεχ' ἄλσος εὔφυλλον Burges: κατάχαλκος εὐφύλλῳ L

1249 ἄμφεπε Seidler: ἀμφέπει L ⟨τε⟩ χθόνιον ⟨ἔδραν⟩
Page: μαντεῖον χθόνιον L

1250 σὺ δέ νιν Nauck, τότε νιν Diggle

289

ἔκανες, ὦ Φοῖβε, μαντείων δ' ἐπέβας ζαθέων
τρίποδί τ' ἐν χρυσέῳ θάσσεις, ἐν ἀψευδεῖ θρόνῳ
1255 μαντείας βροτοῖς θεσφάτων νέμων
ἀδύτων ὕπο, Κασταλίας ῥεέθρων γείτων, μέσον
γᾶς ἔχων μέλαθρον.

ἀντ.

Θέμιν δ' ἐπεὶ Γαῖαν
1260 παῖδ' ἀπενάσσατο <Λατῷος> ἀπὸ ζαθέων.
χρηστηρίων, νύχια
Χθὼν ἐτεκνώσατο φάσματ' ὀνείρων,
οἳ πολέσιν μερόπων τά τε πρῶτα
1265 τά τ' ἔπειθ' ὅσ' ἔμελλε τυχεῖν
ὕπνῳ κατὰ δνοφερὰς χαμεύ-
νας ἔφραζον· Γαῖα δὲ τὰν
μαντείων ἀφείλετο τι-
μὰν Φοῖβον φθόνῳ θυγατρός.
1270 ταχύπους δ' ἐς Ὄλυμπον ὁρμαθεὶς ἄναξ
χέρα παιδνὸν ἕλιξεν ἐκ Διὸς θρόνων,
Πυθίων δόμων χθονίαν ἀφελεῖν μῆνιν θεᾶς.
γέλασε δ' ὅτι τέκος ἄφαρ ἔβα
1275 πολύχρυσα θέλων λατρεύματα σχεῖν·
ἐπὶ δ' ἔσεισεν κόμαν παῦσαι νυχίους ἐνοπάς,

1255 βροτοῖς Seidler: βροτοῖς ἀναφαίνων L   νέμων
Musgrave: ἐμῶν L   1259 Γαῖαν Bruhn: Γᾶς ἰὼν L
1260 <Λατῷος> Mekler   1265 ὅσ' Burges: ὅσα τ' L
1266 ὕπνῳ Markland: -ου L   χαμεύνας Linder: γᾶς εὐνὰς
L   1267 Γαῖα, quae post Χθὼν (1262) abundat, in susp. voc.
Willink, qui τᾷδε coni.: fort. αἶψα

you killed him, Phoebus, and stepped as conqueror upon
    the oracular shrine,
and now you sit on the tripod of gold, from your truthful
    throne
dispensing prophecies of divine decrees to mortals
from your inmost chamber next to the streams of
    Castalia,
having your shrine at earth's midpoint.

But when ⟨Leto's son⟩ had removed Themis,
Earth's daughter, from the holy
oracular shrine, Earth
begot nightly dream apparitions,
which on their night couches in sleep
revealed to the mass of mortals both things that once
    were
and things destined to later fulfilment.
Thus Earth robbed Phoebus
of his oracular office
in jealousy for her daughter.
Speeding on swift feet to Olympus Lord Apollo
coiled his young arm about Zeus's throne,
begging him to free the Pythian temple from the wrath
    of the goddess Earth.
Zeus laughed that his son had come so quickly
in eagerness to possess gold-rich worship.
A shake of his locks brought an end to the nightly voices,

1268 μαντείων Seidler: -εῖον L   1272 μῆνιν θεᾶς Wila-
mowitz: θ- μ- L   1276 ἐπὶ δ' ἔσεισεν … παῦσαι Badham: ἐπεὶ
δ' ἔσεισε … παῦσε L   ἐνοπάς Burges: ὀνείρους L

ὑπὸ δ' ἀλαθοσύναν νυκτωπὸν ἐξεῖλεν βροτῶν,
1280 καὶ τιμὰς πάλιν θῆκε Λοξίᾳ·
πολυάνορι τ' ἐν ξενόεντι θρόνῳ θάσσει βροτοῖς
θεσφάτων ἀοιδός.

ΑΓΓΕΛΟΣ

ὦ ναοφύλακες βωμοί τ' ἐπιστάται,
1285 Θόας ἄναξ γῆς τῆσδε ποῦ κυρεῖ βεβώς;
καλεῖτ' ἀναπτύξαντες εὐγόμφους πύλας
ἔξω μελάθρων τῶνδε κοίρανον χθονός.

ΧΟΡΟΣ

τί δ' ἔστιν, εἰ χρὴ μὴ κελευσθεῖσαν λέγειν;

ΑΓΓΕΛΟΣ

βεβᾶσι φροῦδοι δίπτυχοι νεανίαι
1290 Ἀγαμεμνονείας παιδὸς ἐκ βουλευμάτων
φεύγοντες ἐκ γῆς τῆσδε καὶ σεμνὸν βρέτας
λαβόντες ἐν κόλποισιν Ἑλλάδος νεώς.

ΧΟΡΟΣ

ἄπιστον εἶπας μῦθον· ὃν δ' ἰδεῖν θέλεις
ἄνακτα χώρας, φροῦδος ἐκ ναοῦ συθείς.

ΑΓΓΕΛΟΣ

1295 ποῖ; δεῖ γὰρ αὐτὸν εἰδέναι τὰ δρώμενα.

ΧΟΡΟΣ

οὐκ ἴσμεν· ἀλλὰ στεῖχε καὶ δίωκέ νιν
ὅπου κυρήσας τούσδ' ἀπαγγελεῖς λόγους.

and he filched the night visions' truthfulness from
    mortals
and restored his office to Loxias.
Now on his throne, thronged with foreign guests, he sits
    and for mortals
chants his decrees.

Enter by Eisodos A a member of Thoas' retinue as MES-
SENGER.

MESSENGER
(*addressing those within*) Guardians of the temple and at-
tendants of the altar, where is King Thoas to be found?
Open up these bossed doors and call the country's king out
of the temple!

CHORUS LEADER
What is wrong, if I may speak unbidden?

MESSENGER
The two young men have escaped: they have fled the coun-
try by the design of Agamemnon's daughter and taken the
holy image with them in the hold of a Greek ship.

CHORUS LEADER
What an astonishing story! But the king you wish to see has
left the temple in a hurry.

MESSENGER
Where has he gone? He must learn what has happened.

CHORUS LEADER
I don't know. But go and pursue him and when you find
him you can report this tale.

---

¹²⁸³ ἀοιδός Nauck: -αῖς L   ¹²⁸⁵ ποῖ Elmsley

ΑΓΓΕΛΟΣ

ὁρᾶτ᾽ ἄπιστον ὡς γυναικεῖον γένος·
μέτεστι χὐμῖν τῶν πεπραγμένων μέρος.

ΧΟΡΟΣ

1300   μαίνῃ· τί δ᾽ ἡμῖν τῶν ξένων δρασμοῦ μέτα;
οὐκ εἶ κρατούντων πρὸς πύλας ὅσον τάχος;

ΑΓΓΕΛΟΣ

οὔ, πρίν γ᾽ ἂν εἴπῃ τοὔπος ἑρμηνεὺς τόδε,
εἴτ᾽ ἔνδον εἴτ᾽ οὐκ ἔνδον ἀρχηγὸς χθονός.
ὠή, χαλᾶτε κλῇθρα, τοῖς ἔνδον λέγω,
1305   καὶ δεσπότῃ σημήναθ᾽ οὕνεκ᾽ ἐν πύλαις
πάρειμι, καινῶν φόρτον ἀγγέλλων κακῶν.

ΘΟΑΣ

τίς ἀμφὶ δῶμα θεᾶς τόδ᾽ ἵστησιν βοήν,
πύλας ἀράξας καὶ ψόφον πέμψας ἔσω;

ΑΓΓΕΛΟΣ

ψευδῶς λέγουσαί μ᾽ αἵδ᾽ ἀπήλαυνον δόμων,
1310   ὡς ἐκτὸς εἴης· σὺ δὲ κατ᾽ οἶκον ἦσθ᾽ ἄρα.

ΘΟΑΣ

τί προσδοκῶσαι κέρδος ἢ θηρώμεναι;

ΑΓΓΕΛΟΣ

αὖθις τὰ τῶνδε σημανῶ· τὰ δ᾽ ἐν ποσὶν
παρόντ᾽ ἄκουσον. ἡ νεᾶνις ἡ ᾽νθάδε
βωμοῖς παρίστατ᾽, Ἰφιγένει᾽, ἔξω χθονὸς

1299 χὐμῖν Markland: θ᾽ ὑμῖν L
1309 λέγουσαί μ᾽ αἵδ᾽ Pierson: ἔλεγον αἴδε καί μ᾽ L

MESSENGER

See how treacherous the female sex is! You too had a hand in these events!

CHORUS LEADER

You're crazy! What did we have to do with the foreigners' escape? Go to your master's door as quickly as you can!

MESSENGER

No, not until someone makes it clear to me whether the king is inside or not.

(*pounding on the door*) Ho, undo the bars, you inside, and tell your master that I am at the door, with a cargo of calamity to report!

Enter from the skene THOAS *with retinue.*

THOAS

Who is raising this clamor near the goddess' temple, pounding on the door and causing a din inside?

MESSENGER

These women tried to drive me away from the temple by telling lies, saying you were elsewhere. But you were inside all along!

THOAS

What did they think they could gain from that? What were they after?

MESSENGER

I will tell you about them later. You must hear what immediately concerns you. The young woman, who used to preside at the altar here, Iphigenia, has left the country

EURIPIDES

1315 σὺν τοῖς ξένοισιν οἴχεται, σεμνὸν θεᾶς
ἄγαλμ' ἔχουσα· δόλια δ' ἦν καθάρματα.

ΘΟΑΣ
πῶς φής; τί πνεῦμα συμφορᾶς κεκτημένη;

ΑΓΓΕΛΟΣ
σῴζουσ' Ὀρέστην· τοῦτο γὰρ σὺ θαυμάσῃ.

ΘΟΑΣ
τὸν ποῖον; ἆρ' ὃν Τυνδαρὶς τίκτει κόρη;

ΑΓΓΕΛΟΣ
1320 ὃν τοῖσδε βωμοῖς θεᾷ καθωσιώσατο.

ΘΟΑΣ
ὦ θαῦμα· πῶς σφε μεῖζον ὀνομάσας τύχω;

ΑΓΓΕΛΟΣ
μὴ 'νταῦθα τρέψῃς σὴν φρέν', ἀλλ' ἄκουέ μου·
σαφῶς δ' ἀθρήσας καὶ κλυὼν ἐκφρόντισον
διωγμὸν ὅστις τοὺς ξένους θηράσεται.

ΘΟΑΣ
1325 λέγ'· εὖ γὰρ εἶπας· οὐ γὰρ ἀγχίπλουν πόρον
φεύγουσιν, ὥστε διαφυγεῖν τοὐμὸν δόρυ.

ΑΓΓΕΛΟΣ
ἐπεὶ πρὸς ἀκτὰς ἤλθομεν θαλασσίας,
οὗ ναῦς Ὀρέστου κρύφιος ἦν ὡρμισμένη,
ἡμᾶς μέν, οὓς σὺ δεσμὰ συμπέμπεις ξένων
1330 ἔχοντας, ἐξένευσ' ἀποστῆναι πρόσω

1320 θεᾷ Musurus: θεὰ L

296

with the two foreigners and has taken the goddess' statue!
The purification was a trick!

THOAS

What are you saying? What favoring breeze of circum-
stance was hers?

MESSENGER

She was rescuing Orestes: that is something to amaze you.

THOAS

What Orestes? The son of Tyndareus' daughter?

MESSENGER

The man she consecrated to the goddess at this altar.

THOAS

Astounding! What greater name can I call it?

MESSENGER

Listen to me! Do not turn your attention that way! See and
hear clearly and then think out a way of pursuing and
catching the foreigners!

THOAS

That is good advice: say on. Their flight is no short journey,
and they cannot escape my armed might.

MESSENGER

When we came to the seashore where Orestes' ship was
secretly anchored, Agamemnon's daughter ordered us, the
men you sent with shackles for the foreigners, to stand

1321 σφε Diggle: σε L   μεῖον Markland
1324 διωγμὸν Hermann: -ὸς L

Ἀγαμέμνονος παῖς, ὡς ἀπόρρητον φλόγα
θύουσα καὶ καθαρμὸν ὃν μετῴχετο,
αὐτὴ δ' ὄπισθε δέσμ' ἔχουσα τοῖν ξένοιν
ἔστειχε χερσί. καὶ τάδ' ἦν ὕποπτα μέν,
1335 ἤρεσκε μέντοι σοῖσι προσπόλοις, ἄναξ.
χρόνῳ δ', ἵν' ἡμῖν δρᾶν τι δὴ δοκοῖ πλέον,
ἀνωλόλυξε καὶ κατῇδε βάρβαρα
μέλη μαγεύουσ', ὡς φόνον νίζουσα δή.
ἐπεὶ δὲ δαρὸν ἦμεν ἥμενοι χρόνον,
1340 ἐσῆλθεν ἡμᾶς μὴ λυθέντες οἱ ξένοι
κτάνοιεν αὐτὴν δραπέται τ' οἰχοίατο.
φόβῳ δ' ἃ μὴ χρῆν εἰσορᾶν καθήμεθα
σιγῇ· τέλος δὲ πᾶσιν ἦν αὐτὸς λόγος,
στείχειν ἵν' ἦσαν, καίπερ οὐκ ἐωμένοις.
1345 κἀνταῦθ' ὁρῶμεν Ἑλλάδος νεὼς σκάφος
†ταρσῷ κατήρει† πίτυλον ἐπτερωμένον,
ναύτας τε πεντήκοντ' ἐπὶ σκαλμῶν πλάτας
ἔχοντας, ἐκ δεσμῶν δὲ τοὺς νεανίας
ἐλευθέρους πρύμνηθεν ἑστῶτας νεώς.
1350 κοντοῖς δὲ πρῷραν εἶχον, οἱ δ' ἐπωτίδων
ἄγκυραν ἐξανῆπτον, οἱ δὲ κλίμακα
σπεύδοντες ἦγον διὰ χερῶν πρύμνης τ' ἄπο
πόντῳ διδόντες τῇ ξένῃ καθίεσαν.
ἡμεῖς δ' ἀφειδήσαντες, ὡς ἐσείδομεν
1355 δόλια τεχνήματ', εἰχόμεσθα τῆς ξένης
πρυμνησίων τε, καὶ δι' εὐθυντηρίας
οἴακας ἐξηροῦμεν εὐπρύμνου νεώς.

aside at a distance: it was a secret sacrificial flame and a secret purification she was in quest of. She herself walked behind the strangers, holding the shackles in her hands. This was suspicious, but your servants, my lord, made no objection.

Time passed, and in order that we might think she was accomplishing something, she raised the sacrificial shout and intoned barbarian songs, playing the role of magus, as if she were cleansing blood guilt. But when we had sat idle for a long time, the thought came into our minds that the strangers might have slipped their bonds, killed the girl, and run away. Yet for fear of seeing what was forbidden we sat in silence. Finally, however, we all had the same idea, to go where they were, even though we had been forbidden to do so.

There we saw a Greek ship, winged on either side with oars, and fifty sailors holding their oarblades upon the tholepins, and the two youths, freed from their shackles, standing on the stern of the ship. Some of the sailors were holding the prow with poles, others were tying the anchor to the catheads, while others in haste were carrying a ladder and letting it down from the stern into the sea for the foreign girl.

Having seen her trickery, we were pitiless and took hold of the girl and the hawsers, and we set about removing the well-made ship's steering oars, pulling them

---

1332 θύσουσα Reiske   1346 κατήρη Bothe

1349 post h. v. lac. indic. Bruhn   1351 κλίμακα Kirchhoff: -κας L   1352 πρύμνης τ' ἄπο Musgrave: πρυμνήσια L

1353 διδόντες Kirchhoff: δὲ δόντες L   τῇ ξένῃ Musgrave: τὴν -ην L

λόγοι δ᾽ ἐχώρουν· Τίνι λόγῳ πορθμεύετε
κλέπτοντες ἐκ γῆς ξόανα καὶ θυηπόλους;
1360 τίνος τίς ὢν ⟨σὺ⟩ τήνδ᾽ ἀπεμπολᾷς χθονός;
ὁ δ᾽ εἶπ᾽· Ὀρέστης, τῆσδ᾽ ὅμαιμος, ὡς μάθῃς,
Ἀγαμέμνονος παῖς, τήνδ᾽ ἐμὴν κομίζομαι
λαβὼν ἀδελφήν, ἣν ἀπώλεσ᾽ ἐκ δόμων.
ἀλλ᾽ οὐδὲν ἧσσον εἰχόμεσθα τῆς ξένης
1365 καὶ πρός σ᾽ ἕπεσθαι διεβιαζόμεσθά νιν·
ὅθεν τὰ δεινὰ πλήγματ᾽ ἦν γενειάδων.
κεῖνοί τε γὰρ σίδηρον οὐκ εἶχον χεροῖν
ἡμεῖς τε· πυγμαί δ᾽ ἦσαν ἐγκροτούμεναι,
καὶ κῶλ᾽ ἀπ᾽ ἀμφοῖν τοῖν νεανίαιν ἅμα
1370 ἐς πλευρὰ καὶ πρὸς ἧπαρ ἠκοντίζετο,
ὥστε ξυναλγεῖν καὶ συναποκαμεῖν μέλη.
δεινοῖς δὲ σημάντροισιν ἐσφραγισμένοι
ἐφεύγομεν πρὸς κρημνόν, οἱ μὲν ἐν κάρᾳ
κάθαιμ᾽ ἔχοντες τραύμαθ᾽, οἱ δ᾽ ἐν ὄμμασιν·
1375 ὄχθοις δ᾽ ἐπισταθέντες εὐλαβεστέρως
ἐμαρνάμεσθα καὶ πέτροις ἐβάλλομεν.
ἀλλ᾽ εἶργον ἡμᾶς τοξόται πρύμνης ἔπι
σταθέντες ἰοῖς, ὥστ᾽ ἀναστεῖλαι πρόσω.
      κἂν τῷδε (δεινὸς γὰρ κλύδων ὤκειλε ναῦν
1380 πρὸς γῆν, φόβος δ᾽ ἦν ⟨παρθένῳ⟩ τέγξαι πόδα)
λαβὼν Ὀρέστης ὦμον εἰς ἀριστερόν,
βὰς ἐς θάλασσαν κἀπὶ κλίμακος θορών,
ἔθηκ᾽ ἀδελφήν ⟨τ᾽⟩ ἐντὸς εὐσέλμου νεὼς
τό τ᾽ οὐρανοῦ πέσημα, τῆς Διὸς κόρης
1385 ἄγαλμα. ναὸς ⟨δ᾽⟩ ἐκ μέσης ἐφθέγξατο

300

through the tiller hole. Words began to fly: "By what right are you stealing statues and priestesses and taking them from the land? Who are you, and whose son, that you remove this woman from the country?" And he said, "Know this: I am Orestes, this woman's brother and the son of Agamemnon: I am recovering my sister, whom I lost from our house." But for all that we did not stop clinging to the woman and trying to force her to come with us to you. That is why my face is so bruised. They had no swords in their hands, and neither did we. But both young men landed fist blows and kicks on our ribs and livers, so that our limbs were in pain and exhausted. Imprinted with these terrible blows we withdrew to the cliff, some with bleeding wounds on our scalps, others around the eyes. Taking our stand on a hillock we fought more cautiously and pelted them with stones. But archers standing on the stern kept us away with their arrows, and we were forced to retreat.

Meanwhile, a terrible wave brought the ship to land, but ⟨the maiden⟩ was afraid to step into the water. So Orestes put her on his left shoulder, marched into the sea, leaped upon the ladder and put within his good ship both his sister and the thing that fell from the sky, the statue of Zeus's daughter. And from the middle of the ship a voice

---

1359 ξόανα Reiske: -ον L   1360 ⟨σὺ⟩ Markland

1371 ξυναλγεῖν Hermann olim: ξυνάπτειν L

1376 πέτροις Paley: -ους L

1380 ⟨παρθένῳ⟩ Badham

1383 ⟨τ'⟩ Hermann

1384 τ' Markland: δ' L

1385 ⟨δ'⟩ Markland

βοή τις· Ὦ γῆς Ἑλλάδος ναύτης λεώς,
λάβεσθε κώπης ῥόθιά τ᾽ ἐκλευκαίνετε·
ἔχομεν γὰρ ὧνπερ οὕνεκ᾽ ἄξενον πόρον
Συμπληγάδων ἔσωθεν εἰσεπλεύσαμεν.

1390   οἱ δὲ στεναγμὸν ἡδὺν ἐκβρυχώμενοι
ἔπαισαν ἅλμην. ναῦς δ᾽, ἕως μὲν ἐντὸς ἦν
λιμένος, ἐχώρει στόμια, διαπερῶσα δὲ
λάβρῳ κλύδωνι συμπεσοῦσ᾽ ἠπείγετο·
δεινὸς γὰρ ἐλθὼν ἄνεμος ἐξαίφνης νεὼς

1395 ὠθεῖ παλίμπρυμν᾽ ἱστί᾽· οἱ δ᾽ ἐκαρτέρουν
πρὸς κῦμα λακτίζοντες· ἐς δὲ γῆν πάλιν
κλύδων παλίρρους ἦγε ναῦν. σταθεῖσα δὲ
Ἀγαμέμνονος παῖς ηὔξατ᾽· Ὦ Λητοῦς κόρη,
σῶσόν με τὴν σὴν ἱέραν πρὸς Ἑλλάδα

1400 ἐκ βαρβάρου γῆς καὶ κλοπαῖς σύγγνωθ᾽ ἐμαῖς.
φιλεῖς δὲ καὶ σὺ σὸν κασίγνητον, θεά·
φιλεῖν δὲ κἀμὲ τοὺς ὁμαίμονας δόκει.

  ναῦται δ᾽ ἐπευφήμησαν εὐχαῖσιν κόρης
παιᾶνα, γυμνὰς ⟨ὠλένας⟩ ἐπωμίδος

1405 κώπῃ προσαρμόσαντες ἐκ κελεύσματος.
μᾶλλον δὲ μᾶλλον πρὸς πέτρας ᾔει σκάφος·
χὠ μέν τις ἐς θάλασσαν ὡρμήθη ποσίν,
ἄλλος δὲ πλεκτὰς ἐξανῆπτεν ἀγκύλας.
κἀγὼ μὲν εὐθὺς πρὸς σὲ δεῦρ᾽ ἀπεστάλην,

1410 σοὶ τὰς ἐκεῖθεν σημανῶν, ἄναξ, τύχας.

  ἀλλ᾽ ἕρπε, δεσμὰ καὶ βρόχους λαβὼν χεροῖν·
εἰ μὴ γὰρ οἶδμα νήνεμον γενήσεται,
οὐκ ἔστιν ἐλπὶς τοῖς ξένοις σωτηρίας.

cried out, "Sailing men of Greece, grab your oars and make the waves grow white! We have what we came for when we sailed through the Symplegades to the Hostile Sea!"

The men bellowed out a roar of pleasure and struck the brine. The ship, while it was still within the harbor, proceeded to its mouth but, once it had emerged, it met a violent wave and was hard pressed. A terrible wind had arisen suddenly and was pushing the ship astern. But the sailors kept up their effort, futilely kicking against the wave while the inrushing surf carried the ship back to land. Agamemnon's daughter stood up and prayed, "O daughter of Leto, bring me, your priestess, safely back to Hellas from this barbarian land! Forgive my theft! You too, goddess, love your brother: you must expect that I love mine."

In response to her prayer the sailors uttered a paean to Apollo, then, pushing their garments back and baring their ⟨arms⟩, they applied them to the oars at the boatswain's command. But the ship drew nearer and nearer to the rocks: one of our men waded into the water and another prepared to fasten a plaited noose to the boat. I was sent immediately to you, my king, to report what has happened there.

So take fetters and ropes and go: unless the sea swell grows calm, the foreigners have no hope of getting away

---

1386 ναύτης λεώς F. W. Schmidt, Weil: ναῦται νεὼς L
1387 κώπης Reiske: -αις L
1392 διαπερῶσα δὲ στόμα Murray
1395 παλίμπρυμν' ἰστί' Mekler: πάλιν πρυμνήσια L
1404 γυμνὰς ⟨ὠλένας⟩ ἐπωμίδος Hartung: γυμνὰς ἐκ
⟨   ⟩ ἐπωμίδας L

πόντου δ' ἀνάκτωρ Ἴλιόν τ' ἐπισκοπεῖ
1415 σεμνὸς Ποσειδῶν, Πελοπίδαις ἐναντίος,
καὶ νῦν παρέξει τὸν Ἀγαμέμνονος γόνον
σοὶ καὶ πολίταις, ὡς ἔοικεν, ἐν χεροῖν
λαβεῖν ἀδελφήν θ', ἢ φόνου τοῦ 'ν Αὐλίδι
ἀμνημόνευτος θεὰν προδοῦσ' ἁλίσκεται.

ΧΟΡΟΣ

1420 ὦ τλῆμον Ἰφιγένεια, συγγόνου μέτα
θανῇ πάλιν μολοῦσα δεσποτῶν χέρας.

ΘΟΑΣ

ὦ πάντες ἀστοὶ τῆσδε βαρβάρου χθονός,
οὐκ εἶα πώλοις ἐμβαλόντες ἡνίας
παράκτιοι δραμεῖσθε κἀκβολὰς νεὼς
1425 Ἑλληνίδος δέξεσθε, σὺν δὲ τῇ θεῷ
σπεύδοντες ἄνδρας δυσσεβεῖς θηράσετε,
οἱ δ' ὠκυπομποὺς ἕλξετ' ἐς πόντον πλάτας,
ὡς ἐκ θαλάσσης ἔκ τε γῆς ἱππεύμασιν
λαβόντες αὐτοὺς ἢ κατὰ στύφλου πέτρας
1430 ῥίψωμεν ἢ σκόλοψι πήξωμεν δέμας;
    ὑμᾶς δὲ τὰς τῶνδ' ἴστορας βουλευμάτων,
γυναῖκες, αὖθις, ἡνίκ' ἂν σχολὴν λάβω,
ποινασόμεσθα· νῦν δὲ τὴν προκειμένην
σπουδὴν ἔχοντες οὐ μενοῦμεν ἥσυχοι.

ΑΘΗΝΑ

1435 ποῖ ποῖ διωγμὸν τόνδε πορθμεύεις, ἄναξ
Θόας; ἄκουσον τῆσδ' Ἀθηναίας λόγους.
παῦσαι διώκων ῥεῦμά τ' ἐξορμῶν στρατοῦ·

304

safely. Just as the great god Poseidon, the sea's lord, always watches over Ilium and is enemy to the descendants of Pelops, so now, it seems, he will give you and your citizens the chance to lay hold of the son of Agamemnon and his sister. She has forgotten her sacrifice in Aulis and now stands convicted of betraying the goddess.

CHORUS LEADER

Unhappy Iphigenia! You will come once more into your master's hands and will be put to death with your brother!

THOAS

Up, all you citizens of this barbarian land! Put bridles on your horses, gallop to the shore, pick up the wreck of the Greek ship! With the goddess' help hurry and hunt down the godless men! You others, drag swift ships down to the sea so that either catching them on water or chasing them down on horseback we may hurl them down a rough cliff or spit their bodies on stakes!

You women, who were in on these plots: I shall punish you later when I have the time. But I cannot stay here idle: I have pressing business.

He starts to leave in haste. His departure is halted when ATHENA *enters by* mechane, *alighting on the* theologeion.

ATHENA

This haste, King Thoas, where is it taking you? I am Athena: listen to my words. Stop your pursuit, stop this

---

1415 Πελοπίδαις Bothe: Π- δ' L   1418 φόνου τοῦ 'ν Badham: φόνον τὸν L   1419 ἀμνημόνευτος Markland: -τον L θεὰν Badham: θεᾷ L   1433 τῶν προκειμένων Barnes

305

πεπρωμένον γὰρ θεσφάτοισι Λοξίου
δεῦρ' ἦλθ' Ὀρέστης, τόν τ' Ἐρινύων χόλον
1440 φεύγων ἀδελφῆς τ' Ἄργος ἐσπέμψων δέμας
ἄγαλμά θ' ἱερὸν εἰς ἐμὴν ἄξων χθόνα,
1441a τῶν νῦν παρόντων πημάτων ἀναψυχάς.
πρὸς μὲν σ' ὅδ' ἡμῖν μῦθος· ὃν δ' ἀποκτενεῖν
δοκεῖς Ὀρέστην ποντίῳ λαβὼν σάλῳ,
ἤδη Ποσειδῶν χάριν ἐμὴν ἀκύμονα
1445 πόντου τίθησι νῶτα πορθμεύειν πλάτῃ.
μαθὼν δ', Ὀρέστα, τὰς ἐμὰς ἐπιστολάς
(κλύεις γὰρ αὐδὴν καίπερ οὐ παρὼν θεᾶς),
χώρει λαβὼν ἄγαλμα σύγγονόν τε σήν.
ὅταν δ' Ἀθήνας τὰς θεοδμήτους μόλῃς,
1450 χῶρός τις ἔστιν Ἀτθίδος πρὸς ἐσχάτοις
ὅροισι, γείτων δειράδος Καρυστίας,
ἱερός· Ἀλάς νιν οὑμὸς ὀνομάζει λεώς·
ἐνταῦθα τεύξας ναὸν ἵδρυσαι βρέτας,
ἐπώνυμον γῆς Ταυρικῆς πόνων τε σῶν,
1455 οὓς ἐξεμόχθεις περιπολῶν καθ' Ἑλλάδα
οἴστροις Ἐρινύων. Ἄρτεμιν δέ νιν βροτοὶ
τὸ λοιπὸν ὑμνήσουσι Ταυροπόλον θεάν.
νόμον τε θὲς τόνδ'· ὅταν ἑορτάζῃ λεώς,
τῆς σῆς σφαγῆς ἄποιν' ἐπισχέτω ξίφος
1460 δέρῃ πρὸς ἀνδρὸς αἷμά τ' ἐξανιέτω,
ὁσίας ἕκατι θεά θ' ὅπως τιμὰς ἔχῃ.
σὲ δ' ἀμφὶ σεμνάς, Ἰφιγένεια, λείμακας
Βραυρωνίας δεῖ τῇδε κληδουχεῖν θεᾷ·
οὗ καὶ τεθάψῃ κατθανοῦσα, καὶ πέπλων

306

torrent of armed men! It is because Loxias' oracles have
ordained it that Orestes has come here, fleeing the
Erinyes' anger and trying to take his sister to Argos and
bring the holy image into my country to end his present
misery. That is my message to you. As for Orestes, whom
you think you will capture on the billowy sea and put to
death, Poseidon for my sake is already making the sea's
surface calm so that he may cross by ship. You, Orestes, lis-
ten to my behests (for though you are far away you hear a
goddess' voice) and go on your way with the statue and
your sister. When you come to god-built Athens, there is a
place near the borders of Attica, neighboring the cliff of
Carystus, a sacred place: my people call it Halae. There
build a temple and set up the statue: it will be called after
the Taurian land and your woes, the ones you suffered as
you fared over Greece goaded on by the Erinyes. For all
time to come mortals will sing hymns in honor of Artemis
the Taurian-faring goddess. This is the custom you must
establish: when the people keep the feast, to atone for your
sacrifice let them hold a sword to the neck of a man and
draw blood: thus will piety be satisfied and the goddess
receive honor.

And you, Iphigenia, in the holy meadows of Brauron
must serve this goddess as her temple warder. When you
die, you will lie buried here, and they will dedicate for your

1438 πεπρωμένον Monk: -οις L: -ος Hermann

1441a om. P et idcirco edd. vett.

1445 πορθμεύειν Tyrwhitt: -ων L   1453 τεύξας Pierson:
τάξας L   1461 θεά θ' Markland: θεᾶς L

1462 λείμακας Pierson: κλίμακας L

1463 τῇδε . . . θεᾷ Markland: τῆσδε . . . θεᾶς L

307

EURIPIDES

1465 ἄγαλμά σοι θήσουσιν εὐπήνους ὑφάς,
ἃς ἂν γυναῖκες ἐν τόκοις ψυχορραγεῖς
λίπωσ' ἐν οἴκοις. τάσδε δ' ἐκπέμπειν χθονὸς
Ἑλληνίδας γυναῖκας ἐξεφίεμαι
γνώμης δικαίας οὔνεκ'· <εὖ δ' ἐπίσταμαι
σώζειν δικαίους φῶτας,> ἐκσώσασά γε

1470 καὶ πρίν σ' Ἀρείοις ἐν πάγοις ψήφους ἴσας
κρίνασ', Ὀρέστα· καὶ νόμισμ' ἔσται τόδε,
νικᾶν ἰσήρεις ὅστις ἂν ψήφους λάβῃ.
ἀλλ' ἐκκομίζου σὴν κασιγνήτην χθονός,
Ἀγαμέμνονος παῖ. καὶ σὺ μὴ θυμοῦ, Θόας.

ΘΟΑΣ

1475 ἄνασσ' Ἀθάνα, τοῖσι τῶν θεῶν λόγοις
ὅστις κλυὼν ἄπιστος, οὐκ ὀρθῶς φρονεῖ.
ἐγὼ δ' Ὀρέστῃ τ', εἰ φέρων βρέτας θεᾶς
βέβηκ', ἀδελφῇ τ' οὐχὶ θυμοῦμαι· τί γὰρ
πρὸς τοὺς σθένοντας θεοὺς ἁμιλλᾶσθαι καλόν;

1480 ἴτωσαν ἐς σὴν σὺν θεᾶς ἀγάλματι
γαῖαν, καθιδρύσαιντό τ' εὐτυχῶς βρέτας.
πέμψω δὲ καὶ τάσδ' Ἑλλάδ' εἰς εὐδαίμονα
γυναῖκας, ὥσπερ σὸν κέλευσμ' ἐφίεται.
παύσω δὲ λόγχην ἣν ἐπαίρομαι ξένοις

1485 νεῶν τ' ἐρετμά, σοὶ τάδ' ὡς δοκεῖ, θεά.

ΑΘΗΝΑ

αἰνῶ· τὸ γὰρ χρεὼν σοῦ τε καὶ θεῶν κρατεῖ.
ἴτ', ὦ πνοαί, ναυσθλοῦτε τὸν Ἀγαμέμνονος
παῖδ' εἰς Ἀθήνας· συμπορεύσομαι δ' ἐγὼ

308

delight the finely woven garments which women who die
in childbirth leave behind in their houses. As for these
Greek women my orders are to escort them from the coun-
try because of the uprightness of their hearts. <I know well
how to save the righteous,> having saved your life before
now, Orestes, on the Areopagus when I decided the tie
vote. This will be the custom, that when the votes are tied,
the defendant wins his case. So take your sister from the
land, son of Agamemnon. And you, Thoas, do not be angry.

THOAS

Lady Athena, whoever hears the gods' words and disobeys
is mad. I am angry with neither Orestes nor his sister for
departing with the image: how can it be an admirable thing
to strive against the mighty gods? May they go to your
country with the goddess' statue, and may good fortune
attend their establishing it there! And I will send these
women off to the blessed land of Greece, as you have com-
manded me. I will halt the spears and the ships' oars that I
was raising against them, since that is your will, goddess.

ATHENA

I commend you. What is fated has power over both you
and the gods.

Blow, winds, and carry the son of Agamemnon to

1469 post οὕνεκ' lac. indic. Reiske, post 1468 Brodaeus

1469-70 γε ... σ' Willink: σε ... γ' L

1471 ἔσται τόδε Markland: εἰς ταυτό γε L

1473 κασιγνήτην Elmsley: -τον L: σὺν κασιγνήτῃ (sc. αὐτὰς)
Willink

1487-9 Athenae contin. Musurus: Apollini trib. L

σῴζουσ᾿ ἀδελφῆς τῆς ἐμῆς σεμνὸν βρέτας.

1490 ἴτ᾿ ἐπ᾿ εὐτυχίᾳ τῆς σῳζομένης
μοίρας εὐδαίμονες ὄντες.

XOPOΣ

ἀλλ᾿, ὦ σεμνὴ παρά τ᾿ ἀθανάτοις
καὶ παρὰ θνητοῖς, Παλλὰς Ἀθάνα,
δράσομεν οὕτως ὡς σὺ κελεύεις.
1495 μάλα γὰρ τερπνὴν κἀνέλπιστον
φήμην ἀκοαῖσι δέδεγμαι.
[ὦ μέγα σεμνὴ Νίκη, τὸν ἐμὸν
βίοτον κατέχοις
καὶ μὴ λήγοις στεφανοῦσα.]

1490 Athenae contin. edd. vett.: Αθ. L (vide ad 1487-9): Xo.
Seidler et recentiores edd.
1497-9 del. Blomfield

Athens! I shall journey with him, keeping my sister's holy image safe.

(*to all the departing Greeks*) Go in blessedness, prospering because it is your lot to reach home safely!

CHORUS LEADER

Pallas Athena, revered among immortals and mortals alike, we shall do as you command! The words my ears have heard are a great and unexpected blessing! [O most august lady Victory, may you have my life in your charge and never cease garlanding my head!]

Exit ATHENA *by* mechane *from the roof of the* skene, *the* CHORUS *by Eisodos A, and* THOAS *with retinue and* MESSENGER *by Eisodos B.*

ION

INTRODUCTION

In Euripides' dramatization of the Ion myth, Ion is the son of Apollo and the Athenian princess Creusa, whom the god has raped. Creusa exposes her child, but Apollo rescues him and raises him in Delphi, where at the play's beginning he lives as a temple servant, utterly ignorant of his parentage. Apollo, however, has plans for him. Creusa has married a non-Athenian named Xuthus, and Apollo has seen to it that their union is unfruitful. They accordingly come to Delphi to ask the god about having children. In the prologue Hermes tells us that Apollo has guided events to this conclusion so that he may tell Xuthus that Ion is his son and the boy may be taken to Athens and there learn that his real parents are Creusa and Apollo. But events take a turn the god does not foresee.

Creusa, coming ahead of her husband to the temple, meets Ion. Though neither knows that they are related, the two are strangely drawn to one another, each feeling sympathy for the bereft condition of the other. (This would not surprise the audience: the idea that blood will out, that nature is stronger than nurture, pervades Greek myth.) Creusa has come to the temple ahead of her husband in order to consult Apollo about the baby she exposed years ago. She tells Ion that "a friend of mine" was impregnated by Apollo, that this friend exposed her child, and that the god has apparently allowed him to perish. But she is not allowed to consult the oracle because her question brings reproach upon the god in his own temple.

When Xuthus consults the oracle, Apollo tells him that the first person he meets on emerging from the temple will be his son. When he comes out he finds Ion. Their encounter is exactly the opposite of that between Ion and Creusa. Where mother and son, though ignorant of the relation, felt instant sympathy, Ion repels Xuthus' approach to him, and even after hearing about the oracle he keeps a chilly distance from his supposed father. At first he begs Xuthus to be allowed to stay in Delphi, alleging that since he is both illegitimate and a non-Athenian he will be looked down on in pure-bred Athens, whose royal family is sprung from the soil of Attica. Furthermore, he says, Creusa is bound to be upset if her husband has a child and she does not. At last, though, he gives his consent that Xuthus shall bring him to Athens, ostensibly as a mere friend, and thereafter wait for the right moment to install him on the throne as his heir. Xuthus takes Ion away to hold a banquet in his honor.

When Creusa, accompanied by an old retainer, comes back to find out about the oracle to her husband, the Chorus tell her about Xuthus and his supposed son. The Old Man smells a plot: Xuthus must have deliberately fathered this child behind Creusa's back when he guessed she could have none, and is now trying to install him on the throne and supplant the Athenian royal house, Creusa's family. Together they plot to poison the boy at his feast.

The plot is discovered in a way that suggests divine intervention. As Ion is on the point of drinking the poisoned cup, someone utters a chance word of ill omen, and Ion

316

orders everyone to pour out their cups and begin again. Birds alight near the spilled wine, and the one that sips Ion's immediately dies. Ion uncovers the plot and sets off to arraign Creusa on a charge of murder before the Delphians, who condemn her to death. Creusa takes refuge at an altar, and religious law forbids Ion to remove her by force.

With things at this standoff, the Priestess of Apollo, who had raised Ion, enters bringing the wicker cradle in which the baby Ion was transported to Delphi: the god, she says, now wants Ion to have it. Creusa recognizes it and names its contents to Ion, and mother and son achieve mutual recognition. Creusa then reveals to Ion that Apollo is his father. Athena appears and prophesies glory for both him and his descendants the Ionians. Xuthus is not to be disabused of his belief that he is Ion's father. Mother and son go off toward Athens but not before Creusa unsays her earlier criticism of Apollo.

Like Sophocles' *Oedipus at Colonus* and Aeschylus' *Eumenides*, *Ion* is a thoroughly Athenian play, and it is worth considering in what ways it would have appealed to its first audience. First, it contains numerous references to Athenian places (the Acropolis, the Long Rocks, the Erechtheum) and Athenian local custom (the snake necklaces for children). Ion, though he has lived his entire life in Delphi, knows all about Athens and its myths and asks numerous informed questions about it.

Second and more important, the version of the myth Euripides has chosen (and, in some of its aspects, probably invented) reflects the greatest credit on the Athenian people. The Athenians believed that they were autochthonous, that is, that they had never migrated from anywhere else and were the original indigenous population. One myth that reflected this belief was that an early king, Erichthonius, was a son of Earth, actually sprung from the soil of Attica. He and Cecrops, another early king, are represented in art as part snake, the creature of the soil *par excellence*. All throughout the play this earthborn conception of the Athenians is insisted on. The Athenians are closely identified with their land, and no one who is not so descended can claim the right to citizenship, to say nothing of the throne. That this conception of themselves rang true to the Athenians of the fifth and fourth centuries is evident in the way this theme is handled in Athenian display oratory, e.g. Isocrates' *Panegyricus* 23-5 and *Panathenaicus* 124-5.

To the glory of autochthonous origin Euripides' version adds another: a glorious divine progenitor. In Hesiod and other early sources Ion had a human father, Xuthus, son of Hellen. We do not know who first made Ion the son of Apollo, with Xuthus merely his stepfather, and it may even have been Euripides himself. By incorporating or inventing this version Euripides gives Ion (and thus the Athenians) glorious ancestry on both sides. One further innovation concerns the descendants of Xuthus and Creusa. In the Hesiodic genealogy Xuthus, Dorus, and Aeolus, the ancestors of the three principal branches of the Greek race, are all sons of Hellen and grandsons of Zeus. In Euripides, Xuthus, grandson of Zeus, has Dorus and Aeolus by Creusa. This means that the Ionian race, descended from Ion, is older by a generation than the Dorian and Aeolian, and the latter two are descended from an Athenian princess.

It is frequently said of this play that it is the ancestor of the New Comedy of Menander and others, where it commonly happens that babies are exposed at birth and a happy ending ensues when they are identified through tokens. But in spite of its happy ending *Ion* is a tragedy in a very real sense. Just as *Oedipus the King* explores the fragility of mortal life and the limitations of human knowledge in the face of divine malice, so *Ion* depicts erring mortals—who can never have complete knowledge of even their own circumstances—rescued from their misguided actions by divine benevolence. Ion and Creusa, both of them critical of Apollo and distrusting his providence, come perilously close to murdering each other and are rescued only by the god's care.

Indeed, in some ways *Ion* is more tragic than *Oedipus* since it underscores more completely the utter difference between mortal and immortal life. Apollo, to be sure, is watching out for his son and the mother who bore him, but he takes too little cognizance of what it is like to live as a human being. We may well be right to hear an undertone of loss and sadness in the apparent joy at the play's end. Creusa's long years of sorrow are no small portion of her life, and they can never be recalled. This means nothing to a god who lives forever. Ion has greatness ahead of him, but the blessed life of Delphi, where he has been completely immersed in piety and goodness, is to be no more. Though both Ion and Creusa praise Apollo, the impression remains that, as in the first book of the *Iliad*, the world is run by gods on Olympus who do not understand the realities of the mortal condition. That is a good image for the tragedy of human life.

EURIPIDES

SELECT BIBLIOGRAPHY

Editions

U. von Wilamowitz-Moellendorff (Berlin, 1926).
A. S. Owen (Oxford, 1939).
W. Biehl (Leipzig, 1979).
K. H. Lee (Warminster, 1997).

Literary Criticism

A. P. Burnett, "Human Resistance and Divine Persuasion in Euripides' *Ion*," *CP* 57 (1962), 89-103.
—— *Catastrophe Survived: Euripides' Plays of Mixed Reversal* (Oxford, 1971), pp. 101-29.
K. H. Lee, "Shifts of Mood and Concepts of Time in Euripides' *Ion*," in *Tragedy and the Tragic*, ed. M. S. Silk (Oxford, 1996), pp. 85-109.
M. Lloyd, "Divine and Human Action in Euripides' *Ion*," *A&A* 32 (1986), 33-45.
K. Matthiessen, "Der *Ion*—eine Komödie des Euripides?" in *Opes Atticae: Miscellanea Philologica et Historica R. Bogaert et H. Van Looy Oblata*, ed. M. Geerard (The Hague, 1990), pp. 271-91.
F. Wassermann, "Divine Violence and Providence in Euripides' *Ion*," *TAPA* 71 (1940), 587-604.
C. H. Whitman, *Euripides and the Full Circle of Myth* (Cambridge, Mass., 1974), pp. 69-103.

ΕΡΜΗΣ	HERMES
ΙΩΝ	ION, son of Creusa and Apollo
ΧΟΡΟΣ	CHORUS of Creusa's maidservants
ΚΡΕΟΥΣΑ	CREUSA, daughter of Erechtheus and queen of Athens
ΞΟΥΘΟΣ	XUTHUS, Achaean-born husband of Creusa and king of Athens
ΠΡΕΣΒΥΤΗΣ	OLD MAN, servant of Creusa
ΠΡΟΦΗΤΙΣ	PRIESTESS of Apollo
ΑΘΗΝΑ	ATHENA

A *Note on Staging*

The *skene* represents the temple of Apollo in Delphi. Before it is an altar. Eisodos A leads to Xuthus' and Creusa's hosts, the nearby cave of Trophonius, and to Athens, Eisodos B to other altars and the place where Ion's birthday is celebrated.

ΙΩΝ

ΕΡΜΗΣ

Ἄτλας ὁ νώτοις χαλκέοισιν οὐρανόν,
θεῶν παλαιὸν οἶκον, ἐκτρίβων θεῶν
μιᾶς ἔφυσε Μαῖαν, ἥ 'μ' ἐγείνατο
Ἑρμῆν μεγίστῳ Ζηνί, δαιμόνων λάτριν.
5 ἥκω δὲ Δελφῶν τήνδε γῆν, ἵν' ὀμφαλὸν
μέσον καθίζων Φοῖβος ὑμνῳδεῖ βροτοῖς
τά τ' ὄντα καὶ μέλλοντα θεσπίζων ἀεί.
   ἔστιν γὰρ οὐκ ἄσημος Ἑλλήνων πόλις,
τῆς χρυσολόγχου Παλλάδος κεκλημένη,
10 οὗ παῖδ' Ἐρεχθέως Φοῖβος ἔζευξεν γάμοις
βίᾳ Κρέουσαν, ἔνθα προσβόρρους πέτρας
Παλλάδος ὑπ' ὄχθῳ τῆς Ἀθηναίων χθονὸς
Μακρὰς καλοῦσι γῆς ἄνακτες Ἀτθίδος.
ἀγνὼς δὲ πατρί (τῷ θεῷ γὰρ ἦν φίλον)
15 γαστρὸς διήνεγκ' ὄγκον. ὡς δ' ἦλθεν χρόνος,
τεκοῦσ' ἐν οἴκοις παῖδ' ἀπήνεγκεν βρέφος
ἐς ταὐτὸν ἄντρον οὗπερ ηὐνάσθη θεῷ

1 νώτοις χαλκέοισιν Elmsley: χ- ν- L
2-3 μιᾶς / Νυμφῶν Irvine: θεοῦ / ἀλίας Shilleto

322

ION

HERMES

Atlas, who with his bronze back wears out the heavens, ancient abode of the gods, begot Maia by one of the goddesses, and Maia bore me to great Zeus: I am Hermes, the gods' servant. I have come here to Delphi where Phoebus sits upon the earth's very center[1] and ever prophesies to mortals what is and what shall be.

There is a famous Greek city[2] which takes its name from Pallas, goddess of the golden spear. Here Phoebus made forcible love to Creusa, daughter of Erechtheus, at the place where under Pallas' acropolis stand Athens' northern cliffs, the Long Cliffs, as the lords of Attica call them. Without her father's knowledge (for so the god wished it) she carried to term the burden of her belly. When her time came, Creusa gave birth in the house, then carried the child to the same cave where she was ravished

---

[1] Lit. "the earth's navel." Delphi was thought to be at the center of the world, and the story was told that two eagles simultaneously released at earth's eastern and western edges met there. In historical times a stone representation of a navel was the symbol of Delphi's centrality.

[2] Athens, deriving its name from Athena.

Κρέουσα, κἀκτίθησιν ὡς θανούμενον
κοίλης ἐν ἀντίπηγος εὐτρόχῳ κύκλῳ,
20 προγόνων νόμον σῴζουσα τοῦ τε γηγενοῦς
Ἐριχθονίου. κείνῳ γὰρ ἡ Διὸς κόρη
φρουρὼ παραζεύξασα φύλακε σώματος
δισσὼ δράκοντε, παρθένοις Ἀγλαυρίσιν
δίδωσι σῴζειν· ὅθεν Ἐρεχθείδαις ἐκεῖ
25 νόμος τις ἔστιν ὄφεσιν ἐν χρυσηλάτοις
τρέφειν τέκν'. ἀλλ' ἣν εἶχε παρθένος χλιδὴν
τέκνῳ προσάψασ' ἔλιπεν ὡς θανουμένῳ.
   κἄμ' ὢν ἀδελφὸς Φοῖβος αἰτεῖται τάδε·
Ὦ σύγγον', ἐλθὼν λαὸν εἰς αὐτόχθονα
30 κλεινῶν Ἀθηνῶν (οἶσθα γὰρ θεᾶς πόλιν)
λαβὼν βρέφος νεογνὸν ἐκ κοίλης πέτρας
αὐτῷ σὺν ἄγγει σπαργάνοισί θ' οἷς ἔχει
ἔνεγκε Δελφῶν τἀμὰ πρὸς χρηστήρια
καὶ θὲς πρὸς αὐταῖς εἰσόδοις δόμων ἐμῶν.
35 τὰ δ' ἄλλ' (ἐμὸς γάρ ἐστιν, ὡς εἰδῇς, ὁ παῖς)
ἡμῖν μελήσει. Λοξίᾳ δ' ἐγὼ χάριν
πράσσων ἀδελφῷ πλεκτὸν ἐξάρας κύτος
ἤνεγκα καὶ τὸν παῖδα κρηπίδων ἔπι
τίθημι ναοῦ τοῦδ', ἀναπτύξας κύτος
40 ἑλικτὸν ἀντίπηγος, ὡς ὁρῷθ' ὁ παῖς.
   κυρεῖ δ' ἅμ' ἱππεύοντος ἡλίου κύκλῳ
προφήτις ἐσβαίνουσα μαντεῖον θεοῦ·
ὄψιν δὲ προσβαλοῦσα παιδὶ νηπίῳ

---

22 φύλακε Porson: -κὰς L

by the god, and left him to die in the round hollow of a cradle. She kept the custom of her ancestors and of Erichthonius the earthborn. For Zeus's daughter gave him two serpents to guard his body when she handed him for safe keeping to the daughters of Aglauros.[3] And that is why the Athenians have the custom of rearing their children adorned with serpents of beaten gold. Well, the girl put upon the child what adornment she possessed, thinking he would die, and left him.

Then Phoebus, who is my brother, made this request of me: "Brother, go to the people of famous Athens, who are sprung from the land (you know the goddess' city) and taking a newborn child from the hollow cave bring him— cradle, swaddling clothes, and all—to my prophetic shrine in Delphi. There put him near the very entrance to my temple. The rest I shall take care of: the child, you should know, is mine." Complying with my brother Loxias' wish I picked up the wicker cradle and carried it and put the child upon the steps of this temple, opening the plaited basket so that the boy would be visible.

Now it happened that, just as the sun's orb began to ride in the heavens, a priestess was entering the temple of the god. Her glance fell on the babe. Astonished that some

---

[3] Aglauros, wife of Cecrops, an early king of Athens, had three daughters, Aglauros, Herse, and Pandrosos. (For the daughters, see below, lines 268-74.)

---

24 ἐκεῖ] ἔτι Barnes
33 ἔνεγκε Δελφῶν Reiske: ἔνεγκ᾽ ἀδελφῷ L
41 ἅμ᾽ ἱππεύοντος Musgrave: ἀνιππ- L

ἐθαύμασ᾽ εἴ τις Δελφίδων τλαίη κόρη
45 λαθραῖον ὠδῖν᾽ ἐς θεοῦ ῥῖψαι δόμον,
ὑπέρ τε θυμέλας διορίσαι πρόθυμος ἦν·
οἴκτῳ δ᾽ ἀφῆκεν ὠμότητα—καὶ θεὸς
συνεργὸς ἦν τῷ παιδὶ μὴ ᾽κπεσεῖν δόμων—
τρέφει δέ νιν λαβοῦσα. τὸν σπείραντα δὲ
50 οὐκ οἶδε Φοῖβον οὐδὲ μητέρ᾽ ἧς ἔφυ,
ὁ παῖς τε τοὺς τεκόντας οὐκ ἐπίσταται.
    νέος μὲν οὖν ὢν ἀμφὶ βωμίους τροφὰς
ἠλᾶτ᾽ ἀθύρων· ὡς δ᾽ ἀπηνδρώθη δέμας,
Δελφοί σφ᾽ ἔθεντο χρυσοφύλακα τοῦ θεοῦ
55 ταμίαν τε πάντων πιστόν, ἐν δ᾽ ἀνακτόροις
θεοῦ καταζῇ δεῦρ᾽ ἀεὶ σεμνὸν βίον.
Κρέουσα δ᾽ ἡ τεκοῦσα τὸν νεανίαν
Ξούθῳ γαμεῖται συμφορᾶς τοιᾶσδ᾽ ὕπο·
ἦν ταῖς Ἀθήναις τοῖς τε Χαλκωδοντίδαις,
60 οἳ γῆν ἔχουσ᾽ Εὐβοῖδα, πολέμιος κλύδων·
ὃν συμπονήσας καὶ συνεξελὼν δορὶ
γάμων Κρεούσης ἀξίωμ᾽ ἐδέξατο,
οὐκ ἐγγενὴς ὤν, Αἰόλου δὲ τοῦ Διὸς
γεγὼς Ἀχαιός. χρόνια δὲ σπείρας λέχη
65 ἄτεκνός ἐστι καὶ Κρέουσ᾽· ὧν οὕνεκα
ἥκουσι πρὸς μαντεῖ᾽ Ἀπόλλωνος τάδε
ἔρωτι παίδων. Λοξίας δὲ τὴν τύχην
ἐς τοῦτ᾽ ἐλαύνει, κοὐ λέληθεν, ὡς δοκεῖ.

---

46 τε Kirchhoff: δὲ L   47 χὢ Dindorf
51 del. Herwerden   68 λέληθέ μ᾽ Schoemann

Delphian girl had dared to cast upon the god's temple the child she had borne in secret, she wanted to put it beyond the altar precinct. But out of pity she put cruelty from her heart—and the god too had a hand in his son's not being expelled from the temple—and she took him and is raising him. She is unaware that Phoebus is his father or who is the mother that bore him, and the child likewise does not know his parents.

As a young child the boy wandered in play around about the altars that gave him his nourishment. But when he became a man, the Delphians made him the steward and trusted chamberlain of all the god's possessions, and from then until now he has lived a holy and respected life in the god's temple. Creusa, the young man's mother, married Xuthus under circumstances I will describe. The surge of war broke upon the Athenians and the Chalcodontidae, who inhabit the land of Euboea. Xuthus helped to bring the war to an end with his spear and thus was deemed worthy to marry Creusa although he was a foreigner, being an Achaean and the son of Aeolus, Zeus's son.[4] Though he has been Creusa's husband for a long time, he and Creusa are childless. Hence they have come to this prophetic shrine of Apollo longing for children. Loxias is directing events to this conclusion, and contrary to appearances he has not

[4] The usual genealogy made Hellen (ancestor of all the Greeks) the father of Xuthus, Aeolus, and Dorus (ancestors respectively of the Ionian, Aeolian, and Dorian Greeks). Euripides' genealogical innovation means that, while Xuthus has a respectable lineage, he is clearly a foreigner, whose marriage to Creusa was made necessary by the war with Euboea.

δώσει γὰρ εἰσελθόντι μαντεῖον τόδε

70 Ξούθῳ τὸν αὑτοῦ παῖδα καὶ πεφυκέναι
κείνου σφε φήσει, μητρὸς ὡς ἐλθὼν δόμους
γνωσθῇ Κρεούσῃ καὶ γάμοι τε Λοξίου
κρυπτοὶ γένωνται παῖς τ᾽ ἔχῃ τὰ πρόσφορα.
Ἴωνα δ᾽ αὐτόν, κτίστορ᾽ Ἀσιάδος χθονός,

75 ὄνομα κεκλῆσθαι θήσεται καθ᾽ Ἑλλάδα.
ἀλλ᾽ ἐς δαφνώδη γύαλα βήσομαι τάδε,
τὸ κρανθὲν ὡς ἂν ἐκμάθω παιδὸς πέρι.
ὁρῶ γὰρ ἐκβαίνοντα Λοξίου γόνον
τόνδ᾽, ὡς πρὸ ναοῦ λαμπρὰ θῇ πυλώματα

80 δάφνης κλάδοισιν. ὄνομα δ᾽, οὗ μέλλει τυχεῖν,
Ἴων᾽ ἐγώ ⟨νιν⟩ πρῶτος ὀνομάζω θεῶν.

ΙΩΝ

ἅρματα μὲν τάδε λαμπρὰ τεθρίππων
Ἥλιος ἤδη κάμπτει κατὰ γῆν,
ἄστρα δὲ φεύγει πυρὶ τῷδ᾽ αἰθέρος

85 ἐς νύχθ᾽ ἱεράν·
Παρνασιάδες δ᾽ ἄβατοι κορυφαὶ
καταλαμπόμεναι τὴν ἡμερίαν
ἁψῖδα βροτοῖσι δέχονται.
σμύρνης δ᾽ ἀνύδρου καπνὸς εἰς ὀρόφους

90 Φοίβου πέτεται.
θάσσει δὲ γυνὴ τρίποδα ζάθεον
Δελφίς, ἀείδουσ᾽ Ἕλλησι βοάς,
ἃς ἂν Ἀπόλλων κελαδήσῃ.
ἀλλ᾽, ὦ Φοίβου Δελφοὶ θέραπες,

forgotten. For he means to give his own son to Xuthus
when he enters this shrine and say that Xuthus is the
father. In this way the boy will enter the house of Creusa
his mother and be recognized by her: thus not only will
Loxias' liaison be kept a secret but also the boy will receive
what belongs to him. Apollo will cause his name through-
out Greece to be called Ion, founder of the cities of Asia.

Well, I shall go into this laurel grove so that I can ob-
serve what fate has ordained for the boy. For here I see the
son of Loxias coming out with boughs of laurel to clean the
entrance gate of the temple. I call him Ion, his destined
name, and am the first of the gods to do so.

Exit HERMES *by Eisodos A. From the* skene *enter* ION,
*armed with a bow and arrows and carrying a broom of
laurel branches and a ewer of water. He is accompanied by
temple servants.*

ION

Now Helios bends the course of his bright chariot here to-
ward the earth, and the stars, banished by his flame, flee
into the holy night. The trackless peaks of Parnassus gleam
with light and receive for mortals the sun's chariot wheels.
The smoke of dry incense rises up to Phoebus' rafters.
Upon her holy tripod sits the Delphian priestess, who
cries aloud to the Greeks whatever Apollo utters. So, you
Delphian servants of Apollo, go to the silvery streams of

---

81 ⟨νιν⟩ Scaliger

83 κάμπτει Matthiae et Wakefield: λάμπει L

95 τὰς Κασταλίας ἀργυροειδεῖς
βαίνετε δίνας, καθαραῖς δὲ δρόσοις
ἀφυδρανάμενοι στείχετε ναούς·
στόμα δ' εὔφημοι φρουρεῖτ' ἀγαθόν,
φήμας ἀγαθὰς
100 τοῖς ἐθέλουσιν μαντεύεσθαι
γλώσσης ἰδίας ἀποφαίνειν.
ἡμεῖς δέ, πόνους οὓς ἐκ παιδὸς
μοχθοῦμεν ἀεί, πτόρθοισι δάφνης
στέφεσίν θ' ἱεροῖς ἐσόδους Φοίβου
105 καθαρὰς θήσομεν ὑγραῖς τε πέδον
ῥανίσιν νοτερόν· πτηνῶν τ' ἀγέλας,
αἳ βλάπτουσιν σέμν' ἀναθήματα,
τόξοισιν ἐμοῖς φυγάδας θήσομεν·
ὡς γὰρ ἀμήτωρ ἀπάτωρ τε γεγὼς
110 τοὺς θρέψαντας
Φοίβου ναοὺς θεραπεύω.

στρ.

ἄγ', ὦ νεηθαλὲς ὦ
καλλίστας προπόλευμα δάφνας,
ἃ τὰν Φοίβου θυμέλαν
115 σαίρεις ὑπὸ ναοῖς,
κάπων ἐξ ἀθανάτων,
ἵνα δρόσοι τέγγουσ' ἱεραί,
γαίας ἀέναον
παγὰν ἐκπροϊεῖσαι,
120 μυρσίνας ἱερὰν φόβαν·
ᾇ σαίρω δάπεδον θεοῦ

330

Castalia, and when you have bathed in the pure water,
return to the temple. Keep pious silence and guard the
goodness of your lips, so that to those who wish to consult
the god you may utter words of good omen.

The temple servants exit by Eisidos A.

As for me, I shall perform the tasks I have ever performed
since childhood: with boughs of laurel and their holy bind-
ings I shall purify the entrance to Phoebus' house and
cleanse the floor with sprinklings of water. The flocks of
birds, which harm the sacred offerings, I shall put to flight
with my bow. As one who is without mother or father I
serve the temple of Phoebus that has given me nurture.

Come, O broom fresh-grown,
servant made of lovely laurel,
sweeper of Phoebus' altar
near his temple,
you that are sprung from groves immortal,
where the holy springs,
gushing forth from earth
a stream ever-flowing,
water the holy myrtle growing in profusion:
with you I sweep the god's temple floor

---

⁹⁸ δ' Kirchhoff: τ' L   εὔφημοι Camper: -ον L
⁹⁹ φήμας Hermann: φήμας τ' L
¹¹⁸ γαίας Diggle: τὰν L

παναμέριος ἅμ᾽ ἁλίου πτέρυγι θοᾷ
λατρεύων τὸ κατ᾽ ἦμαρ.
125 ὦ Παιὰν ὦ Παιάν,
εὐαίων εὐαίων
εἴης, ὦ Λατοῦς παῖ.

ἀντ.

καλόν γε τὸν πόνον, ὦ
Φοῖβε, σοὶ πρὸ δόμων λατρεύω,
130 τιμῶν μαντεῖον ἕδραν·
κλεινὸς δ᾽ ὁ πόνος μοι
θεοῖσιν δούλαν χέρ᾽ ἔχειν
οὐ θνατοῖς ἀλλ᾽ ἀθανάτοις·
εὐφάμους δὲ πόνους
135 μοχθεῖν οὐκ ἀποκάμνω.
Φοῖβός μοι γενέτωρ πατήρ·
τὸν βόσκοντα γὰρ εὐλογῶ,
τὸν δ᾽ ὠφέλιμον ἐμοὶ πατέρος ὄνομα λέγω
140 Φοῖβον τὸν κατὰ ναόν.
ὦ Παιὰν ὦ Παιάν,
εὐαίων εὐαίων
εἴης, ὦ Λατοῦς παῖ.

ἀλλ᾽ ἐκπαύσω γὰρ μόχθους
145 δάφνας ὁλκοῖς,
χρυσέων δ᾽ ἐκ τευχέων ῥίψω

134 εὐφάμους ... πόνους Porson: -οις ... οις L
135 μοχθῶν Wakefield

all the day long as the sun wings swiftly through the sky,
performing my daily service.
O Paian, O Paian,
blessed, blessed
may you be, son of Leto!

Fair is the toil, O Phoebus,
I do for you before your house,
honoring your prophetic seat.
Glorious is the task I have,
keeping my hands in service to gods,
not mortals but immortal beings.
Labor of such fair name
I do not grow weary to perform.
Phoebus is the father that begot me:
for I extol the one who feeds me,
and I call my benefactor by the name of father,
Phoebus, lord of the temple.
O Paian, O Paian,
blessed, blessed
may you be, son of Leto!

*He lays aside his laurel broom and takes up the ewer of
water.*

But I shall cease my labor
of sweeping with these laurel branches,
and from a vessel of gold I shall cast

---

139 τὸ Musgrave
140 Φοῖβον τὸν Heath: -ον τοῦ L

γαίας παγάν,
ἃν ἀποχεύονται
Κασταλίας δῖναι,
νοτερὸν ὕδωρ βάλλων,
150 ὅσιος ἀπ᾽ εὐνᾶς ὤν.
εἴθ᾽ οὕτως αἰεὶ Φοίβῳ
λατρεύων μὴ παυσαίμαν,
ἢ παυσαίμαν ἀγαθᾷ μοίρᾳ.

ἔα ἔα·
φοιτῶσ᾽ ἤδη λείπουσίν τε
155 πτανοὶ Παρνασοῦ κοίτας.
αὐδῶ μὴ χρίμπτειν θριγκοὺς
μηδ᾽ ἐς χρυσήρεις οἴκους.
μάρψω σ᾽ αὖ τόξοις, ὦ Ζηνὸς
κῆρυξ, ὀρνίθων γαμφηλαῖς
160 ἰσχὺν νικῶν.
ὅδε πρὸς θυμέλας ἄλλος ἐρέσσει
κύκνος. οὐκ ἄλλᾳ φοινικοφαῆ
πόδα κινήσεις;
οὐδέν σ᾽ ἁ φόρμιγξ ἁ Φοίβου
165 σύμμολπος τόξων ῥύσαιτ᾽ ἄν.
πάραγε πτέρυγας·
λίμνας ἐπίβα τᾶς Δηλιάδος·
αἱάξεις, εἰ μὴ πείσῃ,
τὰς καλλιφθόγγους ᾠδάς.
170 ἔα ἔα·

the water the earth produces,
which gushes out
from the eddies of Castalia.
I scatter its moisture around,
I who have risen pure from my bed.
Thus always for Phoebus
may I not stop toiling—
or stop but with heaven's blessing!

But look!
They are coming, the birds, leaving
their nests on Parnassus!
Do not come near the coping stones
or the golden temple of Apollo!
My bow will bring you down as well, herald
of Zeus, although your beak
routs the strength of other birds!
Here toward the temple wings another,
a swan! Take your feet that show red against your belly
and go elsewhere!
The lyre of Apollo
that accompanies your song cannot save you from my
     bow!
Fly off to somewhere else!
Alight upon the lake at Delos!
Your tuneful song will change
to shrieks of pain if you do not obey!
See, see!

---

¹⁵⁶ θριγκοὺς Wilamowitz: -οῖς L
¹⁶⁸ αἰάξεις Nauck: αἱμάξ- L

τίς ὅδ' ὀρνίθων καινὸς προσέβα;
μῶν ὑπὸ θριγκοὺς εὐναίας
καρφυρὰς θήσων τέκνοις;
ψαλμοί σ' εἴρξουσιν τόξων.
οὐ πείσῃ; χωρῶν δίνας
175 τὰς Ἀλφειοῦ παιδούργει
ἢ νάπος Ἴσθμιον,
ὡς ἀναθήματα μὴ βλάπτηται
ναοί τ' ‹εὔθριγκ›οι Φοίβου.
κτείνειν δ' ὑμᾶς αἰδοῦμαι
180 τοὺς θεῶν ἀγγέλλοντας φήμας
θνατοῖς· οἷς δ' ἔγκειμαι μόχθοις
Φοίβῳ δουλεύσω κοὐ λήξω
τοὺς βόσκοντας θεραπεύων.

ΧΟΡΟΣ

στρ. α
—οὐκ ἐν ταῖς ζαθέαις Ἀθά-
185 ναις εὐκίονες ἦσαν αὐ-
λαὶ θεῶν μόνον, οὐδ' ἀγυι-
άτιδες θεραπεῖαι·
ἀλλὰ καὶ παρὰ Λοξίᾳ
τῷ Λατοῦς διδύμων προσώ-
πων καλλιβλέφαρον φῶς.
190—ἰδού, τᾷδ' ἄθρησον·

174-5 δίνας τὰς Badham: -αις ταῖς L
178 ναοί τ' ‹εὔθριγκ›οι Φοίβου Diggle: ναοί θ' οἱ Φ- L
190 τᾷδ' Dobree: τάνδ' L

ION

What strange bird is this that comes?
Does he mean to make under the gable
a nest of straw for his young?
The twang of my bowstring will prevent you!
Obey! Go to the eddies
of the Alpheus to hatch your brood,
or the groves of the Isthmus!
Thus the offerings and the ⟨fair-gabled⟩
temple of Phoebus will remain unfouled.
Yet I hesitate to kill you,
who convey the gods' words
to mortals. But I shall duly perform
the tasks I am devoted to for Phoebus and never cease
serving him who feeds me.

Exit ION *into the* skene. *Enter by Eisodos A Creusa's maid-
servants as* CHORUS. *Their song is initially divided among
the individual chorus members.*

CHORUS
—Not only in holy Athens, then,
are gods' fair-columned
temples to be found
or homage paid to Aguieus.[5]
Also at the shrine of Loxias,
Leto's son, the temple's twin façades
gleam with fair-eyed loveliness.
—See, look here!

---

[5] Aguieus was a cult title of Apollo as protector of roads.

Λερναῖον ὕδραν ἐναίρει
χρυσέαις ἅρπαις ὁ Διὸς παῖς·
φίλα, πρόσιδ᾽ ὄσσοις.

ἀντ. α

—ὁρῶ. καὶ πέλας ἄλλος αὐ-
195 τοῦ πανὸν πυρίφλεκτον αἴ-
ρει τις· ἆρ᾽ ὃς ἐμαῖσι μυ-
θεύεται παρὰ πήναις,
ἀσπιστὰς Ἰόλαος, ὃς
κοινοὺς αἱρόμενος πόνους
200 Δίῳ παιδὶ συναντλεῖ;
—καὶ μὰν τόνδ᾽ ἄθρησον
πτεροῦντος ἔφεδρον ἵππου·
τὰν πῦρ πνέουσαν ἐναίρει
τρισώματον ἀλκάν.

στρ. β

205—πάντᾳ τοι βλέφαρον διώ-
κω. σκέψαι κλόνον ἐν †τείχε-
σι† λαΐνοισι Γιγάντων.
—†ὧδε δερκόμεσθ᾽, ὦ φίλαι.†
—λεύσσεις οὖν ἐπ᾽ Ἐγκελάδῳ
210 γοργωπὸν πάλλουσαν ἴτυν . . . ;

203 πῦρ Reiske: πυρὶ L
206 τύποισι L. Dindorf: τέχναισι Willink
208 ὧδε δερκόμεθ᾽, ὦ γυναῖκες Wecklein

The hydra of Lerna he slays
with a sickle of gold, does Zeus's son.[6]
Friend, look over here!

—I see him. And near him another
raises the blazing torch!
Is it he whose story I heard
as I plied my loom,
shield-bearing Iolaus, who
took up shared labors with
the son of Zeus and helped him to endure them?
—But see here
the man upon the winged horse:
he is slaying the fire-breathing
three-bodied monster.[7]

—My eyes dart in all directions.
Look at the rout of the Giants[8]
carved on the stonework!
—I see them, my friends!
—Do you see her, shaking over Enceladus
her fierce-visaged shield[9] . . .

---

[6] Heracles cuts off the hydra's many heads. His companion
Iolaus, mentioned below, cauterizes the stumps with a torch to
prevent them from growing back.

[7] Bellerophon, riding the winged horse Pegasus, kills the Chimaera, who is part lioness, part goat, and part snake.

[8] The Giants were Earth's monstrous offspring who rose up
against the Olympian gods and were defeated at Phlegra with the
assistance of Heracles.

[9] The shield of Athena had the head of the Gorgon depicted
on it.

—λεύσσω Παλλάδ᾽, ἐμὰν θεόν.

—τί γάρ; κεραυνὸν ἀμφίπυρον
ὄβριμον ἐν Διὸς
ἐκηβόλοισι χερσίν;

—ὁρῶ· τὸν δάιον

215 Μίμαντα πυρὶ καταιθαλοῖ.

—καὶ Βρόμιος ἄλλον ἀπολέμοι-
σι κισσίνοισι βάκτροις
ἐναίρει Γᾶς τέκνων ὁ Βακχεύς.

ἀντ. β

CHORUS
XOPOΣ

σέ τοι, τὸν παρὰ ναὸν αὐ-
220 δῶ· θέμις γυάλων ὑπερ-
βῆναι λευκῷ ποδί γ᾽ ⟨οὐδόν⟩;

ΙΩΝ

οὐ θέμις, ὦ ξέναι.

ΧΟΡΟΣ

αὐδὰν δ᾽ ἐκ σέθεν ἂν πυθοίμαν;

ΙΩΝ

τίνα τήνδε θέλεις;

ΧΟΡΟΣ

ἆρ᾽ ὄντως μέσον ὀμφαλὸν
γᾶς Φοίβου κατέχει δόμος;

---

221 ⟨οὐδόν⟩ Lindau: ⟨τοῖχον⟩ omisso γ᾽ Willink
222 αὐδὰν δ᾽ . . . πυθοίμαν Kovacs: οὐδ᾽ ἂν . . . πυθοίμαν
αὐδάν L   223 τήνδε Musgrave: δὲ L

340

—I see Pallas, my goddess.
—And do you see the thunderbolt with flame on either
    end?
Zeus holds the mighty weapon
in his far-hurling hands.
—I see it. With its flame he burns to ash
Mimas his foeman.
—And Bromius, the Bacchic god
with his unwarlike wand of ivy
slays another of the giant sons of Earth.

Enter ION *from the* skene. *The Chorus now sing as a
group.*

CHORUS

You there, I speak
to you by the temple: may we cross
with pale foot the sanctuary's ⟨bound⟩?

ION

Foreign ladies, you may not.

CHORUS

Well, may I hear from you some word?

ION

What word is it that you want?

CHORUS

Does Phoebus' temple truly stand
upon Earth's midmost navel?

ΙΩΝ

στέμμασί γ᾽ ἐνδυτόν, ἀμφὶ δὲ Γοργόνες.

ΧΟΡΟΣ

225 οὕτω καὶ φάτις αὐδᾷ.

ΙΩΝ

εἰ μὲν ἐθύσατε πέλανον πρὸ δόμων
καί τι πυθέσθαι χρῄζετε Φοίβου,
πάριτ᾽ ἐς θυμέλας· ἐπὶ δ᾽ ἀσφάκτοις
μήλοισι δόμων μὴ πάριτ᾽ ἐς μυχόν.

ΧΟΡΟΣ

230 ἔχω μαθοῦσα· θεοῦ δὲ νόμον
οὐ παραβαίνομεν,
ἃ δ᾽ ἐκτὸς ὄμμα τέρψει.

ΙΩΝ

πάντα θεᾶσθ᾽, ὅ τι καὶ θέμις, ὄμμασι.

ΧΟΡΟΣ

μεθεῖσαν δεσπόται
με θεοῦ γύαλα τάδ᾽ εἰσιδεῖν.

ΙΩΝ

δμωαὶ δὲ τίνων κλῄζεσθε δόμων;

ΧΟΡΟΣ

235 Παλλάδι σύνοικα τρόφιμα μέλα-

224 ἐνδυτόν Musgrave: -τός L
233 με θεοῦ Hermann: θεοῦ με L
235 Παλλάδι σύνοικα Badham: -δος ἔνοικα L

342

ION

Yes, the navel stone is wrapped in fillets and surrounded by Gorgons.

CHORUS

That is what I have heard tell.

ION

If you have sacrificed the holy cake before the temple and wish to ask a question of Phoebus, go to the shrine. Do not go into the inmost recess without sacrificing a sheep.

CHORUS

I have heard what you say. I do not transgress
the law of the gods:
what is outside will delight my eyes.

ION

Look at everything the law permits.

CHORUS

My mistress has allowed me
to view the god's precincts here.

ION

Of what house are you called the slaves?

CHORUS

The house that reared my mistress

θρα τῶν ἐμῶν τυράννων·
παρούσας δ᾿ ἀμφὶ τάσδ᾿ ἐρωτᾷς.

ΙΩΝ

⟨ὦ χαῖρ᾿, ἄνασσα· καὶ γὰρ οὖν μορφῇ τ᾿ ἔνι⟩
γενναιότης σοι, καὶ τρόπων τεκμήριον
τὸ σχῆμ᾿ ἔχεις τόδ᾿, ἥτις εἶ ποτ᾿, ὦ γύναι.
γνοίη δ᾿ ἂν ὡς τὰ πολλά γ᾿ ἀνθρώπου πέρι
240   τὸ σχῆμ᾿ ἰδών τις εἰ πέφυκεν εὐγενής.
      ἔα·
ἀλλ᾿ ἐξέπληξάς μ᾿, ὄμμα συγκλήσασα σὸν
δακρύοις θ᾿ ὑγράνασ᾿ εὐγενῆ παρηίδα,
ὡς εἶδες ἁγνὰ Λοξίου χρηστήρια.
τί ποτε μερίμνης ἐς τόδ᾿ ἦλθες, ὦ γύναι;
245   οὗ πάντες ἄλλοι γύαλα λεύσσοντες θεοῦ
χαίρουσιν, ἐνταῦθ᾿ ὄμμα σὸν δακρυρροεῖ;

ΚΡΕΟΥΣΑ

ὦ ξένε, τὸ μὲν σὸν οὐκ ἀπαιδεύτως ἔχει
ἐς θαύματ᾿ ἐλθεῖν δακρύων ἐμῶν πέρι·
ἐγὼ δ᾿ ἰδοῦσα τούσδ᾿ Ἀπόλλωνος δόμους
250   μνήμην παλαιὰν ἀνεμετρησάμην τινά·
ἐκεῖσε τὸν νοῦν ἔσχον ἐνθάδ᾿ οὖσά περ.
ὦ τλήμονες γυναῖκες· ὦ τολμήματα
θεῶν. τί δῆτα; ποῖ δίκην ἀνοίσομεν,
εἰ τῶν κρατούντων ἀδικίαις ὀλούμεθα;

237 ante h. v. lac. indic. et suppl. Lloyd-Jones
248 del. Cropp   251 ἐκεῖσε Owen: οἴκοι δὲ L
περ Dobree, Hermann: που L

makes one dwelling with that of Pallas.[10]
But she whom you ask about is here.

Enter CREUSA by Eisodos A.

‹My greeting, O queen! For in your appearance› there is
nobility, and your bearing gives evidence of who you are,
lady. For the most part someone can tell by a person's bear-
ing whether he is well born. (*Creusa turns her face away in
obvious distress.*)

But what is this? It startles me that when you look on
the holy shrine of Loxias you shut your eyes tight and
moisten your noble cheek with tears. Why are you so dis-
traught, lady? Where all others are glad to see the god's
sanctuary, can it be that there your eyes run with tears?

Stranger, your attitude—your wondering at my tears—
is well bred. Looking at Apollo's temple I remembered
something that happened long ago. Though I was here, my
mind was elsewhere.

O unhappy women! O the criminal deeds of the gods!
What is to happen? To what tribunal can we appeal when
we are being done to death by the injustice of our masters?

---

[10] The house of Erechtheus on the Acropolis (where the
Erechtheum stood) was shared by Erechtheus and Athena Polias:
cf. *Odyssey* 7.80-1.

ΙΩΝ

255 τί χρῆμ᾽ ἀνερμήνευτα δυσθυμῇ, γύναι;

ΚΡΕΟΥΣΑ

οὐδέν· μεθῆκα τόξα· τἀπὶ τῷδε δὲ
ἐγώ τε σιγῶ καὶ σὺ μὴ φρόντιζ᾽ ἔτι.

ΙΩΝ

τίς δ᾽ εἶ; πόθεν γῆς ἦλθες; ἐκ ποίου πατρὸς
πέφυκας; ὄνομα τί σε καλεῖν ἡμᾶς χρεών;

ΚΡΕΟΥΣΑ

260 Κρέουσα μέν μοι τοὔνομ᾽, ἐκ δ᾽ Ἐρεχθέως
πέφυκα, πατρὶς γῆ δ᾽ Ἀθηναίων πόλις.

ΙΩΝ

ὦ κλεινὸν οἰκοῦσ᾽ ἄστυ γενναίων τ᾽ ἄπο
τραφεῖσα πατέρων, ὥς σε θαυμάζω, γύναι.

ΚΡΕΟΥΣΑ

τοσαῦτα κεὐτυχοῦμεν, ὦ ξέν᾽, οὐ πέρα.

ΙΩΝ

265 πρὸς θεῶν ἀληθῶς, ὡς μεμύθευται βροτοῖς . . .

ΚΡΕΟΥΣΑ

τί χρῆμ᾽ ἐρωτᾷς, ὦ ξέν᾽, ἐκμαθεῖν θέλων;

ΙΩΝ

. . . ἐκ γῆς πατρός σου πρόγονος ἔβλαστεν πατήρ;

---

258 ποίου πατρὸς L. Dindorf: ποίας πάτρας L
261 fort. πατρός   264 τοσαῦτά γ᾽ Musgrave
266 θέλων Badham: -ω L

ION

Why are you so strangely unhappy, lady?

CREUSA

It's nothing. I have let my shaft fly. As for what my words imply, I say nothing, and you too should think no more of it.

ION

Who are you? From what part of the world do you come? Who is your father? What name am I to call you?

CREUSA

Creusa is my name, my father was Erechtheus, and my native land is the city of Athens.

ION

What a glorious city you live in, and how noble are the forebears who nurtured you! I honor you, lady!

CREUSA

Yes, in this I am fortunate, but in nothing else.

ION

Tell me, by the gods, is it true, as men say . . .

CREUSA

What does your question strive to learn?

ION

. . . that your father's forebear sprang from the earth?

ΚΡΕΟΥΣΑ

Ἐριχθόνιός γε· τὸ δὲ γένος μ' οὐκ ὠφελεῖ.

ΙΩΝ

ἦ καί σφ' Ἀθάνα γῆθεν ἐξανείλετο;

ΚΡΕΟΥΣΑ

270 ἐς παρθένους γε χεῖρας, οὐ τεκοῦσά νιν.

ΙΩΝ

δίδωσι δ', ὥσπερ ἐν γραφῇ νομίζεται . . .

ΚΡΕΟΥΣΑ

Κέκροπός γε σῴζειν παισὶν οὐχ ὁρώμενον.

ΙΩΝ

ἤκουσα λῦσαι παρθένους τεῦχος θεᾶς.

ΚΡΕΟΥΣΑ

τοιγὰρ θανοῦσαι σκόπελον ἥμαξαν πέτρας.

ΙΩΝ

275 εἶέν·
τί δαὶ τόδ'; ἆρ' ἀληθὲς ἢ μάτην λόγος;

ΚΡΕΟΥΣΑ

τί χρῆμ' ἐρωτᾷς; καὶ γὰρ οὐ κάμνω σχολῇ.

ΙΩΝ

πατὴρ Ἐρεχθεὺς σὰς ἔθυσε συγγόνους;

275 δ' αὖ Porson

348

CREUSA

Yes, Erichthonius.[11] But my ancestry does me no good.

ION

And did Athena take him up from the earth?

CREUSA

Yes, into her maidenly embrace: she was not his mother.

ION

And did she give him, as paintings often show . . .

CREUSA

Yes, to Cecrops' daughters to keep without looking at him.

ION

I have heard that the girls opened the goddess' vessel.

CREUSA

And that is why they perished, spattering their blood on the cliffside.

ION

Well, then, what of the other story? Is it true or false?

CREUSA

What is it you ask? I have leisure and to spare.

ION

Did your father Erechtheus sacrifice your sisters?

---

11 Hephaestus, the story went, tried to ravish Athena, but she escaped his grasp, and his seed fell on the ground. Earth was impregnated, she bore Erichthonius (the name seems to mean "very earthy"), and gave him to Athena. Athena in turn entrusted the child, hidden in a chest and guarded by snakes, to the three daughters of King Cecrops with instructions that they should not look at him. Two of them disobeyed, and all three perished, leaping in madness from the Acropolis.

ΚΡΕΟΥΣΑ

ἔτλη πρὸ γαίας σφάγια παρθένους κτανεῖν.

ΙΩΝ

σὺ δ' ἐξεσώθης πῶς κασιγνήτων μόνη;

ΚΡΕΟΥΣΑ

280   βρέφος νεογνὸν μητρὸς ἦν ἐν ἀγκάλαις.

ΙΩΝ

πατέρα δ' ἀληθῶς χάσμα σὸν κρύπτει χθονός;

ΚΡΕΟΥΣΑ

πληγαὶ τριαίνης ποντίου σφ' ἀπώλεσαν.

ΙΩΝ

Μακραὶ δὲ χῶρός ἐστ' ἐκεῖ κεκλημένος;

ΚΡΕΟΥΣΑ

τί δ' ἱστορεῖς τόδ'; ὥς μ' ἀνέμνησάς τινος.

ΙΩΝ

285   τιμᾷ κεραυνός σφ' ἀστραπαί τε Πύθιαι.

ΚΡΕΟΥΣΑ

τιμᾷ; τί τιμᾷ; μήποτ' ὤφελόν σφ' ἰδεῖν.

ΙΩΝ

τί δὲ στυγεῖς σὺ τοῦ θεοῦ τὰ φίλτατα;

285 κεραυνός σφ' Diggle: σφε Πύθιος L
286 τιμᾷ; τί τιμᾷ Hermann: τιμᾷ τιμᾷ ὡς L

CREUSA

He brought himself to kill the girls for the country's sake.[12]

ION

How was it that you alone of the sisters survived?

CREUSA

I was a newborn child in my mother's arms.

ION

Is it true that your father lies covered in a cleft in the earth?

CREUSA

The blow of the sea god's trident killed him.

ION

Is that spot called the Long Rocks?

CREUSA

Why do you ask about that? How you stir my memory!

ION

The place is honored by Apollo's lightning and thunder.[13]

CREUSA

Honored? What honor? I wish I had never seen it!

ION

But why do you hate what the god loves?

12 When Eumolpus, son of Poseidon, invaded Attica, an oracle announced that the city could be saved only by the sacrifice of noble virgins. Erechtheus and his wife Praxithea agreed to sacrifice their daughters. The story was treated by Euripides in his (lost) *Erechtheus* (c. 423 B.C.).

13 From a spot on the acropolis, here identified with the Long Rocks, the Athenians looked north toward Mt. Parnes three days each month for lightning, and when it appeared an embassy was sent to Delphi.

ΚΡΕΟΥΣΑ

οὐδέν· ξύνοιδ᾽ ἄντροισιν αἰσχύνην τινά.

ΙΩΝ

πόσις δὲ τίς σ᾽ ἔγημ᾽ Ἀθηναίων, γύναι;

ΚΡΕΟΥΣΑ

290   οὐκ ἀστὸς ἀλλ᾽ ἐπακτὸς ἐξ ἄλλης χθονός.

ΙΩΝ

τίς; εὐγενῆ νιν δεῖ πεφυκέναι τινά.

ΚΡΕΟΥΣΑ

Ξοῦθος, πεφυκὼς Αἰόλου Διός τ᾽ ἄπο.

ΙΩΝ

καὶ πῶς ξένος σ᾽ ὢν ἔσχεν οὖσαν ἐγγενῆ;

ΚΡΕΟΥΣΑ

Εὔβοι᾽ Ἀθήναις ἔστι τις γείτων πόλις.

ΙΩΝ

295   ὅροις ὑγροῖσιν, ὡς λέγουσ᾽, ὡρισμένη.

ΚΡΕΟΥΣΑ

ταύτην ἔπερσε Κεκροπίδαις κοινῷ δορί.

ΙΩΝ

ἐπίκουρος ἐλθών; κᾆτα σὸν γαμεῖ λέχος;

ΚΡΕΟΥΣΑ

φερνάς γε πολέμου καὶ δορὸς λαβὼν γέρας.

ΙΩΝ

σὺν ἀνδρὶ δ᾽ ἥκεις ἢ μόνη χρηστήρια;

CREUSA

It's nothing. I know a disgraceful deed done in that cave.

ION

Who of the Athenians is your husband, lady?

CREUSA

My husband is no citizen: he comes from another land.

ION

Who? He must be someone of high birth.

CREUSA

Xuthus, sprung from Aeolus[14] and from Zeus.

ION

And how could a foreigner marry you, an Athenian born?

CREUSA

Athens has a neighboring city, Euboea.

ION

Yes, bounded by water, they say.

CREUSA

He helped the sons of Cecrops to conquer it.

ION

As their ally? And then married you?

CREUSA

Yes, as the dowry of war and the prize his spear won.

ION

Have you come to the oracle with your husband or alone?

14 See note on line 63 above.

---

295 ὅροις ⟨γ᾽⟩ Cobet

ΚΡΕΟΥΣΑ

300   σὺν ἀνδρί. σηκοῖς δ' ὑστερεῖ Τροφωνίου.

ΙΩΝ

πότερα θεατὴς ἢ χάριν μαντευμάτων;

ΚΡΕΟΥΣΑ

κείνου τε Φοίβου θ' ἓν θέλων μαθεῖν ἔπος.

ΙΩΝ

καρποῦ δ' ὕπερ γῆς ἥκετ' ἢ ποίων πέρι;

ΚΡΕΟΥΣΑ

ἄπαιδές ἐσμεν, χρόνι' ἔχοντ' εὐνήματα.

ΙΩΝ

305   οὐδ' ἔτεκες οὐδὲν πώποτ' ἀλλ' ἄτεκνος εἶ;

ΚΡΕΟΥΣΑ

ὁ Φοῖβος οἶδε τὴν ἐμὴν ἀπαιδίαν.

ΙΩΝ

ὦ τλῆμον, ὡς τἄλλ' εὐτυχοῦσ' οὐκ εὐτυχεῖς.

ΚΡΕΟΥΣΑ

σὺ δ' εἶ τίς; ὥς σου τὴν τεκοῦσαν ὤλβισα.

ΙΩΝ

τοῦ θεοῦ καλοῦμαι δοῦλος, εἰμί τ', ὦ γύναι.

ΚΡΕΟΥΣΑ

310   ἀνάθημα πόλεως ἤ τινος πραθεὶς ὕπο;

---

300 σηκοῖς Scaliger: -ους L   ὑστερεῖ Badham: εὖ στρέφει L   303 ποίων Diggle: παίδων L
304 ἄπαιδ' ἔτ' Naber

ION

CREUSA

With my husband. But he is tarrying in the precincts of
Trophonius.[15]

ION

To see his shrine or to get oracles?

CREUSA

From him and from Phoebus he wants to learn one thing.

ION

Have you come on behalf of the land's crops, or what is
your errand?

CREUSA

We are childless, though long married.

ION

You have never been a mother, then? You are childless?

CREUSA

(*darkly*) Apollo knows my childlessness.

ION

Poor lady! Though your fortune in other things is good, you
are unfortunate!

CREUSA

But who are you? How blessed in my eyes is your mother!

ION

I am called the god's servant, and that is what I am, lady.

CREUSA

Were you offered to the god by your city or sold to him by
some man?

15 The hero Trophonius, who gave oracles, was worshiped in a
cave in Lebedaea not far from Delphi.

ΙΩΝ

οὐκ οἶδα πλὴν ἕν· Λοξίου κεκλήμεθα.

ΚΡΕΟΥΣΑ

ἡμεῖς σ᾽ ἄρ᾽ αὖθις, ὦ ξέν᾽, ἀντοικτίρομεν.

ΙΩΝ

ὡς μὴ εἰδόθ᾽ ἥτις μ᾽ ἔτεκεν ἐξ ὅτου τ᾽ ἔφυν.

ΚΡΕΟΥΣΑ

ναοῖσι δ᾽ οἰκεῖς τοισίδ᾽ ἢ κατὰ στέγας;

ΙΩΝ

315   ἅπαν ⟨τὸ⟩ θεοῦ μοι δῶμ᾽, ἵν᾽ ἂν λάβῃ μ᾽ ὕπνος.

ΚΡΕΟΥΣΑ

παῖς δ᾽ ὢν ἀφίκου ναὸν ἢ νεανίας;

ΙΩΝ

βρέφος λέγουσιν οἱ δοκοῦντες εἰδέναι.

ΚΡΕΟΥΣΑ

καὶ τίς γάλακτί σ᾽ ἐξέθρεψε Δελφίδων;

ΙΩΝ

οὐπώποτ᾽ ἔγνων μαστόν· ἡ δ᾽ ἔθρεψέ με . . .

ΚΡΕΟΥΣΑ

320   τίς, ὦ ταλαίπωρ᾽; ὡς νοσοῦσ᾽ ηὗρον νόσους.

ΙΩΝ

. . . Φοίβου προφῆτιν μητέρ᾽ ὡς νομίζομεν.

ΚΡΕΟΥΣΑ

ἐς δ᾽ ἄνδρ᾽ ἀφίκου τίνα τροφὴν κεκτημένος;

ION

I only know that I am called Apollo's.

CREUSA

So I in my turn, stranger, pity you.

ION

Yes, since I do not know who my mother and father are.

CREUSA

Do you live in this temple or in a house?

ION

All the god's precinct, wherever I fall asleep, is home to me.

CREUSA

Did you come to the shrine as a boy or as a young man?

ION

Those who are thought to know say as a babe.

CREUSA

And which of the Delphian women suckled you?

ION

I never knew the breast. But the one who raised me up . . .

CREUSA

Who, poor boy? What troubles I find, though I have troubles of my own!

ION

. . . was Phoebus' priestess. I regard her as my mother.

CREUSA

But how did you come to manhood? On what did you live?

---

315 ⟨τὸ⟩ Seidler
321 προφῆτιν Reiske: -τις L

ΙΩΝ

βωμοί μ' ἔφερβον οὔπιών τ' ἀεὶ ξένος.

ΚΡΕΟΥΣΑ

τάλαινά σ' ἡ τεκοῦσα· τίς ποτ' ἦν ἄρα;

ΙΩΝ

325 ἀδίκημά του γυναικὸς ἐγενόμην ἴσως.

ΚΡΕΟΥΣΑ

ἔχεις δὲ βίοτον· εὖ γὰρ ἤσκησαι πέπλοις.

ΙΩΝ

τοῖς τοῦ θεοῦ κοσμούμεθ' ᾧ δουλεύομεν.

ΚΡΕΟΥΣΑ

οὐδ' ἦξας εἰς ἔρευναν ἐξευρεῖν γονάς;

ΙΩΝ

ἔχω γὰρ οὐδέν, ὦ γύναι, τεκμήριον.

ΚΡΕΟΥΣΑ

330 φεῦ·
πέπονθέ τις σῇ μητρὶ ταὔτ' ἄλλη γυνή.

ΙΩΝ

τίς; εἰ πόνου μοι ξυλλάβοι, χαίροιμεν ἄν.

ΚΡΕΟΥΣΑ

ἧς οὕνεκ' ἦλθον δεῦρο πρὶν πόσιν μολεῖν.

ΙΩΝ

ποῖόν τι χρῄζουσ'; ὡς ὑπουργήσω, γύναι.

ΚΡΕΟΥΣΑ

μάντευμα κρυπτὸν δεομένη Φοίβου μαθεῖν.

ION

The altars and the stream of foreigners fed me.

CREUSA

How I pity your poor mother! Who could she be?

ION

I am perhaps the offspring of some woman wronged.

CREUSA

You have means to live: you are well dressed.

ION

I am clothed in the livery of the god I serve.

CREUSA

But have you never tried to find your parents?

ION

No: I have no evidence who they are, lady.

CREUSA

Ah me! Another woman suffered as your mother did.

ION

Who? If she could share my trouble, I would be glad.

CREUSA

She for whose sake I came here before my husband.

ION

What is your errand? I shall help you, lady.

CREUSA

I want to receive a secret oracle from Phoebus.

324-5 post 329 trai. Herwerden
324 τεκοῦσα· τίς ποτ' Jodrell: τεκοῦσ' ἤ τίς ποτ' L
331 sic Yxem: τίς εἶπον εἴ μοι ξυλλάβη L

ΙΩΝ

335 λέγοις ἄν· ἡμεῖς τἆλλα προξενήσομεν.

ΚΡΕΟΥΣΑ

ἄκουε δὴ τὸν μῦθον· ἀλλ᾽ αἰδούμεθα.

ΙΩΝ

οὔ τἄρα πράξεις οὐδέν· ἀργὸς ἡ θεός.

ΚΡΕΟΥΣΑ

Φοίβῳ μιγῆναί φησί τις φίλων ἐμῶν.

ΙΩΝ

Φοίβῳ γυνὴ γεγῶσα; μὴ λέγ᾽, ὦ ξένη.

ΚΡΕΟΥΣΑ

340 καὶ παῖδά γ᾽ ἔτεκε τῷ θεῷ λάθρᾳ πατρός.

ΙΩΝ

οὐκ ἔστιν· ἀνδρὸς ἀδικίαν αἰσχύνεται.

ΚΡΕΟΥΣΑ

οὔ φησιν αὐτή· καὶ πέπονθεν ἄθλια.

ΙΩΝ

τί χρῆμα δράσασ᾽, εἰ θεῷ συνεζύγη;

ΚΡΕΟΥΣΑ

τὸν παῖδ᾽ ὃν ἔτεκεν ἐξέθηκε δωμάτων.

ΙΩΝ

345 ὁ δ᾽ ἐκτεθεὶς παῖς ποῦ ᾽στιν; εἰσορᾷ φάος;

342 οὔ Seager: ὃ L

ION

ION
Tell me: I shall do all else for you.

CREUSA
Hear then the story. But I feel shame!

ION
Then you will accomplish nothing. For she is a do-nothing goddess.[16]

CREUSA
One of my friends claims she lay with Apollo.

ION
A woman with Apollo? Say not so, lady!

CREUSA
Yes, and she bore the god a child without her father's knowledge.

ION
Impossible: she is ashamed some man has wronged her.

CREUSA
She says it is not so. And her suffering has been dreadful.

ION
What became of her if the god was her lover?

CREUSA
She put from her house the child she bore, exposed him.

ION
And the exposed child, where is he? Is he alive?

---

[16] Euripides, like many Greeks, often personifies as goddesses certain abstract qualities. Here the goddess is Shame, and she is said to do nothing because shame often inhibits people from doing what they want or ought to do.

ΚΡΕΟΥΣΑ

οὐκ οἶδεν οὐδείς. ταῦτα καὶ μαντεύομαι.

ΙΩΝ

εἰ δ᾽ οὐκέτ᾽ ἔστι, τίνι τρόπῳ διεφθάρη;

ΚΡΕΟΥΣΑ

θῆράς σφε τὸν δύστηνον ἐλπίζει κτανεῖν.

ΙΩΝ

ποίῳ τόδ᾽ ἔγνω χρωμένη τεκμηρίῳ;

ΚΡΕΟΥΣΑ

350   ἐλθοῦσ᾽ ἵν᾽ αὐτὸν ἐξέθηκ᾽ οὐχ ηὗρ᾽ ἔτι.

ΙΩΝ

ἦν δὲ σταλαγμὸς ἐν στίβῳ τις αἵματος;

ΚΡΕΟΥΣΑ

οὔ φησι. καίτοι πόλλ᾽ ἐπεστράφη πέδον.

ΙΩΝ

χρόνος δὲ τίς τῷ παιδὶ διαπεπραγμένῳ;

ΚΡΕΟΥΣΑ

354   σοὶ ταὐτὸν ἥβης, εἴπερ ἦν, εἶχ᾽ ἂν μέτρον.

ΙΩΝ

357   τί δ᾽ εἰ λάθρᾳ νιν Φοῖβος ἐκτρέφει λαβών;

ΚΡΕΟΥΣΑ

358   τὰ κοινὰ χαίρων οὐ δίκαια δρᾷ μόνος.

357-8 post 354 trai. Diggle

CREUSA

No one knows. That is the very question I am asking
Apollo.

ION

If he is dead, how did he die?

CREUSA

The woman thinks beasts killed the hapless child.

ION

What reason did she have for thinking this?

CREUSA

When she went to where she had left him, she could not
find him again.

ION

Were there any drops of blood on the path?

CREUSA

She says there were not. And she searched the ground
carefully.

ION

How much time has passed since the child was made away
with?

CREUSA

If he were living, he would be the same age as you.

ION

But what if Phoebus has taken him to raise in secret?

CREUSA

Then he does wrong in enjoying alone a pleasure that is to
be shared.

ΙΩΝ

355 ἀδικεῖ νυν ὁ θεός· ἡ τεκοῦσα δ᾽ ἀθλία.

ΚΡΕΟΥΣΑ

356 οὔκουν ἔτ᾽ ἄλλον ⟨γ᾽⟩ ὕστερον τίκτει γόνον.

ΙΩΝ

359 οἴμοι· προσῳδὸς ἡ τύχη τὠμῷ πάθει.

ΚΡΕΟΥΣΑ

360 καὶ σ᾽, ὦ ξέν᾽, οἶμαι μητέρ᾽ ἀθλίαν ποθεῖν.

ΙΩΝ

ἃ μή μ᾽ ἐπ᾽ οἶκτον ἔξαγ᾽ οὗ ᾽λελήσμεθα.

ΚΡΕΟΥΣΑ

σιγῶ· πέραινε δ᾽ ὧν σ᾽ ἀνιστορῶ πέρι.

ΙΩΝ

οἶσθ᾽ οὖν ὃ κάμνει τοῦ λόγου μάλιστά σοι;

ΚΡΕΟΥΣΑ

τί δ᾽ οὐκ ἐκείνῃ τῇ ταλαιπώρῳ νοσεῖ;

ΙΩΝ

365 πῶς ὁ θεὸς ὃ λαθεῖν βούλεται μαντεύσεται;

ΚΡΕΟΥΣΑ

εἴπερ καθίζει τρίποδα κοινὸν Ἑλλάδος.

ΙΩΝ

αἰσχύνεται τὸ πρᾶγμα· μὴ ᾽ξέλεγχέ νιν.

ΚΡΕΟΥΣΑ

ἀλγύνεται δέ γ᾽ ἡ παθοῦσα τῇ τύχῃ.

ION

So the god is guilty: the mother is in misery.

CREUSA

At any rate, she never bore another child.

ION

Ah me! This chimes in with my own misfortune!

CREUSA

I imagine you miss your poor mother, too.

ION

Ah, do not make me weep for what I have forgotten!

CREUSA

I say no more. But bring to completion what I asked you about.

ION

Well, do you know where your request is weakest?

CREUSA

What part of that poor woman's life is not in trouble?

ION

Will the god prophesy a thing he wants concealed?

CREUSA

Surely he will if he sits on the tripod all Hellas consults.

ION

Shame is what he feels at this matter. Do not show him up!

CREUSA

But pain is what she feels, she who suffered this blow!

---

355 νυν Page: νιν L   356 ⟨γ'⟩ Badham
361 ἃ μή μ' ἐπ' οἶκτον Nauck: καὶ μή γ' ἐπ' οἶκτόν μ' L

ΙΩΝ

οὐκ ἔστιν ὅστις σοι προφητεύσει τάδε.
370 ἐν τοῖς γὰρ αὑτοῦ δώμασιν κακὸς φανεὶς
Φοῖβος δικαίως τὸν θεμιστεύοντά σοι
δράσειεν ἄν τι πῆμ'. ἀπαλλάσσου, γύναι.
τῷ γὰρ θεῷ τἀναντί' οὐ μαντευτέον.
ἐς γὰρ τοσοῦτον ἀμαθίας ἔλθοιμεν ἄν,
375 εἰ τοὺς θεοὺς ἑκόντες ἐκπονήσομεν
φράζειν ἃ μὴ θέλουσιν ἢ προβωμίοις
σφαγαῖσι μήλων ἢ δι' οἰωνῶν πτεροῖς.
ἃν γὰρ βίᾳ σπεύδωμεν ἀκόντων θεῶν,
ἀνόνητα κεκτήμεσθα τἀγάθ', ὦ γύναι·
380 ἃ δ' ἂν διδῶσ' ἑκόντες, ὠφελούμεθα.

ΧΟΡΟΣ

πολλαί γε πολλοῖς εἰσι συμφοραὶ βροτῶν,
μορφαὶ δὲ διαφέρουσιν· ἕνα δ' ἂν εὐτυχῆ
μόλις ποτ' ἐξεύροι τις ἀνθρώπων βίον.

ΚΡΕΟΥΣΑ

ὦ Φοῖβε, κἀκεῖ κἀνθάδ' οὐ δίκαιος εἶ
385 ἐς τὴν ἀποῦσαν, ἧς πάρεισιν οἱ λόγοι·
ὅς γ' οὔτ' ἔσωσας τὸν σὸν ὃν σῶσαί σ' ἐχρῆν
οὔθ' ἱστορούσῃ μητρὶ μάντις ὢν ἐρεῖς,
ὡς, εἰ μὲν οὐκέτ' ἔστιν, ὀγκωθῇ τάφῳ,
εἰ δ' ἔστιν, ἔλθῃ μητρὸς εἰς ὄψιν ποτέ.

374-7 del. Holthoefer
375 ἑκόντες Wakefield: -ας L
379 ἀνόνητα Stephanus: ἄκοντα L

ION

There is no one who will act for you in this. For if Phoebus
in his own house were convicted of baseness, he would
quite properly punish the man who acted as your spokes-
man. Desist, lady. We must not put questions to the god
that are contrary to his will. It would be equally foolish if,
knowing they did not wish to do so, we were to try to get
the gods to speak either by means of slaughtered sheep
offered at altars or by bird omens.[17] Whatever blessings we
pursue by force, against the will of the gods, these we find
are of no use. It is what they give us willingly that helps us.

CHORUS LEADER

Mortals are many, and many their fortunes and of many
shapes. Yet a human life of unbroken blessedness—that
you will hardly find.

CREUSA

O Phoebus, you are unjust both then and now to the absent
woman whose plea is here. You did not save your child, as
you should have done, and prophet though you are you will
give no answer to the mother's question, so that if he is
dead, he may receive a burial, but if alive, may come to the

---

17 Ion's point in this comparison is that consulting an oracle is
no different from trying to learn the future by looking at entrails
or the flight of birds. Although in consulting an oracle the wor-
shiper seems to enjoy more initiative than those who wait for signs
the gods send them, in fact in neither case can he force the gods to
reveal what they do not want to reveal.

381-3 del. Irvine
382 ἕνα δ' ἂν εὐτυχῇ Heath: ἓν δ' ἂν εὐτυχὲς L

EURIPIDES

390 †ἀλλ' ἐὰν χρὴ τάδ'†, εἰ πρὸς τοῦ θεοῦ
κωλυόμεσθα μὴ μαθεῖν ἃ βούλομαι.
ἀλλ', ὦ ξέν', εἰσορῶ γὰρ εὐγενῆ πόσιν
Ξοῦθον πέλας δὴ τόνδε, τὰς Τροφωνίου
λιπόντα θαλάμας, τοὺς λελεγμένους λόγους
395 σίγα πρὸς ἄνδρα, μή τιν' αἰσχύνην λάβω
διακονοῦσα κρυπτά, καὶ προβῇ λόγος
οὐχ ἧπερ ἡμεῖς αὐτὸν ἐξειλίσσομεν.
τὰ γὰρ γυναικῶν δυσχερῆ πρὸς ἄρσενας,
κἂν ταῖς κακαῖσιν ἀγαθαὶ μεμειγμέναι
400 μισούμεθ'· οὕτω δυστυχεῖς πεφύκαμεν.

ΞΟΥΘΟΣ
πρῶτον μὲν ὁ θεὸς τῶν ἐμῶν προσφθεγμάτων
λαβὼν ἀπαρχὰς χαιρέτω, σύ τ', ὦ γύναι.
μῶν χρόνιος ἐλθών σ' ἐξέπληξ' ὀρρωδίᾳ;

ΚΡΕΟΥΣΑ
οὐδέν γ'· ἀφίγμην δ' ἐς μέριμναν. ἀλλά μοι
405 λέξον, τί θέσπισμ' ἐκ Τροφωνίου φέρεις,
παίδων ὅπως νῷν σπέρμα συγκραθήσεται;

ΞΟΥΘΟΣ
οὐκ ἠξίωσε τοῦ θεοῦ προλαμβάνειν
μαντεύμαθ'· ἓν δ' οὖν εἶπεν· οὐκ ἄπαιδά με
πρὸς οἶκον ἥξειν οὐδέ σ' ἐκ χρηστηρίων.

390 fort. ἀλλ' αἰνέσαι (Badham) χρεῶν (Heimsoeth) τάδ'
397 fort. οἷσπερ
404 ἀφίγμην Badham: ἀφίκου L

368

sight of his mother. Well, I must let it pass since the god prevents my learning what I want.

Enter by Eisodos A XUTHUS *with retinue.*

But I see my noble husband Xuthus nearby, just come from the cave of Trophonius. Say nothing to him, stranger, about what I have said so that my secret errand may not bring me into disgrace and the story reach other ears than I intended. Women's lot in regard to men is difficult: good and bad women are lumped together and both alike hated. So unblest are we by nature!

XUTHUS

Greetings, Apollo! My first words are to you! Greetings also to you, dear wife! Have I caused you great fear by coming so late?

CREUSA

No: I had just begun to worry. But tell me, what oracle do you bring from Trophonius about how our marriage may be fruitful?

XUTHUS

He did not think it right to anticipate the god's prophecy. But he did say this, that neither you nor I would return home from the oracle without children.

---

406 συγκραθήσεται Wakefield: συγκαθ- L
408 δ' οὖν Seager: γοῦν L

ΚΡΕΟΥΣΑ

410 ὦ πότνια Φοίβου μῆτερ, εἰ γὰρ αἰσίως
ἔλθοιμεν, ἅ τε νῷν συμβόλαια πρόσθεν ἦν
ἐς παῖδα τὸν σὸν μεταπέσοι βελτίονα.

ΞΟΥΘΟΣ
ἔσται τάδ'· ἀλλὰ τίς προφητεύει θεοῦ;

ΙΩΝ
ἡμεῖς τά γ' ἔξω, τῶν ἔσω δ' ἄλλοις μέλει,
415 οἳ πλησίον θάσσουσι τρίποδος, ὦ ξένε,
Δελφῶν ἀριστῆς, οὓς ἐκλήρωσεν πάλος.

ΞΟΥΘΟΣ
καλῶς· ἔχω δὴ πάνθ' ὅσων ἐχρῄζομεν.
στείχοιμ' ἂν εἴσω· καὶ γάρ, ὡς ἐγὼ κλύω,
χρηστήριον πέπτωκε τοῖς ἐπήλυσιν
420 κοινὸν πρὸ ναοῦ· βούλομαι δ' ἐν ἡμέρᾳ
τῇδ' (αἰσία γάρ) θεοῦ λαβεῖν μαντεύματα.
σὺ δ' ἀμφὶ βωμούς, ὦ γύναι, δαφνηφόρους
λαβοῦσα κλῶνας, εὐτέκνους εὔχου θεοῖς
χρησμούς μ' ἐνεγκεῖν ἐξ Ἀπόλλωνος δόμων.

ΚΡΕΟΥΣΑ
425 ἔσται τάδ', ἔσται. Λοξίας δ' ἐὰν θέλῃ
νῦν ἀλλὰ τὰς πρὶν ἀναλαβεῖν ἁμαρτίας,
ἅπας μὲν οὐ γένοιτ' ἂν εἰς ἡμᾶς φίλος,
ὅσον δὲ χρῄζει (θεὸς γάρ ἐστι) δέξομαι.

428 χρήσῃ G. Schmid

ION

CREUSA

O lady mother of Phoebus, I pray that our coming may be
propitious and that our previous relations with your son
may take a turn for the better!

XUTHUS

So shall it be! But who is the god's spokesman?

ION

That is my role outside the temple, stranger: inside the
temple others who sit near the tripod will handle matters,
Delphian noblemen chosen by lot.

XUTHUS

Good! I have all I wanted. I shall go in. And in fact I have
learned that a sacrificial victim on behalf of all visitors
has already been slaughtered before the temple. I intend
today (for the day is a propitious one) to hear the god's
oracles. You, dear wife, take laurel branches, go to the
altars, and pray that I may receive from Apollo's temple an
oracle promising children.

Exit XUTHUS into the skene.

CREUSA

I shall do as you say. If Loxias is willing now at last to make
good his sins, though he would not be completely a friend
to me, still I will accept his will since he is a god.

Exit CREUSA by Eisodos B.

ΙΩΝ

τί ποτε λόγοισιν ἡ ξένη πρὸς τὸν θεὸν
430   κρυπτοῖσιν αἰεὶ λοιδοροῦσ᾽ αἰνίσσεται;
ἤτοι φιλοῦσά γ᾽ ἧς ὕπερ μαντεύεται,
ἢ καί τι σιγῶσ᾽ ὧν σιωπᾶσθαι χρεών;
    ἀτὰρ θυγατρὸς τῆς Ἐρεχθέως τί μοι
μέλει; προσήκει γ᾽ οὐδέν. ἀλλὰ χρυσέαις
435   πρόχοισιν ἐλθὼν εἰς ἀπορραντήρια
δρόσον καθήσω. νουθετητέος δέ μοι
Φοῖβος, τί πάσχει· παρθένους βίᾳ γαμῶν
προδίδωσι; παῖδας ἐκτεκνούμενος λάθρᾳ
θνήσκοντας ἀμελεῖ; μὴ σύ γ᾽· ἀλλ᾽, ἐπεὶ κρατεῖς,
440   ἀρετὰς δίωκε. καὶ γὰρ ὅστις ἂν βροτῶν
κακὸς πεφύκῃ, ζημιοῦσιν οἱ θεοί.
πῶς οὖν δίκαιον τοὺς νόμους ὑμᾶς βροτοῖς
γράψαντας αὐτοὺς ἀνομίαν ὀφλισκάνειν;
εἰ δ᾽ (οὐ γὰρ ἔσται, τῷ λόγῳ δὲ χρήσομαι)
445   δίκας βιαίων δώσετ᾽ ἀνθρώποις γάμων
σὺ καὶ Ποσειδῶν Ζεύς θ᾽ ὃς οὐρανοῦ κρατεῖ,
ναοὺς τίνοντες ἀδικίας κενώσετε.
τὰς ἡδονὰς γὰρ τῆς προμηθίας πέρα
σπεύδοντες ἀδικεῖτ᾽. οὐκέτ᾽ ἀνθρώπους κακοὺς
450   λέγειν δίκαιον, εἰ τὰ τῶν θεῶν καλὰ
μιμούμεθ᾽, ἀλλὰ τοὺς διδάσκοντας τάδε.

ΧΟΡΟΣ

στρ.

σὲ τὰν ὠδίνων λοχιᾶν

ION

Why does this foreign woman keep hurling abuse and dark
hints at the god? Is it because she loves the woman on
whose behalf she asks oracles? Or does she have a secret
that must be kept quiet?

But what does the daughter of Erechtheus matter to
me? She is no relation of mine! I shall go to the vessels of
purification and with ewers of gold fill them with water. I
must rebuke Apollo: what is wrong with him? Ravishing
unwedded girls and abandoning them? Begetting children
and then sitting idly while they die? Do not act this way!
Since you have power, pursue goodness! Any mortal who is
base is punished by the gods. So how is it right that you
who prescribe laws for mortals should yourselves be guilty
of lawlessness? It will never happen, but I say it anyway: if
you pay recompense to mortals for your rapes, you and
Poseidon and Zeus, the ruler of heaven, you will empty
your temples in paying for your crimes. You are guilty of
pursuing your own pleasures and taking no thought for the
future! No more should one call men wicked for imitating
what the gods consider acceptable: blame men's teachers!

Exit ION *by Eisodos A.*

CHORUS

I entreat you, Athena, my goddess,

---

434 γ᾽ οὐδέν Reiske: τοῦδας L
448 πέρα Conington: πέρας t: πάρος L

ἀνειλείθυιαν, ἐμὰν
Ἀθάναν, ἱκετεύω,
455 Προμηθεῖ Τιτᾶνι λοχευ-
θεῖσαν κατ' ἀκροτάτας
κορυφᾶς Διός, ὄλβιε Νίκα,
μόλε Πύθιον οἶκον, Οὐ-
λύμπου ⟨'κ⟩ χρυσέων θαλάμων
460 πταμένα πρὸς ἀγυιάς,
Φοιβήιος ἔνθα γᾶς
μεσόμφαλος ἑστία
παρὰ χορευομένῳ τρίποδι
μαντεύματα κραίνει,
465 σὺ καὶ παῖς ἁ Λατογενής,
δύο θεαὶ δύο παρθένοι,
κασίγνηται σεμνόταται Φοίβου.
ἱκετεύσατε δ', ὦ κόραι,
τὸ παλαιὸν Ἐρεχθέως
470 γένος εὐτεκνίας χρονίου καθαροῖς
μαντεύμασι κῦρσαι.

ἀντ.

ὑπερβαλλούσας γὰρ ἔχει
θνατοῖς εὐδαιμονίας
ἀκίνητον ἀφορμάν,

457 ὄλβιε Willink: ὦ μάκαιρα L
459 Οὐλύμπου Willink: Ὀλύμπου L   ⟨'κ⟩ Dobree
461 γᾶς Reiske: γᾶ L
467 σεμνόταται Fritzsche: σεμναὶ L

374

you who never had part
in the pangs of childbed,
brought to birth from the forehead
of Zeus by Prometheus the Titan:[18]
come, blessed goddess of victory,
come to the Pythian temple,
from the golden chambers of Olympus
winging your way to the city's streets
where Phoebus' altar
at the world's midmost navel,
near the tripod where they dance,
brings oracles to pass.
Come, you and Leto's daughter,
two goddesses, both virgin,
sisters most holy of Phoebus.
Plead with him, O maids,
that the ancient stock of Erechtheus
may win with clear oracles
the long-delayed gift of fair children.

It means a fund unshakable
of surpassing
happiness for mortals
when in their ancestral chambers there gleams

---

[18] Athena was the daughter of Zeus and Metis (good counsel). After he had impregnated Metis, he learned of an oracle that his child by Metis would depose him. He therefore swallowed Metis, Athena being carried to term in Zeus's head. In the usual version of the story it is Hephaestus who splits Zeus's skull with an ax in order to allow her to be born. Athena came also to be identified with Nike, goddess of victory.

475 τέκνων οἷς ἂν καρποφόροι
λάμπωσιν ἐν θαλάμοις
πατρίοισι νεάνιδες ἧβαι,
διαδέκτορα πλοῦτον ὡς
ἕξοντες ἐκ πατέρων
480 ἑτέροις ἐπὶ τέκνοις.
ἄλκαρ τε γὰρ ἐν κακοῖς
σύν τ' εὐτυχίαις φίλον
δορί τε γᾷ πατρίᾳ φέρει
σωτήριον ἀλκάν.
485 ἐμοὶ μὲν πλούτου τε πάρος
βασιλικῶν τ' εἶεν θαλάμων
τροφαὶ κήδειοι τεκέων κεδνῶν.
τὸν ἄπαιδα δ' ἀποστυγῶ
βίον, ᾧ τε δοκεῖ ψέγω·
490 μετὰ δὲ κτεάνων μετρίων βιοτᾶς
εὔπαιδος ἐχοίμαν.

ἐπῳδ.

ὦ Πανὸς θακήματα καὶ
παραυλίζουσα πέτρα
μυχώδεσι Μακραῖς,
495 ἵνα χοροὺς στείβουσι ποδοῖν
Ἀγλαύρου κόραι τρίγονοι
στάδια χλοερὰ πρὸ Παλλάδος
ναῶν συρίγγων ⟨θ'⟩

---

475 καρποφόροι Diggle: -τρόφοι L   481 ἄλκαρ Dawe et
Willink: ἀλκά L   487 τεκέων κεδνῶν post Fritzsche (τεκέων)
Willink: κεδνῶν γε τέκνων L   498 ⟨θ'⟩ Page

376

the prime of youthfulness
that bears fruit,
for these will have from their fathers
wealth hereditary
to give to children in turn.
A bulwark are they in misfortune,
in prosperity much loved,
and with the spear they bring to their country
defense and life.
May I have in preference to wealth
and kingly halls
the careful nurture of dear children!
The life without children I hate,
and him whom it pleases I praise not.
Give me but moderate possessions
and with them lovely children!

O resting place of Pan
and cliff that lies near
the Long Rocks full of caverns!
There they tread the measure,
Aglauros' daughters three,[19]
over the grassy sward before the temple
of Pallas ⟨and⟩ sing

[19] Aglauros, wife of Cecrops, was mother of Aglauros, Herse, and Pandrosos, the three girls mentioned above in lines 271-4. The daughters are here conceived of as haunting the Acropolis, where the younger Aglauros had a shrine (Herodotus 8.53).

ὑπ᾽ αἰόλας ἰαχᾶς
500 ὑμνοῦσ᾽ ὅτ᾽ ἀναλίοις
συρίζεις, ὦ Πάν,
τοῖσι σοῖς ἐν ἄντροις,
ἵνα τεκοῦσά τις
παρθένος μελέα βρέφος
Φοίβῳ πτανοῖς ἐξόρισεν
505 θοίναν θηρσί τε φοινίαν
δαῖτα, πικρῶν γάμων ὕβριν·
οὔτ᾽ ἐπὶ κερκίσιν οὔτε †λόγοις† φάτιν
ἄιον εὐτυχίας μετέχειν θεόθεν τέκνα θνατοῖς.

ΙΩΝ

510 πρόσπολοι γυναῖκες, αἱ τῶνδ᾽ ἀμφὶ κρηπῖδας δόμων
θυοδόκων φρούρημ᾽ ἔχουσαι δεσπότιν φυλάσσετε,
ἐκλέλοιπ᾽ ἤδη τὸν ἱερὸν τρίποδα καὶ χρηστήριον
Ξοῦθος ἢ μίμνει κατ᾽ οἶκον ἱστορῶν ἀπαιδίαν;

ΧΟΡΟΣ

ἐν δόμοις ἔστ᾽, ὦ ξέν᾽· οὔπω δῶμ᾽ ὑπερβαίνει τόδε.
515 ὡς δ᾽ ἐπ᾽ ἐξόδοισιν ὄντος, τῶνδ᾽ ἀκούομεν πυλῶν
δοῦπον, ἐξιόντα τ᾽ ἤδη δεσπότην ὁρᾶν πάρα.

500 ὑμνοῦσ᾽ Page: ὕμνων L
503 μελέα Badham: ὦ μ- L
507 οὔτε χοροῖς Reiske
511 ἔχουσαι Stephanus: ἔχοντα L   δεσπότιν Richards: -την L
514 ἔτ᾽ Cobet

to the shimmering sound of piping
when in your cave
shaded from the sun, O Pan,
you play your pipes.
There it was that some
poor maid, who bore a child
to Phoebus, cast it out for the birds
and wild beasts as a bloody
feast, the violent fruit of her bitter union.
Neither in story at my loom nor in song[20] have I heard it
    told
that children from the gods ever meant for mortals a
    share of blessing.

Enter by Eisodos A ION.

ION

You serving women who keep watch about the steps of
this incense-fragrant temple and guard your mistress, has
Xuthus already left the sacred tripod and the oracle, or is
he still in the temple enquiring about his childlessness?

CHORUS LEADER

He is still in the temple, my foreign friend: he has not yet
come out. But I hear the clang of the doors here, as if he is
about to emerge. Look, it is our master coming out.

Enter XUTHUS from the skene.

---

[20] I give the sense that seems to be required.

ΞΟΥΘΟΣ

ὦ τέκνον, χαῖρ'· ἡ γὰρ ἀρχὴ τοῦ λόγου πρέπουσά
μοι.

ΙΩΝ

χαίρομεν· σὺ δ' εὖ φρόνει γε, καὶ δύ' ὄντ' εὖ πρά-
ξομεν.

ΞΟΥΘΟΣ

δὸς χερὸς φίλημά μοι σῆς σώματός τ' ἀμφιπτυχάς.

ΙΩΝ

520   εὖ φρονεῖς μέν; ἤ σ' ἔμηνεν θεοῦ τις, ὦ ξένε,
βλάβη;

ΞΟΥΘΟΣ

οὐ φρονῶ, τὰ φίλταθ' εὑρὼν εἰ θιγεῖν ἐφίεμαι;

ΙΩΝ

παῦε, μὴ ψαύσας τὰ τοῦ θεοῦ στέμματα ῥήξῃς χερί.

ΞΟΥΘΟΣ

ἅψομαι· κοὐ ῥυσιάζω, τἀμὰ δ' εὑρίσκω φίλα.

ΙΩΝ

οὐκ ἀπαλλάξῃ, πρὶν εἴσω τόξα πλευμόνων λαβεῖν;

ΞΟΥΘΟΣ

525   ὡς τί δὴ φεύγεις με σαυτοῦ γνωρίσαι τὰ φίλτατα;

521 οὐ φρονῶ Jacobs cl. El. 569: σωφρονῶ L   θιγεῖν
Musgrave: φυγεῖν L: φιλεῖν Tr²
525 γνωρίσαι Page: -ίσας L

XUTHUS

My son, I wish you joy! That is the proper way for me to
begin my speech.

ION

Joy I have. But you, show modest good sense, and the two
of us will both fare well.

XUTHUS

Allow me to kiss your hand and to embrace you!

He moves to embrace Ion.

ION

Are you quite sane? Or has some god-sent derangement
afflicted you?

XUTHUS

Am I not sane if having found my heart's desire I am eager
to touch him?

ION

Stop! If you touch the god's fillets you may break them with
your hand!

XUTHUS

I shall put my hands on them: I am no robber but am
finding one I love.

ION

Get away before you get an arrow in your chest!

XUTHUS

Why do you shrink from seeing in me what you hold
dearest?

ΙΩΝ

οὐ φιλῶ φρενοῦν ἀμούσους καὶ μεμηνότας ξένους.

ΞΟΥΘΟΣ

κτεῖνε καὶ πίμπρη· πατρὸς γάρ, ἢν κτάνῃς, ἔσῃ
    φονεύς.

ΙΩΝ

ποῦ δέ μοι πατὴρ σύ; ταῦτ᾽ οὖν οὐ γέλως κλυεῖν
    ἐμοί;

ΞΟΥΘΟΣ

οὔ· τρέχων ὁ μῦθος ἄν σοι τἀμὰ σημήνειεν ἄν.

ΙΩΝ

530   καὶ τί μοι λέξεις;

ΞΟΥΘΟΣ

πατὴρ σός εἰμι καὶ σὺ παῖς ἐμός.

ΙΩΝ

τίς λέγει τάδ᾽;

ΞΟΥΘΟΣ

ὅς σ᾽ ἔθρεψεν ὄντα Λοξίας ἐμόν.

ΙΩΝ

μαρτυρεῖς σαυτῷ.

ΞΟΥΘΟΣ

τὰ τοῦ θεοῦ γ᾽ ἐκμαθὼν χρηστήρια.

ΙΩΝ

ἐσφάλης αἴνιγμ᾽ ἀκούσας.

ION

I do not like to admonish mad and ill-bred strangers.

XUTHUS

Kill and burn me! Then you will be your father's murderer!

ION

How can you be my father? Is this not a laughable story?

XUTHUS

No: as the tale proceeds it will make plain what I am saying.

ION

Whatever can you mean?

XUTHUS

I am your father and you are my son.

ION

Who says so?

XUTHUS

Loxias, who raised you though you were mine.

ION

You testify in your own behalf.

XUTHUS

Yes: I have received the god's oracle.

ION

You misinterpreted the riddle.

ΞΟΥΘΟΣ

οὐκ ἄρ᾽ ὀρθ᾽ ἀκούομεν.

ΙΩΝ

ὁ δὲ λόγος τίς ἐστι Φοίβου;

ΞΟΥΘΟΣ

τὸν συναντήσαντά μοι . . .

ΙΩΝ

535 τίνα συνάντησιν;

ΞΟΥΘΟΣ

. . . δόμων τῶνδ᾽ ἐξιόντι τοῦ θεοῦ . . .

ΙΩΝ

συμφορᾶς τίνος κυρῆσαι;

ΞΟΥΘΟΣ

. . . παῖδ᾽ ἐμὸν πεφυκέναι.

ΙΩΝ

σὸν γεγῶτ᾽, ἢ δῶρον ἄλλως;

ΞΟΥΘΟΣ

δῶρον, ὄντα δ᾽ ἐξ ἐμοῦ.

ΙΩΝ

πρῶτα δῆτ᾽ ἐμοὶ ξυνάπτεις πόδα σόν;

ΞΟΥΘΟΣ

οὐκ ἄλλῳ, τέκνον.

ΙΩΝ

ἡ τύχη πόθεν ποθ᾽ ἥκει;

XUTHUS

Then my hearing is not good.

ION

But what did Phoebus say?

XUTHUS

That the one who met me . . .

ION

What meeting is this?

XUTHUS

. . . as I came out of this temple of the god . . .

ION

What would happen to him?

XUTHUS

. . . is my son.

ION

Your own son, or merely a gift to you?

XUTHUS

A gift, but my own true son.

ION

And I am the first person in your path?

XUTHUS

You and no other, my son.

ION

How in the world did this come about?

---

537 ἄλλων Dobree   δ' Musgrave: τ' Lᵃᶜ ut vid.: σ' Lᵖᶜ

ΞΟΥΘΟΣ

δύο μίαν θαυμάζομεν.

ΙΩΝ

540 ἐκ τίνος δέ σοι πέφυκα μητρός;

ΞΟΥΘΟΣ

οὐκ ἔχω φράσαι.

ΙΩΝ

οὐδὲ Φοῖβος εἶπε;

ΞΟΥΘΟΣ

τερφθεὶς τοῦτο, κεῖν᾽ οὐκ ἠρόμην.

ΙΩΝ

γῆς ἄρ᾽ ἐκπέφυκα μητρός;

ΞΟΥΘΟΣ

οὐ πέδον τίκτει τέκνα.

ΙΩΝ

πῶς ἂν οὖν εἴην σός;

ΞΟΥΘΟΣ

οὐκ οἶδ᾽, ἀναφέρω δ᾽ ἐς τὸν θεόν.

ΙΩΝ

φέρε λόγων ἀψώμεθ᾽ ἄλλων.

ΞΟΥΘΟΣ

τοῦτ᾽ ἄμεινον, ὦ τέκνον.

ΙΩΝ

545 ἦλθες ἐς νόθον τι λέκτρον;

ION

XUTHUS
The same event astonishes us both.

ION
But from what mother was I born to you?

XUTHUS
I cannot say.

ION
Did not Phoebus say either?

XUTHUS
In joy at this news I did not ask that question.

ION
So was I born from earth as my mother?

XUTHUS
The ground does not give birth to children.

ION
Then how can I be your son?

XUTHUS
I do not know. But my authority is the god.

ION
Come, let us take a different tack.

XUTHUS
That is a good idea, son.

ION
Did you ever have an illicit affair?

---

540 ἐκ Bothe: ἔα L
544 τοῦτ' Herwerden: ταῦτ' L

ΞΟΥΘΟΣ

μωρίᾳ γε τοῦ νέου.

ΙΩΝ

πρὶν κόρην λαβεῖν Ἐρεχθέως;

ΞΟΥΘΟΣ

οὐ γὰρ ὕστερόν γέ πω.

ΙΩΝ

ἆρα δῆτ᾽ ἐκεῖ μ᾽ ἔφυσας;

ΞΟΥΘΟΣ

τῷ χρόνῳ γε συντρέχει.

ΙΩΝ

κᾆτα πῶς ἀφικόμεσθα δεῦρο . . .

ΞΟΥΘΟΣ

τοῦτ᾽ ἀμηχανῶ.

ΙΩΝ

. . . διὰ μακρᾶς ἐλθὼν κελεύθου;

ΞΟΥΘΟΣ

τοῦτο κἄμ᾽ ἀπαιολᾷ.

ΙΩΝ

550 Πυθίαν δ᾽ ἦλθες πέτραν πρίν;

ΞΟΥΘΟΣ

ἐς φανάς γε Βακχίου.

⁵⁴⁸ τοῦτ᾽ Hermann: ταῦτ᾽ L

XUTHUS

Yes, in the folly of my youth.

ION

Before you married Erechtheus' daughter?

XUTHUS

Yes: never after that.

ION

So that was the place of my begetting?

XUTHUS

Well, the time at least agrees.

ION

Then how did I come here . . .

XUTHUS

I have no idea.

ION

. . . traveling such a long journey?

XUTHUS

I too am defeated by this question.

ION

Did you ever come to the Pythian cliff before?

XUTHUS

Yes, to the torch feast of Dionysus.[21]

---

21 Dionysus was worshiped in a torchlight ceremony at Delphi in the winter months when Apollo was thought to be absent.

ΙΩΝ

προξένων δ᾽ ἔν του κατέσχες;

ΞΟΥΘΟΣ

ὅς με Δελφίσιν κόραις . . .

ΙΩΝ

ἐθιάσευσ᾽, ἢ πῶς τάδ᾽ αὐδᾷς;

ΞΟΥΘΟΣ

Μαινάσιν γε Βακχίου.

ΙΩΝ

ἔμφρον᾽ ἢ κάτοινον ὄντα;

ΞΟΥΘΟΣ

Βακχίου πρὸς ἡδοναῖς.

ΙΩΝ

τοῦτ᾽ ἐκεῖν᾽· ἵν᾽ ἐσπάρημεν . . .

ΞΟΥΘΟΣ

. . . ὁ πότμος ἐξηῦρεν, τέκνον.

ΙΩΝ

555 πῶς δ᾽ ἀφικόμεσθα ναούς;

ΞΟΥΘΟΣ

ἔκβολον κόρης ἴσως.

ΙΩΝ

ἐκπεφεύγαμεν τὸ δοῦλον.

551 του L. Dindorf: τῷ L
554 ἐκεῖν᾽ ἵν᾽ Elmsley: ἐκεῖ νῦν L   v. dist. Dobree

ION

Did you stay at the house of some official host?[22]

XUTHUS

Yes, the one who put me with the Delphian girls . . .

ION

What do you mean? Initiated you?

XUTHUS

Yes, into the circle of Bacchus' maenads.

ION

Were you sober or drunk?

XUTHUS

I felt the pleasure Bacchus gives.

ION

This is the answer to our question. The place of my begetting . . .

XUTHUS

. . . fate has brought to light, my son.

ION

But how did I come to the temple?

XUTHUS

Perhaps the girl abandoned you.

ION

I have escaped servile birth.

---

22 The *proxenoi* at Delphi were those who provided official hospitality.

ΞΟΥΘΟΣ

πατέρα νυν δέχου, τέκνον.

ΙΩΝ

τῷ θεῷ γοῦν οὐκ ἀπιστεῖν εἰκός.

ΞΟΥΘΟΣ

εὖ φρονεῖς ἄρα.

ΙΩΝ

καὶ τί βουλόμεσθά γ' ἄλλο . . .

ΞΟΥΘΟΣ

νῦν ὁρᾷς ἃ χρή σ' ὁρᾶν.

ΙΩΝ

. . . ἢ Διὸς παιδὸς γενέσθαι παῖς;

ΞΟΥΘΟΣ

ὃ σοί γε γίγνεται.

ΙΩΝ

560 ἦ θίγω δῆθ' οἵ μ' ἔφυσαν;

ΞΟΥΘΟΣ

πιθόμενός γε τῷ θεῷ.

ΙΩΝ

χαῖρέ μοι, πάτερ . . .

ΞΟΥΘΟΣ

φίλον γε φθέγμ' ἐδεξάμην τόδε.

ΙΩΝ

. . . ἡμέρα θ' ἡ νῦν παροῦσα.

XUTHUS

So greet your father, my son.

ION

At any rate, one should not disbelieve the god.

XUTHUS

You are quite sensible.

ION

And what else do I want . . .

XUTHUS

Now you see things in their proper light.

ION

. . . than to be the son of Zeus's offspring?

XUTHUS

That is your fate.

ION

Shall I embrace my father, then?

XUTHUS

Yes, in obedience to the god.

ION

Hail, father . . .

XUTHUS

How welcome these words are to hear!

ION

. . . and hail, sun that now shines!

---

559 παίδων Kraus cl. 1099-1100
560 ὅς μ' ἔφυσας Bothe

ΞΟΥΘΟΣ

μακάριόν γ' ἔθηκέ με.

ΙΩΝ

ὦ φίλη μῆτερ, πότ' ἆρα καὶ σὸν ὄψομαι δέμας;
νῦν ποθῶ σε μᾶλλον ἢ πρίν, ἥτις εἶ ποτ', εἰσιδεῖν.
565 ἀλλ' ἴσως τέθνηκας, ἡμεῖς δ' οὐδ' ὄναρ δυναίμεθ'
 ἄν.

ΧΟΡΟΣ

κοιναὶ μὲν ἡμῖν δωμάτων εὐπραξίαι·
ὅμως δὲ καὶ δέσποιναν ἐς τέκν' εὐτυχεῖν
ἐβουλόμην ἂν τούς τ' Ἐρεχθέως δόμους.

ΞΟΥΘΟΣ

ὦ τέκνον, ἐς μὲν σὴν ἀνεύρεσιν θεὸς
570 ὀρθῶς ἔκρανε, καὶ συνῆψ' ἐμοί τε σὲ
σύ τ' αὖ τὰ φίλταθ' ηὗρες οὐκ εἰδὼς πάρος.
ὃ δ' ἦξας ὀρθῶς, τοῦτο κἄμ' ἔχει πόθος,
ὅπως σύ τ', ὦ παῖ, μητέρ' εὑρήσεις σέθεν
ἐγώ θ' ὁποίας μοι γυναικὸς ἐξέφυς.
575 χρόνῳ δὲ δόντες ταῦτ' ἴσως εὕροιμεν ἄν.
ἀλλ' ἐκλιπὼν θεοῦ δάπεδ' ἀλητείαν τε σὴν
ἐς τὰς Ἀθήνας στεῖχε κοινόφρων πατρί,
οὗ σ' ὄλβιον μὲν σκῆπτρον ἀναμένει πατρός,
πολὺς δὲ πλοῦτος· οὐδὲ θάτερον νοσῶν
580 δυοῖν κεκλήσῃ δυσγενὴς πένης θ' ἅμα,
ἀλλ' εὐγενής τε καὶ πολυκτήμων βίου.
 σιγᾷς; τί πρὸς γῆν ὄμμα σὸν βαλὼν ἔχεις

XUTHUS

Yes, it has made me blessed!

ION

O dear mother, when shall I see you as well? Now I long more than ever to look upon you, whoever you are! But perhaps you are dead, and I cannot see you even in a dream.

CHORUS LEADER

I share in the good fortune of the house. But I would have preferred that my mistress and the house of Erechtheus also were enjoying good fortune as regards children.

XUTHUS

My son, the god has acted well in causing you to be found. He has brought you to me, and you for your part have found a beloved father you never knew. What you naturally long for, I too desire, my son, that you should find your mother and I should learn who it was that gave me you as my son. Perhaps if we let time bring forth the truth we will discover this. So leave the god's precincts and your homeless life, join purposes with your father, and come to Athens. There your father's prosperous power and great wealth await you. You will suffer from neither of two disabilities by being called ignobly born and poor: you will be called high-born and rich.

Ion looks down at the ground and does not reply.

Silence? Why do you keep your eyes fixed on the

---

565 οὐδ' ὄναρ δυναίμεθ' ἄν Harry, Parmentier: οὐδὲν ἄρ δυναίμεθα L   572 οἷ Herwerden   578-81 del. Diggle

ἐς φροντίδας τ᾽ ἀπῆλθες, ἐκ δὲ χαρμονῆς
πάλιν μεταστὰς δεῖμα προσβάλλεις πατρί;

ΙΩΝ

585 οὐ ταὐτὸν εἶδος φαίνεται τῶν πραγμάτων
πρόσωθεν ὄντων ἐγγύθεν θ᾽ ὁρωμένων.
ἐγὼ δὲ τὴν μὲν συμφορὰν ἀσπάζομαι,
πατέρα σ᾽ ἀνευρών· ὧν δὲ γιγνώσκω †πέρι†
ἄκουσον. εἰναί φασι τὰς αὐτόχθονας
590 κλεινὰς Ἀθήνας οὐκ ἐπείσακτον γένος,
ἵν᾽ ἐσπεσοῦμαι δύο νόσω κεκτημένος,
πατρός τ᾽ ἐπακτοῦ καὐτὸς ὢν νοθαγενής.
καὶ τοῦτ᾽ ἔχων τοὔνειδος, ἀσθενὴς μένων
<αὐτὸς τὸ> μηδὲν κοὐδένων κεκλήσομαι.
595 [ἢν δ᾽ ἐς τὸ πρῶτον πόλεος ὁρμηθεὶς ζυγὸν
ζητῶ τις εἶναι, τῶν μὲν ἀδυνάτων ὕπο
μισησόμεσθα· λυπρὰ γὰρ τὰ κρείσσονα.
ὅσοι δέ, χρηστοὶ δυνάμενοί τ᾽ εἶναι σοφοί,
σιγῶσι κοὐ σπεύδουσιν ἐς τὰ πράγματα,
600 γέλωτ᾽ ἐν αὐτοῖς μωρίαν τε λήψομαι
οὐχ ἡσυχάζων ἐν πόλει φόβου πλέα.
τῶν δ᾽ αὖ †λογίων τε† χρωμένων τε τῇ πόλει
ἐς ἀξίωμα βὰς πλέον φρουρήσομαι
ψήφοισιν. οὕτω γὰρ τάδ᾽, ὦ πάτερ, φιλεῖ·
605 οἳ τὰς πόλεις ἔχουσι κἀξιώματα,
τοῖς ἀνθαμίλλοις εἰσὶ πολεμιώτατοι.]

583 τ᾽ Dindorf: δ᾽ L
588 πάτερ Dobree: πέρας Willink: δυσθυμῶ πέρι Wecklein

ground? Why begin to worry? Why change from joy and
make your father afraid?

Things do not look the same close up as from a distance.
For my part, I welcome this turn of fortune, my finding
that you are my father. But hear my reflections. They say
that the famous Athenians, born from the soil, are no im-
migrant race. I would be suffering from two disabilities if I
were cast there, both the foreignness of my father and my
own bastardy. With this blot upon my name I would remain
powerless and be called a nobody <myself> and the son of
nobodies.

[If I attempt to be somebody by aspiring to the city's
helm, I shall be hated by the powerless: men always hate
what is above them. As for all those who are of good char-
acter and have an aptitude for wisdom but live quietly and
do not exert themselves in public affairs, they will think I
am laughably foolish not to keep quiet in a city full of fear.
But if I invade the prestige of those who speak in public
and engage in politics, by their votes I will be kept in check
even more. That is the way things usually happen, father.
Those who hold office in their cities are always most hostile
to their competitors.]

---

589 οἰκεῖν φασι τοὺς αὐτόχθονας G. Müller
593 μένων Musgrave: μὲν ὢν L
594 <αὐτὸς τὸ> Badham
595-606 del. Kovacs
601 ψόγου Musgrave: φθόνου Badham
602 δοκούντων Wecklein: λεγόντων Schaefer

ἐλθὼν δ' ἐς οἶκον ἀλλότριον ἔπηλυς ὢν
γυναῖκά θ' ὡς ἄτεκνον, ἡ κοινουμένη
τῆς συμφορᾶς σοι πρόσθεν ἀπολαχοῦσα νῦν
610 αὐτὴ καθ' αὑτὴν τὴν τύχην οἴσει πικρῶς,
πῶς οὐχ ὑπ' αὐτῆς εἰκότως μισήσομαι,
ὅταν παραστῶ σοὶ μὲν ἐγγύθεν ποδός,
ἡ δ' οὖσ' ἄτεκνος τὰ σὰ φίλ' εἰσορᾷ πικρῶς,
κᾆτ' ἢ προδοὺς σύ μ' ἐς δάμαρτα σὴν βλέπῃς
615 ἢ τἀμὰ τιμῶν δῶμα συγχέας ἔχῃς;
[ὅσας σφαγὰς δὴ φαρμάκων ⟨τε⟩ θανασίμων
γυναῖκες ηὗρον ἀνδράσιν διαφθοράς.]
ἄλλως τε τὴν σὴν ἄλοχον οἰκτίρω, πάτερ,
ἄπαιδα γηράσκουσαν· οὐ γὰρ ἀξία
620 πατέρων ἀπ' ἐσθλῶν οὖσ' ἀπαιδίᾳ νοσεῖν.
[τυραννίδος δὲ τῆς μάτην αἰνουμένης
τὸ μὲν πρόσωπον ἡδύ, τἀν δόμοισι δὲ
λυπηρά· τίς γὰρ μακάριος, τίς εὐτυχής,
ὅστις δεδοικὼς καὶ περιβλέπων βίαν
625 αἰῶνα τείνει; δημότης ἂν εὐτυχὴς
ζῆν ἂν θέλοιμι μᾶλλον ἢ τύραννος ὤν,
ᾧ τοὺς πονηροὺς ἡδονὴ φίλους ἔχειν,
ἐσθλοὺς δὲ μισεῖ κατθανεῖν φοβούμενος.
εἴποις ἂν ὡς ὁ χρυσὸς ἐκνικᾷ τάδε,
630 πλουτεῖν τε τερπνόν· οὐ φιλῶ ψόφους κλύειν
ἐν χερσὶ σῴζων ὄλβον οὐδ' ἔχειν πόνους·
εἴη γ' ἐμοὶ ⟨μὲν⟩ μέτρια μὴ λυπουμένῳ.]
ἃ δ' ἐνθάδ' εἶχον ἀγάθ' ἄκουσόν μου, πάτερ·
τὴν φιλτάτην μὲν πρῶτον ἀνθρώποις σχολὴν

Then suppose I come, as a foreigner, to a house that is not mine and to your childless wife. She previously shared in your sorrow but now is excluded from your joy and will feel bitterly a misfortune she must bear by herself. Will she not naturally hate me when I take my stand beside you while she, being childless, looks with bitterness at what gives you joy? Then either you must have regard for your wife and abandon me or honor me and bring confusion upon your house. [How many times have wives killed husbands by poison or the knife!] Besides I feel pity for your wife, father, growing old without children. Her lineage is noble, and she does not deserve to suffer from childlessness.

[Mortals foolishly praise kingship, but though its façade is pleasant, what it holds indoors is painful. What man is blessed or fortunate who lives his life in fear, constantly looking out for violence? I would rather live as a happy commoner than as a tyrant. The tyrant finds his pleasure in the friendship of the base and hates men of good character, since he is afraid of being killed. You might argue that money overcomes these disabilities and that to be rich is pleasant. But I do not enjoy hearing noises as I guard my wealth, nor do I like to work so hard. My prayer is for modest means without pain.]

Hear, father, what good things I have enjoyed here. First, I have had a peaceful life, one with little trouble, a

---

609 τῆς συμφορᾶς Diggle: τὰς συμφοράς L
616-7 del. Dindorf   616 ⟨τε⟩ Heath   621-32 del. Kovacs
630 ψόγους commemorat Brodaeus
632 ⟨μὲν⟩ ed. Brubach.
634 ἀνθρώποις Dobree: -ων L: -ῳ Wakefield

635 ὄχλον τε μέτριον, οὐδέ μ᾽ ἐξέπληξ᾽ ὁδοῦ
πονηρὸς οὐδείς· κεῖνο δ᾽ οὐκ ἀνασχετόν,
εἴκειν ὁδοῦ χαλῶντα τοῖς κακίοσιν.
θεῶν δ᾽ ἐν εὐχαῖς ἢ λόγοισιν ἢ βροτῶν,
ὑπηρετῶν χαίρουσιν, οὐ γοωμένοις.

640 καὶ τοὺς μὲν ἐξέπεμπον, οἱ δ᾽ ἧκον ξένοι,
ὥσθ᾽ ἡδὺς αἰεὶ καινὸς ἐν καινοῖσιν ἦ.
ὃ δ᾽ εὐκτὸν ἀνθρώποισι, κἂν ἄκουσιν ἦ,
δίκαιον εἶναί μ᾽ ὁ νόμος ἡ φύσις θ᾽ ἅμα
παρεῖχε τῷ θεῷ. ταῦτα συννοούμενος

645 κρείσσω νομίζω τἀνθάδ᾽ ἢ τἀκεῖ, πάτερ.
ἔα δέ μ᾽ αὐτοῦ ζῆν· ἴση γὰρ ἡ χάρις
μεγάλοισι χαίρειν σμικρά θ᾽ ἡδέως ἔχειν.

ΧΟΡΟΣ

καλῶς ἔλεξας, εἴπερ οὓς ἐγὼ φιλῶ
ἐν τοῖσι σοῖσιν εὐτυχήσουσιν φίλοις.

ΞΟΥΘΟΣ

650 παῦσαι λόγων τῶνδ᾽, εὐτυχεῖν δ᾽ ἐπίστασο.
θέλω γὰρ οὗπέρ σ᾽ ηὗρον ἄρξασθαι, τέκνον,
κοινῆς τραπέζης, δαῖτα πρὸς κοινὴν πεσών,
θῦσαί θ᾽ ἅ σου πρὶν γενέθλι᾽ οὐκ ἐθύσαμεν.
καὶ νῦν μὲν ὡς δὴ ξένον ἄγων σ᾽ ἐφέστιον

655 δείπνοισι τέρψω, τῆς δ᾽ Ἀθηναίων χθονὸς
ἄξω θεατὴν δῆθεν, οὐχ ὡς ὄντ᾽ ἐμόν.
καὶ γὰρ γυναῖκα τὴν ἐμὴν οὐ βούλομαι
λυπεῖν ἄτεκνον οὖσαν αὐτὸς εὐτυχῶν.

638 λόγοισιν ἢ Musgrave: γόοισιν ἢ L

thing mortals hold most dear. Unworthy people do not
shove me forcibly from the road—and to step out of the
path and make way for those beneath me is something I
cannot endure. I have spent my time in prayer to the gods
or in conversation with mortals, serving those who are in
joy, not sorrow. When I sent one set of foreign guests off,
another set arrived, and so I was always welcome as a fresh
face among fresh faces. Furthermore, mine was a thing
men should pray to have even against their will: both the
law and my nature joined in making me righteous in the
eyes of the god. As I consider these things I think it is
better here than in Athens, father. Let me live here! One
can take just as much delight in humble blessings as in high
position.

CHORUS LEADER

What you have said is good since the joy you choose means
that my beloved mistress will be happy.

XUTHUS

No more of this! Learn to be fortunate! I want to begin our
table fellowship in the very place where I found you and
recline at a shared feast. I mean to hold the sacrifice I omit-
ted before, in celebration of your birth. For the present I
shall take you to my lodging as a foreign friend and give
you the pleasure of a feast. Thereafter I shall take you to
Athens as a visitor, not as my own son. I do not want my
own good fortune to cause my wife grief in her childless-

---

646 δέ μ᾽ αὐτοῦ Badham: δ᾽ ἐμαυτῷ L, quo servato ζῆν ‹μ᾽›
Dindorf

656 οὐχ ὡς Badham: ὡς οὐκ L

EURIPIDES

χρόνῳ δὲ καιρὸν λαμβάνων προσάξομαι
660 δάμαρτ᾽ ἐᾶν σε σκῆπτρα τἄμ᾽ ἔχειν χθονός.
Ἴωνα δ᾽ ὀνομάζω σε τῇ τύχῃ πρέπον,
ὁθούνεκ᾽ ἀδύτων ἐξιόντι μοι θεοῦ
ἴχνος συνῆψας πρῶτος. ἀλλὰ τῶν φίλων
πλήρωμ᾽ ἀθροίσας βουθύτῳ σὺν ἡδονῇ
665 πρόσειπε, μέλλων Δελφίδ᾽ ἐκλιπεῖν πόλιν.
ὑμῖν δὲ σιγᾶν, δμωίδες, λέγω τάδε,
ἢ θάνατον εἰπούσαισι πρὸς δάμαρτ᾽ ἐμήν.

ΙΩΝ

στείχοιμ᾽ ἄν. ἓν δὲ τῆς τύχης ἄπεστί μοι·
εἰ μὴ γὰρ ἥτις μ᾽ ἔτεκεν εὑρήσω, πάτερ,
670 ἀβίωτον ἡμῖν. εἰ δ᾽ ἐπεύξασθαι χρεών,
ἐκ τῶν Ἀθηνῶν μ᾽ ἡ τεκοῦσ᾽ εἴη γυνή,
ὥς μοι γένηται μητρόθεν παρρησία.
καθαρὰν γὰρ ἤν τις ἐς πόλιν πέσῃ ξένος,
κἂν τοῖς λόγοισιν ἀστὸς ᾖ, τό γε στόμα
675 δοῦλον πέπαται κοὐκ ἔχει παρρησίαν.

ΧΟΡΟΣ

στρ.

ὁρῶ δάκρυα καὶ πενθίμους
⟨ἀλαλαγὰς⟩ στεναγμάτων τ᾽ ἐσβολάς,
ὅταν ἐμὰ τύραννος εὐπαιδίαν
πόσιν ἔχοντ᾽ εἰδῇ,
680 αὐτὴ δ᾽ ἄπαις ᾖ καὶ λελειμμένη τέκνων.
τίν᾽, ὦ παῖ πρόμαντι Λατοῦς, ἔχρη-
σας ὑμνῳδίαν;

402

ness. But as time passes I will find occasion and win my wife's consent to your assuming my kingly power.

I name you Ion, a name to suit your fate. For when I was coming out of the god's shrine you were the first to meet me.[23] So gather all your friends and with the cheer of the ox-slaughtering feast bid them farewell since you are leaving Delphi.

You servants, say nothing about these matters: the penalty for telling my wife is death.

ION

I will go! Now only one thing is missing from my lot. Unless I find my mother, my life will be no life at all, father. If it is right to do so, I pray my mother may be Athenian, so that I may have free speech as my maternal inheritance! For if a foreigner, even though nominally a citizen, comes into that pure-bred city, his tongue is enslaved and he has no freedom of speech.

Exit by Eisodos B ION *and* XUTHUS *with retinue.*

CHORUS

I see tears, mournful ⟨cries⟩
of pain and the onset of groaning
when my queen learns
that her husband enjoys fair offspring
while she herself has none and is bereft of children.
O prophetic son of Leto, what song was this
you uttered in prophecy?

---

23 Ion's name is here derived from the verb "to come/go."

677 ⟨ἀλαλαγὰς⟩ Hermann

πόθεν ὁ παῖς ὅδ᾽ ἀμφὶ ναοὺς σέθεν
τρόφιμος ἐξέβα; γυναικῶν τίνος;
685 οὐ γάρ με σαίνει θέσφατα μή τιν᾽ ἔχῃ δόλον.
δειμαίνω συμφοράν,
ἐφ᾽ ὅ ποτε βάσεται ⟨κακόν⟩.
690 ἄτοπος ἄτοπα γὰρ παραδίδωσί μοι
τάδε θεοῦ φήμα.
ἔχει δόλον τέχναν θ᾽ ὁ παῖς
ἄλλων τραφεὶς ἐξ αἱμάτων.
τίς οὐ τάδε ξυνοίσεται;

ἀντ.

695 φίλαι, πότερ᾽ ἐμᾷ δεσπότει
τάδε τορῶς ἐς οὓς γεγωνήσομεν
πόσιν, ἐν ᾧ τὰ πάντ᾽ ἔχουσ᾽ ἐλπίδων
μέτοχος ἦν, τολμᾶν;
νῦν δ᾽ ἡ μὲν ἔρρει συμφοραῖς, ὁ δ᾽ εὐτυχεῖ,
700 πολιὸν ἐσπεσοῦσα γῆρας πόσει τ᾽
ἀτίετος φίλῳ.
μέλεος, ὃς θυραῖος ἐλθὼν δόμους
μέγαν ἐς ὄλβον οὐκ ἴσωσεν τύχας.
705 ὄλοιτ᾽ ὄλοιτο πότνιαν ἐξαπαφὼν ἐμάν,
καὶ θεοῖσιν μὴ τύχοι
καλλίφλογα πέλανον ἐπὶ πυ⟨ρὸς

689 ⟨κακόν⟩ Willink
691 τάδε θεοῦ φήμα Nauck: τόδε τ᾽ εὔφημα L
692 ἔχει] πλέκει Diggle   τέχναν Schoemann: τύχαν L
695 δεσπότει Diggle: δεσποίνᾳ L
698 τολμᾶν Page: τλάμων L

404

This boy nursed about your altars,
from whence did he come? From what woman?
This oracle is not to my liking: perchance it may involve
    deceit.
I fear what may yet come,
in what ⟨calamity⟩ it may end.
Strange is the word of the god and strange
the things it reports to me.
There is some clever trickery in this boy
raised here and begotten elsewhere.
Who would deny it?

My friends, shall I speak this
clearly in my mistress' ear,
that the husband in whom her all was bound up,
the sharer of her hopes, has dared this deed?
Now while he is blessed, she is ruined by misfortune,
cast into grey old age and unhonored
by her dear husband.
The wretch: he came to the house from outside,
entered on its great wealth, yet he did not make her
    fortunes equal to his own.
A curse, a curse on him for deceiving my mistress!
May he not have success as before the gods
he lays in sacrifice the bright-flamed cake upon the fire

700-1 πόσει τ' . . . φίλῳ Diggle: πόσις δ' . . . φίλων L
702 δόμων Wecklein: δόμου Musgrave
704 ἴσωσεν Wakefield: ἔσωσε L
707-8 πυ⟨ρὸς χε⟩ρὶ Willink

χε>ρὶ καθαγνίσας· τὸ δ' ἐμὸν εἴσεταί
<τις ὅσον ἀρχαίας
710 ἔφυν> τυραννίδος φίλα.
ἤδη πέλας δείπνων κυρεῖ
παῖς καὶ πατὴρ νέος νέων.

ἐπῳδ.

ἰὼ δειράδες Παρνασοῦ πέτρας
715 ἔχουσαι σκόπελον οὐράνιόν θ' ἕδραν,
ἵνα Βάκχιος ἀμφιπύρους ἀνέχων πεύκας
λαιψηρὰ πηδᾷ νυκτιπόλοις ἅμα σὺν Βάκχαις,
μή <τί> ποτ' εἰς ἐμὰν πόλιν ἵκοιθ' ὁ παῖς,
720 νέαν δ' ἀμέραν ἀπολιπὼν φθάνοι.
στεγομένα γὰρ ἂν πόλις ἔχοι σκῆψιν
ξενικὸν ἐσβολάν·
ἅλις ἔασεν ὁ πάρος ἀρχαγὸς ὢν
Ἐρεχθεὺς ἄναξ.

ΚΡΕΟΥΣΑ

725 ὦ πρέσβυ παιδαγώγ' Ἐρεχθέως πατρὸς
τοὐμοῦ ποτ' ὢν τόθ' ἡνίκ' ἦν ἔτ' ἐν φάει,
ἔπαιρε σαυτὸν πρὸς θεοῦ χρηστήρια,
ὥς μοι συνησθῇς, εἴ τι Λοξίας ἄναξ
θέσπισμα παίδων ἐς γονὰς ἐφθέγξατο.
730 σὺν τοῖς φίλοις γὰρ ἡδὺ μὲν πράσσειν καλῶς·
ὃ μὴ γένοιτο δ', εἴ τι τυγχάνοι κακόν,

710 ante h. v. lac. indic. Canter, suppl. Willink
711 πέλας Seidler: πελάσας L   δεινῶν Diggle
712 νέου Burges   719 <τί> Hermann

with his hand! As for me, ⟨people⟩ will know
⟨how close to the ancient⟩
royal house I stand in friendship.
Now the new father and son
are already near their newmade feast.

Hail, peaks of the cliff of Parnassus
with your sharp crag and your seat high in the heavens!
There Dionysus, holding aloft twin torches,
leaps nimbly about in company with his night-ranging
    maenads.
Never may the boy come to my city:
ere then may he leave his young life behind.
The city would have good reason
to keep off an incursion of strangers.
Enough have been admitted by our old ruler,
King Erechtheus.

Enter by Eisodos B CREUSA *and* OLD MAN.

CREUSA

Aged tutor to my father Erechtheus while he was still alive,
climb up to the god's oracular shrine to share in my joy if
lord Loxias has prophesied the birth of children. It is a
pleasure to share good fortune with those we love. But if—
as I pray may not happen—some trouble comes, the sight

---

720 φθάνοι Herwerden: θάν- L
721 στεγομένα Grégoire: στεν- L
723 ἅλις ἔασεν post Scaliger (ἅλις) Willink: ἁλίσας L
726 ὧν τόθ' Wecklein: ὄντος L

ἐς ὄμματ᾽ εὔνου φωτὸς ἐμβλέψαι γλυκύ.
ἐγὼ δέ σ᾽, ὥσπερ καὶ σὺ πατέρ᾽ ἐμόν ποτε,
δέσποιν᾽ ὅμως οὖσ᾽ ἀντικηδεύω πατρός.

ΠΡΕΣΒΥΤΗΣ

735 ὦ θύγατερ, ἄξι᾽ ἀξίων γεννητόρων
ἤθη φυλάσσεις κοὐ καταισχύνασ᾽ ἔχεις
τοὺς σούς, παλαιῶν ἐκγόνους αὐτοχθόνων.
ἕλχ᾽ ἕλκε πρὸς μέλαθρα καὶ κόμιζέ με.
αἰπεινά μοι μαντεῖα· τοῦ γήρως δέ μοι
740 συνεκπονοῦσα κῶλον ἰατρὸς γενοῦ.

ΚΡΕΟΥΣΑ

ἕπου νυν· ἴχνος δ᾽ ἐκφύλασσ᾽ ὅπου τίθης.

ΠΡΕΣΒΥΤΗΣ

ἰδού·
τὸ τοῦ ποδὸς μὲν βραδύ, τὸ τοῦ δὲ νοῦ ταχύ.

ΚΡΕΟΥΣΑ

βάκτρῳ δ᾽ ἐρείδου· περιφερὴς στίβος χθονός.

ΠΡΕΣΒΥΤΗΣ

καὶ τοῦτο τυφλόν, ὅταν ἐγὼ βλέπω βραχύ.

ΚΡΕΟΥΣΑ

745 ὀρθῶς ἔλεξας· ἀλλὰ μὴ παρῇς κόπῳ.

ΠΡΕΣΒΥΤΗΣ

οὔκουν ἑκών γε· τοῦ δ᾽ ἀπόντος οὐ κρατῶ.

---

737 παλαιῶν ... αὐτοχθόνων Jackson: -οὺς ... -χθόνας L
739 μοι Barnes: δέ μοι L: μὲν Badham

of a friendly face is soothing. Though I am your mistress, I take care of you as I would a father, just as you cared for my father.

OLD MAN

My daughter, your character is worthy of your worthy ancestors, and you do not disgrace your kin, who are descended from ancient stock sprung from the soil. Pull, pull me to the temple: bring me along! To the mantic seat it is a hard climb for me. Support my limbs and be healer to my old age.

CREUSA

Come with me, then. Careful where you plant your steps.

OLD MAN

I do as you say. Though my feet are slow, my mind at least is quick.

CREUSA

Let your staff take your weight. The path winds back and forth.

OLD MAN

When I fail to see my way, this staff too is blind.

CREUSA

You are right. But do not quit from weariness.

OLD MAN

Not if I can help it! But what is not in my power I cannot control.

---

743 περιφερὴς στίβος Diggle: -ῆ στίβον L, quibus servatis ἐρεύνα Schoemann   745 μὴ παρῆς κόπῳ Tyrwhitt (πάρες κόπῳ) et Paley: μὴ 'πάρεκέ πω L
746 ἀπόντος Reiske: ἄκοντος L

ΚΡΕΟΥΣΑ

γυναῖκες, ἱστῶν τῶν ἐμῶν καὶ κερκίδος
δούλευμα πιστόν, τίνα τύχην λαβὼν πόσις
βέβηκε παίδων, ὧνπερ οὕνεχ' ἥκομεν;
750 σημήνατ'· εἰ γὰρ ἀγαθά μοι μηνύσετε,
οὐκ εἰς ἀπίστους δεσπότας βαλεῖς χάριν.

ΧΟΡΟΣ

ἰὼ δαῖμον.

ΠΡΕΣΒΥΤΗΣ

τὸ φροίμιον μὲν τῶν λόγων οὐκ εὐτυχές.

ΧΟΡΟΣ

ἰὼ τλᾶμον.

ΠΡΕΣΒΥΤΗΣ

755 ἀλλ' ἦ τι θεσφάτοισι δεσποτῶν νοσῶ;

ΧΟΡΟΣ

αἰαῖ· τί δρῶμεν θάνατος ὧν κεῖται πέρι;

ΚΡΕΟΥΣΑ

τίς ἥδε μοῦσα, χὠ φόβος τίνων πέρι;

ΧΟΡΟΣ

εἴπωμεν ἢ σιγῶμεν ἢ τί δράσομεν;

ΚΡΕΟΥΣΑ

εἴφ'· ὡς ἔχεις γε συμφοράν τιν' εἰς ἐμέ.

ΧΟΡΟΣ

760 εἰρήσεταί τοι, κεἰ θανεῖν μέλλω διπλῇ.

---

751 χάριν Elmsley: χαράν L

ION

CREUSA

Women, trusty servants who toil at loom and shuttle, what hope of children did my husband take from the shrine, the hope that has brought us here? Tell me. If you report good news, you will not be wasting kindness on a mistress who is ungrateful.

CHORUS LEADER

Ah, miserable fate!

OLD MAN

The prelude at least sounds like misfortune.

CHORUS LEADER

Ah, poor lady!

OLD MAN

Are my mistress' oracles bringing me grief?

CHORUS LEADER

Ah me! What shall we do? The penalty is death.

CREUSA

What tune is this you sing? What are you afraid of?

CHORUS LEADER

Shall we speak or be silent? What are we to do?

CREUSA

Tell me: you have some disaster to report.

CHORUS LEADER

Well, I will tell, even if I must die twice over. My lady, it

---

753, 755n Πρ. Hermann: Χο. L: Κρ. Canter
756 αἰαῖ F. W. Schmidt: εἶεν L

411

οὐκ ἔστι σοι, δέσποιν᾽, ἐπ᾽ ἀγκάλαις λαβεῖν
τέκν᾽ οὐδὲ μαστῷ σῷ προσαρμόσαι ποτέ.

ΠΡΕΣΒΥΤΗΣ

ὤμοι θάνοιμι, θύγατερ.

ΚΡΕΟΥΣΑ

ὦ τάλαιν᾽ ἐγὼ συμφορᾶς,
ἔλαβον ἔπαθον ἄχος ἀβίοτον, φίλαι.

ΠΡΕΣΒΥΤΗΣ

765 διοιχόμεσθα, τέκνον.

ΚΡΕΟΥΣΑ

αἰαιαί· διανταῖος ἔτυ-
πεν ὀδύνα με πλευμόνων τῶνδ᾽ ἔσω.

ΠΡΕΣΒΥΤΗΣ

μήπω στενάξῃς . . .

ΚΡΕΟΥΣΑ

ἀλλὰ πάρεισι γόοι.

ΠΡΕΣΒΥΤΗΣ

770 . . . πρὶν ἂν μάθωμεν . . .

ΚΡΕΟΥΣΑ

ἀγγελίαν τίνα μοι;

ΠΡΕΣΒΥΤΗΣ

. . . εἰ ταὐτὰ πράσσων δεσπότης τῆς συμφορᾶς
κοινωνός ἐστιν ἢ μόνη σὺ δυστυχεῖς.

ΧΟΡΟΣ

κείνῳ μέν, ὦ γεραιέ, παῖδα Λοξίας

cannot be that you will ever take children into your arms or
suckle them at your breast.

OLD MAN

Ah! Death take me, daughter!

CREUSA

How unblest am I in this fate!
My friends, I have received, have suffered grief my life
    cannot endure!

OLD MAN

We are dead, my child!

CREUSA

Ah, ah, ah! Straight through the heart
goes the pain deep within!

OLD MAN

Do not groan aloud . . .

CREUSA

But there is reason to weep!

OLD MAN

. . . until we learn . . .

CREUSA

What message?

OLD MAN

. . . whether my master has the same lot and shares in your
fate or whether you alone are unblest.

CHORUS LEADER

To him, old sir, Loxias has given a child, and on his own,

---

762 ποτέ Jacobs: τάδε L

775 ἔδωκεν, ἰδίᾳ δ' εὐτυχεῖ ταύτης δίχα.

ΚΡΕΟΥΣΑ

τόδ' ἐπὶ τῷδε κακὸν ἄκρον ἔλακες ⟨ἔλακες⟩
ἄχος ἐμοὶ στένειν.

ΠΡΕΣΒΥΤΗΣ

πότερα δὲ φῦναι δεῖ γυναικὸς ἔκ τινος
τὸν παῖδ' ὃν εἶπας ἢ γεγῶτ' ἐθέσπισεν;

ΧΟΡΟΣ

780 ἤδη πεφυκότ' ἐκτελῆ νεανίαν
δίδωσιν αὐτῷ Λοξίας· παρῇ δ' ἐγώ.

ΚΡΕΟΥΣΑ

πῶς φῄς; ἄφατον αὖ φάτιν, ἀναύδατον
λόγον, ἐμοὶ θροεῖς.

ΠΡΕΣΒΥΤΗΣ

785 κἄμοιγε. πῶς δ' ὁ χρησμὸς ἐκπεραίνεται
σαφέστερόν μοι φράζε χὤστις ἔσθ' ὁ παῖς.

ΧΟΡΟΣ

ὅτῳ ξυναντήσειεν ἐκ θεοῦ συθεὶς
πρώτῳ πόσις σός, παῖδ' ἔδωκ' αὐτῷ θεός.

ΚΡΕΟΥΣΑ

790 ὀτοτοτοῖ· τὸν ἐμὸν ἄτεκνον ἄτεκνον ἔλακ'
ἄρα βίοτον, ἐρημίᾳ δ' ὀρφανοὺς
δόμους οἰκήσω.

776 ⟨ἔλακες⟩ Seidler
783 αὖ φάτιν Murray: ἄφατον (iterum) L

414

apart from her, he enjoys good fortune.

CREUSA

You tell, ‹you tell› of great sorrow upon great sorrow,
a grief for me to bewail!

OLD MAN

But did the god say that a woman was to bear this child you
speak of or that he was already born?

CHORUS LEADER

Loxias gave him a child already born, a young man full-
grown. I was there.

CREUSA

What is this you say? It is a tale unspeakable, a word
unutterable you tell me!

OLD MAN

Yes, unspeakable. But tell me more plainly how the oracle
was fulfilled and who the child is.

CHORUS LEADER

The god gave Xuthus as his son whomever he first encoun-
tered on leaving the temple.

CREUSA

O woe! So Apollo has said my life will be childless,
     childless,
and in desolation I shall dwell
in a house bereft!

---

790 τὸν Badham: τὸ δ᾽ L   ἔλακ᾽ post Murray (ἔλακεν)
Conomis: ἔλαβεν L

ΠΡΕΣΒΥΤΗΣ

τίς οὖν ἐχρήσθη; τῷ συνῆψ' ἴχνος ποδὸς
πόσις ταλαίνης; πῶς δὲ ποῦ νιν εἰσιδών;

ΧΟΡΟΣ

οἶσθ', ὦ φίλη δέσποινα, τὸν νεανίαν
795 ὃς τόνδ' ἔσαιρε ναόν; οὗτος ἔσθ' ὁ παῖς.

ΚΡΕΟΥΣΑ

ὑγρὰν ἀμπταίην ἀν' αἰθέρα πρόσω
γᾶς Ἑλλανίας ἀστέρας ἑσπέρους,
οἷον οἷον ἄλγος ἔπαθον, φίλαι.

ΠΡΕΣΒΥΤΗΣ

800 ὄνομα δὲ ποῖον αὐτὸν ὀνομάζει πατήρ;
οἶσθ', ἢ σιωπῇ τοῦτ' ἀκύρωτον μένει;

ΧΟΡΟΣ

Ἴων', ἐπείπερ πρῶτος ἤντησεν πατρί.
μητρὸς δ' ὁποίας ἐστὶν οὐκ ἔχω φράσαι.
φροῦδος δ', ἵν' εἰδῇς πάντα τἀπ' ἐμοῦ, γέρον,
805 παιδὸς προθύσων ξένια καὶ γενέθλια
σκηνὰς ἐς ἱερὰς τῆσδε λαθραίως πόσις,
κοινὴν ξυνάψων δαῖτα παιδὶ τῷ νέῳ.

ΠΡΕΣΒΥΤΗΣ

δέσποινα, προδεδόμεσθα (σὺν γάρ σοι νοσῶ)
τοῦ σοῦ πρὸς ἀνδρὸς καὶ μεμηχανημένως
810 ὑβριζόμεσθα δωμάτων τ' Ἐρεχθέως

796 ὑγρὰν ... ἀν' αἰθέρα Willink: ἀν' ὑγρὸν ... αἰθέρα L
797 γᾶς Weil: γαίας L

OLD MAN

Who was meant by the oracle, then? Whom did this poor
woman's husband meet? How did he see him and where?

CHORUS LEADER

Dear mistress, do you know the young man who was
sweeping the temple? That is the boy.

CREUSA

Oh, would that I could fly through the moist upper air
far from the land of Hellas to the stars in the west!
Such is the grief I have suffered, my friends!

OLD MAN

But by what name did his father call him? Do you know, or
was this left undetermined, with nothing said?

CHORUS LEADER

"Ion" he called him, since he was the first to go to meet his
father. But I cannot tell you who the mother is. To tell you
all I know, old man, about this woman's husband, he has
gone off without telling her to the sacred tent to make a
sacrifice in honor of their friendship and his birth. He
means to share the feast with his new son.

OLD MAN

Mistress, we have been betrayed by your husband! (I share
in your grief.) He has done us a premeditated outrage, and
we are being ejected from the house of Erechtheus! I do

---

798 ἑσπέρους Seidler: -ρίου L

417

ἐκβαλλόμεσθα. καὶ σὸν οὐ στυγῶν πόσιν
λέγω, σὲ μέντοι μᾶλλον ἢ κεῖνον φιλῶν·
ὅστις σε γήμας ξένος ἐπεισελθὼν πόλιν
καὶ δῶμα καὶ σὴν παραλαβὼν παγκληρίαν
815 ἄλλης γυναικὸς παῖδας ἐκκαρπούμενος
λάθρᾳ πέφηνεν· ὡς λάθρᾳ δ᾽, ἐγὼ φράσω.
ἐπεί σ᾽ ἄτεκνον ᾔσθετ᾽, οὐκ ἔστεργέ σοι
ὅμοιος εἶναι τῆς τύχης τ᾽ ἴσον φέρειν,
λαβὼν δὲ δοῦλα λέκτρα νυμφεύσας λάθρᾳ
820 τὸν παῖδ᾽ ἔφυσεν, ἐξενωμένον δέ τῳ
Δελφῶν δίδωσιν ἐκτρέφειν. ὁ δ᾽ ἐν θεοῦ
δόμοισιν ἄφετος, ὡς λάθοι, παιδεύεται.
νεανίαν δ᾽ ὡς ᾔσθετ᾽ ἐκτεθραμμένον,
ἐλθεῖν σ᾽ ἔπεισε δεῦρ᾽ ἀπαιδίας χάριν.
825 κᾆθ᾽ ὁ θεὸς οὐκ ἐψεύσαθ᾽, ὅδε δ᾽ ἐψεύσατο
πάλαι τρέφων τὸν παῖδα, κἄπλεκεν πλοκὰς
τοιάσδ᾽· ἁλοὺς μὲν ἀνέφερ᾽ ἐς τὸν δαίμονα,
λαβὼν δὲ καιρόν, χρόνον ἀμύνεσθαι θέλων,
τυραννίδ᾽ αὐτῷ περιβαλεῖν ἔμελλε γῆς.
830 [καινὸν δὲ τοὔνομ᾽ ἀνὰ χρόνον πεπλασμένον
Ἴων, ἰόντι δῆθεν ὅτι συνήντετο.]

⟨ΧΟΡΟΣ⟩

οἴμοι, κακούργους ἄνδρας ὡς αἰεὶ στυγῶ,
οἳ συντιθέντες τἄδικ᾽ εἶτα μηχαναῖς
κοσμοῦσι. φαῦλον χρηστὸν ἂν λαβεῖν φίλον
835 θέλοιμι μᾶλλον ἢ κακὸν σοφώτερον.

not say this from hatred of your husband but because I love
you more than him. He came as a foreigner to the city,
married you, and received your house and your patrimony,
but now it is clear he has reaped in secret a harvest of chil-
dren by another woman. How he did so in secret I will tell
you. When he learned that you were childless, he was not
content to be like you and to bear an equal fortune. He
took some slave woman, lay with her in secret, and begot
this boy. He took him out of the country and gave him to
some Delphian to raise. For concealment the boy was
raised in the god's temple, like an animal dedicated to the
god. When Xuthus learned that the young man was full
grown, he persuaded you to come here to ask about your
childlessness. So the god was no liar. Xuthus was the liar,
raising the boy for so long, and this was the device he
concocted: if he was detected, he meant to throw responsi-
bility on the god. Otherwise, he meant to ward off the reve-
lations of Time and seize any chance to make him the
country's king.[24] [In the course of time the new name "Ion"
was invented for him because he met him as he went.]

⟨CHORUS LEADER⟩

Oh, oh! How I hate villainous men, who plot injustice and
then make their handiwork look fair with clever ruses! I
would prefer to have someone ordinary but honest for a
friend rather than a clever knave.

24 The text here is uncertain.

828 λαβὼν (vel εὑρὼν) δὲ καιρόν Jacobs cl. 659: ἐλθὼν δὲ καὶ
τὸν L
830-1 del. Dindorf
832-5 Choro trib. Bothe: Seni contin. L

⟨ΠΡΕΣΒΥΤΗΣ⟩

καὶ τῶνδ᾽ ἁπάντων ἔσχατον πείσῃ κακόν·
ἀμήτορ᾽, ἀναρίθμητον, ἐκ δούλης τινὸς
γυναικὸς ἐς σὸν δῶμα δεσπότην ἄγει.
ἁπλοῦν ἂν ἦν γὰρ τὸ κακόν, εἰ παρ᾽ εὐγενοῦς
840 μητρός, πιθών σε, σὴν λέγων ἀπαιδίαν,
ἐσῴκισ᾽ οἴκους· εἰ δέ σοι τόδ᾽ ἦν πικρόν,
τῶν Αἰόλου νιν χρῆν ὀρεχθῆναι γάμων.
ἐκ τῶνδε δεῖ σε δὴ γυναικεῖόν τι δρᾶν.
[ἢ γὰρ ξίφος λαβοῦσαν ἢ δόλῳ τινὶ
845 ἢ φαρμάκοισι σὸν κατακτεῖναι πόσιν
καὶ παῖδα, πρὶν σοὶ θάνατον ἐκ κείνων μολεῖν.
εἰ γάρ γ᾽ ὑφήσεις τοῦδ᾽, ἀπαλλάξῃ βίου.
δυοῖν γὰρ ἐχθροῖν εἰς ἓν ἐλθόντοιν στέγος,
ἢ θάτερον δεῖ δυστυχεῖν ἢ θάτερον.
850 ἐγὼ μὲν οὖν σοι καὶ συνεκπονεῖν θέλω
καὶ συμφονεύειν παῖδ᾽ ὑπεισελθὼν δόμους
οὗ δαῖθ᾽ ὁπλίζει καὶ τροφεῖα δεσπόταις
ἀποδοὺς θανεῖν τε ζῶν τε φέγγος εἰσορᾶν.
ἐν γάρ τι τοῖς δούλοισιν αἰσχύνην φέρει,
855 τοὔνομα· τὰ δ᾽ ἄλλα πάντα τῶν ἐλευθέρων
οὐδὲν κακίων δοῦλος, ὅστις ἐσθλὸς ᾖ.

ΧΟΡΟΣ

κἀγώ, φίλη δέσποινα, συμφορὰν θέλω
κοινουμένη τήνδ᾽ ἢ θανεῖν ἢ ζῆν καλῶς.]

836 κὰκ Dobree
838 ἄγει Hermann: -ειν L

420

⟨OLD MAN⟩

And here is the crowning blow. He is bringing into your
house as its master a boy with no mother, someone of no
consequence, born from some slave woman. Your misfor-
tune would have been single if he had brought into the
house a boy from some noble mother, pressing the point of
your childlessness and thus winning your consent. And if
that was unwelcome to you, he should have sought the
hand of an Aeolian.[25] As a result you must do a womanly
deed. [By sword or trick or poison you must kill your hus-
band and this boy before they kill you. If you flinch from
this you will die. If two enemies come under one roof, one
or the other of them must suffer misfortune. For my part, I
am willing to share with you in the work of murdering the
boy, slipping into the house where he is preparing the
feast. I am ready to repay my masters for my raising and
then to die or to live. Only one thing brings shame to
slaves, the name. In all else a slave who is valiant is not at
all inferior to free men.

CHORUS LEADER

I too, my lady, am willing to share in what befalls and to die
or live nobly.]

25 Who could be expected to be more accepting than an Athe-
nian princess.

844-58 del. post Murray (qui 843-58 suspectos habuit) Diggle,
qui etiam fieri posse arbitratur ut hi vv. pro genuinis suppositi sint,
si minus, 832-5 post 843 ponendos: fort. etiam 836-43 delendi

851 ὑπεισελθών Wakefield: ἐπ- L

856 οὐδὲν Dobree: οὐδεὶς L

857-8 συμφορᾶς ... τῆσδ' Wecklein

421

ΚΡΕΟΥΣΑ

ὦ ψυχά, πῶς σιγάσω;
860 πῶς δὲ σκοτίας ἀναφήνω
εὐνάς, αἰδοῦς δ᾽ ἀπολειφθῶ;

τί γὰρ ἐμπόδιον κώλυμ᾽ ἔτι μοι;
πρὸς τίν᾽ ἀγῶνας τιθέμεσθ᾽ ἀρετῆς;
οὐ πόσις ἡμῶν προδότης γέγονεν;
865 στέρομαι δ᾽ οἴκων, στέρομαι παίδων,
φροῦδαι δ᾽ ἐλπίδες, ἃς διαθέσθαι
χρῄζουσα καλῶς οὐκ ἐδυνήθην,
σιγῶσα γάμους,
σιγῶσα τόκους πολυκλαύτους.
870 ἀλλ᾽ οὐ τὸ Διὸς πολύαστρον ἕδος
καὶ τὴν ἐπ᾽ ἐμοῖς σκοπέλοισι θεὰν
λίμνης τ᾽ ἐνύδρου Τριτωνιάδος
πότνιαν ἀκτήν,
οὐκέτι κρύψω λέχος, ὃ στέρνων
875 ἀπονησαμένη ῥᾴων ἔσομαι.
στάζουσι κόραι δακρύοισιν ἐμαί,
ψυχὴ δ᾽ ἀλγεῖ κακοβουλευθεῖσ᾽
ἔκ τ᾽ ἀνθρώπων ἔκ τ᾽ ἀθανάτων,
οὓς ἀποδείξω
880 λέκτρων προδότας ἀχαρίστους.

ὦ τᾶς ἑπταφθόγγου μέλπων
κιθάρας ἐνοπάν, ἅτ᾽ ἀγραύλοις
κεράεσσιν ἐν ἀψύχοις ἀχεῖ

ION

My heart, how shall I keep silent?
But how shall I reveal the secret
union and lose my sense of shame?

What stands in my way to halt me? With whom am I contending for the prize of goodness? Has not my husband betrayed me? I am being robbed of my house, robbed of children, my hopes are gone. Though I wished to achieve these hopes by saying nothing of the rape or of my tearful childbirth, I could not. No, by the starry seat of Zeus, by the goddess who dwells on my high hill, and by the lordly shore of Lake Triton's deep waters,[26] I shall no more conceal this union! Lifting this load from my breast I shall feel relief! My eyes run with tears, and my soul is pained by the evil machinations of men and gods. I shall reveal that they are ungrateful betrayers of my bed!

O you that cause the voice
of the seven-stringed lyre to resound, which on the
    rustic
lifeless horn[27] echoes forth

[26] The goddess is Athena, and Lake Triton is the place where she was born or first alighted.

[27] Horn (once belonging to an animal but now lifeless) was used for parts of the lyre.

---

861 εὐνάς] κοίτας Willink
863 ἀγῶνας Musgrave: -να L
864 οὖ Dobree
874 ὃ Reiske: ὡς L

423

μουσᾶν ὕμνους εὐαχήτους,
885 σοὶ μομφάν, ὦ Λατοῦς παῖ,
πρὸς τάνδ᾽ αὐγὰν αὐδάσω.
ἦλθές μοι χρυσῷ χαίταν
μαρμαίρων, εὖτ᾽ ἐς κόλπους
κρόκεα πέταλα φάρεσιν ἔδρεπον,
890 †ἀνθίζειν χρυσανταυγῆ†·
λευκοῖς δ᾽ ἐμφὺς καρποῖσιν
χειρῶν εἰς ἄντρου κοίτας
κραυγὰν Ὦ μᾶτέρ μ᾽ αὐδῶσαν
θεὸς ὁμευνέτας
895 ἆγες ἀναιδείᾳ
Κύπριδι χάριν πράσσων.
τίκτω δ᾽ ἁ δύστανός σοι
κοῦρον, τὸν φρίκᾳ ματρὸς
βάλλω τὰν σὰν εἰς εὐνάν,
900 ἵνα μ᾽ ἐν λέχεσιν μελέαν μελέοις
ἐζεύξω τὰν δύστανον.
οἴμοι· καὶ νῦν ἔρρει πτανοῖς
ἁρπασθεὶς θοίνα παῖς μοι—
905 καὶ σός, τλᾶμον· σὺ δ᾽ ⟨ἀεὶ⟩ κιθάρᾳ
κλάζεις παιᾶνας μέλπων.
ὠή, τὸν Λατοῦς αὐδῶ,
ὅστ᾽ ὀμφὰν κληροῖς
πρὸς χρυσέους ⟨ἐλθοῦσιν⟩ θάκους

---

890 ἀνθιζομένα dubitanter Diggle   χρυσαυγῆ Paley
891 ἐμφὺς Reiske: ἐμφύσας L

the Muses' lovely hymns,
to you, O son of Leto,
by the light of day I utter my reproach!
You came to me with your hair
gold-gleaming as into the folds of my gown
I was plucking flowers of saffron hue
reflecting the golden light.
Seizing me by my pale white wrists
as I cried out "Mother!"
into the cave that was your bed
you took me, divine ravisher,
without pity,
doing what gladdens Cypris' heart.
I, the unblest, bore to you
a son whom, in fear of my mother,
I cast upon your couch
where in sorrow upon a bed of sorrow
you yoked my wretched self.
Ah me! And now he is gone, seized
by creatures of the air for their feast, my son—
and yours, hard-hearted one! Yet you ⟨forever⟩ with
      your lyre
go on playing "O Paian"!
You there, I mean the son of Leto,
who allot your oracles
to those ⟨who come⟩ to your golden seat

---

899 sic Bothe: εἰς εὐνὰν β- τὰν σάν L   900 μ' ἐν Heath: με
L   902 οἴμοι Willink: οἴμοι μοι L   904 μου Willink
905 δ' ⟨ἀεὶ⟩ Willink: δὲ L: δὲ ⟨καὶ⟩ Diggle
908 ὅστ' Herwerden: ὃς L: ⟨θνατοῖσιν⟩ ὃς Willink
909 ⟨ἐλθοῦσιν⟩ Page

910 καὶ γαίας μεσσήρεις ἕδρας,
ἐς φῶς αὐδὰν καρύξω·
Ἰὼ ⟨ἰὼ⟩ κακὸς εὐνάτωρ,
ὃς τῷ μὲν ἐμῷ νυμφεύτᾳ
χάριν οὐ προλαβὼν
915 παῖδ᾽ εἰς οἴκους οἰκίζεις·
ὁ δ᾽ ἐμὸς γενέτας
καὶ σός ⟨γ᾽⟩, ἀμαθὴς ⟨θεός⟩, οἰωνοῖς
ἔρρει συλαθείς, οἰκεῖα
σπάργανα ματέρος ἐξαλλάξας.
μισεῖ σ᾽ ἁ Δᾶλος καὶ δάφνας
920 ἔρνεα φοίνικα παρ᾽ ἁβροκόμαν,
ἔνθα λοχεύματα σέμν᾽ ἐλοχεύσατο
Λατὼ Δίοισί σε κάποις.

ΧΟΡΟΣ

οἴμοι, μέγας θησαυρὸς ὡς ἀνοίγνυται
κακῶν, ἐφ᾽ οἷσι πᾶς ἂν ἐκβάλοι δάκρυ.

ΠΡΕΣΒΥΤΗΣ

925 ὦ θύγατερ, οἴκτου σὸν βλέπων ἐμπίμπλαμαι
πρόσωπον, ἔξω δ᾽ ἐγενόμην γνώμης ἐμῆς.
κακῶν γὰρ ἄρτι κῦμ᾽ ὑπεξαντλῶν φρενί,
πρύμνηθεν αἴρει μ᾽ ἄλλο σῶν λόγων ὕπο,
οὓς ἐκβαλοῦσα τῶν παρεστώτων κακῶν
930 μετῆλθες ἄλλων πημάτων κακὰς ὁδούς.
τί φῄς; τίνα λόγον Λοξίου κατηγορεῖς;

911 φῶς Wilamowitz: οὓς L   912 ⟨ἰὼ⟩ Paley
916 ⟨γ᾽⟩ Tr   917 ⟨θεός⟩ Willink

426

and to the earth's midmost resting place!
To the light of day I make this proclamation:
Oh, ungrateful lover!
Though you had no previous favor
from my husband
you gave him a child for his house;
yet my son
and yours, unfeeling ⟨god,⟩ has vanished
taken as prey for birds, leaving
his own mother's swaddling bands behind.
You are hated by Delos and the shoots
of laurel that stand beside the palm tree's delicate
    fronds,
there where in holy childbed
Leto bore you in the bower sent by Zeus.

CHORUS LEADER

Ah, what a great storehouse of misery is opening, misery to
make everyone weep!

OLD MAN

My daughter, as I look at your face I am filled with pity and
have wandered from the thread of my thoughts. As I was
trying to bail this wave of misfortune out of my mind, an-
other comes from astern and lifts my vessel aloft because
of your words: in uttering them you go from our present
misfortunes down the woeful path of other sorrows. What
are you saying? What accusation are you making against

---

922 κάποις Kirchhoff: καρποῖς L
925 οἴκτου Nauck: οὔτοι L
930 καινὰς Musgrave

ποῖον τεκεῖν φὴς παῖδα; ποῦ 'κθεῖναι πόλεως
θηρσὶν φίλον τύμβευμ'; ἄνελθέ μοι πάλιν.

ΚΡΕΟΥΣΑ

αἰσχύνομαι μέν σ', ὦ γέρον, λέξω δ' ὅμως.

ΠΡΕΣΒΥΤΗΣ

935 ὡς συστενάζειν γ' οἶδα γενναίως φίλοις.

ΚΡΕΟΥΣΑ

ἄκουε τοίνυν· οἶσθα Κεκροπίων πετρῶν
πρόσβορρον ἄντρον, ἃς Μακρὰς κικλήσκομεν;

ΠΡΕΣΒΥΤΗΣ

οἶδ', ἔνθα Πανὸς ἄδυτα καὶ βωμοὶ πέλας.

ΚΡΕΟΥΣΑ

ἐνταῦθ' ἀγῶνα δεινὸν ἠγωνίσμεθα.

ΠΡΕΣΒΥΤΗΣ

940 τίν'; ὡς ἀπαντᾷ δάκρυά μοι τοῖς σοῖς λόγοις.

ΚΡΕΟΥΣΑ

Φοίβῳ ξυνῆψ' ἄκουσα δύστηνον γάμον.

ΠΡΕΣΒΥΤΗΣ

ὦ θύγατερ, ἆρ' ἦν ταῦθ' ἅ γ' ᾐσθόμην ἐγώ;

ΚΡΕΟΥΣΑ

οὐκ οἶδ'· ἀληθῆ δ' εἰ λέγεις φαῖμεν ἄν.

ΠΡΕΣΒΥΤΗΣ

νόσον κρυφαίαν ἡνίκ' ἔστενες λάθρᾳ.

---

932 'κθεῖναι Dobree: θεῖναι L   934 σ' del. Dobree: cf.
El. 900   936 Κεκροπίων πετρῶν Page: -ίας πέτρας L

428

Loxias? What child do you say you gave birth to? Where in the city did you expose him to be a corpse welcome to the wild beasts? Start at the beginning!

CREUSA

Though I feel shame before you, old sir, still I will speak.

OLD MAN

I know how to be generous in sharing my friends' griefs, you may be sure.

CREUSA

Listen then! Do you know the north-facing cave in the Cliffs of Cecrops, which we call Long Rocks?

OLD MAN

I know it: the shrine and altar of Pan are nearby.

CREUSA

In that place I underwent a terrible struggle.

OLD MAN

What struggle? Tears well up in my eyes at your words.

CREUSA

Against my will I was coupled with Phoebus on a bed of misery.

OLD MAN

My child, was that what I noticed?

CREUSA

I do not know. But I will tell you whether what you say is true.

OLD MAN

The time when you were lamenting a secret illness by yourself.

ΚΡΕΟΥΣΑ

945 τότ᾽ ἦν ἃ νῦν σοι φανερὰ σημαίνω κακά.

ΠΡΕΣΒΥΤΗΣ

κᾆτ᾽ ἐξέκλεψας πῶς Ἀπόλλωνος γάμους;

ΚΡΕΟΥΣΑ

ἔτεκον· ἀνάσχου ταῦτ᾽ ἐμοῦ κλυών, γέρον.

ΠΡΕΣΒΥΤΗΣ

ποῦ; τίς λοχεύει σ᾽; ἢ μόνη μοχθεῖς τάδε;

ΚΡΕΟΥΣΑ

μόνη κατ᾽ ἄντρον οὗπερ ἐζεύχθην γάμοις.

ΠΡΕΣΒΥΤΗΣ

950 ὁ παῖς δὲ ποῦ ᾽στιν; ἵνα σὺ μηκέτ᾽ ᾖς ἄπαις.

ΚΡΕΟΥΣΑ

τέθνηκεν, ὦ γεραιέ, θηρσὶν ἐκτεθείς.

ΠΡΕΣΒΥΤΗΣ

τέθνηκ᾽; Ἀπόλλων δ᾽ ὁ κακὸς οὐδὲν ἤρκεσεν;

ΚΡΕΟΥΣΑ

οὐκ ἤρκεσ᾽· Ἅιδου δ᾽ ἐν δόμοις παιδεύεται.

ΠΡΕΣΒΥΤΗΣ

τίς γάρ νιν ἐξέθηκεν; οὐ γὰρ δὴ σύ γε.

ΚΡΕΟΥΣΑ

955 ἡμεῖς, ἐν ὄρφνῃ σπαργανώσαντες πέπλοις.

945 τότ᾽ L. Dindorf: τοῦτ᾽ L
948 ᾽μόχθεις Valckenaer
948-9 del. Wiskemann: cf. 16

430

CREUSA

That was the time of those troubles I am now revealing.

OLD MAN

Then how did you conceal your union with Apollo?

CREUSA

I gave birth: do not be shocked at my words, old sir.

OLD MAN

Where? Who delivered you? Or did you do this by yourself?

CREUSA

By myself in the cave where I was joined to the god.

OLD MAN

But the child, where is he? You need not be childless.

CREUSA

He is dead, old sir, exposed to the wild beasts.

OLD MAN

Dead? Then cowardly Apollo did not help him?

CREUSA

No, he did not. The child is being reared in the house of Hades.

OLD MAN

But who exposed him? Surely not you.

CREUSA

It was I: in the darkness I swaddled him in a garment.

ΠΡΕΣΒΥΤΗΣ

οὐδὲ ξυνῄδει σοί τις ἔκθεσιν τέκνου;

ΚΡΕΟΥΣΑ

αἱ ξυμφοραί γε καὶ τὸ λανθάνειν μόνον.

ΠΡΕΣΒΥΤΗΣ

καὶ πῶς ἐν ἄντρῳ παῖδα σὸν λιπεῖν ἔτλης;

ΚΡΕΟΥΣΑ

πῶς; οἰκτρὰ πολλὰ στόματος ἐκβαλοῦσ᾽ ἔπη.

ΠΡΕΣΒΥΤΗΣ

960 φεῦ·
τλήμων σὺ τόλμης, ὁ δὲ θεὸς μᾶλλον σέθεν.

ΚΡΕΟΥΣΑ

εἰ παῖδά γ᾽ εἶδες χεῖρας ἐκτείνοντά μοι.

ΠΡΕΣΒΥΤΗΣ

μαστὸν διώκοντ᾽ ἢ πρὸς ἀγκάλαις πεσεῖν;

ΚΡΕΟΥΣΑ

ἐνταῦθ᾽ ἵν᾽ οὐκ ὢν ἄδικ᾽ ἔπασχεν ἐξ ἐμοῦ.

ΠΡΕΣΒΥΤΗΣ

σοὶ δ᾽ ἐς τί δόξ᾽ ἐσῆλθεν ἐκβαλεῖν τέκνον;

ΚΡΕΟΥΣΑ

965 ὡς τὸν θεὸν σώσοντα τόν γ᾽ αὑτοῦ γόνον.

ΠΡΕΣΒΥΤΗΣ

οἴμοι, δόμων σῶν ὄλβος ὡς χειμάζεται.

959 πῶς; Matthiae: πῶς δ᾽ L   962 ἢ Bruhn
964 δόξ᾽ ἐσῆλθεν Dobree, Hermann: δόξης ἦλθεν L

OLD MAN

And was no one privy to your exposing the child?

CREUSA

Only Misfortune and Stealth.

OLD MAN

How could you bear to leave your child in the cave?

CREUSA

How? With many words of pity on my lips!

OLD MAN

Ah me! You were hard-hearted, but the god even more so.

CREUSA

If you had seen the child stretching forth its hands to me!

OLD MAN

Seeking your breast and to lie in your arms?

CREUSA

Yes, the place I wrongfully refused him.

OLD MAN

Why did you think to cast the child out?

CREUSA

I thought the god would save his own son.

OLD MAN

Ah me, what a storm has troubled the happiness of your house!

He covers his head with his garments.

---

965 σώσοντα Wakefield: σῴζ- L

ΚΡΕΟΥΣΑ

τί κρᾶτα κρύψας, ὦ γέρον, δακρυρροεῖς;

ΠΡΕΣΒΥΤΗΣ

σὲ καὶ πατέρα σὸν δυστυχοῦντας εἰσορῶν.

ΚΡΕΟΥΣΑ

τὰ θνητὰ τοιαῦτ᾽· οὐδὲν ἐν ταὐτῷ μένει.

ΠΡΕΣΒΥΤΗΣ

970 μή νυν ἔτ᾽ οἴκτων, θύγατερ, ἀντεχώμεθα.

ΚΡΕΟΥΣΑ

τί γάρ με χρὴ δρᾶν; ἀπορία τὸ δυστυχεῖν.

ΠΡΕΣΒΥΤΗΣ

τὸν πρῶτον ἀδικήσαντά σ᾽ ἀποτίνου θεόν.

ΚΡΕΟΥΣΑ

καὶ πῶς τὰ κρείσσω θνητὸς οὖσ᾽ ὑπερδράμω;

ΠΡΕΣΒΥΤΗΣ

πίμπρη τὰ σεμνὰ Λοξίου χρηστήρια.

ΚΡΕΟΥΣΑ

975 δέδοικα· καὶ νῦν πημάτων ἄδην ἔχω.

ΠΡΕΣΒΥΤΗΣ

τὰ δυνατά νυν τόλμησον, ἄνδρα σὸν κτανεῖν.

ΚΡΕΟΥΣΑ

αἰδούμεθ᾽ εὐνὰς τὰς τόθ᾽ ἡνίκ᾽ ἐσθλὸς ἦν.

ΠΡΕΣΒΥΤΗΣ

νῦν δ᾽ ἀλλὰ παῖδα τὸν ἐπὶ σοὶ πεφηνότα.

CREUSA

Why do you hide your head, old man, and weep?

OLD MAN

Since I see you and your father in misfortune.

CREUSA

Such is our mortal life. Nothing remains unchanged.

OLD MAN

Well, let us not cling any longer to our tears.

CREUSA

Why, what should I do? Misfortune means helplessness.

OLD MAN

Revenge yourself on the aggressor, the god who wronged you!

CREUSA

But how can I, a mortal, overcome one more powerful?

OLD MAN

Burn down the holy temple of Loxias!

CREUSA

I am afraid to: I already have enough trouble.

OLD MAN

Well then dare what is in your power: kill your husband!

CREUSA

The thought of our earlier marriage, when he was good, inhibits me.

OLD MAN

Well at least kill the child who has come to rule over you.

ΚΡΕΟΥΣΑ

πῶς; εἰ γὰρ εἴη δυνατόν· ὡς θέλοιμί γ᾽ ἄν.

ΠΡΕΣΒΥΤΗΣ

980 ξιφηφόρους σοὺς ὁπλίσασ᾽ ὀπάονας.

ΚΡΕΟΥΣΑ

στείλαιμ᾽ ἄν· ἀλλὰ ποῦ γενήσεται τόδε;

ΠΡΕΣΒΥΤΗΣ

ἱεραῖσιν ἐν σκηναῖσιν οὗ θοινᾷ φίλους.

ΚΡΕΟΥΣΑ

ἐπίσημον ὁ φόνος καὶ τὸ δοῦλον ἀσθενές.

ΠΡΕΣΒΥΤΗΣ

ὤμοι, κακίζῃ· φέρε, σύ νυν βούλευέ τι.

ΚΡΕΟΥΣΑ

985 καὶ μὴν ἔχω γε δόλια καὶ δραστήρια.

ΠΡΕΣΒΥΤΗΣ

ἀμφοῖν ἂν εἴην τοῖνδ᾽ ὑπηρέτης ἐγώ.

ΚΡΕΟΥΣΑ

ἄκουε τοίνυν· οἶσθα γηγενῆ μάχην;

ΠΡΕΣΒΥΤΗΣ

οἶδ᾽, ἣν Φλέγρᾳ Γίγαντες ἔστησαν θεοῖς.

ΚΡΕΟΥΣΑ

ἐνταῦθα Γοργόν᾽ ἔτεκε Γῆ, δεινὸν τέρας.

981 στείλαιμ᾽ Herwerden: στείχοιμ᾽ L

436

CREUSA

How? May it be possible! How much I wish to!

OLD MAN

Arm your servants with weapons.

CREUSA

I will do so: but where will this take place?

OLD MAN

In the holy tent where he is entertaining his friends.

CREUSA

Murder is hard to hide. Servants are weak.

OLD MAN

Oh, now you are being a coward! Come, you make a plan!

CREUSA

I have one, one that is cunning and effective.

OLD MAN

Both kinds of plan I shall help to carry out.

CREUSA

Listen, then. Have you heard of the Battle of the Earth-born?[28]

OLD MAN

Yes, when the Giants fought the gods in Phlegra.

CREUSA

It was there that Earth gave birth to the Gorgon, a terrible monster.

---

[28] See note on line 207 above.

ΠΡΕΣΒΥΤΗΣ

990 ἦ παισὶν αὐτῆς σύμμαχον, θεῶν πόνον;

ΚΡΕΟΥΣΑ

991 ναί· καί νιν ἔκτειν' ἡ Διὸς Παλλὰς θεά.

ΠΡΕΣΒΥΤΗΣ

994 ἆρ' οὗτός ἐσθ' ὁ μῦθος ὃν κλύω πάλαι;.

ΚΡΕΟΥΣΑ

995 ταύτης ⟨γ'⟩ Ἀθάναν δέρος ἐπὶ στέρνοις ἔχειν.

ΠΡΕΣΒΥΤΗΣ

ἣν αἰγίδ' ὀνομάζουσι, Παλλάδος στολήν;

ΚΡΕΟΥΣΑ

997 τόδ' ἔσχεν ὄνομα, θεῶν ὅτ' ᾖξεν ἐς δόρυ.

ΠΡΕΣΒΥΤΗΣ

992 ποῖόν τι μορφῆς σχῆμ' ἔχουσαν ἀγρίας;

ΚΡΕΟΥΣΑ

993 θώρακ' ἐχίδνης περιβόλοις ὡπλισμένον.

ΠΡΕΣΒΥΤΗΣ

998 τί δῆτα, θύγατερ, τοῦτο σοῖς ἐχθροῖς βλάβος;

ΚΡΕΟΥΣΑ

Ἐριχθόνιον οἶσθ' ἢ ⟨οὔ⟩; τί δ' οὐ μέλλεις, γέρον;

ΠΡΕΣΒΥΤΗΣ

1000 ὃν πρῶτον ὑμῶν πρόγονον ἐξανῆκε γῆ;

990 θεοῖς Hermann   992-3 post 997 trai. Kirchhoff
995 ⟨γ'⟩ Hartung
997 ᾖξεν nescioquis apud Paley cl. *El.* 844: ἦλθεν L

438

OLD MAN

To aid her sons and trouble the gods?

CREUSA

Yes. The goddess Pallas, Zeus's daughter, killed her.

OLD MAN

Is this the story that I heard long ago?

CREUSA

Yes, that Athena wears the pelt upon her breast.

OLD MAN

Pallas' armament, the thing they call the aegis?

CREUSA

Yes: it got that name when she rushed into the ranks of the gods.[29]

OLD MAN

What kind of wild appearance does it have?

CREUSA

A breastplate armed with the coils of snakes.

OLD MAN

Well, daughter, what harm does this do our enemies?

CREUSA

Have you heard of Erichthonius? But how could you not, old man?

OLD MAN

Our earliest ancestor, whom the earth put forth?

---

[29] The name *aigis* is here derived from *aïsso*, "to rush."

999 ⟨οὔ⟩ Badham

ΚΡΕΟΥΣΑ

τούτῳ δίδωσι Παλλὰς ὄντι νεογόνῳ . . .

ΠΡΕΣΒΥΤΗΣ

τί χρῆμα; μέλλον γάρ τι προσφέρεις ἔπος.

ΚΡΕΟΥΣΑ

. . . δισσοὺς σταλαγμοὺς αἵματος Γοργοῦς ἄπο.

[ΠΡΕΣΒΥΤΗΣ

ἰσχὺν ἔχοντας τίνα πρὸς ἀνθρώπου φύσιν;

ΚΡΕΟΥΣΑ

1005 τὸν μὲν θανάσιμον, τὸν δ᾽ ἀκεσφόρον νόσων.]

ΠΡΕΣΒΥΤΗΣ

ἐν τῷ καθάψασ᾽ ἀμφὶ παιδὶ σώματος;

ΚΡΕΟΥΣΑ

χρυσοῖσι δεσμοῖς· ὁ δὲ δίδωσ᾽ ἐμῷ πατρί.

ΠΡΕΣΒΥΤΗΣ

κείνου δὲ κατθανόντος ἐς σ᾽ ἀφίκετο;

ΚΡΕΟΥΣΑ

ναί· κἀπὶ καρπῷ γ᾽ αὔτ᾽ ἐγὼ χερὸς φέρω.

ΠΡΕΣΒΥΤΗΣ

1010 πῶς οὖν κέκρανται δίπτυχον δῶρον θεᾶς;

ΚΡΕΟΥΣΑ

κοίλης μὲν ὅστις φλεβὸς ἀπέσταξεν φόνος . . .

[1002] χρῆμ᾽; ἄδηλον Herwerden
[1004-5] suspectos habuit Wecklein propter 1010-5, del.
Grégoire   [1004] ἔχοντας Reiske: ἔχοι γ᾽ ἂν L

CREUSA

When he was a newborn babe, Pallas gave him . . .

OLD MAN

What did she give? Your words are hesitant.

CREUSA

. . . two drops of blood from the Gorgon.

[OLD MAN

What is their effect on the human frame?

CREUSA

The one is deadly, the other cures diseases.]

OLD MAN

By what did he attach them to the child's body?

CREUSA

By golden chains. And Erichthonius gave them to my father.

OLD MAN

And after his death they passed to you?

CREUSA

Yes: I carry them upon my wrist.

OLD MAN

This double gift of the goddess—how is it fashioned?

CREUSA

The blood that dripped from the beast's principal vein . . .

ΠΡΕΣΒΥΤΗΣ

τί τῷδε χρῆσθαι; δύναμιν ἐκφέρει τίνα;

ΚΡΕΟΥΣΑ

. . . νόσους ἀπείργει καὶ τροφὰς ἔχει βίου.

ΠΡΕΣΒΥΤΗΣ

ὁ δεύτερος δ᾽ ἀριθμὸς ὢν λέγεις τί δρᾷ;

ΚΡΕΟΥΣΑ

1015 κτείνει, δρακόντων ἰὸς ὢν τῶν Γοργόνος.

ΠΡΕΣΒΥΤΗΣ

ἐς ἓν δὲ κραθέντ᾽ αὐτὸν ἢ χωρὶς φορεῖς;

ΚΡΕΟΥΣΑ

χωρίς· κακῷ γὰρ ἐσθλὸν οὐ συμμείγνυται.

ΠΡΕΣΒΥΤΗΣ

ὦ φιλτάτη παῖ, πάντ᾽ ἔχεις ὅσων σε δεῖ.

ΚΡΕΟΥΣΑ

τούτῳ θανεῖται παῖς· σὺ δ᾽ ὁ κτείνων ἔσῃ.

ΠΡΕΣΒΥΤΗΣ

1020 ποῦ καὶ τί δράσας; σὸν λέγειν, τολμᾶν δ᾽ ἐμόν.

ΚΡΕΟΥΣΑ

ἐν ταῖς Ἀθήναις, δῶμ᾽ ὅταν τοὐμὸν μόλῃ.

ΠΡΕΣΒΥΤΗΣ

οὐκ εὖ τόδ᾽ εἶπας· καὶ σὺ γὰρ τοὐμὸν ψέγεις.

1012 δύναμιν Calder: -ασιν L
1014 ὢν Nauck: ὂν L
1015 Γοργόνος Dobree, Bothe: -ων L

442

OLD MAN

Of what use is it? What effect does it have?

CREUSA

. . . wards off disease and nourishes life.

OLD MAN

And the second you mention, what does it do?

CREUSA

It kills: it is the venom of the Gorgon's snakes.

OLD MAN

Do you carry them mixed together or separately?

CREUSA

Separately: bad does not mingle with good.

OLD MAN

Dearest daughter, you have everything you need!

CREUSA

By this means the boy will be killed. You will be the killer.

OLD MAN

Where and how? It is for you to command and for me to dare the deed.

CREUSA

In Athens, when he comes to my house.

OLD MAN

That is not a good suggestion. You also found fault with my plan.

ΚΡΕΟΥΣΑ

πῶς; ἆρ᾽ ὑπείδου τοῦθ᾽ ὃ κἄμ᾽ ἐσέρχεται;

ΠΡΕΣΒΥΤΗΣ

σὺ παῖδα δόξεις διολέσαι, κεἰ μὴ κτενεῖς.

ΚΡΕΟΥΣΑ

1025 ὀρθῶς· φθονεῖν γάρ φασι μητρυιὰς τέκνοις.

ΠΡΕΣΒΥΤΗΣ

αὐτοῦ νυν αὐτὸν κτεῖν᾽, ἵν᾽ ἀρνήσῃ φόνους.

ΚΡΕΟΥΣΑ

προλάζυμαι γοῦν τῷ χρόνῳ τῆς ἡδονῆς.

ΠΡΕΣΒΥΤΗΣ

καὶ σόν γε λήσεις πόσιν ἅ σε σπεύδει λαθεῖν.

ΚΡΕΟΥΣΑ

οἶσθ᾽ οὖν ὃ δρᾶσον· χειρὸς ἐξ ἐμῆς λαβὼν
1030 χρύσωμ᾽ Ἀθάνας τόδε, παλαιὸν ὄργανον,
ἐλθὼν ἵν᾽ ἡμῶν βουθυτεῖ λάθρᾳ πόσις,
δείπνων ὅταν λήγωσι καὶ σπονδὰς θεοῖς
μέλλωσι λείβειν, ἐν πέπλοις ἔχων τόδε
κάθες βαλὼν ἐς πῶμα τῷ νεανίᾳ,
1035 ἰδίᾳ δέ, μή <τι> πᾶσι, χωρίσας ποτὸν
τῷ τῶν ἐμῶν μέλλοντι δεσπόζειν δόμων.
κἄνπερ διέλθῃ λαιμόν, οὔποθ᾽ ἵξεται
κλεινὰς Ἀθήνας, κατθανὼν δ᾽ αὐτοῦ μενεῖ.

1028 λαθεῖν Stephanus: λαβ- L   1031 ἡμῶν Battezzato:
ἡμῖν L   1034 λαθὼν West
1035 <τι> Wakefield   v. del. Paley

444

CREUSA

What do you mean? Have you detected what also occurs
to me?

OLD MAN

People will think you have killed the boy even if you did
not.

CREUSA

You are right. Stepmothers, they say, wish children ill.

OLD MAN

Kill him here, then, where you can deny the murder.

CREUSA

Good! Then I can taste my joy the sooner!

OLD MAN

Yes, and you will fool your husband where he wants to fool
you.

CREUSA

Here is what you must do. Take this golden vessel of
Athena, ancient workmanship, from my hand and go to
where my husband is secretly holding his sacrifice. When
they have finished their meal and are about to pour liba-
tions to the gods, keeping this hidden in your garments put
it into the young man's cup, but his alone, not everyone's,
reserving this drink for the one who means to lord it over
my house. If it passes down his throat, he will never come
to glorious Athens but will die and remain here.

She gives him a golden vial.

EURIPIDES

ΠΡΕΣΒΥΤΗΣ

σὺ μέν νυν εἴσω προξένων μέθες πόδα·
1040 ἡμεῖς δ' ἐφ' ᾧ τετάγμεθ' ἐκπονήσομεν.
ἄγ', ὦ γεραιὲ πούς, νεανίας γενοῦ
ἔργοισι, κεἰ μὴ τῷ χρόνῳ πάρεστί σοι.
ἐχθρὸν δ' ἐπ' ἄνδρα στεῖχε δεσποτῶν μέτα
καὶ συμφόνευε καὶ συνεξαίρει δόμων.
1045 τὴν δ' εὐσέβειαν εὐτυχοῦσι μὲν καλὸν
τιμᾶν· ὅταν δὲ πολεμίους δρᾶσαι κακῶς
θέλῃ τις, οὐδεὶς ἐμποδὼν κεῖται νόμος.

ΧΟΡΟΣ

στρ. α

Εἰνοδία θύγατερ Δάματρος, ἃ τῶν
νυκτιπόλων ἐφόδων ἀνάσσεις,
1050 καὶ μεθαμερίων
ὅδωσον δυσθανάτων
κρατήρων πληρώματ' ἐφ' οἷσι πέμπει
πότνια πότνι' ἐμὰ χθονίας
1055 Γοργοῦς λαιμοτόμων ἀπὸ σταλαγμῶν
τῷ τῶν Ἐρεχθεϊδᾶν
δόμων ἐφαπτομένῳ·
μηδέ ποτ' ἄλλος ἄλλων ἀπ' οἴ-
κων πόλεως ἀνάσσοι
1060 πλὴν τῶν εὐγενετᾶν Ἐρεχθειδᾶν.

1045 εὐτυχοῦσι] fort. ἔν γ' ἔταισι

446

OLD MAN

Proceed then to your hosts' house. I shall carry out the task
I have been assigned. Come, aged feet, become young in
action, if not in years! Become your mistress' ally and
march against the foe! Join her in slaughtering him and
driving him out of the house! For those who are enjoying
good fortune it is a fine thing to honor piety. But when a
man wants to harm an enemy, no law stands in the way.

Exit CREUSA *by Eisodos A,* OLD MAN *by Eisodos B.*

CHORUS

Enodia,[30] daughter of Demeter, who rule
over the goings of the night,
direct also by day
the filling of the cup
of lingering death to him against whom
my mistress, my mistress, sends it filled
with drops from the severed neck of the earthborn
    Gorgon,
against the one who upon Erechtheus' house
would lay his hands!
May no one else from another house come
and rule the city,
none save the noble Erechtheids!

---

[30] Enodia is the goddess of crossroads. She is sometimes iden-
tified with Hecate, who has connections with sorcery, but here she
is called daughter of Demeter, i.e. Persephone, who is patroness
of the Eleusinian Mysteries, alluded to below.

ἀντ. α

εἰ δ' ἀτελὴς θάνατος σπουδαί τε δεσποί-
νας ὅ τε καιρὸς ἄπεισι τόλμας,
ὧν νῦν ἐλπίσι φέρ-
βεται, θηκτὸν ξίφος ἢ
1065 λαιμῶν ἐξάψει βρόχον ἀμφὶ δειράν,
πάθεσι πάθεα δ' ἐξανύτουσ'
εἰς ἄλλας βιότου κάτεισι μορφάς.
οὐ γὰρ δόμων γ' ἑτέρους
1070 ἄρχοντας ἀλλοδαποὺς
ζῶσά ποτ' ὄμμασιν <θεοῦ 'ν> φαεν-
ναῖς ἀνέχοιτ' ἂν αὐγαῖς
ἃ τῶν εὐπατριδᾶν γεγῶσ' οἴκων.

στρ. β

αἰσχύνομαι τὸν πολύ-
1075 μνον θεόν, εἰ παρὰ Καλλιχόροισι παγαῖς
λαμπάδα θεωρὸς εἰκάδων
ἐννύχιον ἄυπνος ὄψεται,
ὅτε καὶ Διὸς ἀστερωπὸς
ἀνεχόρευσεν αἰθήρ,
1080 χορεύει δὲ σελάνα
καὶ πεντήκοντα κόραι

1063 ὧν olim Wecklein: ὦ L   ἐλπίσι φέρβεται post
Headlam (ἐφέρβετ') Willink: ἐλπὶς φέρετ' ἢ L
1064 θηκτὸν] θήξει Kock
1068 κάτεισι μορφάς Hermann: μ- κ- L
1071 <θεοῦ 'ν> Willink
1076 θεωρὸς Musgrave: -ὸν L

448

If my mistress' murderous design miscarries,
and the hour for the daring deed passes by,
the hope of which nourishes her heart,
she will take the sharp sword or
fasten the neck halter about her throat:
making a sorrowful end to her sorrows
she will go down to another mode of life.
For never, while she lives,
can her eyes bear to see, in the ⟨god's⟩ bright
sunlight, foreigners
ruling over her house,
since she is begotten of noble lineage.

I feel shame before the god
of many hymns,[31] if beside the spring of Callichoroe
the boy as sleepless onlooker beholds
the all-night torch of the twentieth day
when the star-gleaming heaven of Zeus
strikes up the dance
and the moon dances
and also the fifty daughters

[31] The Chorus here contemplates the shame of an outsider taking part in the Eleusinian Mysteries. "The god of many hymns" is Iacchus (cf. Hom. *Hymn.* 26.7), who is the personification of the mystic shout (*iakchê*) and is identified with Dionysus. On the twentieth day of the month Boedromion was the procession from Athens to Eleusis preceded by an all-night festival of torches.

1077 ἐννύχιον ἄυπνος ὄψεται Musgrave (ἐννύχιον) et Hartung: ὄψεται ἐννύχιος ἄυπνος L

†Νηρέος αἱ κατὰ† πόντον
ἀείνων τ᾽ ἃμ ποταμῶν
δίνας χορευόμεναι
1085 τὰν χρυσοστέφανον κόραν
καὶ ματέρα σεμνάν·
ἵν᾽ ἐλπίζει βασιλεύ-
σειν ἄλλων πόνον ἐσπεσὼν
ὁ Φοίβειος ἀλάτας.

ἀντ. β
1090 ὁρᾶθ᾽ ὅσοι δυσκελάδοι-
σιν κατὰ μοῦσαν ἰόντες ἀείδεθ᾽ ὕμνοις
ἀμέτερα λέχεα καὶ γάμους
Κύπριδος ἀθέμιτος ἀνοσίους,
ὅσον εὐσεβίᾳ κρατοῦμεν
1095 ἄδικον ἄροτον ἀνδρῶν.
παλίμφαμος ἀοιδὰ
καὶ μοῦσ᾽ εἰς ἄνδρας ἴτω
δυσκέλαδος ἀμφὶ λέκτρων.
δείκνυσι γὰρ Διὸς οὐκ
1100 παίδων ἀμνημοσύναν,
οὐ κοινὰν τεκέων τύχαν
οἴκοισι φυτεύσας
δεσποίνᾳ· πρὸς δ᾽ Ἀφροδί-
ταν ἄλλαν θέμενος χάριν
1105 νόθου παιδὸς ἔκυρσεν.

1082 Νηρέος ἑλικτὰ Willink: fort. Νηρῆδες ἀμφὶ
1083 ἀείνων Fix: ἀενάων L   τ᾽ ἃμ Willink: τε L

of Nereus, in the sea
and in the eddies
of everflowing rivers, dance
in honor of the maid of golden garland
and her august mother.
This is the place where he hopes
to invade the work of others and reign,
this wandering boy of Phoebus.

All you that with defaming songs
travel the path of minstrelsy,
singing of the unholy unions
and unlawful loves of our sex,
see how in piety we excel
the unrighteous brood of males!
Let song reverse its course,
and the muse of blame
assail men for their amours!
The offspring of Zeus's offspring
is showing ingratitude:
he did not sire for my mistress
the shared blessing of children
for the house. Favoring
another woman's love
he has a bastard child.

Enter by Eisodos B a SERVANT *of Creusa.*

1093 ἀθέμιτος Bayfield: -τας L
1099 Διὸς οὐκ Hartung: ὁ Διὸς ἐκ L
1100 ἀγνωμοσύναν Canter

451

EURIPIDES

ΘΕΡΑΠΩΝ

κεδναὶ γυναῖκες, ποῦ κόρην Ἐρεχθέως
δέσποιναν εὕρω; πανταχῇ γὰρ ἄστεως
⟨κἀκεῖσε καὶ τὸ δεῦρο καμπίμους δρόμους⟩
ζητῶν νιν ἐξέπλησα κοὐκ ἔχω λαβεῖν.

ΧΟΡΟΣ

τί δ᾽ ἔστιν, ὦ ξύνδουλε; τίς προθυμία
1110 ποδῶν ἔχει σε καὶ λόγους τίνας φέρεις;

ΘΕΡΑΠΩΝ

θηρώμεθ᾽· ἀρχαὶ δ᾽ ἀπιχώριοι χθονὸς
ζητοῦσιν αὐτὴν ὡς θάνῃ πετρουμένη.

ΧΟΡΟΣ

οἴμοι, τί λέξεις; οὔτι που λελήμμεθα
κρυφαῖον ἐς παῖδ᾽ ἐκπορίζουσαι φόνον;

ΘΕΡΑΠΩΝ

1115 ἔγνως· μεθέξεις οὐκ ἐν ὑστάτοις κακοῦ.

ΧΟΡΟΣ

ὤφθη δὲ πῶς τὰ κρυπτὰ μηχανήματα;

ΘΕΡΑΠΩΝ

[τὸ μὴ δίκαιον τῆς δίκης ἡσσώμενον]
ἐξηῦρεν ὁ θεός, οὐ μιανθῆναι θέλων.

ΧΟΡΟΣ

πῶς; ἀντιάζω σ᾽ ἱκέτις ἐξειπεῖν τάδε.
1120 πεπυσμέναι γάρ, εἰ θανεῖν ἡμᾶς χρεών,
ἥδιον ἂν θάνοιμεν, εἴθ᾽ ὁρᾶν φάος.

ION

SERVANT

Trusty women, where can I find my mistress, Erechtheus'
daughter? I have been going down ⟨the winding streets,
now this way, now that,⟩ searching for her all over the town
but I cannot find her.

CHORUS LEADER

What is it, my fellow slave? Why such eagerness of foot?
What is your message?

SERVANT

They are after us! The local authorities are looking for her
to stone her to death!

CHORUS LEADER

Ah, what can you mean? Have we been caught trying to
murder the boy by stealth?

SERVANT

Exactly. You will be among the first to be punished.

CHORUS LEADER

But how was the secret plot detected?

SERVANT

[Injustice was worsted by justice.] The god exposed it, not
wishing to be polluted by it.

CHORUS LEADER

How? I beg you to tell me. For when I have learned the
truth, if die I must I shall die content—or live and see the
light.

1106 κεδναὶ Bayfield: κλειναὶ L   1108 ante h. v. lac. indic.
Badham, suppl. Diggle cl. *IT* 81, *Phoen.* 265-6
   1115 sic Porson: ἐγνώσμεθ᾽ ἐξ ἴσου· κἐν ὑστάτοις κακοῖς L
   1117 del. Kvíčala

EURIPIDES

ἐπεὶ θεοῦ μαντεῖον ᾤχετ᾽ ἐκλιπὼν
πόσις Κρεούσης παῖδα τὸν καινὸν λαβὼν
πρὸς δεῖπνα θυσίας θ᾽ ἃς θεοῖς ὡπλίζετο,

1125 Ξοῦθος μὲν ᾤχετ᾽ ἔνθα πῦρ πηδᾷ θεοῦ
βακχεῖον, ὡς σφαγαῖσι Διονύσου πέτρας
δεύσειε δισσὰς παιδὸς ἀντ᾽ ὀπτηρίων,
λέξας· Σὺ μὲν νῦν, τέκνον, ἀμφήρεις μένων
σκηνὰς ἀνίστη τεκτόνων μοχθήμασιν.

1130 θύσας δὲ γενέταις θεοῖσιν ἦν μακρὸν χρόνον
μείνω, παροῦσι δαῖτες ἔστωσαν φίλοις.
    λαβὼν δὲ μόσχους ᾤχεθ᾽· ὁ δὲ νεανίας
σεμνῶς ἀτοίχους περιβολὰς σκηνωμάτων
ὀρθοστάταις ἱδρύεθ᾽, ἡλίου βολὰς

1135 καλῶς φυλάξας, οὔτε πρὸς μέσας φλογὸς
ἀκτῖνας οὔτ᾽ αὖ πρὸς τελευτώσας βίον,
πλέθρου σταθμήσας μῆκος εἰς εὐγωνίαν,
μέτρημ᾽ ἔχουσαν τοὐν μέσῳ γε μυρίων
ποδῶν ἀριθμόν, ὡς λέγουσιν οἱ σοφοί,

1140 ὡς πάντα Δελφῶν λαὸν ἐς θοίνην καλῶν.
    λαβὼν δ᾽ ὑφάσμαθ᾽ ἱερὰ θησαυρῶν πάρα
κατεσκίαζε, θαύματ᾽ ἀνθρώποις ὁρᾶν.
πρῶτον μὲν ὀρόφῳ πτέρυγα περιβάλλει πέπλων,
ἀνάθημα Δίου παιδός, οὓς Ἡρακλῆς

1145 Ἀμαζόνων σκυλεύματ᾽ ἤνεγκεν θεῷ.

1125 Ξοῦθος] fort. αὐτὸς
1131 μείνω Diggle: μενῶ L

454

ION

When Creusa's husband Xuthus left the god's shrine, taking his new son to the dinner and the sacrifices he was preparing for the gods, he himself departed for the place where the god's Bacchic fire leaps up,[32] so that he might sprinkle with victims' blood the twin peaks of Dionysus in place of birth offerings for his son. He said, "My son, stay here and have carpenters raise high a tent all around this space. If I am a long time in sacrificing to the gods of birth, let your friends who are here begin the feast."

So he took his sacrificial animals and went off. In solemn fashion the young man raised on pillars the perimeter of the tent, as yet unwalled, taking good account of the rays of the sun so as to avoid both its midday and its dying beams. He measured off the length of a *plethron* to form a square with an interior area (as the experts tell us) of ten thousand feet,[33] so that he might invite the whole population of Delphi to dine.

Then he took sacred tapestries from the storerooms and draped them for shade over the frame, a marvelous sight for men to see. First on the top he put a covering of garments dedicated by Heracles, garments which the son of Zeus offered the god as spoils from the Amazons.[34] On

---

[32] One of the twin peaks of Parnassus was dedicated to Dionysus. Flashes of light visible about those peaks at sunset were said to be the torches of Bacchants dancing upon the mountain.

[33] A *plethron* is one hundred feet.

[34] See *Heracles* 408-18.

1134-5 βολὰς . . . φλογὸς A. Schmidt: φ- . . . β- L
1138-9 del. Paley

ἐνῆν δ' ὑφανταὶ γράμμασιν τοιοῖσδ' ὑφαί·
Οὐρανὸς ἀθροίζων ἄστρ' ἐν αἰθέρος κύκλῳ·
ἵππους μὲν ἤλαυν' ἐς τελευταίαν φλόγα
Ἥλιος, ἐφέλκων λαμπρὸν Ἑσπέρου φάος·
1150 μελάμπεπλος δὲ Νὺξ ἀσείρωτον ζυγοῖς
ὄχημ' ἔπαλλεν, ἄστρα δ' ὡμάρτει θεᾷ·
Πλειὰς μὲν ᾔει μεσοπόρου δι' αἰθέρος
ὅ τε ξιφήρης Ὠρίων, ὕπερθε δὲ
Ἄρκτος στρέφουσ' οὐραῖα χρυσήρη πόλῳ·
1155 κύκλος δὲ πανσέληνος ἠκόντιζ' ἄνω
μηνὸς διχήρης, Ὑάδες τε, ναυτίλοις
σαφέστατον σημεῖον, ἥ τε φωσφόρος
Ἕως διώκουσ' ἄστρα. τοίχοισιν δ' ἔπι
ἤμπισχεν ἄλλα βαρβάρων ὑφάσματα·
1160 εὐηρέτμους ναῦς ἀντίας Ἑλληνίσιν
καὶ μιξόθηρας φῶτας ἱππείας τ' ἄγρας
ἐλάφων λεόντων τ' ἀγρίων θηράματα.
κατ' εἰσόδους δὲ Κέκροπα θυγατέρων πέλας
σπείραισιν εἱλίσσοντ', Ἀθηναίων τινὸς
1165 ἀνάθημα· χρυσέους τ' ἐν μέσῳ συσσιτίῳ
κρατῆρας ἔστησ'. ἐν δ' ἄκροισι βὰς ποσὶν
κῆρυξ ἀνεῖπε τὸν θέλοντ' ἐγχωρίων
ἐς δαῖτα χωρεῖν. ὡς δ' ἐπληρώθη στέγη,
στεφάνοισι κοσμηθέντες εὐόχθου βορᾶς
1170 ψυχὴν ἐπλήρουν. ὡς δ' ἀνεῖσαν ἡδονὴν
⟨δαιτός,⟩ παρελθὼν πρέσβυς ἐς μέσον πέδον
ἔστη, γέλων δ' ἔθηκε συνδείπνοις πολύν,

them were woven the following. Heaven was mustering the stars in the circle of the sky. Helios was driving his horses toward his final gleaming, bringing on the brightness of Eveningstar. Night, robed in black, was making her chariot, drawn by a pair with no trace horses, swing forward, and the stars were accompanying the goddess. The Pleiades were passing through mid heaven and so was Orion with his sword, while above them the Bear turned its golden tail about the Pole. The circle of the full moon, as at mid month, darted her beams, and there were the Hyades, clearest sign for sailors, and Dawn the Daybringer putting the stars to flight. On the walls of the tent he spread as a covering other tapestries, barbarian work: there were finely oared ships facing ships of the Greeks, half-beast men, horsemen chasing hinds, and the hunting of wild lions. Near the entrance he put Cecrops, winding himself in coils,[35] standing next to his daughters, a work dedicated by an Athenian. In the middle of the dining hall he put golden mixing bowls. A herald, drawing himself up to his full height, invited to the feast all of the inhabitants who wished to come. When the hall was filled, they garlanded their heads and took their hearts' fill of the plentiful feast. When they had satisfied their desire ‹for food›, an old man came forward and took his place in the middle of the floor, and he caused much laughter among the feasters by his

---

[35] Cecrops, who was born from the earth, was a snake from the waist down.

1146 τοιοῖσδ' Dobree: τοιαίδ' L   1152 μεσοπόρος Barnes
1154 χρυσήρει Stephanus   1166 fort. ἄκροις βεβὼς
1171 ‹δαιτός› Reiske

EURIPIDES

πρόθυμα πράσσων· ἔκ τε γὰρ κρωσσῶν ὕδωρ
χεροῖν ἔπεμπε νίπτρα κἀξεθυμία
1175 σμύρνης ἱδρῶτα χρυσέων τ' ἐκπωμάτων
ἦρχ', αὐτὸς αὐτῷ τόνδε προστάξας πόνον.
ἐπεὶ δ' ἐς αὐλοὺς ἦκον ἐς κρατῆρά τε
κοινόν, γέρων ἔλεξ'· Ἀφαρπάζειν χρεὼν
οἰνηρὰ τεύχη σμικρά, μεγάλα δ' ἐσφέρειν,
1180 ὡς θᾶσσον ἔλθωσ' οἵδ' ἐς ἡδονὰς φρενῶν.
ἦν δὴ φερόντων μόχθος ἀργυρηλάτους
χρυσέας τε φιάλας· ὁ δὲ λαβὼν ἐξαίρετον,
ὡς τῷ νέῳ δὴ δεσπότῃ χάριν φέρων,
ἔδωκε πλῆρες τεῦχος, εἰς οἶνον βαλὼν
1185 ὅ φασι δοῦναι φάρμακον δραστήριον
δέσποιναν, ὡς παῖς ὁ νέος ἐκλίποι φάος·
κοὐδεὶς τάδ' ᾔδειν. ἐν χεροῖν ἔχοντι δὲ
[σπονδὰς μετ' ἄλλων παιδὶ τῷ πεφηνότι]
βλασφημίαν τις οἰκετῶν ἐφθέγξατο·
1190 ὁ δ', ὡς ἐν ἱερῷ μάντεσίν τ' ἐσθλοῖς τραφείς,
οἰωνὸν ἔθετο κἀκέλευσ' ἄλλον νέον
κρατῆρα πληροῦν· τὰς δὲ πρὶν σπονδὰς θεοῦ
δίδωσι γαίᾳ πᾶσί τ' ἐκσπένδειν λέγει.
σιγὴ δ' ὑπῆλθεν. ἐκ δ' ἐπίμπλαμεν δρόσου
1195 κρατῆρας ἱεροὺς Βιβλίνου τε πώματος.
κἀν τῷδε μόχθῳ πτηνὸς ἐσπίπτει δόμους

1177 ἦκον Dobree: -εν L   1178 κοινόν Musgrave: καιν- L
1179 τεύχη Wakefield: σκεύη L
1180 φρενῶν] fort. θεοῦ: cf. 553

458

eager bustling. From the water jars he kept bringing water
for the guests to wash their hands, burned myrrh resin
as incense, and had charge of the golden drinking cups,
having assigned this duty to himself.

When they came to the playing of the pipe and to the
common mixing bowl,[36] the old man said, "We must take
away these small wine vessels and bring in large ones, so
that these guests may more quickly find their hearts' joy."
There was a bustling as servants brought silver and gold
cups. Then he took a special cup, as if doing honor to his
new master, and gave it to him filled with wine, slipping
into it the deadly drug they say my mistress gave him,
meaning to kill this newfound son. No one noticed this.
But as the boy held it in his hand, [holding the libation
along with others, this newly appeared boy,] one of the ser-
vants uttered a word of evil omen. Since he had been
brought up in the temple and among good seers, he took it
as a sign and gave the order to fill another mixing bowl. The
first libations to the god he poured out upon the ground
and told everyone to do the same. Silence fell while we
filled the holy mixing bowls with water and Bibline wine.[37]
While this task was being performed, a riotous band of

36 At a Greek feast, the guests first ate, then sang a paean ac-
companied by a reed pipe, and then proceeded to the symposium,
wine being served to them from a large bowl where it was mixed
with water.

37 A strong and fragrant wine, probably of Thrace.

1188 del. Paley
1191 νέους Wilamowitz
1196 δόμους Badham: -οις L: στέγην Page

κῶμος πελειῶν (Λοξίου γὰρ ἐν δόμοις
ἄτρεστα ναίουσ'), ὡς δ' ἀπέσπεισαν μέθυ,
ἐς αὐτὸ χείλη πώματος κεχρημέναι
1200 καθῆκαν, εἷλκον δ' εὐπτέρους ἐς αὐχένας.
καὶ ταῖς μὲν ἄλλαις ἄνοσος ἦν λοιβὴ θεοῦ·
ἡ δ' ἕζετ' ἔνθ' ὁ καινὸς ἔσπεισεν γόνος
ποτοῦ τ' ἐγεύσατ', εὐθὺς εὔπτερον δέμας
ἔσεισε κἀβάκχευσεν, ἐκ δ' ἔκλαγξ' ὄπα
1205 ἀξύνετον αἰάζουσ'· ἐθάμβησεν δὲ πᾶς
θοινατόρων ὅμιλος ὄρνιθος πόνους.
θνῄσκει δ' ἀπασπαίρουσα, φοινικοσκελεῖς
χηλὰς παρεῖσα. γυμνὰ δ' ἐκ πέπλων μέλη
ὑπὲρ τραπέζης ἦχ' ὁ μαντευτὸς γόνος,
1210 βοᾷ δέ· Τίς μ' ἔμελλεν ἀνθρώπων κτανεῖν;
σήμαινε, πρέσβυ· σὴ γὰρ ἡ προθυμία
καὶ πῶμα χειρὸς σῆς ἐδεξάμην πάρα.
εὐθὺς δ' ἐρευνᾷ γραῖαν ὠλένην λαβών,
ἐπ' αὐτοφώρῳ πρέσβυν ὡς ἔχονθ' ἕλοι
⟨βαιόν τι τεῦχος φαρμάκων κακῶν γέμον⟩.
1215 ὤφθη δὲ καὶ κατεῖπ' ἀναγκασθεὶς μόλις
τόλμας Κρεούσης πώματός τε μηχανάς.
θεῖ δ' εὐθὺς ἔξω συλλαβὼν θοινάτορας
ὁ πυθόχρηστος Λοξίου νεανίας,
κἀν κοιράνοισι Πυθικοῖς σταθεὶς λέγει·
1220 Ὦ γαῖα σεμνή, τῆς Ἐρεχθέως ὕπο,
ξένης γυναικός, φαρμάκοισι θνῄσκομεν.
Δελφῶν δ' ἄνακτες ὥρισαν πετρορριφῆ

doves came flying into the tent: these dwell unmolested in
Loxias' temple. Since drink had been poured out, they put
their beaks down into it, being thirsty, and drew it up into
their feathered throats. Most of them were unharmed by
the god's libation. But one bird settled where the new-
found son had poured out his drink, and no sooner had she
tasted the wine than her feathered body was shaken and
convulsed like a Bacchant, and she uttered a cry of distress
hard to interpret. As the whole company of feasters looked
in astonishment at the bird's agony, she gasped away her
life and died, her red legs and feet all limp. Then the son
named by the god bared his arms from his cloak as he
shot them over the table and cried, "Who has been trying
to kill me? Tell me, old man. You were the one who served
so eagerly, and it was from your hand that I received the
drink." Immediately he seizes the old man by the arm and
searches him, expecting to catch him red-handed with ‹a
vial of deadly poison›. It was found, and under hard duress
he confessed Creusa's act of daring and the drink plot. Im-
mediately the young man named by Loxias ran outside
with the guests, and standing in the midst of the rulers of
Delphi said, "Rulers of this revered land, the daughter of
Erechtheus, a foreign woman, has tried to poison me!" The
lords of Delphi voted in double ballot[38] that my mistress

[38] Lit. "not by one vote," which could imply, as Wilamowitz
said, that two charges, murder and sacrilege, were voted on. It
could also mean "overwhelmingly." There is something to be said
for Reiske's emendation, "by a single (i.e. undivided, unanimous)
vote."

1214 post h. v. lac. indic. Herwerden

θανεῖν ἐμὴν δέσποιναν οὐ ψήφῳ μιᾷ,
τὸν ἱερὸν ὡς κτείνουσαν ἔν τ᾽ ἀνακτόροις
1225 φόνον τιθεῖσαν. πᾶσα δὲ ζητεῖ πόλις
τὴν ἀθλίως σπεύσασαν ἀθλίαν ὁδόν·
παίδων γὰρ ἐλθοῦσ᾽ εἰς ἔρον Φοίβου πάρα
τὸ σῶμα κοινῇ τοῖς τέκνοις ἀπώλεσεν.

ΧΟΡΟΣ
οὐκ ἔστ᾽ οὐκ ἔστιν θανάτου
1230 παρατροπὰ μελέα μοι·
φανερὰ γὰρ φανερᾶς τάδ᾽ ἤ-
δη ᾽κ σπονδὰς Διονύσου
βοτρύων ὀλοοῖς ἐχίδνας
σταγόσι μειγνυμένας φόνου.
1235 φανερὰ θύματα νερτέρων,
συμφοραὶ μὲν ἐμῷ βίῳ,
λεύσιμοι δὲ καταφθοραὶ δεσποίνᾳ.
τίνα φυγὰν πτερόεσσαν ἢ
χθονὸς ὑπὸ σκοτίους μυχοὺς πορευθῶ,
1240 θανάτου λεύσιμον ἄταν
ἀποφεύγουσα, τεθρίππων
ὠκιστᾶν χαλᾶν ἐπιβᾶσ᾽
ἢ πρύμνας ἐπὶ ναῶν;

1223 ἐν ψ- Reiske: cf. Aesch. *Su.* 942-3
1231 φανερᾶς Willink: φανερὰ L
1232 ᾽κ σπονδὰς post Bothe (σπονδᾶς) Willink: σπονδὰς ἐκ L
1233 ὀλοοῖς post Nauck (ὀλοᾶς) Willink: θοᾶς L
1234 φόνου Reiske: -ῳ L

should be put to death by stoning, seeing that she tried to kill someone dedicated to the god and tried to desecrate the sanctuary with murder. All the city is looking for her, a woman who has sorrily rushed down a sorry road. She wanted Phoebus to give her children, but instead as well as children she has lost her own life.

Exit SERVANT *by Eisodos A.*

CHORUS

Luckless as I am, I have no way
to turn death aside.
All too plain is this fact
from the all too plain libation
of Dionysus' vine mingled with
the deadly gore of the serpent:
the victims for the world below stand plainly revealed,
a misfortune for my life
and death by stoning for my mistress.
What winged flight shall I take,
what path to the dark recesses of the earth,
to escape death
by stoning, mounting
the swift hooves of a chariot team
or the stern of a ship?

1237 δεσποίνᾳ Hermann: δέσποινα L
1239 σκοτίους μυχοὺς Hartung: -ων -ῶν L

—οὐκ ἔστι λαθεῖν, ὅτε μὴ χρῄζων
1245 θεὸς ἐκκλέπτει.
τί ποτ᾽, ὦ μελέα δέσποινα, μένει
ψυχῇ σε παθεῖν; ἆρα θέλουσαι
δρᾶσαί τι κακὸν τοὺς πέλας αὐταὶ
πεισόμεθ᾽ ὥσπερ τὸ δίκαιον;

ΚΡΕΟΥΣΑ

1250 πρόσπολοι, διωκόμεσθα θανασίμους ἐπὶ σφαγάς,
Πυθίᾳ ψήφῳ κρατηθεῖσ᾽, ἔκδοτος δὲ γίγνομαι.

ΧΟΡΟΣ

ἴσμεν, ὦ τάλαινα, τὰς σὰς συμφοράς, ἵν᾽ εἶ τύχης.

ΚΡΕΟΥΣΑ

ποῖ φύγω δῆτ᾽; ἐκ γὰρ οἴκων προύλαβον μόλις
πόδα
μὴ θανεῖν, κλοπῇ δ᾽ ἀφῖγμαι διαφυγοῦσα πολε-
μίους.

ΧΟΡΟΣ

1255 ποῖ δ᾽ ἂν ἄλλοσ᾽ ἢ 'πὶ βωμόν;

ΚΡΕΟΥΣΑ

καὶ τί μοι πλέον τόδε;

ΧΟΡΟΣ

ἱκέτιν οὐ θέμις φονεύειν.

ΚΡΕΟΥΣΑ

τῷ νόμῳ δέ γ᾽ ὄλλυμαι.

ION

CHORUS LEADER

It is not possible to hide unless a god should be willing to
steal us from view. Poor mistress, what suffering awaits
your heart? We tried to harm others: shall we not justly suf-
fer harm ourselves?

Enter CREUSA *in haste by Eisodos A.*

CREUSA

Serving women, I have been condemned by the Del-
phians' verdict! They are looking for me to put me to
death! My life is forfeit!

CHORUS LEADER

We know, poor lady, where you stand in misfortune.

CREUSA

Where shall I take refuge? I barely ran out of the house in
time to escape death. I gave my enemies the slip and came
here by stealth.

CHORUS LEADER

Where else but at the altar?

CREUSA

What good will that do me?

CHORUS LEADER

It is unlawful to slay a suppliant.

CREUSA

But the law is putting me to death!

1253 προύβαλον G. Schmid

ΧΟΡΟΣ

χειρία γ᾿ ἁλοῦσα.

ΚΡΕΟΥΣΑ

καὶ μὴν οἵδ᾿ ἀγωνισταὶ πικροὶ
δεῦρ᾿ ἐπείγονται ξιφήρεις.

ΧΟΡΟΣ

ἵζε νυν πυρᾶς ἔπι.
κἂν θάνῃς γὰρ ἐνθάδ᾿ οὖσα, τοῖς ἀποκτείνασί σε
1260 προστρόπαιον αἷμα θήσεις· οἰστέον δὲ τὴν τύχην.

ΙΩΝ

ὦ ταυρόμορφον ὄμμα Κηφισοῦ πατρός,
οἵαν ἔχιδναν τήνδ᾿ ἔφυσας ἢ πυρὸς
δράκοντ᾿ ἀναβλέποντα φοινίαν φλόγα,
ᾗ τόλμα πᾶσ᾿ ἔνεστιν οὐδ᾿ ἥσσων ἔφυ
1265 Γοργοῦς σταλαγμῶν, οἷς ἔμελλέ με κτενεῖν.
1269 ἐσθλοῦ δ᾿ ἔκυρσα δαίμονος, πρὶν ἐς πόλιν
1270 μολεῖν Ἀθηνῶν χὐπὸ μητρυιὰν πεσεῖν.
ἐν συμμάχοις γὰρ ἀνεμετρησάμην φρένας
τὰς σάς, ὅσον μοι πῆμα δυσμενής τ᾿ ἔφυς·
ἔσω γὰρ ἄν με περιβαλοῦσα δωμάτων
1274 ἄρδην ἂν ἐξέπεμψας εἰς Ἅιδου δόμους.
1266 λάζυσθ᾿, ἵν᾿ αὐτῆς τοὺς ἀκηράτους πλόκους
1267 κόμης καταξήνωσι Παρνασοῦ πλάκες,
1268 ὅθεν πετραῖον ἅλμα δισκηθήσεται.

1266-8 post 1274 trai. Kovacs

466

CHORUS LEADER

Yes, if it can capture you.

Enter by Eisodos B ION *with a group of Delphians armed with swords.*

CREUSA

But see, here they come on hurrying feet, sword in hand, my hated adversaries.

CHORUS LEADER

Then sit upon the altar. If you are killed there, you will stain your killers with a suppliant's blood. You must endure your fate.

Creusa begins to move toward the altar, then stops.

ION

O Cephisus, bull-faced river god,[39] her ancestor, what a viper you have begotten in her, a snake with murderous fire in its glance! She stops at nothing and is more dangerous than the drops of Gorgon blood with which she meant to kill me! My guardian spirit did me a good turn before I came to Athens and fell under the power of a stepmother. While I had allies about me I took the measure of your mind and learned what a menace and enemy you are to me. If you had trapped me in your house, you would have destroyed me utterly. Seize her so that she may be hurled from the peaks of Parnassus and her unsullied tresses smashed on the rocks!

---

[39] The Greeks often imagined river gods in the form of bulls. The Cephisus was one of the rivers of Attica.

1279 ἴδεσθε τὴν πανοῦργον, ἐκ τέχνης τέχνην
1280 οἵαν ἔπλεξε· βωμὸν ἔπτηξεν θεοῦ
1281 ὡς οὐ δίκην δώσουσα τῶν εἰργασμένων.
1275 ἀλλ' οὔτε βωμὸς οὔτ' Ἀπόλλωνος δόμος
   σώσει σ'· ὁ δ' οἶκτος †ὁ σὸς† ἐμοὶ κρείσσων πάρα
   καὶ μητρὶ τἠμῇ· καὶ γὰρ εἰ τὸ σῶμά μοι
1278 ἄπεστιν αὐτῆς, τοὔνομ' οὐκ ἄπεστί πω.

ΚΡΕΟΥΣΑ

1282 ἀπεννέπω σε μὴ κατακτείνειν ἐμὲ
   ὑπέρ τ' ἐμαυτῆς τοῦ θεοῦ θ' ἵν' ἔσταμεν.

ΙΩΝ

   τί δ' ἐστὶ Φοίβῳ σοί τε κοινὸν ἐν μέσῳ;

ΚΡΕΟΥΣΑ

1285 ἱερὸν τὸ σῶμα τῷ θεῷ δίδωμ' ἔχειν.

ΙΩΝ

   κἄπειτ' ἔκαινες φαρμάκοις τὸν τοῦ θεοῦ;

ΚΡΕΟΥΣΑ

   ἀλλ' οὐκέτ' ἦσθα Λοξίου, πατρὸς δὲ σοῦ.

ΙΩΝ

   ἀλλ' ἐγενόμεσθα· πατρὸς ἀπουσίᾳ λέγω.

ΚΡΕΟΥΣΑ

   οὐκοῦν τότ' ἦσθα· νῦν δ' ἐγώ, σὺ δ' οὐκέτι.

1275-8 post 1281 trai. Musgrave, del. Diggle
1286 ἔκαινες Duport: ἔκτανες L
1288 πατρὸς Canter: π- δ' L ἀπουσίᾳ Kirchhoff: οὐσίαν
L: sed fort. delendi sunt 1287-8

Creusa runs to the altar and takes her seat on it.

See the wicked creature, weaving guile upon guile! She is cowering at the altar of the god, thinking that thus she will escape punishment! But neither the altar nor the temple of Apollo will save you. Any pity owed to you belongs to me in greater measure—and to my mother. For even though she is physically absent, in name she is not far off.

CREUSA
Do not kill me! I forbid you in my name and in that of the god in whose precincts we stand!

ION
Why, what do you and Phoebus have in common?

CREUSA
I have given myself over to the god as sacrosanct.

ION
You tried to kill me. Was I not the god's boy?

CREUSA
You were no longer Loxias' boy but your father's.

ION
But I became his boy. I mean while my father was absent.

CREUSA
Well, at that time you were. But now it is I, not you, who belong to the god.

EURIPIDES

ΙΩΝ

1290 οὐκ εὐσεβεῖς δέ· τἀμὰ δ' εὐσεβῆ τότ' ἦν.

ΚΡΕΟΥΣΑ

ἔκτεινά σ' ὄντα πολέμιον δόμοις ἐμοῖς.

ΙΩΝ

οὔτοι σὺν ὅπλοις ἦλθον ἐς τὴν σὴν χθόνα.

ΚΡΕΟΥΣΑ

μάλιστα· κἀπίμπρης γ' Ἐρεχθέως δόμους.

ΙΩΝ

ποίοισι πανοῖς ἢ πυρὸς ποίᾳ φλογί;

ΚΡΕΟΥΣΑ

1295 ἔμελλες οἰκεῖν τἀμ', ἐμοῦ βίᾳ λαβών.

ΙΩΝ

1300 κἄπειτα τοῦ μέλλειν μ' ἀπέκτεινες φόβῳ;

ΚΡΕΟΥΣΑ

1301 ὡς μὴ θάνοιμί γ', εἰ σὺ μὴ μέλλων τύχοις.

ΙΩΝ

1302 φθονεῖς ἄπαις οὖσ', εἰ πατὴρ ἐξηῦρέ με.

ΚΡΕΟΥΣΑ

1303 σὺ τῶν ἀτέκνων δῆτ' ἀναρπάσεις δόμους;

1290 δέ West: γε L
1300-3 post 1295 trai. Nauck

470

ION

But I was pious, and you are guilty of impiety.[40]

CREUSA

I tried to kill you as the foe of my house.

ION

I did not march into your land with weapons, you know.

CREUSA

You most certainly did, and you were trying to set fire to the house of Erechtheus!

ION

With what torch and what flame?

CREUSA

You intended to control what is mine, taking it from me by force.

ION

So for fear of "intentions" you tried to kill me?

CREUSA

Yes, so that I would not be killed in case you ceased merely "intending."

ION

Just because you are childless you begrudge my father's finding me.

CREUSA

So you'd seize the houses of the childless, would you?

---

40 I. e. by attempting to commit murder. In her next line Creusa tries to maintain that the situation was one of war in which killing an enemy is not impious.

ΙΩΝ

1296 πατρός γε γῆν διδόντος ἣν ἐκτήσατο.

ΚΡΕΟΥΣΑ

τοῖς Αἰόλου δὲ πῶς μετῆν τῆς Παλλάδος;

ΙΩΝ

ὅπλοισιν αὐτήν, οὐ λόγοις, ἐρρύσατο.

ΚΡΕΟΥΣΑ

1299 ἐπίκουρος οἰκήτωρ γ' ἂν οὐκ εἴη χθονός.

ΙΩΝ

1304 ἡμῖν δέ γ' ἅμα ⟨τῷ⟩ πατρὶ γῆς οὐκ ἦν μέρος;

ΚΡΕΟΥΣΑ

1305 ὅσ' ἀσπὶς ἔγχος θ'· ἥδε σοι παμπησία.

ΙΩΝ

ἔκλειπε βωμὸν καὶ θεηλάτους ἕδρας.

ΚΡΕΟΥΣΑ

τὴν σὴν ὅπου σοι μητέρ' ἐστὶ νουθέτει.

ΙΩΝ

σὺ δ' οὐχ ὑφέξεις ζημίαν κτείνουσ' ἐμέ;

ΚΡΕΟΥΣΑ

ἤν γ' ἐντὸς ἀδύτων τῶνδέ με σφάξαι θέλῃς.

ΙΩΝ

1310 τίς ἡδονή σοι θεοῦ θανεῖν ἐν στέμμασιν;

1297 τῆς Musurus: τῶν L
1304 ἅμα ⟨τῷ⟩ Page: ἀλλὰ L
1306 θεοδμήτους Heiland: θυηπόλους Diggle

472

ION

Yes, since my father is giving me the land which he won.

CREUSA

What did the sons of Aeolus have to do with Pallas' land?

ION

He came to its rescue with arms, not words.

CREUSA

A mere ally may not dwell in the land as his own.

ION

But surely I have a share in the land together with my father?

CREUSA

Yes, a shield and spear's worth: that is your whole estate.

ION

Leave the altar, this holy place in which you sit!

CREUSA

Give that counsel to your mother, wherever she may be!

ION

Shall you not pay the penalty for murdering me?

CREUSA

Yes, if you are willing to cut my throat within this holy place.

ION

What pleasure do you find in dying amidst the god's wreaths?

ΚΡΕΟΥΣΑ

λυπήσομέν τιν᾽ ὧν λελυπήμεσθ᾽ ὕπο.

ΙΩΝ

φεῦ.

δεινόν γε, θνητοῖς τοὺς νόμους ὡς οὐ καλῶς
ἔθηκεν ὁ θεὸς οὐδ᾽ ἀπὸ γνώμης σοφῆς·
τοὺς μὲν γὰρ ἀδίκους βωμὸν οὐχ ἵζειν ἐχρῆν
1315 ἀλλ᾽ ἐξελαύνειν· οὐδὲ γὰρ ψαύειν καλὸν
θεῶν πονηρᾷ χειρί, τοῖσι δ᾽ ἐνδίκοις·
ἱερὰ καθίζειν ⟨δ᾽⟩ ὅστις ἠδικεῖτ᾽ ἐχρῆν,
καὶ μὴ ᾽πὶ ταὐτὸ τοῦτ᾽ ἰόντ᾽ ἔχειν ἴσον
τόν τ᾽ ἐσθλὸν ὄντα τόν τε μὴ θεῶν πάρα.

ΠΡΟΦΗΤΙΣ

1320 ἐπίσχες, ὦ παῖ· τρίποδα γὰρ χρηστήριον
λιποῦσα θριγκὸν τόνδ᾽ ὑπερβάλλω ποδὶ
Φοίβου προφῆτις, τρίποδος ἀρχαῖον νόμον
σῴζουσα, πασῶν Δελφίδων ἐξαίρετος.

ΙΩΝ

χαῖρ᾽, ὦ φίλη μοι μῆτερ, οὐ τεκοῦσά περ.

ΠΡΟΦΗΤΙΣ

1325 ἀλλ᾽ οὖν λεγόμεθά γ᾽· ἡ φάτις δ᾽ οὔ μοι πικρά.

ΙΩΝ

ἤκουσας ὥς μ᾽ ἔκτεινεν ἥδε μηχαναῖς;

1316 πονηρᾷ χειρί Owen: -ὰν χεῖρα L
1317 ⟨δ᾽⟩ Owen
1321 θριγκὸν τόνδ᾽ Dindorf: -οῦ τοῦδ᾽ L

CREUSA

I will cause grief to one of those who caused me grief.

ION

Ah, it is monstrous how bad and unintelligent are the laws
the god has made for mortals! He ought not to let the
wicked sit at his altar but drive them away. It is not right for
an evil hand to touch the gods but only a righteous one.
Those who are wronged should be given a seat: just and
unjust should not come to the same place and receive the
same treatment from the gods.

Enter from the skene *the* PRIESTESS *carrying a wicker
cradle.*

PRIESTESS

Stop, my son! I, Phoebus' priestess, chosen out of all the
women of Delphi to preserve the tripod's ancient law, have
left the oracular tripod and crossed this threshold.

ION

Dear mother in all but birth, I greet you!

PRIESTESS

That is what I am called, and I do not find the name unwel-
come.

ION

Have you heard how this woman tried to murder me by
guile?

1325 λεγόμεθά γ' Elmsley: λεγόμεσθ' L

EURIPIDES

ΠΡΟΦΗΤΙΣ

ἤκουσα· καὶ σὺ δ' ὠμὸς ὢν ἁμαρτάνεις.

ΙΩΝ

οὐ χρή με τοὺς κτείνοντας ἀνταπολλύναι;

ΠΡΟΦΗΤΙΣ

προγόνοις δάμαρτες δυσμενεῖς ἀεί ποτε.

ΙΩΝ

1330 ἡμεῖς δὲ μητρυιαῖς γε πάσχοντες κακῶς.

ΠΡΟΦΗΤΙΣ

μὴ ταῦτα· λείπων ἱερὰ καὶ στείχων πάτραν . . .

ΙΩΝ

τί δή με δρᾶσαι νουθετούμενον χρεών;

ΠΡΟΦΗΤΙΣ

. . . καθαρὸς Ἀθήνας ἔλθ' ὑπ' οἰωνῶν καλῶν.

ΙΩΝ

καθαρὸς ἅπας τοι πολεμίους ὃς ἂν κτάνῃ.

ΠΡΟΦΗΤΙΣ

1335 μὴ σύ γε· παρ' ἡμῶν δ' ἔκλαβ' οὓς ἔχω λόγους.

ΙΩΝ

λέγοις ἄν· εὔνους δ' οὖσ' ἐρεῖς ὅσ' ἂν λέγῃς.

ΠΡΟΦΗΤΙΣ

ὁρᾷς τόδ' ἄγγος χερὸς ὑπ' ἀγκάλαις ἐμαῖς;

ΙΩΝ

ὁρῶ παλαιὰν ἀντίπηγ' ἐν στέμμασιν.

PRIESTESS

I have heard. But you too are wrong to be savage.

ION

Should I not kill those who try to kill me?

PRIESTESS

Wives are always ill-disposed to earlier children.

ION

And I, when ill treated, to stepmothers.

PRIESTESS

Do not be so. As you leave the temple and go to your home-
land . . .

ION

What should I do? What is your advice?

PRIESTESS

. . . go to Athens with pure hands and good omens.

ION

Everyone who kills the enemy is pure.

PRIESTESS

Don't! Listen to what I have to say.

ION

Speak. Whatever you say will be said in good will.

PRIESTESS

Do you see this vessel I'm holding?

ION

I see an old cradle decked with wool.

1327 δ' Hermann: γ' L   1333 καθαρὸς Porson: -ῶς L
1335 ἔκμαθ' Hartung   1337 ὑπαγκάλισμ' ἐμῆς Elmsley

ΠΡΟΦΗΤΙΣ

ἐν τῇδέ σ᾽ ἔλαβον νεόγονον βρέφος ποτέ.

ΙΩΝ

1340 τί φῄς; ὁ μῦθος εἰσενήνεκται νέος.

ΠΡΟΦΗΤΙΣ

σιγῇ γὰρ εἶχον αὐτά· νῦν δὲ δείκνυμεν.

ΙΩΝ

πῶς οὖν ἔκρυπτες τάδε λαβοῦσ᾽ ἡμᾶς πάλαι;

ΠΡΟΦΗΤΙΣ

ὁ θεὸς ἐβούλετ᾽ ἐν δόμοις <σ᾽> ἔχειν λάτριν.

ΙΩΝ

νῦν δ᾽ οὐχὶ χρῄζει; τῷ τόδε γνῶναί με χρή;

ΠΡΟΦΗΤΙΣ

1345 πατέρα κατειπὼν τῆσδέ σ᾽ ἐκπέμπει χθονός.

ΙΩΝ

σὺ δ᾽ ἐκ κελευσμῶν ἢ πόθεν σῴζεις τάδε;

ΠΡΟΦΗΤΙΣ

ἐνθύμιόν μοι τότε τίθησι Λοξίας . . .

ΙΩΝ

τί χρῆμα δρᾶσαι; λέγε, πέραινε σοὺς λόγους.

ΠΡΟΦΗΤΙΣ

. . . σῶσαι τόδ᾽ εὕρημ᾽ ἐς τὸν ὄντα νῦν χρόνον.

1342 τάδε Fix: τόδε L
1343 θεὸς Badham: θεός σ᾽ L   <σ᾽> Badham
1348 δρᾶσαι Musgrave: -σειν L

ION

PRIESTESS

It was in this that I received you as an infant long ago.

ION

What? This is a story I have not heard before.

PRIESTESS

I said nothing about these objects, but now I reveal them.

ION

Why did you not tell me that you had received them long ago?

PRIESTESS

The god wanted to have you in his temple as his servant.

ION

But now he does not wish to? How can I be sure of this?

PRIESTESS

By naming your father he is sending you out of the country.

ION

Why did you save these things? Were you told to?

PRIESTESS

Loxias at that time put the thought in my mind . . .

ION

To do what? Continue your story.

PRIESTESS

. . . to keep what I had found until the present moment.

ΙΩΝ

1350 ἔχει δέ μοι τί κέρδος ἢ τίνα βλάβην;

ΠΡΟΦΗΤΙΣ

ἐνθάδε κέκρυπται σπάργαν᾽ οἷς ἐνῆσθα σύ.

ΙΩΝ

μητρὸς τάδ᾽ ἡμῖν ἐκφέρεις ζητήματα;

ΠΡΟΦΗΤΙΣ

ἐπεί γ᾽ ὁ δαίμων βούλεται· πάροιθε δ᾽ οὔ.

ΙΩΝ

ὦ μακαρία μοι φασμάτων ἥδ᾽ ἡμέρα.

ΠΡΟΦΗΤΙΣ

1355 λαβών νυν αὐτὰ τὴν τεκοῦσαν ἐκπόνει.

ΙΩΝ

πᾶσάν γ᾽ ἐπελθὼν Ἀσιάδ᾽ Εὐρώπης θ᾽ ὅρους.

ΠΡΟΦΗΤΙΣ

γνώσῃ τάδ᾽ αὐτός. τοῦ θεοῦ δ᾽ ἕκατί σε
ἔθρεψά τ᾽, ὦ παῖ, καὶ τάδ᾽ ἀποδίδωμί σοι,
ἃ κεῖνος ἀκέλευστόν μ᾽ ἐβουλήθη λαβεῖν.
1360 σῶσαί θ᾽· ὅτου δέ γ᾽ οὕνεκ᾽ οὐκ ἔχω λέγειν.
ᾔδει δὲ θνητῶν οὔτις ἀνθρώπων τάδε
ἔχοντας ἡμᾶς οὐδ᾽ ἵν᾽ ἦν κεκρυμμένα.
καὶ χαῖρ᾽· ἴσον γάρ σ᾽ ὡς τεκοῦσ᾽ ἀσπάζομαι.
[ἄρξαι δ᾽ ὅθεν σὴν μητέρα ζητεῖν σε χρή·
1365 πρῶτον μὲν εἴ τις Δελφίδων τεκοῦσά σε

1351 σπάργαν᾽ οἷς ἐνῆσθα Reiske: σπαργάνοισιν οἶσθα L

480

ION

What benefit or what harm does it hold for me?

PRIESTESS

In it are hid the infant clothes you wore.

ION

Are you bringing them out as clues to find my mother?

PRIESTESS

Yes, since that is the god's will. Before it was not so.

ION

O day blessed with revelations!

PRIESTESS

Take this, therefore, and search diligently for your mother.

She gives him the cradle.

ION

Yes, over the bounds of Europe and all of Asia!

PRIESTESS

You must make that choice. It was by the god's will that I
raised you and give these things to you. He wished me of
my own accord to take and save these things. Why he
wished so, I cannot say. No mortal man knew that I had
them or where they were hidden. Farewell! I greet you as a
mother would! [As to the point where you must begin the
search for your mother, first see if any unmarried Delphian

1354 μακαρία Hermann: -ίων L   1356 γ' Kirchhoff: δ' L
1357-62 suspectos habet Diggle, 1359-62 Kraus
1360 δέ γ' οὕνεκ' Badham: δ' ἐβούλεθ' οὕνεκ' L
1364-8 del. Hirzel

ἐς τούσδε ναοὺς ἐξέθηκε παρθένος,
ἔπειτα δ᾽ εἴ τις Ἑλλάς. ἐξ ἡμῶν δ᾽ ἔχεις
ἅπαντα Φοίβου θ᾽, ὃς μετέσχε τῆς τύχης.]

ΙΩΝ

φεῦ φεῦ· κατ᾽ ὄσσων ὡς ὑγρὸν βάλλω δάκρυ,
1370 ἐκεῖσε τὸν νοῦν δοὺς ὅθ᾽ ἡ τεκοῦσά με
κρυφαῖα νυμφευθεῖσ᾽ ἀπημπόλα λάθρᾳ
καὶ μαστὸν οὐκ ἐπέσχεν· ἀλλ᾽ ἀνώνυμος
ἐν θεοῦ μελάθροις εἶχον οἰκέτην βίον.
τὰ τοῦ θεοῦ μὲν χρηστά, τοῦ δὲ δαίμονος
1375 βαρέα· χρόνον γὰρ ὅν μ᾽ ἐχρῆν ἐν ἀγκάλαις
μητρὸς τρυφῆσαι καί τι τερφθῆναι βίου
ἀπεστερήθην φιλτάτης μητρὸς τροφῆς.
τλήμων δὲ χἡ τεκοῦσά μ᾽· ὡς ταὐτὸν πάθος
πέπονθε, παιδὸς ἀπολέσασα χαρμονάς.
1380 καὶ νῦν λαβὼν τήνδ᾽ ἀντίπηγ᾽ οἴσω θεῷ
ἀνάθημ᾽, ἵν᾽ εὕρω μηδὲν ὧν οὐ βούλομαι.
εἰ γάρ με δούλη τυγχάνει τεκοῦσά τις,
εὑρεῖν κάκιον μητέρ᾽ ἢ σιγῶντ᾽ ἐᾶν.
ὦ Φοῖβε, ναοῖς ἀνατίθημι τήνδε σοῖς.
1385 καίτοι τί πάσχω; τοῦ θεοῦ προθυμίᾳ
πολεμῶ, τὰ μητρὸς σύμβολ᾽ ὃς σέσωκέ μοι.
ἀνοικτέον τάδ᾽ ἐστὶ καὶ τολμητέον·
τὰ γὰρ πεπρωμέν᾽ οὐχ ὑπερβαίην ποτ᾽ ἄν.
ὦ στέμμαθ᾽ ἱερά, τί ποτέ μοι κεκεύθατε,
1390 καὶ σύνδεθ᾽ οἷσι τἄμ᾽ ἐφρουρήθη φίλα;

1372 οὐκ ἐπέσχεν Dobree: οὐχ ὑπέσχεν L

woman gave birth to you and exposed you in the temple, then whether any Greek woman. You have everything from me and from Phoebus, who had a share in your fate.]

She embraces him. Exit PRIESTESS *into the* skene.

ION

Ah me! My eyes run with tears as I cast my mind back to the time when my mother, after a clandestine affair, disposed of me in secret without giving me her breast. Instead, nameless in the god's temple I had the life of a servant. Though the god has been good to me, my fate has been heavy. At the time when I ought to have lived a life of luxurious enjoyment in my mother's arms, I was deprived of my dear mother's nurture. But my mother too was unblest. How similar is her suffering to mine, since she lost the joy of her child!

Now I will take this cradle and dedicate it to the god, so that I may not make an unwelcome discovery. If some slave woman bore me, it is worse to find my mother than to say nothing and let matters be. Phoebus, I dedicate this cradle in your temple!

Yet what is wrong with me? I am fighting against the purposes of the god, who saved these tokens of my mother for me. I must have the courage to unwrap them. I will never be able to avoid my fate. What do you conceal for me, you holy fillets and clasps that have kept safe what is

---

1378 χή Schaefer: θ' ή L
1385 τῆ Wilamowitz
1386 σέσωκέ Dobree: ἔσωσε L
1388 οὐχ Nauck: οὐδ' L

ἰδοὺ περίπτυγμ᾽ ἀντίπηγος εὐκύκλου
ὡς οὐ γεγήρακ᾽ ἔκ τινος θεηλάτου,
εὐρώς τ᾽ ἄπεστι πλεγμάτων· ὁ δ᾽ ἐν μέσῳ
χρόνος πολὺς δὴ τοῖσδε θησαυρίσμασιν.

ΚΡΕΟΥΣΑ

1395 τί δῆτα φάσμα τῶν ἀνελπίστων ὁρῶ;

ΙΩΝ

σίγα σύ· πῆμα καὶ πάροιθεν ἦσθά μοι.

ΚΡΕΟΥΣΑ

οὐκ ἐν σιωπῇ τἀμά· μή με νουθέτει.
ὁρῶ γὰρ ἄγγος ᾧ ᾽ξέθηκ᾽ ἐγώ ποτε
σέ γ᾽, ὦ τέκνον μοι, βρέφος ἔτ᾽ ὄντα νήπιον,
1400 Κέκροπος ἐς ἄντρα καὶ Μακρὰς πετρηρεφεῖς.
λείψω δὲ βωμὸν τόνδε, κεἰ θανεῖν με χρή.

ΙΩΝ

λάζυσθε τήνδε· θεομανὴς γὰρ ἥλατο
βωμοῦ λιποῦσα ξόανα· δεῖτε δ᾽ ὠλένας.

ΚΡΕΟΥΣΑ

σφάζοντες οὐ λήγοιτ᾽ ἄν· ὡς ἀνθέξομαι
1405 καὶ τῆσδε καὶ σοῦ τῶν γ᾽ ἔσω κεκρυμμένων.

ΙΩΝ

τάδ᾽ οὐχὶ δεινά; ῥυσιάζομαι λόγῳ.

1396 πῆμα Broadhead: πολλὰ L   ἦσθά Musgrave: οἶσθά
L   1399 del. Cobet   1405 γ᾽ ἔσω post Whitman (γε iam P)
et Tyrwhitt (τ᾽ ἔσω) Kovacs: τε σῶν L
1406 δόλῳ Jacobs

484

precious to me? See! The covering of this round cradle has miraculously not grown old. Its wicker weaving shows no decay. Yet a long time has passed since these things were stored away.

CREUSA

What startling vision do I see?

ION

Quiet! You caused me grief before as well.

CREUSA

This is no time for me to be silent. Do not admonish me. I see the vessel in which I long ago exposed you, my son, as a newborn babe at the cave of Cecrops and the Long Cliffs. I will leave this altar, even if I must die.

She leaves the altar and runs toward Ion.

ION

Seize her! Deranged by some god she has leapt from the altar, leaving the statue behind! Bind her hands!

Some of the Delphians seize her.

CREUSA

Go on, cut my throat! For I dispute with both you and her your claim to what is hidden within.

ION

Is this not monstrous? Her words rob me of what is mine!

ΚΡΕΟΥΣΑ

οὔκ, ἀλλὰ σοῖς φίλοισιν εὑρίσκῃ φίλος.

ΙΩΝ

ἐγὼ φίλος σός; κᾆτά μ' ἔκτεινες λάθρᾳ;

ΚΡΕΟΥΣΑ

παῖς γ', εἰ τόδ' ἐστὶ τοῖς τεκοῦσι φίλτατον.

ΙΩΝ

1410 παῦσαι ⟨πλοκὰς⟩ πλέκουσα· λήψομαί σ' ἐγώ.

ΚΡΕΟΥΣΑ

ἐς τοῦθ' ἱκοίμην, τοῦδε τοξεύω, τέκνον.

ΙΩΝ

κενὸν τόδ' ἄγγος ἢ στέγει πλήρωμά τι;

ΚΡΕΟΥΣΑ

σά γ' ἔνδυθ', οἷσί σ' ἐξέθηκ' ἐγώ ποτε.

ΙΩΝ

καὶ τοὔνομ' αὐτῶν ἐξερεῖς πρὶν εἰσιδεῖν;

ΚΡΕΟΥΣΑ

1415 κἂν μὴ φράσω γε, κατθανεῖν ὑφίσταμαι.

ΙΩΝ

λέγ'· ὡς ἔχει τι δεινὸν ἥ γε τόλμα σου.

ΚΡΕΟΥΣΑ

σκέψασθ' ὃ παῖς ποτ' οὖσ' ὕφασμ' ὕφην' ἐγώ.

ΙΩΝ

ποῖόν τι; πολλὰ παρθένων ὑφάσματα.

ION

CREUSA

No: you are shown to be dear to your own.

ION

I dear to you, who tried to kill me by stealth?

CREUSA

Yes, dear as my son, if that is what is dearest to a parent.

ION

Stop weaving ⟨guile⟩! I shall catch you!

CREUSA

Yes, I pray that you may! That is my goal, my son!

ION

Is this vessel empty or is there something inside it?

CREUSA

It holds the clothes in which I exposed you.

ION

And will you tell me what they are before you see them?

CREUSA

Yes, and if I fail, I consent to my death.

ION

Say on: your boldness inspires awe.

CREUSA

See, all of you, the weaving I did as a girl.

ION

What kind of weaving? Maidens weave many things.

1408 σοι Hermann   1410 ⟨πλοκὰς⟩ Herwerden σ' Tyr-
whitt: δ' L   ἐγώ Herwerden: ἐγὼ καλῶς L
    1416 ἥ γε τόλμα Jodrell: ἡ τ- γε L

EURIPIDES

KΡΕΟΥΣΑ

οὐ τέλεον, οἷον δ᾽ ἐκδίδαγμα κερκίδος.

IΩN

1420 μορφὴν ἔχον τίν'; ὥς με μὴ ταύτῃ λάβῃς.

KΡΕΟΥΣΑ

Γοργὼ μὲν ἐν μέσοισιν ἠτρίοις πέπλων.

IΩN

ὦ Ζεῦ, τίς ἡμᾶς ἐκκυνηγετεῖ πότμος;

KΡΕΟΥΣΑ

κεκρασπέδωται δ᾽ ὄφεσιν αἰγίδος τρόπον.

IΩN

ἰδού·
τόδ᾽ ἔσθ᾽ ὕφασμα †θέσφαθ᾽ ὡς εὑρίσκομεν†.

KΡΕΟΥΣΑ

1425 ὦ χρόνιον ἱστῶν παρθένευμα τῶν ἐμῶν.

IΩN

ἔστιν τι πρὸς τῷδ᾽ ἢ μόνον τόδ᾽ εὐτυχεῖς;

KΡΕΟΥΣΑ

δράκοντες, ἀρχαίῳ τι πάγχρυσον γένει
δώρημ᾽ Ἀθάνας, οἷς τέκν᾽ ἐντρέφειν λέγει,
Ἐριχθονίου γε τοῦ πάλαι μιμήματα.

IΩN

1430 τί δρᾶν, τί χρῆσθαι, φράζε μοι, χρυσώματι;

1421 Γοργὼ L. Dindorf: Γοργὼν L   ἠτρίοις Musgrave:
-ίων L   1424 ἔφησθα θ᾽ ὡς εὑρίσκομεν A. Y. Campbell

488

CREUSA

One not finished: you could call it my shuttle's apprentice
work.

ION

And its design? Don't try to trick me here!

CREUSA

In the middle of the warp it has a Gorgon.

ION

O Zeus, what is this fate that tracks me down?

CREUSA

And it is fringed with serpents like an aegis.

ION

(*Holding it up*) See! Here is the weaving! I find you speak
the truth!

CREUSA

O maiden loomwork, woven so long ago!

ION

Is there anything else, or does your luck stop here?

CREUSA

Snakes, Athena's gift all-golden to my ancient family: she
bids us raise our children dressed in these, in imitation of
ancient Erichthonius.

ION

What use does she bid you make of this golden ornament?

1426 μόνον τόδ' Usener: μόνῳ τῷδ' L   1427 ἀρχαίῳ . . .
πάγχρυσον Wilamowitz: ἀρχαῖον . . . παγχρύσῳ L
    1428 οἷς Page: ἢ L
    1430 χρυσώματι L. Dindorf: -ώμια L

ΚΡΕΟΥΣΑ

δέραια παιδὶ νεογόνῳ φέρειν, τέκνον.

ΙΩΝ

ἔνεισιν οἵδε· τὸ δὲ τρίτον ποθῶ μαθεῖν.

ΚΡΕΟΥΣΑ

1433 στέφανον ἐλαίας ἀμφέθηκά σοι τότε,
1435 ὃς εἴπερ ἐστίν, οὔποτ' ἐκλείπει χλόην,
1436 θάλλει δ', ἐλαίας ἐξ ἀκηράτου γεγὼς
1434 ἣν πρῶτ' Ἀθάνας σκόπελος ἐξηνέγκατο.

ΙΩΝ

ὦ φιλτάτη μοι μῆτερ, ἄσμενός σ' ἰδὼν
πρὸς ἀσμένας πέπτωκα σὰς παρηίδας.

ΚΡΕΟΥΣΑ

ὦ τέκνον, ὦ φῶς μητρὶ κρεῖσσον ἡλίου
1440 (συγγνώσεται γὰρ ὁ θεός), ἐν χεροῖν σ' ἔχω,
ἄελπτον εὕρημ', ὃν κατὰ γᾶς ἐνέρων
χθονίων μέτα Περσεφόνας τ' ἐδόκουν ναίειν.

ΙΩΝ

ἀλλ', ὦ φίλη μοι μῆτερ, ἐν χεροῖν σέθεν
ὁ κατθανών τε κοὐ θανὼν φαντάζομαι.

ΚΡΕΟΥΣΑ

1445 ἰὼ ἰὼ λαμπρᾶς αἰθέρος ἀμπτυχαί,
τίν' αὐδὰν ἀύσω βοάσω; πόθεν μοι
συνέκυρσ' ἀδόκητος ἡδονά;

1434 post 1436 trai. Kraus   1436 ἀγηράτου Badham
1438 ἀσμένης L. Dindorf   1442 χθονίων Bothe: χθόνιον L

CREUSA

As a necklace for the newborn child to wear, my son.

ION

The snakes are there. But I long to hear of a third thing.

CREUSA

On that day I put on you a garland of olive leaves. If it is this garland, it has not lost its green but still grows, being sprung from the inviolable olive tree that Athena's crag first produced.

ION

(*running to embrace Creusa*) O mother most dear to me, with what joy do I see you! What joy is in your cheeks I rush to kiss!

CREUSA

O my child, dearer than sunlight to your mother
(the god will forgive my saying this), I have you in my
　　arms,
a finding I had not looked for, a child I thought
dwelt below with the shades and with Persephone!

ION

Well, dear mother, now I have come to your arms, I who died and am now alive!

CREUSA

Oh, oh, radiant expanse of heaven,
what word shall I speak or cry out? From whence
did this pleasure unlooked for come?

491

πόθεν ἐλάβομεν χαράν;

ΙΩΝ

1450 ἐμοὶ γενέσθαι πάντα μᾶλλον ἄν ποτε,
μῆτερ, παρέστη τῶνδ', ὅπως σός εἰμ' ἐγώ.

ΚΡΕΟΥΣΑ

ἔτι φόβῳ τρέμω.

ΙΩΝ

μῶν οὐκ ἔχειν μ' ἔχουσα;

ΚΡΕΟΥΣΑ

τὰς γὰρ ἐλπίδας
ἀπέβαλον πρόσω.
ἰὼ γύναι·
πόθεν ἔλαβες ἐμὸν βρέφος ἐς ἀγκάλας;
1455 τίν' ἀνὰ χέρα δόμους ἔβα Λοξίου;

ΙΩΝ

θεῖον τόδ'· ἀλλὰ τἀπίλοιπα τῆς τύχης
εὐδαιμονοῖμεν, ὡς τὰ πρόσθε δυστυχῆ.

ΚΡΕΟΥΣΑ

τέκνον, οὐκ ἀδάκρυτος ἐκλοχεύῃ,
γόοις δὲ ματρὸς ἐκ χερῶν ὁρίζῃ·
1460 νῦν δὲ γενειάσιν παρὰ σέθεν πνέω
μακαριωτάτας τυχοῦσ' ἡδονᾶς.

ΙΩΝ

τοὐμὸν λέγουσα καὶ τὸ σὸν κοινῶς λέγεις.

1449 πόθεν ⟨τάνδ'⟩ Willink

ION

Whence did I receive such joy?

ION

I would have thought anything more likely than this,
mother, that I am your son.

CREUSA

I am still trembling with fear.

ION

Fear that you have me but have me not?

CREUSA

Yes, for my hopes
I have lost ere now.
You there, priestess within!
From where did you take my child into your arms?
By whose hand did he come to the house of Loxias?

ION

This was the god's doing. But let us henceforth enjoy our
good fortune, just as our previous luck was bad.

CREUSA

My son, your birth was a tearful one,
and with wailing you were separated from my arms.
But now with your cheek against mine I am alive
and have found delight most blessed!

ION

You name my fortune as you name your own.

1454 πόθεν semel Hartung: bis L
1458 ὦ τέκνον, οὐκ ἄδακρυς Hermann
1462 κοινῇ Diggle

ΚΡΕΟΥΣΑ

ἄπαιδες οὐκέτ᾽ ἐσμὲν οὐδ᾽ ἄτεκνοι·
δῶμ᾽ ἑστιοῦται, γᾶ δ᾽ ἔχει τυράννους·
1465 ἀνηβᾷ δ᾽ Ἐρεχθεύς,
ὅ τε γηγενέτας δόμος οὐκέτι νύκτα δέρκεται,
ἀελίου δ᾽ ἀναβλέπει λαμπάσιν.

ΙΩΝ

μῆτερ, παρών μοι καὶ πατὴρ μετασχέτω
τῆς ἡδονῆς τῆσδ᾽ ἧς ἔδωχ᾽ ὑμῖν ἐγώ.

ΚΡΕΟΥΣΑ

1470 ὦ τέκνον,
τί φῄς; οἷον οἷον ἀνελέγχομαι.

ΙΩΝ

πῶς εἶπας;

ΚΡΕΟΥΣΑ

ἄλλοθεν γέγονας, ἄλλοθεν.

ΙΩΝ

ὤμοι· νόθον με παρθένευμ᾽ ἔτικτε σόν;

ΚΡΕΟΥΣΑ

οὐχ ὑπὸ λαμπάδων οὐδὲ χορευμάτων
1475 ὑμέναιος ἐμὸς σὸν ἔτικτε κάρα, τέκνον.

ΙΩΝ

αἰαῖ· πέφυκα δυσγενής; μῆτερ, πόθεν;

1464 δῶμ᾽ Hermann: δῶμα δ᾽ L
1466 νύκτα Markland: -ας L
1472 ⟨σὺ⟩ γέγονας Dindorf

494

CREUSA

No longer am I childless, barren!
The house has its hearth, the land its kings!
Erechtheus is young once more!
The house of the earthborn race no longer looks upon
    night
but recovers its sight in the rays of the sun!

ION

Mother, my father should be here with me to share the
happiness I have brought you both.

CREUSA

My son,
What do you mean? Oh, how great is my disgrace!

ION

What disgrace?

CREUSA

Another is your father, another!

ION

Ah! Did you bear me in girlhood? Am I a bastard?

CREUSA

The marriage that begot you, my son,
was blessed by no torches or dances.

ION

Ah, ah! Am I ignobly born? Mother, who is my father?

1475 sic Willink: ἐμός, τέκνον, ἔτικτε σὸν κάρα L

ΚΡΕΟΥΣΑ

ἴστω Γοργοφόνα . . .

ΙΩΝ

τί τοῦτ᾽ ἔλεξας;

ΚΡΕΟΥΣΑ

. . . ἃ σκοπέλοις ἐπ᾽ ἐμοῖς

1480 τὸν ἐλαιοφυῆ πάγον θάσσει· . . .

ΙΩΝ

⟨μῆτερ,⟩ λέγεις μοι σκολιὰ κοὐ σαφῆ τάδε.

ΚΡΕΟΥΣΑ

. . . παρ᾽ ἀηδόνιον πέτραν Φοίβῳ . . .

ΙΩΝ

τί Φοῖβον αὐδᾷς;

ΚΡΕΟΥΣΑ

. . . κρυπτόμενον λέχος ηὐνάσθην . . .

ΙΩΝ

1485 λέγ᾽· ὡς ἐρεῖς τι κεδνὸν εὐτυχές τέ μοι.

ΚΡΕΟΥΣΑ

. . . δεκάτῳ δέ σε μηνὸς ἐν κύκλῳ
κρύφιον ὠδῖν᾽ ἔτεκον Φοίβῳ.

1481 ⟨μῆτερ⟩ Wilamowitz   σκολιὰ Herwerden: δόλια L

ION

CREUSA

I call to witness her who slew the Gorgon . . .

ION

What is this you have said?

CREUSA

. . . who on my crag

sits upon the olive-bearing hill: . . .

ION

‹Mother,› what you say to me is riddling and unclear.

CREUSA

. . . near the cliff where the nightingales throng, with
Phoebus . . .

ION

Why do you mention Phoebus?

CREUSA

. . . I lay in illicit love . . .

ION

Say on: what you say will bring me blessing!

CREUSA

. . . and in the tenth circling of the moon[41]
I bore you in secret travail to Phoebus.

---

[41] The ancients spoke of human gestation as lasting ten
months, counting inclusively.

ΙΩΝ

ὦ φίλτατ᾽ εἰποῦσ᾽, εἰ λέγεις ἐτήτυμα.

ΚΡΕΟΥΣΑ

παρθένια δ᾽ ἐμᾶς ⟨λάθρᾳ⟩ ματέρος
1490 σπάργανά σοι τάδ᾽ ἀμφίβολ᾽ ἀνῆψα, κερ-
κίδος ἐμᾶς πλάνους.
γάλακτι δ᾽ οὐκ ἐπέσχον οὐδὲ μαστῷ
τροφεῖα ματρὸς οὐδὲ λουτρὰ χερσίν,
ἀνὰ δ᾽ ἄντρον ἔρημον οἰωνῶν
1495 γαμφηλαῖς φόνευμα θοίναμά τ᾽ εἰς
Ἅιδαν ἐκβάλλῃ.

ΙΩΝ

ὦ δεινὰ τλᾶσα μῆτερ.

ΚΡΕΟΥΣΑ

ἐν φόβῳ, τέκνον,
καταδεθεῖσα σὰν ἀπέβαλον ψυχάν.
1500 ἔκτεινά σ᾽ ἄκουσ᾽.

ΙΩΝ

†ἐξ ἐμοῦ τ᾽ οὐχ ὅσι᾽ ἔθνῃσκες†.

ΚΡΕΟΥΣΑ

ἰὼ ⟨ἰώ⟩· δειναὶ μὲν ⟨αἱ⟩ τότε τύχαι,

1489 ⟨λάθρᾳ⟩ Murray: ⟨ἑκὰς⟩ Jackson   1490 σπάργανά
σοι τάδ᾽ ἀμφ- Diggle: σπάργαν᾽ ἀμφ- σοι τάδ᾽ L   ἀνῆψα
Paley: ἐν- L   1493 χερσίν Wilamowitz: χεροῖν L
1498-9 sic Wilamowitz: καταδεθεῖσα σὰν ψυχὰν ἀπέβαλον,
τέκνον L
1500 ἔθνῃσκες] ἔτλης Maas   ⟨Ιων⟩ ἔκτεινας ἄκουσ᾽, οἷ᾽

ION

ION

What welcome news you tell me, if it is true!

CREUSA

⟨Without⟩ my mother's ⟨knowledge⟩ I wrapped
the work of my maiden hands about you,
my loom's unsteady weaving.
I did not hold you to the milk of my breast,
a mother's nurturing, nor did I bathe you,
but in a lonely cave, for the talons
of birds a thing to kill and feast on,
you were cast out to die.

ION

What a dreadful deed that was, mother!

CREUSA

My son, by fear
was I constrained when I cast away your life!
I killed you against my will!

ION

And against my intention I tried to murder you impiously!

CREUSA

Oh, oh! Terrible were my fortunes then,

ἔθνῃσκες ἐξ ἐμοῦ post Diggle (⟨Ἴων⟩ ἔκτεινας) Kovacs ne in hoc
episodio hic tantum cantet Ion
    1501 ⟨ἰώ⟩ Hermann   ⟨αἱ⟩ Matthiae

EURIPIDES

δεινὰ δὲ καὶ τάδ᾽· ἑλισσόμεσθ᾽ ἐκεῖθεν
1505 ἐνθάδε δυστυχίαισιν εὐτυχίαις τε πάλιν,
μεθίσταται δὲ πνεύματα.
μενέτω· τὰ πάροιθεν ἅλις κακά· νῦν
δὲ γένοιτό τις οὖρος ἐκ κακῶν, ὦ παῖ.

ΧΟΡΟΣ

1510 μηδεὶς δοκείτω μηδὲν ἀνθρώπων ποτὲ
ἄελπτον εἶναι πρὸς τὰ τυγχάνοντα νῦν.

ΙΩΝ

ὦ μεταβαλοῦσα μυρίους ἤδη βροτῶν
καὶ δυστυχῆσαι καὖθις αὖ πρᾶξαι καλῶς
τύχη, παρ᾽ οἵαν ἤλθομεν στάθμην βίου
1515 μητέρα φονεῦσαι καὶ παθεῖν ἀνάξια.
φεῦ·
ἆρ᾽ ἐν φαενναῖς ἡλίου περιπτυχαῖς
ἔνεστι πάντα τάδε καθ᾽ ἡμέραν μαθεῖν;
   φίλον μὲν οὖν σ᾽ εὕρημα, μῆτερ, ηὕρομεν,
καὶ τὸ γένος οὐδὲν μεμπτόν, ὡς ἡμῖν, τόδε·
1520 τὰ δ᾽ ἄλλα πρὸς σὲ βούλομαι μόνην φράσαι.
δεῦρ᾽ ἔλθ᾽· ἐς οὖς γὰρ τοὺς λόγους εἰπεῖν θέλω
καὶ περικαλύψαι τοῖσι πράγμασι σκότον.
ὅρα σύ, μῆτερ, μὴ σφαλεῖσ᾽ ἃ παρθένοις
ἐγγίγνεται νοσήματ᾽ ἐς κρυπτοὺς γάμους
1525 ἔπειτα τῷ θεῷ προστίθης τὴν αἰτίαν,
καὶ τοὐμὸν αἰσχρὸν ἀποφυγεῖν πειρωμένη
Φοίβῳ τεκεῖν με φῄς, τεκοῦσ᾽ οὐκ ἐκ θεοῦ.

but no less terrible these last events: we are tossed
  hither
and thither by bad fortune and again by good,
and the winds of luck veer around!
Let them now stay! Our previous woes suffice: now
let there be a fair wind after our troubles, my son!

CHORUS LEADER

In the light of what has just happened let no one think any-
thing impossible.

ION

O fortune, you have brought countless mortals to misery
and then to blessedness again! How close I came to killing
my own mother and suffering undeserved woe! Ah, can
one not see events such as this every day in this sun-lit
world?

Now in finding you, mother, I have certainly made a
joyful discovery, and I cannot find fault with such lineage.
But there are other things I want to say to you by yourself.
Come here: my words are for your ears alone, and I want
this matter to be kept a secret. (*Creusa comes closer.*)
Might it not be, mother, that you misstepped, as maidens
do, in illicit love, and then fastened the blame on the god?
That in trying to escape the disgrace of me you claimed
that you bore me to Phoebus, though my father was not
divine?

1509 δὲ γένοιτο Wilamowitz: δ' ἐγένετο L
1523 σφαλεῖσ' ἃ παρθένοις Musgrave: -σα παρθένος L

ΚΡΕΟΥΣΑ

μὰ τὴν παρασπίζουσαν ἅρμασίν ποτε
Νίκην Ἀθάναν Ζηνὶ γηγενεῖς ἔπι,
1530 οὐκ ἔστιν ὅστις σοι πατὴρ θνητῶν, τέκνον,
ἀλλ' ὅσπερ ἐξέθρεψε Λοξίας ἄναξ.

ΙΩΝ

πῶς οὖν τὸν αὑτοῦ παῖδ' ἔδωκ' ἄλλῳ πατρὶ
Ξούθου τέ φησι παῖδά μ' ἐκπεφυκέναι;

ΚΡΕΟΥΣΑ

πεφυκέναι μὲν οὐχί, δωρεῖται δέ σε
1535 αὑτοῦ γεγῶτα· καὶ γὰρ ἂν φίλος φίλῳ
δοίη τὸν αὑτοῦ παῖδα δεσπότην δόμων.

ΙΩΝ

ὁ θεὸς ἀληθὴς ἢ μάτην μαντεύεται;
ἐμοῦ ταράσσει, μῆτερ, εἰκότως φρένα.

ΚΡΕΟΥΣΑ

ἄκουε δή νυν ἅμ' ἐσῆλθεν, ὦ τέκνον·
1540 εὐεργετῶν σε Λοξίας ἐς εὐγενῆ
δόμον καθίζει· τοῦ θεοῦ δὲ λεγόμενος
οὐκ ἔσχες ἄν ποτ' οὔτε παγκλήρους δόμους
οὔτ' ὄνομα πατρός. πῶς γάρ, οὗ γ' ἐγὼ γάμους
ἔκρυπτον αὐτὴ καί σ' ἀπέκτεινον λάθρᾳ;
1545 ὁ δ' ὠφελῶν σε προστίθησ' ἄλλῳ πατρί.

ΙΩΝ

οὐχ ὧδε φαύλως αὔτ' ἐγὼ μετέρχομαι,
ἀλλ' ἱστορήσω Φοῖβον εἰσελθὼν δόμους
εἴτ' εἰμὶ θνητοῦ πατρὸς εἴτε Λοξίου.

CREUSA

By Athena, goddess of victory, who stood in battle beside
Zeus's chariot against the earthborn foe, no mortal begot
you, my son: lord Apollo, who raised you, is your father.

ION

Then why did he give his own son to another father? Why
say I am the son of Xuthus?

CREUSA

He did not say you are his son: he merely gave him his own
son as a present, just as a man might give a friend his son to
be his heir.

ION

Is the god truthful, or does he prophesy falsely? With good
reason this question troubles my mind, mother.

CREUSA

Listen, then, to what I think, my son. It was for your good
that Loxias settles you in a noble house. If you were called
the god's son, you would not have had a house as your in-
heritance or a father's name. How could you, seeing that I
hid my liaison and tried to kill you secretly? But he is doing
you good by making you over to another father.

ION

I will investigate these things more vigorously than this: I
will go to the temple and ask Phoebus whether I have a
mortal or Loxias for a father.

1530 ὅστις] οὐδείς Diggle
1537 interrogationis notam add. Wilamowitz
1538 ἐμοὶ Paley

ἔα· τίς οἴκων θυοδόκων ὑπερτελὴς
1550 ἀντήλιον πρόσωπον ἐκφαίνει θεῶν;
φεύγωμεν, ὦ τεκοῦσα, μὴ τὰ δαιμόνων
ὁρῶμεν, εἰ μὴ καιρός ἐσθ᾽ ἡμᾶς ὁρᾶν.

ΑΘΗΝΑ

μὴ φεύγετ᾽· οὐ γὰρ πολεμίαν με φεύγετε
ἀλλ᾽ ἔν τ᾽ Ἀθήναις κἀνθάδ᾽ οὖσαν εὐμενῆ.
1555 ἐπώνυμος δὲ σῆς ἀφικόμην χθονὸς
Παλλάς, δρόμῳ σπεύσασ᾽ Ἀπόλλωνος πάρα,
ὃς ἐς μὲν ὄψιν σφῷν μολεῖν οὐκ ἠξίου,
μὴ τῶν πάροιθε μέμψις ἐς μέσον μόλῃ,
ἡμᾶς δὲ πέμπει τοὺς λόγους ὑμῖν φράσαι·
1560 ὡς ἥδε τίκτει σ᾽ ἐξ Ἀπόλλωνος πατρός,
δίδωσι δ᾽ οἷς ἔδωκεν, οὐ φύσασί σε,
ἀλλ᾽ ὡς κομίζῃ 'ς οἶκον εὐγενέστατον.
ἐπεὶ δ᾽ ἀνεῴχθη πρᾶγμα μηνυθὲν τόδε,
θανεῖν σε δείσας μητρὸς ἐκ βουλευμάτων
1565 καὶ τήνδε πρὸς σοῦ, μηχαναῖς ἐρρύσατο.
ἔμελλε δ᾽ αὐτὰ διασιωπήσας ἄναξ
ἐν ταῖς Ἀθήναις γνωριεῖν ταύτην τε σοὶ
σέ θ᾽ ὡς πέφυκας τῆσδε καὶ Φοίβου πατρός.
ἀλλ᾽ ὡς περαίνω πρᾶγμα καὶ χρησμοὺς θεοῦ,
1570 ἐφ᾽ οἷσιν ἔζευξ᾽ ἅρματ᾽, εἰσακούσατον.
λαβοῦσα τόνδε παῖδα Κεκροπίαν χθόνα
χώρει, Κρέουσα, κἀς θρόνους τυραννικοὺς
ἵδρυσον. ἐκ γὰρ τῶν Ἐρεχθέως γεγὼς
δίκαιος ἄρχειν τῆς ἐμῆς ὅδε χθονός,

ION

Enter ATHENA *by* mechane, *alighting on the* theologeion.

But look! Which of the gods is showing a sun-like countenance above the incense-laden temple? Let's get away from here, mother, and not look on the gods—unless it is time for us to see.

ATHENA

Do not run away! It is not an enemy you are fleeing but one who is your friend both here and in Athens. I, Pallas, who gave my name to your land, have come here, sent in haste by Apollo. He has not thought it best to come to see you lest reproach for what happened before come between him and you. He has sent me to tell you that this woman is your mother and Apollo your father. He has bestowed you on one who is not your father so that you may take your place in a noble house. When the matter was revealed and brought to light, he was afraid that you would be killed by your mother's contrivance and she by you, and so he found the means to rescue you. Lord Apollo intended to keep all this quiet and in Athens to reveal your mother to you and that you were her son by Phoebus.

But I must bring the business of the god's oracles to a conclusion: hear why I have yoked my chariot. Take this son of yours, Creusa, and go to the land of Cecrops and set him upon the royal throne. Since he is of the line of Erechtheus it is right that he should rule my land, and he

---

1549 θυοδόκων Pierson: θεοδότων L

1562 κομίζῃ 's post Lenting (κομίζῃ σ') et Reiske (νομίζῃ 's) Wilamowitz: νομίζῃς L

1567 σοὶ Kuiper: σήν L

1574 τῆς Hartung: τῆσδ' L

1575 ἔσται δ' ἀν' Ἑλλάδ' εὐκλεής. οἱ τοῦδε γὰρ
παῖδες γενόμενοι τέσσαρες ῥίζης μιᾶς
ἐπώνυμοι γῆς κἀπιφυλίων χθονὸς
λαῶν ἔσονται, σκόπελον οἳ ναίουσ' ἐμόν.
Γελέων μὲν ἔσται πρῶτος· εἶτα δεύτερος
<τρίτος τ' ἔσονται παῖδες ὧν ἐπώνυμοι>
1580 Ὅπλητες Ἀργαδῆς τ', ἐμῆς τ' ἀπ' αἰγίδος
ἐν φῦλον ἕξουσ' Αἰγικορῆς. οἱ τῶνδε δ' αὖ
παῖδες γενόμενοι σὺν χρόνῳ πεπρωμένῳ
Κυκλάδας ἐποικήσουσι νησαίας πόλεις
χέρσους τε παράλους, ὃ σθένος τἠμῇ χθονὶ
1585 δίδωσιν· ἀντίπορθμα δ' ἠπείροιν δυοῖν
πεδία κατοικήσουσιν, Ἀσιάδος τε γῆς
Εὐρωπίας τε· τοῦδε δ' ὀνόματος χάριν
Ἴωνες ὀνομασθέντες ἕξουσιν κλέος.
Ξούθῳ δὲ καὶ σοὶ γίγνεται κοινὸν γένος,
1590 Δῶρος μέν, ἔνθεν Δωρὶς ὑμνηθήσεται
πόλις κατ' αἶαν Πελοπίαν· ὁ δεύτερος
Ἀχαιός, ὃς γῆς παραλίας Ῥίου πέλας
τύραννος ἔσται, κἀπισημανθήσεται
κείνου κεκλῆσθαι λαὸς ὄνομ' ἐπώνυμον.
1595 καλῶς δ' Ἀπόλλων πάντ' ἔπραξε· πρῶτα μὲν
ἄνοσον λοχεύει σ', ὥστε μὴ γνῶναι φίλους·
ἐπεὶ δ' ἔτικτες τόνδε παῖδα κἀπέθου
ἐν σπαργάνοισιν, ἁρπάσαντ' ἐς ἀγκάλας
Ἑρμῆν κελεύει δεῦρο πορθμεῦσαι βρέφος,
1600 ἔθρεψέ τ' οὐδ' εἴασεν ἐκπνεῦσαι βίον.

506

will be renowned in Hellas. His sons, four born from a
single stock, will give their names to the land and to the
peoples in their tribes who inhabit my rock. Geleon will
be the first. The second ⟨and third are the sons who will
give their name to⟩ the Hopletes and Argades, and the
Aigikores named from my aegis shall possess their separate
tribe. When the appointed time comes children born of
these shall come to dwell in the island cities of the
Cyclades and the coastal cities of the mainland, which will
give strength to my land. They shall dwell in the plains in
two continents on either side of the dividing sea, Asia and
Europe. They shall be called Ionians after this boy and win
glory. But you and Xuthus shall have children together:
Dorus, who will cause the city of Doris[42] to be glorified in
Pelops' land, and secondly Achaeus, who will be ruler of
the coastland about Rhium, and the people will be marked
by the same name as his.

Apollo has done all things well. First, your labor, thanks
to him, was free from sickness, and your family did not
learn of it. And when you had given birth and exposed your
son in his swaddling clothes, he ordered Hermes to snatch
up the child in his arms and convey it here: he raised him
and did not allow him to die.

---

[42] Apparently a reference to Sparta, the Dorian city *par excellence*.

1575 δ' L. Dindorf: τ' L   1577 κἀπιφυλίων Paley: -ίου L
1579 post h. v. lac. indic. Badham
1581 ἐν φῦλον Hermann: ἔμφ- L
1591 ὁ Wilamowitz et Murray quasi ex L: γ' ὁ L
1594 ἐπώνυμον Kirchhoff: -ος L

νῦν οὖν σιώπα παῖς ὅδ᾽ ὡς πέφυκε σός,
ἵν᾽ ἡ δόκησις Ξοῦθον ἡδέως ἔχῃ
σύ τ᾽ αὖ τὰ σαυτῆς ἀγάθ᾽ ἔχουσ᾽ ἴῃς, γύναι.
καὶ χαίρετ᾽· ἐκ γὰρ τῆσδ᾽ ἀναψυχῆς πόνων
1605 εὐδαίμον᾽ ὑμῖν πότμον ἐξαγγέλλομαι.

ΙΩΝ

ὦ Διὸς Παλλὰς μεγίστου θύγατερ, οὐκ ἀπιστίᾳ
σοὺς λόγους ἐδεξάμεσθα· πείθομαι δ᾽ εἶναι πατρὸς
Λοξίου καὶ τῆσδε. καὶ πρὶν τοῦτο δ᾽ οὐκ ἄπιστον
ἦν.

ΚΡΕΟΥΣΑ

τἀμὰ νῦν ἄκουσον· αἰνῶ Φοῖβον οὐκ αἰνοῦσα πρίν,
1610 οὕνεχ᾽ οὗ ποτ᾽ ἠμέλησα παιδὸς ἀποδίδωσί μοι.
αἵδε δ᾽ εὐωποὶ πύλαι μοι καὶ θεοῦ χρηστήρια,
δυσμενῆ πάροιθεν ὄντα. νῦν δὲ καὶ ῥόπτρων χέρας
ἡδέως ἐκκριμνάμεσθα καὶ προσεννέπω πύλας.

ΑΘΗΝΑ

ᾔνεσ᾽ οὕνεκ᾽ εὐλογεῖς θεὸν μεταβαλοῦσ᾽ ἀμείνονα·
1615 χρόνια μὲν τὰ τῶν θεῶν πως, ἐς τέλος δ᾽ οὐκ
ἀσθενῆ.

ΚΡΕΟΥΣΑ

ὦ τέκνον, στείχωμεν οἴκους.

ΑΘΗΝΑ

στείχεθ᾽, ἕψομαι δ᾽ ἐγώ.

1603 ἴῃς Porson: εἴη L
1607 ἐδεξάμεσθα Musgrave: δεξόμεσθα L

ION

Now therefore tell no one that he is your son: Xuthus will enjoy a pleasant delusion and you, lady, will go your way in possession of the blessing that belongs to you. Farewell! Your troubles now are ended, and hereafter, I promise you, your fortune will be good.

ION

Pallas, daughter of great Zeus, I believe what you have said! I am convinced that I am the son of Loxias and this woman. Even before this was not incredible.

CREUSA

Hear now what I have to say. I praise Phoebus, though before I did not praise him, because he has given me back the son I did not take care of. Lovely now in my eyes are the gates of the god's oracular shrine, which I once hated. Now my hands cling with pleasure to the door knocker as I bid the gates farewell.

ATHENA

I appove this change of heart for the better, this praise of the god. Though the gods may be slow to act, yet in the end they are mighty.

CREUSA

My son, let us go home.

ATHENA

Go, both of you, and I shall follow.

1610 ἠμέλησα Heath: -σε L
1614 ἀμείνονα Musgrave: ἀεί που L

ΙΩΝ

ἀξία γ᾽ ἡμῶν ὁδουρός.

⟨ΚΡΕΟΥΣΑ⟩

καὶ φιλοῦσά γε πτόλιν.

ΑΘΗΝΑ

ἐς θρόνους δ᾽ ἷζου παλαιούς.

ΙΩΝ

ἄξιον τὸ κτῆμά μοι.

ΧΟΡΟΣ

1620 ὦ Διὸς Λητοῦς τ᾽ Ἄπολλον, χαῖρ᾽· ὅτῳ δ᾽ ἐλαύνεται
συμφοραῖς οἶκος, σέβοντα δαίμονας θαρσεῖν
χρεών·
ἐς τέλος γὰρ οἱ μὲν ἐσθλοὶ τυγχάνουσιν ἀξίων,
οἱ κακοὶ δ᾽, ὥσπερ πεφύκασ᾽, οὔποτ᾽ εὖ πράξειαν
ἄν.

1617n Ιων Hermann: Κρ. L
1617 αἰσία Musgrave   ⟨Κρ.⟩ Hermann
1618n Ιων Heath: Κρ. L

ION

Yes, a fit guardian of our way.

⟨CREUSA⟩

And one who loves the city.

ATHENA

Mount the ancient throne.

ION

It is right for me to possess it.

CHORUS LEADER

Apollo, son of Zeus and Leto, farewell! Anyone whose house is hard pressed by troubles should worship the gods and be confident: in the end the noble receive their just reward. But the base, as befits their nature, will never prosper.

Exit ATHENA *by* mechane *from the* theologeion, CREUSA, ION, *and* CHORUS *by Eisodos A.*

Composed in ZephGreek and ZephText by
Technologies 'N Typography, Merrimac, Massachusetts.
Printed in Great Britain by St Edmundsbury Press Ltd,
Bury St Edmunds, Suffolk, on acid-free paper.
Bound by Hunter & Foulis Ltd, Edinburgh, Scotland.